LINCOLN'S BODY

*Alexander Gardner's February 5, 1865, portrait
brings out Lincoln's lined and leathery visage.*

Mr. Lincoln's face was so mobile, so sure a reflex of his mood, and his temper had so wide a range, that it is not to be wondered at [that] the portraits [of him] differ so . . . [People] will choose from the multitude of photographs the one that best answers the notion they have formed of the man.

For ourselves, we cannot separate Mr. Lincoln in our minds from the time in which he lived, nor think of him except as a man who, having mental and spiritual organization of extreme delicacy and sensitiveness, was called to bear a load of care, responsibility, and anxiety, that must have left a deep and indelible mark upon his face . . . time left all [its] bitter dealings with him written on that scarred and weather-beaten visage. And this record the true portrait of Mr. Lincoln must have, or miss the final verdict of acceptance. People do not want a "nice" portrait, nor a "handsome" portrait, nor an "ideal" portrait. They want to say, this is the man who suffered and died in our cause. Let flatterers stand aside, and squeamish people. Show us the grim features, the shaggy head, the beetling brow, the big nose, the great mouth. What do we care for his homeliness? His soul transfigures this scarred and craggy face as sunset strikes against a mountain side, and changes rugged cliff, and black ravine, and darkest wood into golden or rosy cloud.

— "FINE ARTS," *NEW YORK TRIBUNE*, DEC. 28, 1866

This retouched print of Gardner's February 5, 1865, image offers an idealized man for the ages.

LINCOLN'S BODY

A Cultural History

Richard Wightman Fox

W. W. NORTON & COMPANY

New York   London

For information about permission to reproduce selections from this book, write to
Permissions, W. W. Norton & Company, Inc., 500 Fifth Avenue, New York, NY 10110

For information about special discounts for bulk purchases, please contact
W. W. Norton Special Sales at specialsales@wwnorton.com or 800-233-4830

Manufacturing by Quad Graphics Fairfield
Book design by Helene Berinsky
Production manager: Julia Druskin

ISBN: 978-0-393-06530-5

W. W. Norton & Company, Inc., 500 Fifth Avenue, New York, N.Y. 10110
www.wwnorton.com
W. W. Norton & Company Ltd., Castle House, 75/76 Wells Street, London W1T 3QT

1 2 3 4 5 6 7 8 9 0

To
Jonah, Oliver, Cornelia, Roscoe, and Jim
and their parents
Christopher and Laura, Rachel and Christophe

Contents

PART THREE

The National Body (1909–2015)

Preface

*I had this image of Lincoln, the living president, haunting his
own White House, just taking strolls up and down the long,
wide corridors of the residence . . . just working things out.
That was one of the first images I had.*
　　　　　　　　　　　　—Steven Spielberg, January 5, 2013 [1]

D EAD FOR A CENTURY and a half, Abraham Lincoln remains
curiously and uniquely alive to millions of Americans. Many
presidents are remembered and admired. Lincoln is cherished
and loved—more deeply, by more people—than any other. He endures
as the model leader other presidents are judged by. For some he persists
as a moral exemplar, a man of saintly disposition unable to hold a grudge
or hate an enemy.

A decade ago, in her engaging *Team of Rivals: The Political Genius
of Abraham Lincoln* (2005), Doris Kearns Goodwin expressed a warm
attachment to him as the gold standard of American presidents. Her
750-page study of his person and his politics beguiled readers across the
country. By 2012, it had sold 1.3 million physical copies, ten times more
than the total sale of David Donald's classic biography *Lincoln* (1995).

Political insiders couldn't resist *Team of Rivals*. During the 2008
presidential campaign, the political elite in Washington took the book as
"totemic." Barack Obama was a brand-new senator from Illinois when he
read it in 2005. He gave Goodwin a call at her home in Massachusetts
and said, "We need to talk." She got on a plane and met him in the Senate

Office Building to discuss Lincoln's outlook and exploits. Hillary Clinton, Obama's chief rival in 2008, also read Goodwin's book. They both understood the historical parallel when President Obama asked her to serve as secretary of state. Abraham Lincoln had offered that post to his main competitor, William Seward. Seward said yes, and so did Hillary Clinton.[2]

Over her three decades of historical writing, Goodwin wrote in her introduction, she had come to know the lives of Franklin Roosevelt, the Kennedys, and Lyndon Johnson (in her twenties, she had actually worked for LBJ). After spending a decade living and breathing Abraham Lincoln, she saw that he surpassed all the others in his "power to captivate the imagination and to inspire emotion." He had drawn her in with his humor, intelligence, fortitude, and self-deprecating composure.[3]

Goodwin's contagious enthusiasm for Lincoln rubbed off on Steven Spielberg. In 1999, after running into Goodwin at a conference on the impending millennium, he asked her what she was writing about. He knew she'd won the Pulitzer Prize in 1995 for *No Ordinary Time*, a study of Franklin and Eleanor Roosevelt during World War II. When she uttered the name "Lincoln," he salivated. He hadn't been looking to make a film on Lincoln, but he'd been fascinated by the sixteenth president since boyhood. Would she consider selling him the movie rights, he asked, even though her book was years away from publication? She was thrilled by the offer, and they shook on it.

A few years later, their partnership doubled into a star-studded four-member team of literary and cinematic artists. Screenwriter Tony Kushner came aboard through the combined persuasion of Spielberg and Goodwin, and actor Daniel Day-Lewis finally signed on after reading a draft of Kushner's script. In 2012, most critics and ticket buyers found their depiction of the president riveting. Without Goodwin the historian—the creator, in *Team of Rivals*, of a gripping story and a carefully chiseled verbal monument to her hero—the movie never would have happened.[4]

Lincoln built upon earlier films (Tony Kushner has expressed special

Daniel Day-Lewis as Lincoln. Billboard ad in south-central Los Angeles, 2012.

fondness for John Ford's *Young Mr. Lincoln*), but *Lincoln* is the first one to deliver a fully embodied presidential Lincoln: politician, chief magistrate, commander in chief, father, and husband whose physical frame carried the load of war and stood in life and death as symbol of the undivided Republic. Spielberg registered the pace and power of that frame in his first brainstorm about what the camera should record: a solitary Lincoln ambling down a White House hallway, silently pondering the nation's fate.

LONG BEFORE the assassination, and even before his presidency, many Americans had taken Lincoln's towering, shambling physique as a symbol of republican simplicity and American self-making. Thanks to photography and other visual arts, his body exerted huge symbolic force during the Civil War. But with his sudden metamorphosis into the nation's martyr in chief in the spring of 1865, his capacity to evoke love and gratitude expanded exponentially. The mythic potency already contained in his living frame was magnified beyond measure in his bruised and rigid corpse.

In the hearts and minds of African Americans and northern whites, Lincoln's body was no longer just a symbol. It was an actual physical bestowal, one that metamorphosed, in the decades to come, into a virtual embodiment of national purpose and glory—still a symbol, but for many people more charged and real than other icons. Uncle Sam was a symbol standing for the nation. Lincoln was a man dying for the nation.

Ever since May 4, 1865, Americans have vied with one another to exploit Lincoln's symbolic power. For a century after his death, African Americans did the most to preserve a continuous memory of Lincoln the emancipator, and they did so by treasuring what they took as the providential meaning of his martyrdom. He had given his life for the nation, but he had also given it especially for *them*. Nowadays, after the reelection of the first African American president, differences in the way blacks and whites see Lincoln have been mostly overcome. The image of Lincoln's body and face, familiar to all, doesn't carry the same nearly sacred meaning it once did.

In 1947, the young historian David Donald could describe the Lincoln "cult" as "almost an American religion," featuring high priests such as Carl Sandburg and a legion of disciples dedicated to celebrating Lincoln's virtues. A measure of that ardor remains, but by the 1970s the image of Lincoln circulated more and more *as* an image, and less and less as a window on the actual man and his sacrifice for the nation. Advertisers had used him to sell products for generations, but for the first time they could satirize him with impunity. Consumers were invited to smile at the ubiquity of his image, to wink at its overuse.[5]

Satire didn't necessarily mean disrespect. It just meant that in the post–Vietnam War era, the use of Lincoln's image wasn't always intended to evoke patriotic sentiments. Ads could now treat consumers as being in the know, too smart and liberated for the Lincoln worship of old.

But who's to say that laughter directed at the globally familiar Lincoln icon prevents people from still taking him as a true hero? They can still cherish a leader who stood up for the principle of equality without fretting about the dangers—without counting, as Lincoln said in 1861, "the chances of his own life."[6]

Circulating as a universally known iconic image, Lincoln's body continues to call to mind, for millions of Americans and many others around the world, his unlikely story of self-making, his implausible blend of forbearance and strength, and his easy familiarity built up with the people he always called "my fellow citizens." He relished his contact with them, whatever the risks.

Since his youth, he'd been entertaining his peers with a stream of tales and jokes. "That reminds me of a story," he would say to White House visitors as they got settled in his office. When journalist Albert D. Richardson of the *New York Tribune* came to see him in 1863, Lincoln recognized him from a brief encounter they'd had in Kansas in 1859. That memory launched him into the tale of a white man out West who once "bought a pony of an Indian, who could not speak much English." The Indian warned the buyer with the words "Oats—no!," "Hay—no!," "Corn—no!," "Cottonwood—yes! Very much!" The white man dismissed the injunction as so much gibberish and put the horse up that night in "a stable built of cottonwood logs," with ample oats, hay, and corn to eat. "The next morning he found the grain and fodder untouched, but the barn was quite empty, with a great hole on one side, which the pony had gnawed his way through!"[7]

Lincoln could summon a story for any occasion. On May 6, 1864, he concocted an intricate tale in the presence of Admiral Charles H. Davis, who recorded it in his diary the next day.

May 7 [1864] Yesterday, while I was in [Assistant Secretary of the Navy Gustavus] Fox's office talking on business, the President came in, and seeing that he interrupted us he said: "I have nothing to say, I did not come in for any object; I was once at a county town, during the session of the court, where there were a great many lawyers present, and a stranger—a countryman—surprised at such a crowd, asked what it meant, and if all these lawyers had business there. 'No,' was the answer; 'they have not come to court because they have any business here, but because they have no business anywhere else.' This," said the President, "is my case. I have nothing to do, and have been over to [Secretary of War Edwin] Stanton's, and have now come here. The fact is, I cannot keep still, I am so anxious to hear something about the army."[8]

Lincoln embedded this joke inside an account of his jittery body and mind. He'd been darting from place to place, trying to get through a nerve-wracking day. He had nothing to say when he got to Fox's office, but he couldn't stop talking. In this case, however, his stash of self-descriptive humor and his comic antics supplied little comfort. Only some good military news from Virginia could have relieved him.

Years earlier, the *New York Herald*'s Henry Villard, covering the presidential candidate from Springfield, had told the paper's hundreds of thousands of readers, "I think it would be hard to find one who tells better jokes, enjoys them better and laughs oftener, than Abraham Lincoln." The president would never stop joking and laughing during the war years, but as Admiral Davis noticed on May 6, 1864, Lincoln's body had its own story to tell. And that story kept unfolding over the last year of his life, and for generations to come.[9]

PART ONE

The Public Body
(1840–1865)

On April 4, 1865, Lincoln took his twelve-year-old son Tad by the hand and plunged into a large Richmond, Virginia, crowd made up mostly of slaves celebrating their first day of de facto freedom. Jubilant at the sight of their president, they marched with him for almost a mile to the Confederate White House—which on April 3 had become Union army headquarters. Photograph of Thomas Nast's 1868 painting, based on his drawing published in Harper's Weekly, *February 24, 1866.*

CHAPTER ONE

Lincoln's Body Politic

A life is never wisely given to save a limb.

—LINCOLN, APRIL 4, 1864

W HEN NORTHERNERS and southern blacks lost their beloved president in 1865, they lost a leader who had put his body at the center of his public life. Many friends had tried to break him of the habit, but it was no use. He loved the byplay with ordinary folks, and he'd learned over decades that it bore political fruit. As president, he thought of his White House office hours as free-flowing focus groups, giving him access to public opinion. It had always worked the other way around too. He wanted to give the people access to him, to let them know how he looked and sounded up close.

His friends and supporters in Illinois had been calling him "Honest Old Abe" since the mid-1840s, and the virile, youthful "rail-splitter" image had taken off in 1860: actual wooden fence rails from the 1830s were carried into the Republican state convention, and amid the foot-stomping delirium of the delegates, he announced that if he hadn't split those exact rails, he had split many others just as good. Yet, as he became known nationally in the 1850s, his reputation as an ugly, uncouth commoner grew apace, and he found it hard to shake. What changed people's minds was getting to see him in person, in conversation or on the lecture platform, when his features would suddenly glow.[1]

"Mr. Lincoln was the homeliest man I ever saw," journalist Donn Piatt recalled after Lincoln's death. "His body seemed to me a huge skeleton in clothes . . . Every movement was awkward in the extreme . . . When in repose, his face was dull, heavy, and repellent. It brightened like a lit lantern when animated. His dull eyes would fairly sparkle with fun, or express as kindly a look as I ever saw, when moved by some matter of human interest."[2]

But some Lincoln admirers found him just plain ugly, whether animated or not. Walt Whitman, one of Lincoln's biggest boosters, thought there was no gainsaying Lincoln's unattractiveness. But in Whitman's eyes this made him all the more endearing. "He has a face like a hoosier Michael Angelo, so awful ugly it becomes beautiful, with its strange mouth, its deep cut, criss-cross lines, and its doughnut complexion."[3]

Occasionally, critics went further and found Lincoln repulsive— usually Democratic detractors who disliked his policies as much as his looks. Colonel Charles Wainwright, scion of the old Hudson River elite, saw the president and Secretary of War Edwin Stanton at the opera in Washington, DC, in 1862, and he tied Lincoln's ugliness to his unrefined behavior. "It would be hard work to find the great man in his face or figure," Wainwright wrote in his diary, "and he is infinitely uglier than any of his pictures. When the audience rose and cheered on his entry, instead of coming forward and bowing like a gentleman, he sat down, stuck his head out over the edge of the box, and grinned like a great baboon. I was ashamed to think that such a gawk was President of the United States."[4]

Ohio Republican Rutherford B. Hayes, a graduate of Harvard Law School and a future president, loved Lincoln's moderate antislavery politics and found the ugliness charge unconvincing. "Homely as Lincoln is," he wrote to his niece Laura Platt in 1861, he is "by no means ill-looking" if you glimpse him "by day light when he is talking." But having just seen the president-elect in Cincinnati, Hayes mocked his physical inelegance. He instructed his niece—about to see Lincoln in Columbus—not to miss his "awkward look when he bows. It can't be caricatured. It beyond compare exceeds caricature. His chin rises—his body breaks in two at the hips—there is a bend of the knees at a queer angle. It's good."[5]

Democratic papers north and south spun Lincoln's looks for laughs as well as political advantage. "If it is his fate to be Chief Magistrate," said the *Newark (Ohio) Advocate* in August 1860, guests at White House public receptions will need "cut-glass prisms, which might, by their distortion, bring Old Abe's features into something not altogether repulsive." "We have seen some faces of the ultra-ugly stamp in our day," wrote the *Petersburg Express* in May 1860, but "the election to the Presidency of . . . this living Black republican specimen of infinite ugliness . . . would be, of itself, cause enough for a dissolution of the Union."[6]

Looking back from the twenty-first century, it's hard to believe that personal appearance mattered so much in nineteenth-century politics, or even that Lincoln could have been seen as so ugly in the first place. The modern viewer may find his looks unusual, but probably not unpleasant and certainly not hideous. In the mid-nineteenth century, everyone seems to have agreed that Lincoln's physiognomy and physique required rigorous scrutiny. The burden of proof seems to have lain on those who thought he wasn't as wretched looking as all that. Albert Richardson loved the man and argued that "the ineffable tenderness which shone through his gentle eyes" made up for the "huge hands and feet, great mouth," and "angular features." He had to concede that Lincoln lacked "symmetry," a key component of beauty.[7]

Even after the assassination—when you'd think people would have stopped harping on physical attributes—eulogists and mourners kept right on calling him ugly. By that time, the mention of his uncomely looks had become the expected lead-in to praise of his animation; the homely start magnified the final winsomeness. When you least expected it, as Donn Piatt put it, Lincoln would pivot from dull heaviness to sparkling fun. Millions were inspired by Lincoln's knowing how to overcome the unfortunate hand nature had dealt him. His repellent features faded from view every time an inner delight flashed across his face.

CAPTIVATED BY new technology, Lincoln gladly sat for photographers as well as painters and sculptors, trusting—as Colonel Wainwright suspected—

that images would elevate the popular estimate of his appearance. In 1860 and 1864, his campaign aides deluged the Republican Party faithful with pictures of him. At the 1860 Republican National Convention in Chicago's Wigwam, they literally showered the delegates with his image, tossing cheap, hand-colored woodcuts of an 1857 Alexander Hesler photograph from the balcony.[8]

Within two weeks, anyone in the country could order a sturdy 19×24-inch engraving of that photo for "15 cents plain, or 25 cents handsomely colored," plus 6 cents postage. Conveniently for Lincoln, inexpensive photographic cartes de visite also appeared in America in 1860, just in time to put Mathew Brady's dashing shot of him—standing erect beside a table, staring intently at the viewer, his left hand posed authoritatively atop two weighty books—into thousands of people's photo albums. Between the Hesler and Brady photos, citizens had Lincoln covered. The 1857 Hesler image presented a rustic western Lincoln—with unruly republican hair above a ramshackle collar—while Brady's 1860 photo (taken when Lincoln came to Manhattan for his famous Cooper Institute speech) offered a polished eastern makeover, with every hair in place and an impeccable high collar.[9]

Meanwhile, Lincoln had been joking freely about his physical fea-

This sheet was flung to the delegates on the floor of the Wigwam in 1860.

tures ever since entering politics in Illinois in 1832, making an asset of what nearly everyone took as his unlovely appearance and unrefined demeanor. Showing he could laugh at his own looks made him likeable and strong at the same time. "Homely" was the nicest adjective people could find to describe him. "Grotesque" was surprisingly common, capturing his almost alien, otherworldly dimensions: six foot four (eight or nine inches taller than the average man of the day), massive head, narrow shoulders, short trunk, and endless legs.[10]

Alexander Hesler's simple man of the heartland.

Lincoln was fond of telling story jokes about himself. In 1856, he cracked up a convention of newspaper editors in Decatur, Illinois, with a tale reported decades later by one of those present, Benjamin Shaw of the *Dixon (Illinois) Telegraph*. Shaw said Lincoln "was in a happy mood" that night and told the group that as an "interloper" amid the journalists, he was reminded of "a man not possessed of features the ladies would call handsome."

Mathew Brady's civilized statesman.

While riding a horse through the woods, the man stopped on the path to let a woman rider pass.

> She stopped in turn, and said, "Well, for land sake, you are the home-liest man I ever saw."
>
> "Yes, madam, but I can't help it."
>
> "No, I suppose not," she said, "but you might stay at home."

Shaw told his 1900 audience he'd always believed Lincoln's man-on-the-horse story to be a "personal reminiscence."[11]

Lincoln didn't mind trying to improve his looks—that's why he grew a beard after winning the 1860 election—but he kept making light of his appearance anyway. Adopting such a confident, carefree pose delighted onlookers, though it didn't stop them from thinking he was ugly. Neither "his new whiskers" nor the rash of recent "popular prints," said the pro-Lincoln *New York World*, had altered the basic picture. His "personal appearance disappointed everybody," even those who "found him better looking than they had ever hoped." "Very homely" at best, added the paper, the president-elect could do nothing about his heavy eyebrows and his "standard" dark complexion of "the western fever and ague districts."[12]

Yet some people thought Lincoln looked *better* than his photos. "I have never seen a picture of him that does anything like justice to the original," contended Henry Villard of the *New York Herald*. Feature by feature, said Villard, Lincoln resembled some very presentable faces. He had the late Massachusetts Whig Rufus Choate's eyes, nose, and cheekbones, and he had his fellow Kentuckian Henry Clay's mouth. And of course, Villard continued, "the frequent relation of his early 'rail splitting' history" had ensured that no one doubted his "muscular qualities."[13]

Into his political maturity, Lincoln kept bantering about his own and other people's physical appearance. In 1858, he told a Springfield audience of the great gap between his measly self and the grand Stephen Douglas, his opponent in the Illinois Senate race. The incumbent enjoyed "world wide renown," said Lincoln. Douglas's Democratic minions dreamed of the patronage positions they would pluck when he rose to the presidency. They beheld in "his round, jolly, fruitful face postoffices, landoffices, marshalships, and cabinet appointments, chargeships and foreign missions, bursting and sprouting out in wonderful exuberance ready to be laid hold of by their greedy hands. [Great laughter.]" As for his own features, Lincoln said, "Nobody has ever expected me to be President. In my poor, lean, lank face, nobody has ever seen that any cabbages were sprouting out. [Tremendous cheering and laughter.]"[14]

Commenting on his overall appearance, Lincoln added with sudden soberness, "I set out in this campaign, with the intention of conducting it strictly as a gentleman, in substance at least, if not in the outside polish. The latter I shall never be, but that which constitutes the inside of a gentleman I hope I understand, and am not less inclined to practice than others. [Cheers.]"[15]

MOST PEOPLE pay little conscious attention to Lincoln's body these days, but once they focus on it they can see how it's been tied to his words and deeds ever since he entered politics. His physicality proved fascinating to his contemporaries, and to following generations, because they realized how much it mattered to him. Lincoln made people care about it by tying it to their national saga. Only in America was self-making possible on such a grand scale, he kept saying, and only in America was a man like him—of such unprepossessing origins, in appearance and social standing—able to rise to such heights of power and respect.

By the mid- to late 1850s, he was a former one-term US congressman (1847–49) eager for a return to Washington as a senator from Illinois. Though he fell short of that goal in 1855 and 1858, he made a national name for himself in scores of impassioned speeches on the subject of slavery. From 1854 on, he was touting the idea that the United States composed a single political *body*—a "body politic," as he labeled it in a major speech in Peoria on October 16 of that year. This was a common phrase in his day, as in ours, but for him the idea took on special importance.[16]

The virtue of a *republican* body politic for Lincoln lay in its vision of an equality uniting the leader and the led. They all counted as members of one vast citizenry, even the person acting temporarily as its head. In this nonmonarchical conception, nothing split the leader off from everyone else—except his status "for the time being," as Lincoln told the New Jersey state senate in 1861, as "the representative man of the nation." A majority of the gentlemen listening to him in Trenton had voted against him for president, he reminded them. They had nevertheless all assembled now to welcome him as "Chief Magistrate," a reception he accepted "more gratefully than I could do did I believe it was tendered to me as an individual."[17]

In his public body as chief magistrate, in other words, he had acquired distinction deriving from his office, not from any personal grandeur. He remained one of the ordinary people, a commoner whose looks and manners, as he kept repeating to all comers, proved his perfect ordinariness. Projecting an aura of contented plainness, he had established impeccable "democratic" credentials since Illinois days. Once that foundation was in place, he could prove his utter uniqueness with little risk of seeming "superior." He got busy commanding one hall after another with verbal dexterity, lawyerly logic, self-deprecation, and physical humor.

After he appeared on the stage of Manhattan's Cooper Institute in 1860, the *New York Tribune*'s editors apologized for the limitations, in the case of Lincoln, of the written text they would immediately distribute for all to read in pamphlet form. For it couldn't possibly capture "the gestures, the kindling eye and the mirth-provoking look" of "Nature's orator." Lincoln had deployed his "rare powers solely and effectively to elucidate and to convince, though their inevitable effect is to delight and electrify as well."[18]

The anti-Republican *New York Herald* was also bowled over by Lincoln's physicality. But the *Herald* found his body off-putting in its "involuntary comical awkwardness." "Unsteady in his gait," this "dark complexioned" out-of-towner had caused unavoidable "merriment" from "the frequent contortions" of his features. The *Herald* and the *Tribune* concurred in tracing Lincoln's oratorical power to his unique blending of body and mind. They just disagreed about his worth. The *Herald* took him as an oddity of nature, not as "Nature's orator."[19]

LINCOLN'S "HOUSE" metaphor for the nation is well known today: "A house divided against itself cannot stand," he told the 1858 Illinois Republican state convention as he accepted its nomination for the US Senate race. But his use of the "body" metaphor for the American Republic is mostly forgotten. In his breakthrough speech in Peoria in October 1854, he found it an indispensable weapon in his assault on Stephen Douglas's notion of popular sovereignty.[20]

Douglas had addressed the crowd for three hours in the afternoon, defending his plan to permit the people of a territory such as Nebraska to decide whether slavery should exist within their borders. That approach, thought Douglas, could split the difference between abolitionists and slave owners, preserving peace between the sections.

Rather than launching into his own three-hour speech at 5:00 p.m., Lincoln asked the crowd if they'd rather break for dinner until 7:00 p.m. If they agreed, he would begin his address at that hour, and he promised Douglas an hour to reply beginning at 10:00 p.m. Lincoln confessed that this offer was not "wholly unselfish." It was the only way to ensure that the Democrats in the audience would stick around for Lincoln's speech. "By giving him the close," Lincoln added, "I felt confident you would stay for the fun of hearing him skin me." The audience "signified their assent to the arrangement," both sides looking forward to the symbolic flaying of Lincoln's flesh.[21]

In his speech, Lincoln objected to the "new position" that popular sovereignty had accorded slavery in the body politic. The "fathers of the republic," in drawing up the Constitution, had permitted slavery only as a matter of necessity, never mentioning it by name, "just as an afflicted man hides away a wen or a cancer, which he dares not cut out at once, lest he bleed to death." They had allowed slavery to continue, all the while upholding liberty as the ruling principle, and rejecting the idea of a "moral right in the enslaving of one man by another." In their eyes, said Lincoln, slavery had been safely placed on the road to eventual extinction. Douglas's doctrine did what the founders had refused to do. It gave moral legitimacy to enslavement.

The body politic conception let Lincoln promote liberty as the lifeblood of an indivisible republic, a living entity with a single circulatory system. Douglas's notion of popular sovereignty avoided any such organic metaphor for the nation, picturing the people as a sum total of individual selves and opinions. The sovereign people in each territory should decide by vote whether slavery was compatible with republican liberty. Nonsense, said Lincoln. Slavery wrecked republican liberty, whether a majority of the people knew it or not.[22]

HAVING LOST the Senate battle to Douglas in 1858, Lincoln beat him handily in the presidential race of 1860 (with almost 40 percent of the popular vote to Douglas's 30 percent, and with 180 electoral votes to Douglas's 12). On his twelve-day preinaugural train ride to Washington in February 1861, he kept up the genial mocking of his own below-par physical appearance. In little town after little town, his train stopped just long enough for him to step out onto the rear platform and announce that he had no speech to make—except to say, as he did at Little Falls, New York, "I have come to see you and allow you to see me [applause]," and with respect to "the Ladies, I have the best of the bargain."[23]

At Westfield, New York, he broke with this repetitive formula but stuck with his odd looks, pausing to applaud the local girl, Grace Bedell, who had written him three months earlier to urge that he grow a beard. She had suggested, Lincoln told the jolly crowd (numbering in the thou-

February 9, 1861, seven days before Lincoln's encounter with Grace Bedell at the Westfield, New York, train station.

sands), "it would improve my physical appearance." He'd followed her advice, and the straggly proof was now visible on his cavernous cheeks. Twelve-year-old Grace was present at the depot that day, and once she was pointed out to him, Lincoln dove into the mass of onlookers to give her "several hearty kisses . . . amid the yells of delight from the excited crowd."[24]

During the 1861 inaugural trip, the president-elect avoided direct comment on public affairs—the "threatening National difficulties," as he called them in Cincinnati on February 12 (his fifty-second birthday). Seven southern states had seceded since December, and on February 8 they had formed the Confederacy, with Jefferson Davis at its head. Addressing citizens and elected officials in the cities on his route, Lincoln said he would defer comment on the crisis until his inaugural address on Monday, March 4. In the meantime, he articulated again and again—as he did at the Trenton statehouse—his idea of the republican body politic.[25]

Becoming president, he said, did not mean abandoning his station as a fellow citizen; he remained one humble member of the national body. The people had given him the helm of the ship of state, and he would pass it back to them when they elected another president. This republican setup continued to give him exactly what he wanted: the distinction of high responsibility without having to give up his unassuming traits. He must have felt at times that this system was too good to be true: interacting day by day with other plain citizens in a simple public life no different in substance from his private life in Springfield. The difference concerned only the magnitude of the decision making, and the sheer number of ordinary people pressing in on him. He didn't have to put on any airs.

The easy fit that Lincoln perceived between his private body and public body—getting to be his true, simple self while fulfilling his public duty—*was* too good to be true. No sooner had he arrived in Philadelphia on the evening of February 21, 1861, than he learned from two independent sources of an apparent assassination plot against him. He would supposedly be killed by a band of ruffians as he passed through Baltimore at midday on February 23. On the brisk early morning of February 22, as he tended to his Washington's birthday tasks at Independence Hall—a flag raising and two short speeches—he had all he could do to keep this chilling news to himself. He did keep quiet about it, but the words he spoke into the frigid air of Chestnut Street, where several thousand citizens had gathered to hear him, showed that his mind was wandering toward whatever awaited him in Baltimore.

As he praised Jefferson's glorious Declaration signed in 1776, he announced how willingly he would trade his life for an assurance that Americans would never renounce the document's principle of liberty. If the country "cannot be saved without giving up that principle, I was about to say I would rather be assassinated on this spot than surrender it [applause]." About to say? Immediately he realized he'd garbled his delivery, and perhaps disclosed too much of what was on his mind. He backpedaled, telling the crowd that maybe he'd "said something indiscreet [cries of 'no, no']. But," he continued, "I have said nothing but what I am willing to live by, and, if the pleasure of Almighty God, die by."[26]

The national press duly quoted his words the next day, without suspecting that anything was amiss. Politicians commonly proclaimed their readiness to die for the people. And angry citizens often dispatched ominous-sounding letters to their chief magistrate, telling him he was ruining the country and his days were numbered. Lincoln collected piles of such letters in Springfield and Washington after his election—so many that it was easy for him to laugh them off as so much hot air.

"May the hand of the devil strike you down before long," went one of the milder ones. "You are destroying the country[.] Damn you—every breath you take—[Signed] Hand of God against you[.]" Another got right to the point: "You will be shot on the 4th of March 1861 by a Louisiana Creole . . . we are decided and our aim is sure. [Signed] A young creole. BEWARE." In mid-nineteenth-century America, politicians openly broached the topic of assassination, and citizens often called for carrying it out, yet almost no one—least of all Lincoln—took the threats seriously.[27]

As William Seward, Lincoln's secretary of state, wrote in 1862 to one of his foreign ambassadors, assassination plots were always being "formed and organized" in the United States, but they amounted to exactly nothing. Assassination was simply "not an American practice or habit." Seward reported that during the humid Washington summers, the president often rode out alone to the Soldiers' Home, three miles from the White House, and the secretary of state followed his example. "I go there unattended at all hours, by daylight and moonlight, by starlight and without any light." A practice as "vicious" and "desperate" as murder could not be "engrafted into our political system," which provides for the removal of unpopular presidents at regular intervals.[28]

With the reported Baltimore plot clogging his mind, Lincoln spent the rest of Washington's birthday putting on a good face as he addressed gatherings in Lancaster and Harrisburg. Late that afternoon, he could finally sit down with his advisers in the Jones House, the Harrisburg hotel where they were all scheduled to spend the night. Mulling the problem over only confirmed that Lincoln was boxed in. Going through Baltimore the next day as planned would put the entire Lincoln family at risk, yet not sticking to the plan would place the president-elect at the mercy of an easily alienated public opinion.

Everyone in the room concurred about the deep-seated public expectations. In the republican body politic, new leaders were bound by a standing code: they were supposed to enter the national capital publicly, placing their ritual passage to power under the symbolic scrutiny of the people. A republican citizenry still sensitive to the arbitrary pretensions and deceptions of monarchs would tolerate nothing less.

Lincoln never wrote or spoke publicly about how seriously he took the assassination danger in Baltimore, but he went along with his advisers: a threat confirmed by two investigations had to be respected, whatever the subsequent public fallout. That evening he snuck onto a night train to Washington and arrived there, without his family, half a day ahead of schedule. Newspapers shortly erupted with calumnious catcalls, heaping scorn on Lincoln's disguise (he actually wore a plain overcoat and a soft woolen cap, but that unobtrusive garb quickly morphed into a laughable Scottish plaid cap and long "military" coat). The simple, transparent republican had supposedly let fear of personal injury turn him into a quivering weakling.

As usual, Lincoln kept his feelings to himself, but he must have been stung by the insinuations of cowardice, even from Republican papers. "How deplorably did he yield to his advisers!" declared the *New York World*, a Republican paper until the following year. The *World* regretted the missed opportunity: Lincoln could have affirmed his physical strength and intrepid spirit at the head of a mounted people's brigade.

> We cannot believe that a man of his bold and open bearing, who has hewn his way with strength of arm, and will, and force of character to his present high position, would blench [*sic*] at the first show of danger . . . Had he known that there were murderers lying in wait for his life in Maryland, he should have refused the shelter of car or of carriage, and mounting a horse, like a man, have called his friends around him, and he would have ridden into Washington with an escort of thousands, and the conqueror of millions of loyal hearts.[29]

One Republican editor issued a full-throated defense of Lincoln's secret passage through Baltimore in 1861. Henry Raymond of the *New York Times* was fed up with all the talk about assassination being incompatible with American values. To the claim of the Democratic *Albany*

Argus that "assassination is not congenial to the American character," the *Times* replied, "As a general statement, this is perfectly true—but it is none the less true, that in a time of excitement there are many men quite forgetful of their 'American character.'"[30]

In Raymond's eyes, Lincoln had courageously put public duty over his own desire to display personal courage to the northern masses. Some people might think they needed a show of bravery from him, but the body politic needed the higher courage of precaution. "He had no right to regard it from a merely personal point of view," said the *Times*, "nor to guide his action in regard to it by his personal feelings or predilections."[31]

CONCEALING HIS IDENTITY on the night of February 22–23, 1861, for what the Republican *New York Evening Post* satirically called his "flight *to* power," marked the first splitting off of Lincoln's private body from his public body. Until then, hail-fellow-well-met sociability had meshed with prepresidential duty. On the train ride east, he'd proven himself the republican leader to a fault: letting the horde of well-wishers see him up close, showing off his simplicity, bantering about his looks, and brushing off the excessive enthusiasm of the crowd inside the Buffalo depot.[32]

When he disembarked in that city on February 16, Lincoln found the platform jammed. He and his aides made for the exit, but the throng swept through the flimsy police barrier and "pressed upon him with a perfect furor," as the *New York Herald* put it, blocking his path to the street. His aides managed to squeeze him out the door and into his carriage, leaving the president "somewhat exhausted" but "in good spirits."[33]

Perhaps the Buffalo fracas influenced his decision a week later to pass secretly through Baltimore on the night train. In any event, the Baltimore decision laid down the precedent for stronger security measures. For the last four years of his life, he grudgingly accepted armed protectors but periodically managed to elude them. He drove Secretary of War Edwin Stanton to distraction by riding off to the Soldiers' Home without his Union Light Guard cavalry escort, heading off to the theater without his police guard, or walking alone at night over to the nearby War Department telegraph office. Stanton huffed and puffed, but he couldn't convince his friend to change his ways.

The president knew he could be attacked, but he thought a determined assassin would probably outwit any cordon of protection. A malefactor might even be spurred to action by a display of concern about the chief magistrate's safety. Lincoln may not have shared Seward's view that republics discouraged assassination by definition (since opponents could vote out an unpopular leader at the next election), but he did think that potential assassins, like other men, acted rationally. They were deterred by the prospect of losing their own lives in the attempt, and by the realization that murdering the president would accomplish little.

The notion of a southern sympathizer taking his life had struck him as silly in 1862. "Do you think the Richmond people would like to have [Vice President] Hannibal Hamlin here any better than myself?" he asked Major Charles Halpine, according to the major's later recollection. "In that one alternative, I have an insurance on my life worth half the prairie land of Illinois." (Hamlin was well known as a more militant antislavery man than Lincoln.) Three years later, with Andrew Johnson serving as vice president, the idea would have struck Lincoln as equally irrational.[34]

But putting himself repeatedly at risk didn't stem from a conscious calculation of the odds of being assaulted. It flowed from a deeper source, political and philosophical. All American politicians claimed to favor open interchange between the leader and the led, but none matched Lincoln in making his body a republican insignia. His physical charisma, his love of male sociability, and his ease in laughing at his looks all lay at the heart of his political life. Meanwhile, a deeply ingrained stoicism brought him to the belief that his living or dying lay beyond his or anyone else's control. He couldn't grasp the notion of actively trying to shield himself from harm. What seemed obvious to Edwin Stanton, to Henry Raymond, or to the president's self-appointed bodyguard Ward Lamon seemed beside the point to the man in question.

Lincoln and Stanton went head-to-head on this subject for the last time in early April 1865. In late March, Lincoln had accepted General Grant's invitation to visit army headquarters at City Point, Virginia. By the end of the month, the war in Virginia was hurtling to a close, and when the city of Petersburg fell to Union forces on April 2, Lincoln took Grant up on the offer to meet him there (fifteen miles west of City Point) the next day.

Stanton was not pleased. He dashed off a cable to the president trying to stop him from getting any closer to "a treacherous and dangerous enemy like the rebel army." Stanton trotted out his heavy artillery: the distinction between Lincoln's private and public bodies. "If it was a question concerning yourself only[,] I should not presume to say a word." But "the political head" of the nation must think twice about exposing the country to possible "disaster to yourself."[35]

Lincoln didn't receive Stanton's appeal until he returned to City Point from Petersburg on the afternoon of April 3. He was so elated by his short trip to Petersburg—where he had seen not just Grant, but a group of African Americans ecstatically celebrating their first day of de facto freedom, and the implausible presence in town of their emancipator—that he determined to head upriver to Richmond the next day with his son Tad. He gave Stanton the news by telegram, lightheartedly dismissing his call for public-minded caution. "It is certain now that Richmond is in our hands," he wrote, "and I think I will go there tomorrow. I will take care of myself."[36]

After arriving at the Richmond dock, Lincoln decided to walk through the downtown streets, rather than wait for an army vehicle to take him to Union General Weitzel's headquarters. Making the three-quarter-mile trek on foot, as reporters noted at the time, affirmed his republican commitment. Once again he was making intimate contact with the people—in this case, thousands of exuberant black Virginians (slaves suddenly free to salute their hero publicly) and hundreds of Union troops. Lincoln's personal predilections and his public duty (as he, not Stanton, defined it) coincided in the streets of Richmond, ten days before his assassination.[37]

NORTHERNERS got wind of Lincoln's memorable walk, and of his safe return to Washington, on the same day (April 10) that they read the news of Lee's surrender to Grant. Gleeful young men from government departments bounded around Washington in packs, beating drums, singing patriotic songs including "Rally 'Round the Flag, Boys," and pulling up at officials' houses to demand rousing speeches. When several groups and a band rendezvoused on the North Lawn of the White House, Lincoln dutifully appeared at a second-floor window under the porte cochere and quipped that if they all forced him to "dribble" out his thoughts on the spot, he would have nothing left to say on the next evening, Tuesday, April 11, when he planned to make a real speech. ("That's too late," one listener protested.)

The White House was so brightly lit by 8:00 p.m. on Tuesday that "the misty drizzle" couldn't obscure "the extent of the vast throng" stretching from the north portico to the sidewalks of Pennsylvania Avenue between Fifteenth and Seventeenth Streets. Former slave Elizabeth Keckley, Mary Lincoln's friend, servant, and "modiste" (dressmaker), remembered looking out a second-floor window at "the swaying motion of the crowd, in the dim uncertain light . . . like the rising and falling of billows—like the ebb and flow of the tide."[38]

Keckley's tide image was apt, since this mass of "thousands of both sexes" was "standing patiently in the deep mud" waiting for the president to appear. "In thorough good humor," they were ready for a festive, jocular victory speech. Instead, Lincoln read them a straightlaced policy statement on "reconstruction." Reminding everyone that "I myself was near the front and had the high pleasure of transmitting much of the good news to you," he launched into a dry defense of his lenient approach to readmitting Confederate states to the Union.[39]

Distinguishing his plan from the Radical Republicans' punitive stance toward the Confederate rebels, Lincoln nevertheless took one step in their direction: for the first time he voiced his preference for giving the vote to some African American men—those with some education ("very intelligent") and those who had fought for the Union. It was the first time *any* American president had publicly recommended extending suffrage to black men. Three days before the end of his life, Lincoln was contemplating black citizenship, and strengthening the affection that African Americans north and south felt for him.

Somewhere in the audience stood twenty-six-year-old John Wilkes Booth, whose work on the Washington stage Lincoln had witnessed in November 1863. Ten days before delivering his address at the Gettysburg battlefield, Lincoln had watched the actor (then in Washington for a series of twelve plays, mostly Shakespeare) perform at Ford's Theatre. The play was the melodrama *The Marble Heart*, and the president had been seated in his regular stage-left box. Sixteen months later, on March 4, 1865, Booth had watched Lincoln's outdoor second inaugural address, looking down at him on the dignitaries' platform from a position near the US Capitol's east entrance. Now, on April 11, Lincoln peered down upon Booth and the rest of the rain-soaked crowd from the second-floor White House window. If this had been daytime and Booth had been standing anywhere near the front of the crowd, the president might have recognized his face.[40]

The actor fumed when he heard the president endorse limited black suffrage. Booth took this as a declaration of war on the sacred American practice of white supremacy ("this country was formed for the *white* not for the black man," Booth had written in November 1864), and on the principle of state rights. Lincoln was subjecting the Confederacy, and the white race, to his autocratic, centralizing rule. "To hate tyranny [and] to love liberty and justice, to strike at wrong and oppression, was the teaching of our fathers," Booth wrote, signing off with pride as "a Confederate." "The study of our early history will not let *me* forget it."[41]

Thus the American assassin of 1865 concurred with one part of the general American consensus on assassination. Republics discouraged it, while tyrannies encouraged it. Lincoln had turned the United States into a tyranny. Booth compared himself to fellow assassins Brutus and William Tell, finding his motives "purer than either of theirs." He believed he cared only about his country, not about himself. Obviously Lincoln was bent on betraying it. According to the recollections of accomplices, Booth swore as he stood on the White House lawn to preserve the white essence of the American Republic by taking the president's life at the first opportunity. [42]

Lincoln and Booth showed on this rainy Tuesday evening that they shared a sense of urgency. Everyone else wanted to cavort, while these two men wished to get serious about defending the Republic. Each of them wished to restore the body politic to health—Booth by returning black people to their proper place in the social order, Lincoln by extending citizen rights to qualified African Americans. Lincoln's speech showed he was in flux on Reconstruction, eager to bring the rebellious states back quickly into their "practical relation" to the Union, but attentive to the danger that haste might just hand power back to the former secessionists. Booth murdered a man mulling over the prospects for linking reunion to a modest rebirth of freedom. [43]

Lincoln knew where he stood on basic principles. The body politic included Americans of all races, and in their "natural" rights they were already equal. Persisting civic inequalities could be removed with the passage of time, as leaders like him pushed for change when conditions permitted. His bold stroke on emancipation—proclaiming the freedom, on January 1, 1863, of slaves held in rebel-controlled territory—showed his skill at stepping through a political minefield. Since 1837 he'd publicly opposed slavery as "founded on both injustice and bad policy," but as president he had sworn to defend the Constitution, not to enact his personal moral convictions. He needed an impersonal, constitutional basis for hitting slavery in the rebellious states, and he found it in the commander in chief's sworn duty to defend the union. [44]

When criticized for unjustifiably turning a war for union into a war for emancipation, and for suspending habeas corpus on his own authority, he replied that he'd done nothing but defend the Union in both cases. "A life is never wisely given to save a limb," he wrote in 1864. Others were willing to sacrifice the nation to preserve their right to own slaves, and to prevent the president from ever detaining, even briefly, those disrupting the war effort. His critics were entitled to their belief (and their prejudice), but they were not entitled to whistle while the Republic burned. No person was permitted to disregard "palpable facts," about which "there can be no caviling."[45]

Lincoln's April 11 speech on Reconstruction suggests that had he lived to complete his second term, this open-minded problem solver devoted to equal chances for all might have found a way, working with congressional Republicans, to bring African Americans a greater measure of political freedom. That was the belief of John Wilkes Booth—hardly the insane sociopath of American myth, but instead the frantically clear-eyed defender of racial hierarchy and the diabolically clever author of a play within the play at Ford's Theatre on the evening of April 14, 1865.

CHAPTER TWO

Last Words, Last Breath

*The collective sense of what had occurred was of a sadness
too noble not somehow to inspire, and it was truly in the air
that . . . we could at least gather round this perfection of a
classic woe.*[1]

—HENRY JAMES, 1914

MARY AND ABRAHAM Lincoln arrived late at Ford's Theatre on Good Friday, April 14, 1865. The president had been
entertaining White House visitors, including Speaker of the
House Schuyler Colfax. An affable Hoosier, nicknamed "Smiler" for his
sunny disposition, Colfax was leaving town the next day on an overland
trip to California. Later he remembered Lincoln telling him he'd love
to see California himself, but could only dream about it since "public
duties chain me down here." Lincoln's comments to the Speaker about
the "pleasures" of the West were among his last spoken words.[2]

Lincoln tried to entice Colfax to join the party headed to Ford's, but
the Speaker begged off, saying he had to pack his bags. He walked beside
Lincoln as the president "took his last steps" from the White House Red
Room to the North Portico. Colfax received "the last grasp of that generous and loving hand, and his last goodbye." With that, Lincoln clambered
into his carriage for the two-block ride to Fifteenth and H Streets, where
he and Mary picked up their two guests, Clara Harris, the daughter of

a New York senator, and her fiancé, Major Henry Rathbone. Then they rode on another eight blocks to Tenth Street, between E and F, where a small crowd, pelted by occasional cloudbursts, was waiting to greet them.[3]

Jiggling along on the unpaved streets, the presidential party got a glimpse of the decorations put up to celebrate Lee's April 9 surrender. The public euphoria had peaked on Thursday night, April 13, with a festive "grand illumination" running into the wee hours. The city's homes, shops, and buildings were now even more lavishly appointed, as the April 14 *Washington Star* catalogued in a five-column survey of the most striking embellishments.

Jaunty or solemn words had been put up all over town. "How are you Lee?" taunted a motto spelled out in gas jets at E. L. Seldner's clothing store at Pennsylvania Avenue and Seventh Street. At the Swiss consulate on A Street South, a sign read, "The old Republic of the Old World greets the new Republic of the New World on the occasion of its new birth." If Lincoln's carriage was traveling east on E Street between Thirteenth and Fourteenth Streets on its way to Ford's, he could have read the large illuminated transparency mounted in front of Grover's Theatre, summing up the trajectory of the rebellion: "April 1861 the cradle, April 1865 the grave."

At Wolfsheimer & Brothers clothiers on Seventh Street, a poem-prayer placed in a large display window petitioned the Lord to protect Lincoln, whose health was widely thought to be failing:

> *Long live our chief, the President,*
> *In glory, peace and health;*
> *Nobly he brought the war to end,*
> *Crushed treason in its wealth.*
> *O God! Preserve his worthy life,*
> *Let never war or civil strife*
> *Again disturb our land.*[4]

The fifty-six-year-old president did look bedraggled during this week of northern jubilation. His face had withered over the previous year:

deep creases beside his nose, sunken eyes, hollowed cheeks, graying temples and beard. The outer man appeared old and frail, but on the inside, as Colfax and other friends testified, Lincoln felt revitalized by Appomattox and by his recent two-week stay at General Grant's headquarters on the James River. The epic April 4 march through Richmond had capped the visit, with thousands of slaves striding through town in the wake of the man they hailed as liberator. Colfax told Lincoln on his return from Virginia that he'd worried about the president's safety in the rebels' fallen capital. Lincoln replied that he would have fretted too if it had been anyone else; for himself, he'd felt no qualms at all.

AROUND 8:30 P.M., the Lincoln party of four made its way up the staircase from the foyer of Ford's Theatre to the dress circle. The audience was already engrossed in the evening's performance of the comedy *Our American Cousin*, but with the gaslights in all likelihood burning bright (dimming the house became customary in American theaters only a generation later) most people in the orchestra seats would have had no trouble catching the Lincolns' entrance. Once they appeared, spectators rose to their feet in applause, actors on stage joined in the welcome, and the orchestra launched into "Hail to the Chief." Seated in his wicker chair in the dress circle, Charles Leale, a twenty-three-year-old army surgeon, noted the presidential couple smiling and bowing as they proceeded to their stage-left box.[5]

When the play resumed, Lincoln's good spirits persisted, for the actors were freely adding humorous lines, for his benefit, to an already funny play. To one character's expressed desire to "escape the draft" of cool air, another answered that she needn't worry: the "draft has just been abolished," as the morning papers on April 14 had announced (referring to the military draft). Treasury Department employee John Deering got a straight-on view of the presidential party from his stage-right seat in the dress circle, and he noticed the "broad smile on Uncle Abraham's face." Actors and audience members were all keeping up the weeklong spirit of levity, and Lincoln was enjoying the party.[6]

Shortly after 10:15 p.m., during the second scene of the third act of
Our American Cousin, Deering heard what sounded like a gunshot.
Later he claimed that upon hearing the report of the weapon, he sensed
a gunman might have attacked the president. If so, he outclassed the rest
of the audience in quick mental work. Hardly anyone realized initially
that Lincoln might have been assaulted, and many did not register the
sharp sound as gunfire. Virtually everyone in 1865 thought about assassination in the abstract, but few were prepared for it as a real prospect.
Lincoln had attended Ford's and Grover's Theatres on many occasions
with no apparent risk, and no security detail.[7]

Grudgingly, after several moments of confusion, the audience began
accepting the idea of an assassination unfolding in their midst. Yet, after
Booth had launched the lead ball from his derringer muzzle-loader into
the back of Abraham Lincoln's head, rendering him instantly and permanently unconscious; and after Booth had slashed the Lincolns' guest
Major Rathbone in the upper arm with a long blade, causing blood to
spurt all over the box as Rathbone kept trying to subdue the assailant;
and after Mary had let out an anguished scream; and after Booth had
vaulted over the balustrade of the box, falling ten or twelve feet to the
stage below and shouting "sic semper tyrannis"—many in the audience
still could not take in what had happened. Witnessing Booth's awkward
landing on the boards, Edwin Bates, a New England businessman sitting in the front row of the orchestra underneath the presidential box,
assumed at first that Booth had crashed onto the stage because someone
had shot at *him*.[8]

The audience at Ford's on that evening inhabited an America funda-
mentally different from the one that came abruptly into being the very
next day—a new dispensation in which freely elected presidents might
succumb to violent attack, not just to illness (like William Henry Harrison in 1841 and Zachary Taylor in 1850). "It seemed," wrote the *Cincinnati Daily Commercial* in a pained, page-one pronouncement four
days later, "as if we had turned over a new page in history, and become
suddenly possessed of new natures and new destinies—the one baleful
and ungovernable, and the other leading to shipwreck."[9]

Newspapers soon scoured the annals of history for the most recent example of an assassinated republican leader, and they settled on Dutch Protestant nobleman William of Orange, shot and killed without warning in 1584 by a French Catholic assassin because he objected to Spanish rule. Almost three hundred years had passed since that murder. Assassination made no sense in a republic, and three centuries of European and American history confirmed it.[10]

The Sunday and Monday papers on April 16 and 17 engraved the entire sequence of events into millions of northern minds: Booth's stealthy approach, the distinct crack of his weapon, the bloody scuffle with Rathbone, Mary's cry, Booth's leap and declaration and escape, the impotent stupor of the audience. The killing lodged in people's memories as a succession of images, as a quickly developing action narrative that couldn't have happened, but did. The implausibility of the event made the theatergoers' anguished confusion vital to the story: their experience could stand for the gaping incomprehension of the entire Union population of twenty-five million. At the center of the sequence sat Lincoln's hulking frame, mute and motionless in his red damask rocking chair.

For villainous flair, John Wilkes Booth has never been surpassed: incensed at the public elation in the North over Lee's surrender to Grant, he waited for the Ford's theatergoers to roar with delight before pulling the trigger. Has any other martyr in history been dispatched while a thousand of his admirers were bent over in stitches? A master of dramatic irony, Booth had also made a careful calculation. The people's glee would slow down their perceptions. They wouldn't know how to react. They'd think the odd noise piercing their laughter had been intentionally added to the play—one more comic bit. Their disorientation would ease his escape. Some in the theater were ashamed of their slow response that night.

What the Ford's audience went through on April 14—a wrenching reversal from mirth to misery—was repeated in northern hamlets and cities in the days to come. It made Lincoln's death all the more inconceivable and all the more searing. For so incomprehensible a killing it was impossible to limit the blame to Booth (immediately named as the assassin in the weekend press), or to the Confederate government that must surely have controlled him, or to a negligent bodyguard from the Washington Metropolitan Police.

Many northerners blamed themselves for letting their guard down after Lincoln's return from Richmond. They had lost focus in celebrating Appomattox day after day since Monday, April 10. They had lulled themselves into believing that if Lincoln had walked unscathed through the former Confederate capital on April 4, he was surely safe in Washington, DC. "Of all the occurrences within the range of possibility," said the shaken and disbelieving *St. Louis Democrat*, "the assassination of our President in Washington, at this triumphant stage of the war, and while he was devoting himself in the most liberal spirit to an adjustment with the rebels, was perhaps the one event never thought of, still less looked for." For those who lived through the assassination, the brutal emotional turnabout from April 14 to 15 forever colored their sense of loss. "Noon and midnight," noted Brooklyn preacher Henry Ward Beecher, "without a space between."[11]

IN LINCOLN'S DAY, Americans were infatuated with the dying sentiments of public officials. Mass-produced lithographs depicted great men's deathbed scenes and printed their parting phrases as captions. The two previous presidents to expire in office—Harrison and Taylor—had declined little by little, giving them the chance to offer solemn last reflections. "Sir," the sixty-eight-year-old Harrison had said to his doctor, "I wish you to understand the true principles of the government. I wish them carried out. I ask nothing more." The sixty-five-year-old Taylor, famous for his exploits in the war with Mexico, spotted his doctor and spoke soldier to soldier: "You have fought a good fight, but you cannot make a stand." To those gathered around his bed, including his wife, Margaret, and his son-in-law Jefferson Davis, he added, "I die. I am ready for the summons. I have endeavored to do my duty. I am sorry to leave my old friends."[12]

During the Civil War, the nation's readers consumed a steady diet of dying phrases spoken by common soldiers and by great leaders, past and present. In its column "Last Words," *Frank Leslie's Illustrated Newspaper*, one of the most popular weeklies of the day, reminded everyone that George Washington's parting declaration was as "firm, cool, and reliant as himself: 'I am about to die, and I am not afraid to die.'" When Lincoln's old nemesis, Stephen Douglas, lay on his deathbed in 1861, his wife put her arms around him and said, "Your boys, Robby and Stevie, and your mother and sister Sarah—have you any message for them?" Douglas replied, "Tell them to obey the laws and support the Constitution of the United States."[13]

In the days ahead, northerners speculated freely about the words Lincoln would have chosen if he'd been given the time. Perhaps he'd have offered a message of reconciliation for North and South, or a Christian word of forgiveness for his attacker. Perhaps he'd have repeated words he'd already spoken elsewhere, like "with malice toward none, with charity for all" from his second inaugural address, delivered only six weeks before the assassination. Newspapers by the hundreds reminded readers of the martyr's favorite poem: the Scottish poet William Knox's fourteen-stanza "Oh, Why Should the Spirit of Mortal Be Proud?" written in the early 1820s. In doing so, they gave it the status of a self-eulogy, Lincoln's virtual last words.

In 1850, at the end of the eulogy he delivered for Zachary Taylor at a public gathering in Chicago, Lincoln had recited six of Knox's last seven stanzas from memory. His oration was soon published, and from that point on Lincoln was frequently taken as the poem's author. With good reason: he recited it to all comers and told them he couldn't remember who *had* written it. He melted at its fatalistic insistence on the universality and unanswerable power of death.

> *So the multitude goes, like the flowers or the weed*
> *That withers away to let others succeed;*
> *So the multitude comes, even those we behold,*
> *To repeat every tale that has often been told.*

'Tis the wink of an eye—'tis the draught of a breath—
From the blossom of health to the paleness of death,
From the gilded saloon to the bier and the shroud
Oh, why should the spirit of mortal be proud?

"I would give all I am worth, and go in debt," Lincoln wrote in 1846, "to write so fine a piece as I think that is."[14]

THE *NEW YORK HERALD* reported that as Booth approached him from behind, Lincoln was bending forward in his rocking chair, eyes fixed on the stage, head resting on his hand in his carefree way, sharing "a hearty laugh" with the audience. Sitting below Lincoln in the orchestra, Julia Adelaide Shepard noticed "how sociable" the event seemed, "like one family sitting around their parlor fire." Lincoln had tried to mingle as best he could from his elevated position. She described him as "a father watching what interests his children, for their pleasure rather than his own . . . How different this from the pomp and show of monarchial Europe."[15]

Many of those who loved Lincoln in 1865 regretted that he had spent his last conscious hours in a theater, in their eyes a morally dubious destination at best. But they took comfort in knowing that to the very end, he had sought out the company of ordinary citizens. He had been sitting among them, relishing their merriment, when he was struck down. Most northerners believed he'd given up his life for them. They took the assassination not as a retroactive martyrdom made possible by Booth's bullet, but as a voluntary self-sacrifice, akin to the death of a soldier in battle. "President Lincoln fell a sacrifice to his country's salvation as absolutely, palpably," said a *New York Tribune* editorial on April 17, "as though he had been struck down while leading an assault on the ramparts of Petersburg."[16]

Lincoln didn't know he had a date with death that night, but he did know that his republican duty entailed an attitude of disinterestedness as to life or death. A confirmed reader of the Bible, if not a professed Christian, he understood the relevance to his republicanism of Matthew 10:28 ("fear not them which kill the body but are not able to kill the soul") and Paul's comment to the Philippians (1:20) that "Christ shall be magnified in my body, whether it be by life, or by death."

He might have said the same about the American Republic being magnified by his dying as much as by his living. Perhaps once in a while President Lincoln came close to imagining the appropriateness, in the midst of all the war losses, of his own death. Schuyler Colfax remembered the president telling him, after spending a sleepless night agonizing over Union fatalities in 1863, "how willingly" he would "exchange places today with the soldier who sleeps on the ground in the Army of the Potomac." On that occasion, Lincoln was plainly aching for a good night's sleep, but he also sensed that solid rest now depended on imagining his body exposed to the risks run by his soldiers.[17]

SITTING in the dress circle forty feet from the president's box, army surgeon Charles Leale was startled like everyone else, not long after 10:15 p.m., by what sounded like a pistol going off. He rushed in the direction of the shot and reached the box before anyone else did. Lincoln sat slumped in his rocking chair, propped up by his wife, unconscious but still breathing. Leale couldn't tell where Lincoln had been wounded, and he quickly laid him out on the floor to examine him. He glanced at Major Rathbone's bleeding arm and inferred that Lincoln, too, might have been stabbed. A bystander with a penknife cut away Lincoln's coat and shirt, revealing no wound.

Running his hands through the victim's thick black hair (Lincoln had likened it to a horse's mane), Leale found the entry point of the derringer ball behind the left ear. Ignorant of microbial transmission, he used his pinky to probe the entry point of the .41-caliber projectile (four-tenths of an inch in diameter). Feeling the cavity convinced Leale that Lincoln had suffered a fatal injury. The surgeon conveyed this news to the people pressing into the box, and it spread quickly through the theater and into the crowd already forming in anger and gloom on Tenth Street.

By this time, a second young army surgeon, Charles Taft (uncle of future president William Howard Taft, then seven years old) had been boosted into the balcony box from the stage below. He concurred with Leale's dire prognosis, as did a third doctor, Albert F. A. King, who soon joined the others. Immediately they turned their attention from saving the president to keeping him alive as long as they could. As the doctors deliberated about what to do next, actress Laura Keene, the star of the show, arrived in the box and got Leale's permission to cradle Lincoln's head in her lap, absorbing drops of Lincoln's blood into the folds of her dress.[18]

Laura Keene was, in effect, sitting in for Mary Lincoln, who was too distraught to stroke her husband's forehead. In the weeks to come, many lithographs were produced to capture the scene in the president's box, but apparently none showed Laura Keene performing the holy service of succoring the dying martyr. Perhaps too many citizens would have taken umbrage at the idea of a "public woman," an actress, playing this poignant familial role. Such judgment did nothing to lessen interest in the bloodstained patches of her dress that she eventually distributed, along with affidavits attesting to their authenticity.[19]

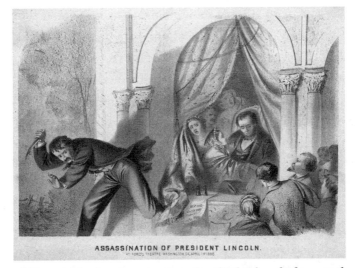

ASSASSINATION OF PRESIDENT LINCOLN.
AT FORD'S THEATRE WASHINGTON DC APRIL 14 1865

Major Rathbone's blood is dripping from Booth's knife as he leaps to the stage, and the top of Lincoln's rocking chair has been squared off to look like a coffin.

Dr. Leale recollected decades later that his only thought at this point was to "remove [the president] to safety." He and the other doctors ruled out a bumpy carriage ride back to the White House, a trip they felt would surely kill him, and chose instead to carry him out into the street in search of shelter. Had protecting his body alone controlled their decision, they might have asked the many soldiers present to clear the theater and make Lincoln as comfortable as they could. Something besides the victim's physical security drove their decision to take him on a jostling journey down the staircase and into a volatile crowd on Tenth Street, where, for all they knew, more danger lurked in the form of another assassin.

Merely moving the president outdoors posed medical risks too: "retaining [Lincoln's] life" as they crossed the street, Dr. Leale recalled, was accomplished only with "great difficulty." They had to keep stopping so that he could remove the clot of blood on the wound, reducing cranial pressure to aid the president's breathing. Dr. Taft was supporting Lincoln's head as the group shuffled along, led by a soldier who parted the crowd with his drawn sword. As Taft later remembered, "the motion of the body in being carried" caused additional oozing, "and my hands, which supported the head, were covered with blood and brain tissue."[20]

Meanwhile, Lincoln's body was barely covered above the waist. William DeMotte, an Illinois state official who'd attended the play and was now watching the Tenth Street spectacle, said the president was "denuded of the upper clothing, not only his face and neck exposed but his breast and arms. His coat or cloak was thrown loosely over his chest." On the evening of April 14, dozens if not hundreds of citizens got a glimpse of Lincoln's head and bare chest as he was carried past them in the open air.[21]

The idea of putting Lincoln in a lodging house on the other side of Tenth Street may have seemed so enticing to Leale, Taft, and King because it offered them a domestic setting where they could temporarily have the dying man to themselves. In a real bedroom they could close the door, keeping family, politicians, and soldiers out of the way as they prepared the president for a proper deathbed vigil. The pull of this enclosable space, where the physicians could perform their medical duties unimpeded, was matched by an equally compelling push factor: relocating Lincoln to a boardinghouse would ensure he didn't die on Good Friday in a setting many Americans considered suspect at best, disgraceful at worst. Realizing that the wound was mortal, the doctors may have sensed that the threat to the "safety" of the president included his moral legacy just as much as his bodily survival for, at best, a few more hours.

For years, Lincoln had been roundly chastised for his regular trips to the theater; one historian counts forty-three such trips during his four years in the White House. He had attended Grover's (later National) Theatre more frequently than Ford's, taking in performances of Shakespeare and of ordinary playwrights like Tom Taylor, author of *Our American Cousin*. For many American Protestants, theaters ranked with gambling dens and dance halls as cesspools of vice, and the president's spending the anniversary of Christ's crucifixion chuckling at an English comedy struck many of them as a lamentable lapse of judgment.[22]

"Multitudes of his best friends," said the Lincolns' own minister, Phineas Gurley, in a public address six weeks later, "would have preferred that he should have fallen in almost any other place. Had he been murdered in his bed, or in his office, or on the street, or on the steps of the Capitol," said Gurley, "the tidings of his death would not have struck the Christian heart of the country quite so painfully." If the public roadway ranked higher than the theater as a respectable place for a president to die, then Drs. Leale, Taft, and King had done Christians a vital service simply by getting the still breathing Lincoln out onto Tenth Street.[23]

IMMIGRANT TAILOR William Petersen owned a three-story, eleven-room house across the street from Ford's Theatre, and he rented out rooms to several young government employees and to Hulda Francis and her husband, George, a dealer in "house furnishing goods" ("cutlery, guns, baskets, brushes, and notions"). About 10:30 p.m., George and Hulda were undressing for bed in their big first-floor room at the rear of the house. Suddenly they heard what George called "a terrible scream" outside, and they ran to the front parlor window looking out on Tenth Street.

At the doorway of Ford's Theatre they saw "some running in, others hurrying out," and they heard "hundreds of voices mingled in the greatest confusion." Buttoning up his clothes and hurrying out the door, George reached the street just as Lincoln was being carried from the theater. Like William DeMotte, Francis registered the unexpected sight of the president's chest only barely covered with a coat. "I could see as the gas light [from the sidewalk streetlamp] fell upon his face," George recalled. The president looked "deathly pale," and "his eyes were closed."[24]

Holding a candle as he stood on the raised front stoop of the Petersen house, fellow boarder Henry Safford called out to Dr. Leale's party, inviting them to bring Lincoln inside. The obvious place to lay him down was the large Francis bedroom, but Leale's group passed it up in favor of a much smaller (10×17-foot) room rented by William Clark, a former soldier in Company D of the Thirteenth Massachusetts Infantry and now a clerk at the Treasury Department. Out for the evening, Clark had left his room neatly made up, and the door unlocked. The gigantic Lincoln was placed diagonally on the black walnut bed, his feet left dangling off the edge of the mattress by the wall, and his head angled toward the door.

This room's spare simplicity would permit an easy transition to the deathbed vigil. Aside from the bed, it contained only a bureau (topped with a crochet) and a small table. The old standards affixed to the wall— prints of J. H. Herring Sr.'s *Barnyard*, *Stable*, and *Village Blacksmith*, and a photo reproduction of Rosa Bonheur's *Horse Fair*—gave grieving visitors some familiar images of prewar rural tranquillity to contemplate as the night wore on.

Almost immediately, the Francis bedroom was pressed into national service too, as soldiers, officials, family, friends, and ordinary citizens converged on the Petersen house. In chaotic fulfillment of republican doctrine, a random detachment of "the people" had swarmed up the steps and followed the president's body onto the premises. Taking for granted the propriety of continued free access to their chief magistrate, they hung about the soon impassable hallway until a soldier was finally delegated to throw them out. Then they blended into the large mass of people squeezed into Tenth Street, where reeling theatergoers had been joined by the same roving bands of young men who'd been publicly celebrating every evening since Lee's surrender to Grant five days earlier.

After the hotheads in their midst had expended themselves with calls to burn down Ford's Theatre and to hang an allegedly anti-Lincoln passerby from a sycamore tree, the informal assembly settled into patient waiting for hard facts to emerge. Whenever a general or politician appeared on the Petersen house steps, the crowd plied him for information. William DeMotte remembered the people on Tenth Street keeping their collective ear literally to the ground. "At intervals during the night the clatter of horses' hoofs was heard as squads of cavalry galloped about the city. Each time there would be quiet and listening of the vast crowd till the direction was determined and as the sound always died away from us we knew the assassin was not found."[25]

Another man standing in the street, Union army officer Roeliff Brinkerhoff, had followed Lincoln's body down the stairway from Ford's dress circle, noticing "a plash of blood on every step." (The blood likely belonged to Major Rathbone, severely gashed by Booth's knife, not to Lincoln, whose head wound bled far less copiously.) Once outdoors, Brinkerhoff found alarm spreading as rumors pulsed through the crowd. Vice President Johnson, Secretary of State Seward, and Secretary of War Stanton had all supposedly been killed. "It looked as if there might be a second Saint Bartholomew [massacre of 1572 in France] in progress," Brinkerhoff wrote later. He ran up Tenth Street to get a look at the signal station atop the five-story Winder Building at Seventeenth and F Streets. When he saw the corpsmen sending a message to "the fortifications," he relaxed, knowing that "any uprising would be quickly suppressed."[26]

The rumors Brinkerhoff had picked up contained some truth. Booth had planned a coordinated assault against Lincoln, Vice President Andrew Johnson, and Secretary of State William Seward. His accomplice Lewis Powell had in fact "assassinated" Seward, since the word then connoted any violent assault, lethal or not, on the life of a public official. Seward and his son Frederick, also wounded by Powell, survived the knife attack. Johnson's designated attacker, George Atzerodt, had gotten cold feet and failed to act.[27]

As a deliberating minipublic, sifting out the truth or falsity of its own rumors, the crowd acted the part of a first-alert apparatus, sending off emissaries armed with the latest intelligence to other parts of the city. Until official word of the assassination was cabled from the War Department to the national press soon after midnight, the Tenth Street citizens operated as an informal broadcasting system.

Lounging with a newspaper in the lobby of the Willard Hotel, several blocks west of Ford's Theatre, Assistant Secretary of the Treasury Maunsell B. Field first learned what had happened when several men ran into the lobby yelling that the president had been shot. He hustled up Tenth Street and began buttonholing members of the crowd, who told him—perhaps grasping at straws of hope based on having seen the president's upper torso—that Lincoln had been shot in the chest and might survive. Field had little trouble pursuing the truth of the matter on his own by talking his way into the still lightly guarded boardinghouse.[28]

Meanwhile, Dr. Leale had cleared William Clark's bedroom of everyone but medical personnel—an order that meant ejecting an inconsolable Mary Lincoln. As Secretary Field stepped inside the house, he found her standing alone in the center of the front parlor, still in her bonnet and gloves, keeping solitary company with a marble-topped table. Three times she repeated the question: "Why didn't he [Booth] shoot me?" Soon she was joined and comforted by her friend Elizabeth Dixon, wife of Connecticut senator James Dixon, who remained with her all night long, and by her pastor, Phineas Gurley. Until the following morning, the front parlor of the Petersen house remained a sanctuary for familial, prayerful mourning.[29]

Having found the president unscathed below the head, yet growing frigid in his extremities, Dr. Leale ordered blankets, hot-water bottles, and "mustard plaster" to increase body temperature (by irritating the skin, the mustard application improved blood circulation). At Dr. Taft's suggestion, Leale forced a sip of diluted brandy between Lincoln's lips, which he swallowed with a struggle. Another teaspoonful of brandy did not go down at all. With that, the doctors settled in for a deathbed vigil of indeterminate length, readmitting mourners while continuing to monitor the victim's breathing and heartbeat.[30]

PRESENTLY, Secretary of War Stanton arrived at the Petersen house, after being apprised of the attack on Lincoln by another man sprinting out from the Tenth Street crowd. Stanton had waved off the advice that he stay clear of Tenth Street—"there [are] thousands of people of all sorts there," warned Major Thomas Eckert as he rode up on horseback beside Stanton's carriage. Once he had pushed his way through the onlookers outside the house, Stanton commandeered the Francis bedroom, turning it into his operations center.[31]

With an all-night flurry of instructions, Stanton—featuring "more of the Bonaparte in his composition than any other man in America," as the *Cleveland Plain Dealer* in his native Ohio said approvingly in 1862— oversaw the interviewing of witnesses from Ford's Theatre, launched the search for more assassins (on the correct theory that a second man, not Lincoln's assailant, had attacked Secretary of State Seward), and dictated a string of pronouncements for military commanders and the national press. A relay team of couriers sped the messages back to the telegraph office at the War Department, ten blocks to the west.[32]

In a spontaneously republican moment, the "people" supplied Stanton with his stenographer. One of his generals had perched on the Petersen house front stoop and barked out to ask if anyone in the Tenth Street crowd could take dictation. Corporal James Tanner was standing on his two artificial legs on the balcony of his boardinghouse next door, watching the throng beneath him. Having lost his limbs to amputation after the Second Battle of Bull Run, he'd learned the Pitman method of "standard phonography" and found work as a clerk in the ordnance section of the

War Department. He answered the general's call and spent the rest of the night by Stanton's side.[33]

Periodically, Stanton and other officials slipped across the hall to William Clark's crowded, stuffy room to stand vigil by the president. Tanner observed Stanton "trying every way to be calm and yet he was very much moved." Embellishing that comment many decades later, Tanner added that looking across the bed at Stanton's face, he observed the twitching of his muscles and "knew it was only by a powerful effort that he restrained himself and that he was near a break."[34]

Struggling to maintain his own composure, Stanton carefully limited the distressed and voluble Mary Lincoln's access to the death chamber. During the night she appeared by the bedside about once an hour. Her arrival would prompt the doctors to gather up the bloody towels and pillowcases under Lincoln's head and replace them with clean ones. On one of her visits, Dr. Taft recalled, she sat beside her husband, entreating him to address her. "Love, live but for one moment to speak to me once—to speak to our children." As she left the room and walked by the Francis bedroom, Tanner overheard her moaning, "O, my God, and have I given my husband to die?" "I tell you," Tanner wrote to a friend, "I never heard so much agony in so few words." Settled back into the front parlor, she resumed "weeping as though her heart would break."[35]

The Lincolns' oldest son, Robert, dressed in his army uniform, arrived at Petersen's from the White House, where Massachusetts senator Charles Sumner, a close family friend, had gone to fetch him. But Stanton denied Mary's agitated request that twelve-year-old Tad be allowed to join them. She pleaded that the voice of Lincoln's beloved young son might provoke the president to speak. Stanton knew Tad well, since the rambunctious boy had had the run of the White House, interrupting his father's business at will. During the war Stanton had fitted the child for a regulation army uniform and given him an honorary second lieutenant's commission and a captured Confederate battle flag. Familiar with his unpredictability, Stanton wasn't about to let him near the Francis bedroom, where business of state was being conducted, or near either of his parents. Stanton made

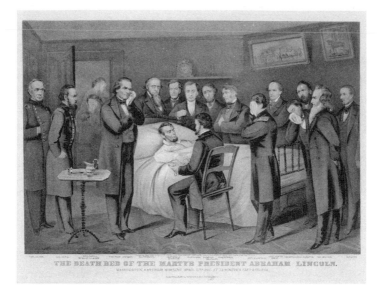

In the spring of 1865, Currier and Ives customers could choose between a public Lincoln deathbed—male officials tending to Lincoln, while Mary, her theater guest Clara Harris, and Tad (whom Stanton had in fact barred from the Petersen house) grieve in the hallway . . .

. . . and a familial one, with officials ceding control to Mary, Tad, and Miss Harris. Lincoln's son Robert, in his soldier's uniform, bridges the public and private scenes, weeping at the foot of the bed in both lithographs. In the actual event, the public deathbed prevailed, with occasional allowance for Mary's bedside mourning.

sure this deathbed ritual remained in the hands of circumspect men of government—political, judicial, military, and medical—and was spared the vagaries of family mourning.

REALIZING FROM the start that Lincoln was dying, Dr. Leale might have settled for keeping him comfortable and waiting for the end. Instead, he said many years later, he led the way in trying to get through to the president, hoping he might speak. Leale had served only briefly at the Armory Square army hospital in Washington (where he oversaw commissioned officers), but he had learned that unconscious patients with severe head wounds sometimes regained "recognition and reason . . . just before departure." We can bet he made this expectation known to the bedside mourners, and that some of them chose to linger by the president all night long because they hoped for that result. Roughly sixty people appeared at Lincoln's bedside during the night, including Vice President Andrew Johnson and all members of the cabinet except the badly injured Seward.[36]

Assorted congressmen also passed through, from Senator Sumner (who stayed until the end, letting Robert Lincoln lean against his shoulder) to Speaker Colfax, whose trip to California had been put on hold. Generals, judges, Illinois political figures, the Reverend Phineas Gurley, friends of Mary Lincoln, Petersen house boarders, Petersen's sixteen-year-old son Fred (the youngest of the bedside attendants), and more than a dozen civilian and government physicians collected in and about the bedroom. Perhaps twenty or thirty people remained at Petersen's all night.

Even if Lincoln couldn't speak, Leale believed his "sense of hearing or feeling" might remain, allowing him to take in the voices or feel the presence of those around him. So the doctor took possession of Lincoln's right hand, trying to let him "in his blindness know, if possible, that he was in touch with humanity and had a wfriend." In 1909, Leale remembered having gripped the hand all through the night, letting go only for a single minute when he went out to summon Mary Lincoln from the front parlor. As long as Leale remained in charge of the president's care (until Lincoln family physician Robert Stone and Surgeon General Joseph Barnes arrived), the possessive twenty-three-year-old allowed other doctors only to take his patient's pulse, not to touch the wound.[37]

Leale realized, forty-four years after the event, that he had played the part of a family member: "I took the place of kindred." He had imitated Laura Keene, who had sat in for Mary Lincoln in the theater box. The young doctor had succored the prostrate president while the stricken twenty-one-year-old Robert Lincoln, only two years his junior, stood a few feet away. Leale also realized, looking back from 1909, how "athletic" and "heroic" Lincoln's body had seemed to him even in the Ford's Theatre box, as the president lay sprawled on the carpeted floor.[38]

Others who caught a glimpse of Lincoln's body at the Petersen house concurred with that judgment when they looked back on the event. Every time a doctor pulled down the sheet to check the heartbeat, the dying man's upper body was exposed. "His brawny chest and immensely muscular arms revealed the hero of many a successful wrestling-match in his youthful days at New Salem," said Maunsell Field. The president's "vital power was prodigious." Field and the others had apparently never before seen him with his shirt off. The awkward man famous for his narrow shoulders now surprised them with his robust torso and limbs.

Secretary of the Navy Gideon Welles, awed by Lincoln's "large arms . . . of a size which one would scarce have expected from his spare appearance," added that the president's facial features had never appeared "to better advantage than for the first hour, perhaps, that I was there." Charles Taft believed "the vitality exhibited by Mr. Lincoln was remarkable." He recalled the surgeons at the Petersen house concurring that "most patients would have died within two hours from the reception of such an injury; yet Mr. Lincoln lingered from 10:30 p.m. until 7:22 a.m.[39]

All this attention paid to Lincoln's physical prowess helped the mourners prepare for the eventuality that he would not speak before dying. If he failed to utter last words, the mourners could appeal to his body for a final gesture. Stretched out for nine hours beneath a hissing gaslight and across a bed that could not contain him, his gargantuan frame rising and falling in steady rhythm, and his face occasionally twitching and looking "as though he was trying to speak" (as Fred Petersen remembered), Lincoln appeared under the guise of an indomitable leader determined to serve the Republic until his last heaving breath.[40]

Doctors, politicians, and ordinary folk were all seeing signs of implausible stamina in their dying hero. Fatally wounded, he revealed moral fortitude as well as unheard-of physical power. The deathbed mourners were inadvertently building a mythic edifice of memory for Lincoln. In his case, dying meant staying alive longer than humanly possible. It also meant giving up the campaign for life just in time to slip away "calmly and silently," as the *New York Herald* reporter, present in the Petersen house since 5:00 a.m. that morning, wrote of Lincoln's departure. There would be no disconcerting death throes—just a stirring struggle for life followed by an honorable surrender.

At 7:22 a.m. on April 15, Lincoln's heart stopped beating, and about ten seconds later, "his muscles relaxed and the spirit of Abraham Lincoln fled from its earthly tabernacle 'to that bourne from which no traveller returns'" (a line from *Hamlet*). On Easter Sunday morning, April 16, hundreds of thousands of newspaper readers found out that when he died, "the countenance of the president was beaming with that characteristic smile which only those who have seen him in his happiest moments can appreciate; and except [for] the blackness of his eyes his face appeared perfectly natural. He died without a struggle, and without even a perceptible motion of a limb."[41]

The next day they read it again. On page one of the *New York Times*, Maunsell Field described a passing with "no apparent suffering, no convulsive action, no rattling of the throat . . . [only] a mere cessation of breathing," and a smile that appeared on Lincoln's face not quite at the moment of death, but fifteen minutes later—"a smile that seemed almost an effort of life. I had never seen upon the President's face an expression more genial and pleasing." In the absence of consciousness, and of last words, Lincoln's body had delivered a parting message of striving for life and contentment with leaving it.[42]

THOSE PRESENT at the end in William Clark's bedroom dropped to their knees as Phineas Gurley, at Stanton's request, offered a prayer for the president's family and country. The secretary of war let his tears flow. The *Herald* man watched as "stoical Stanton," the embodiment of "coolness and self-possession," released "the silent monitors of the inward sorrow which rolled out from his eyes upon his cheeks." All the while, Stanton kept taking care of business: pulling down the window shades, dispatching a courier to order the tolling of city bells, and perhaps murmuring under his breath some now-famous last words of his own—a phrase that no one, neither the *Herald* reporter nor those standing by the bed at the moment of death (including the avid diarists and letter writers Charles Leale, Maunsell Field, Charles Sumner, Gideon Welles, James Tanner, and Phineas Gurley), caught at the time.[43]

"Now he belongs to the ages," Stanton supposedly said, giving voice to the ancient republican dream of time-transcending fame. A republic's leaders die, republics themselves may fall, but public heroes live on, inspiring generations to come. But no one reported in 1865 having heard Stanton utter any such phrase. The first mention of it came twenty-five years later in the ten-volume 1890 biography of Lincoln written by his secretaries John Hay and John Nicolay. They certified those six words as Stanton's authentic deathbed benediction, a secular affirmation allegedly delivered right after Reverend Gurley's well-attested deathbed prayer.[44]

Nearly all historians and biographers who came after Hay and Nicolay gladly accepted the Stanton phrase as genuine, for it truly sums up the course of Lincoln's reputation after 1865. Scholars never pressed for documentary evidence of Stanton's words because the phrase so plainly predicted the future. The report of Stanton's comment in Hay and Nicolay got a free pass because Lincoln *has* belonged to the ages, and because northerners ever since 1865 have so deeply wished that *some* memorable last words had emerged from Lincoln's deathbed.[45]

Whatever Stanton may have said, and whenever he said it, the crowning irony of "now he belongs to the ages" is that this republican pronouncement—one of the main things many twenty-first-century Americans "recall" about the deathbed of Lincoln—was unknown in 1865. Yet the whole episode confirms a deep truth about how Americans experienced Lincoln's death at that time. They were so desperate for *some* final word from Lincoln's deathbed that they kept that yearning alive for a generation, and in 1890 they were rewarded with a momentous *phrase* for the ages.

CHAPTER THREE

The Martyr and His Relics

The blow is . . . felt in every fibre of the body, social and politic.

—New York Journal of Commerce, April 17, 1865 [1]

B Y EARLY APRIL 1865, Lincoln was well on his way to standing on a pedestal all his own as the republican paragon of nineteenth-century America: victorious commander in chief, liquidator of slavery, unschooled orator of nature, gifted popular humorist, and master prose stylist. Heralded for a quarter century as the self-made Honest Old Abe, for half a decade as the virile rail-splitter, and in wartime as Father Abraham ("We Are Coming, Father Abraham, 300,000 More," sang the soldiers), he'd acquired an array of iconic qualities ensuring his lasting fame in the United States and among republicans battling autocrats and aristocrats around the world. He might have suffered political reversals during Reconstruction, but his legacy as wartime leader and "representative" man of the midcentury Republic was secure. [2]

One can imagine him, retired from politics in March 1869, just past his sixtieth birthday, stepping onto the national and global lecture stage and reshaping republican ideas as the era of Reconstruction moved toward its collision with the age of industrialism and class conflict. The nation was deprived of Lincoln's last words on April 14, 1865, but it also lost his first reflections on how to reconcile a republican approach to

*The republican figure Columbia and the religious figure Jesus both
claim a connection to Lincoln in William Wentworth's 1865 lithograph.*

equality—self-improvement for everyone, whatever their race, religion,
or starting rung on the ladder of opportunity—with the bracing conditions of modern farm and factory labor.

Some of Lincoln's speeches and letters suggest how he might have
addressed the problem of modern labor, had he lived past the 1860s.
His speech to the Wisconsin State Fair in 1859 sketches an outlook challenging the modern split between "capital" and "labor," and between the
educated and the uneducated. Lincoln saw hope for modernizing agricultural labor while keeping it family based and infusing it with chances
for lifelong learning. Farming had never appealed to him, but he believed
that equality in the future depended on making farm life an attractive
option for others—a life brimming with "cultivated thought," as well as
"mechanical" knowledge. "Every blade of grass is a study," he said, "and

not grass alone, but soils, seeds, and seasons," all opening up into the wondrous inquiries of botany, chemistry, and natural philosophy.[3]

It's easy to see that Booth's single shot on April 14, 1865, put an end to Lincoln's inquiries on every front, including the most urgent one of Reconstruction. What's harder to see is that it brought a halt to his unfolding *republican* fame. No longer merely a hero of the Union or a champion of self-making, the deceased president emerged from the Petersen house as a nascent *religious* martyr too—shot down and deprived of consciousness, unbelievably, on Good Friday, the very day of Christ's crucifixion.

Many Northern Protestants thought it was obvious: God had selected Lincoln for special service. They didn't think of him as divine, like Jesus—just divinely appointed for a mission of his own. Most didn't sense any conflict between the Christian and republican interpretations of his death—and of the gift he'd made of his body. But his saintly character began shoving his political virtues aside. It became harder and harder to remember him as an ordinary human being with unique talents and unmatched republican accomplishments.

ON THE MORNING of April 15, northerners took in the horrifying news. As soon as they woke up, city dwellers and many country folk living close to telegraph lines learned that Lincoln was dying, or perhaps already dead. Thanks to Edwin Stanton's cable delivered to the Associated Press at 2:15 a.m.—"It is not probable that the President will live throughout the night"—thousands of people across the North and West got word early enough to keep vigil in real time with the Petersen house mourners. In New York City, lawyer and diarist George Templeton Strong received the bleak report around 7:00 a.m., twenty minutes before Lincoln passed away. "I am stunned, as by a fearful personal calamity," he wrote hours later. "Poor Ellie [his wife Ellen Ruggles Strong] is heartbroken, though never an admirer of Lincoln's."[4]

Many northerners got the news as townspeople fanned out to fill them in. Visiting her uncle at his Ida Hill home a mile or two east of Troy, New York, Louise Coffin Smith was sitting in the flower garden after breakfast when "a horseman came up from the city, riding very fast, and as he saw us [he] checked his horse long enough to say, 'President Lincoln was shot last night and died this morning.'" He rode on to spread the news to the "country people," while her uncle, unsure what to believe, "drove down to the city and found it was true."[5]

All day long, people across the North faithfully pursued their pre-scribed roles in a collective ritual of loss. Benefiting from long experience with public mourning, they knew exactly what needed doing to honor a departed hero. They'd done for Henry Clay in 1852 exactly what they set about doing on this dreadful Saturday morning: they put black mourning emblems on their clothes; they placed black cloth and photos of Lincoln on their houses, shops, and buildings; and they gathered at public meet-ings to commiserate and ponder what his passing might portend.

The meetings were open to all, though in many places in the North, home to a quarter million free African Americans, black people often stayed home for their own safety. These customs asserted the whole com-munity's respect for the dead and gave vigilant citizens the pretext for silencing the few anti-Lincoln diehards that dared to speak up. Those even whispering a derogatory word about the president were manhan-dled or beaten, and sometimes arrested for their own protection. Occa-sionally they were tarred and feathered, and a few were killed; in many places they were publicly shamed and forced to recant. A unified north-ern experience of grief was created by compulsion whenever it didn't happen spontaneously.

On their left arms, many people fastened a mourning badge of black crepe (spelled "crape" in 1865) and displayed it for the next thirty days. If they wished to adopt "full mourning"—like the four hundred Illinois residents present in Washington, DC, on April 15 who assembled to pass a formal resolution to that effect—they also placed crepe on their hats for sixty days. By wearing these signs of grief on their bodies, people were building momentum for the processions to follow: the public marches that took place all over the North on the day of Lincoln's national funeral (April 19), and the local parades that accompanied the passage of his body across seven states (April 21–May 4).

Within days, manufacturers had produced a huge selection of mourning paraphernalia tailored to the occasion. The simplest badge or pin cost twenty-five cents. For fifty cents, one could get a satin badge, five inches by one and a half inches, inscribed "In Memory of Abraham Lincoln, April 15, 1865," with "neat pin and likeness [of the president], the whole covered with crepe." For the same price, one could buy a breast pin in a silver-plated oval frame, with eagle, flags, silk streamers, and the inscription "E Pluribus Unum."

On Saturday, with Lincoln dead for only a few hours, the *New York Herald* reported that "black crepe and ribbon, interspersed with the national colors, were worn by almost every person." Many citizens had already stocked up on basic black material during four years of civil war, but by the time of his funeral on April 19, they could wear a photographic likeness of Lincoln's face on their chests or sleeves.[6]

With their bodies properly appointed, northerners draped their dwellings and shops with crepe or some other black fabric. Those without the proper cloth on hand had to scramble for whatever they could find. "The market is swept bare of everything that will answer the purpose," lamented the *Springfield Republican*. "Cambric, broadcloth, cassimeres, serges, calicoes, crepe,

everything black has been put into requisition; the dry goods stores in cities, small and great, have been stripped of all goods that would express the public sorrow; and yet the demand is not half supplied."[7]

On Saturday morning, William DeMotte (who had attended *Our American Cousin* the night before) went out in search of crepe for his door, only to find that the largest dry-goods store in his neighborhood, near Pennsylvania Avenue and Seventh Street, was charging "foolish prices" for everything from "the finest crepe to black muslin." Meanwhile, the poorest African Americans in the national capital scavenged for "the small clippings of crepe and muslin used by their better circumstanced neighbors," stitching the remnants into "little irregular strings of black patch-work" to place on a door or window.[8]

Since many people had already bedecked their homes and businesses with flags to celebrate the fall of Richmond on April 3 and Lee's surrender on April 9, they just added black borders to the red, white, and blue, summing up in that simple act the weekend's crash from exhilaration to devastation. In Nashville, Tennessee, the emotional turnaround was acted out publicly on Saturday morning. It had taken nearly a week for the civil authorities and occupying Union troops to organize a "day of rejoicing" over Appomattox. Extra "star spangled banners" had been brought in from Louisville and Cincinnati, enough to decorate "almost every house."

Twenty thousand soldiers (the equivalent of the town's entire population in 1860) were massed in the streets on Saturday morning, April 15, waiting to march; and military bands were practicing their "lively and patriotic airs." Nashville citizens, previously divided politically, but now pitched toward union, were anticipating the evening's grand illumination and fireworks. Suddenly, at about 9:00 a.m., the disastrous news began coursing through the city. Like the crowd at Ford's Theatre in Washington the night before, most people first took it "as a jest," choosing to believe it only after members of the crowd had run off to check the newspaper bulletin boards. With the information confirmed, dazed soldiers marched back to their quarters, arms reversed, accompanied by bands playing funeral dirges. And soon the black draping appeared on many flags.[9]

In larger northern cities, photos and "mottoes" (handwritten banners) began springing up on Saturday morning, often reflecting people's attachment to the same books they knew Lincoln had loved: the plays of Shakespeare and the King James Bible. New York City, by far the largest metropolis in the nation (over a million residents when combined with Brooklyn—double the size of Philadelphia) erupted "as if by magic" with displays of words and pictures. Broadway from Madison Square to the Battery became a canyon of verbal and visual remembrance.

A store window at 759 Broadway displayed a Lincoln portrait above the words that Hamlet chose to describe his father: "He was a man, take him for all in all." Another shop down the block placed the rest of that passage (from act 1, scene 2, changing "I" to "we") under an image of the president: "We shall not look upon his like again." Wallach's Theatre near Union Square placed a large picture of Lincoln above its entrance, with a long banner stretched underneath offering eight lines from Macbeth's speech (in act 1, scene 7) in praise of King Duncan. This selection appeared so often across the North in the coming days that it became the virtually official slogan of the mourning period: "He hath borne his faculties so meek, hath been so clear in his great office, that his virtues will plead like angels, trumpet-tongued, against the deep damnation of his taking off."

Meanwhile, a shop in the sixth ward on Chatham Street kept up the biblical quotient of the public exhibits, posting a motto drawn from Numbers 23:10 and urging that a martyr is to be imitated: "Let me die the death of the righteous. May my last end be like his." In his establishment at Broadway and Fulton Street, a Mr. Knox joined the secular to the sacred by placing a long passage from Shakespeare's *The Life and Death of King John* (act 4, scene 3) in one window ("All murders past do stand excused . . . by this heinous spectacle") and citing Lamentations 5:15 in the other ("The joy of our heart has ceased; our dance has turned into mourning").[10]

———

WITH THEIR CLOTHES, homes, shops, and buildings marked for grieving, northerners set off on Saturday afternoon and evening for the citizen assemblies, where prayers, hymns, and orations mixed with eulogies and formal resolutions of gratitude to Lincoln. Community-wide meetings alternated over the next week with a full slate of religious, regional, ethnic, fraternal, political, and occupational gatherings, all of them enacting their own resolutions. Many were published in the local press as a way of honoring the president, and of shaping the meanings of his death.

One of the first to reach print was composed by the African Methodist Episcopal church delegates convened in Baltimore. The AME resolutions included a rare explicit reference to the martyrdom of John Brown, who had been hanged by the state of Virginia in 1859 for trying to launch an antislavery rebellion at Harper's Ferry. The delegates saw "the blood of John Brown" as having inaugurated "the meting out of justice to those who had long oppressed the Saviour in the person of the bondman." Lincoln's blood flowed in the same channel as Brown's, sparking "continued work until the Divine mandates, which award death to men-stealers, be fully and literally accomplished."[11]

The Baltimore delegates treated John Brown and Abraham Lincoln as equals in their proven devotion to the divine cause, but a few African Americans and white abolitionists still took Brown as the more heroic martyr of the two. For Brown had put the ideal of freedom ahead of any political calculation, even ahead of self-preservation. Brown had taken the old abolitionists' slogan—"duty is ours; consequences are God's"—and turned it into a warrior's cry, raising his sword against injustice.

In 1860, Lincoln had derided Brown as an "enthusiast" who "fancie[d] himself commissioned by Heaven to liberate" the slaves, only to draw up a plan "so absurd" that even the slaves "with all their ignorance, saw plainly enough it could not succeed." For Lincoln, Brown's obedience to a higher law of his own choosing reeked of anarchism. Lincoln had dismissed the "duty is ours . . ." slogan back in the 1840s. Yet in the eyes of the AME delegates in 1865, the president had found true kinship with Brown: both had died for the freedom of all.[12]

The AME resolution, published on Monday, April 17, shows that a religious slant on Lincoln's martyrdom took hold right after the assassination—and in this case, the religious thrust explicitly embraced the republican one. For the AME delegates, Lincoln's death made sense only in relation to Brown's. Both martyrdoms magnified the divine mandate ensuring the eventual civic and political liberty of black people.

By noon on Saturday, less than five hours after Lincoln's death, thousands of New Yorkers were gathered outside the Custom House on Wall Street. The extensive open space in front of "the old Merchants' Exchange" had served as a citizen's rallying point for many decades. After the April 3 march of Union troops into Richmond, and again after the April 9 news from Appomattox, major celebrations had erupted at that spot. On Friday morning, April 7, visiting Indiana congressman George Julian found an ongoing "blaze of enthusiasm" over the retaking of Richmond, "Wall Street packed with people, singing, shouting . . . people seemed wild with joy."[13]

As the crowd swelled at midday on April 15, many individuals found their numb disarray replaced by focused anger. When George Templeton Strong joined the assemblage sometime before noon, he sensed its surging venom, and felt the same sentiment rising in himself. He found the "temper of the great meeting" grim and uncompromising toward what he called the "woman-flogging aristocracy" of the Confederate states. "Let us henceforth deal with rebels as they deserve," Strong imagined the crowd thinking. "The rose-water treatment does not meet their case. . . . These madmen have murdered the two best friends they had in the world!" (Early press reports assumed William Seward had also been mortally wounded.) It was perfectly obvious to Strong, as it was to leaders in Washington, that the gunman had done the bidding of some entity within the official Confederate apparatus. They couldn't imagine a coordinated attack emerging from the mind of a single vengeful man, and an actor at that.[14]

A self-appointed committee of moderate Republicans and War Democrats, summoned by Simeon Draper, collector of the Port of New York, tried to control the message of the meeting by praising Lincoln, in one of their prepared resolutions, as a champion of "kindness, charity, and a spirit of conciliation toward the enemies of the Republic." But the people on the street showed they wanted not peace, but the sword: they gave a thunderous welcome to prominent Radical Republican Ben Butler, former military governor of New Orleans, who had shown up unannounced and persuaded the committee to open the meeting and let him speak. With the thousands spread out before them chanting "Butler, Butler," the committee had little choice but to accede.[15]

Butler lauded Lincoln as "a great and good man," the "savior" and "redeemer" of his country, but he quickly pushed beyond the plaudits. He painted the savior and redeemer as a naïve sentimentalist unaware of Confederate perfidy. He could have saved *himself*, cried Butler, if he'd only "nerved his heart" and recognized the bleak truth about the rebellion. Crushed militarily, it would naturally resort to assassination as a means of "reviving its soul." Lincoln had become "the first victim" of his own policy of "clemency," dying "with words of forgiveness on his tongue."

Butler nodded to the "inscrutable mysteries of Providence," but they turned out to be easily decoded. God had let Lincoln escape "the plotters against his life at Baltimore" four years earlier, when his inaugural train was taking him to Washington and "a great work lay before him." Now, with the president's task completed, God had passed the mantle to Andrew Johnson, "able, believe me, and determined to treat this rebellion as we want to have it treated . . . Retribution, retribution, swift, unerring, terrible and just." The crowd yelled out "as one man, 'Hang them!' 'Hang them!' 'Vengeance!' 'Vengeance!'"

Shrewdly, Butler politicized the mourning by using Lincoln's murder against him and his moderate Reconstruction policy. Under the guise of bemoaning Lincoln's death, he asserted the president's incapacity to recognize evil when it stared him in the face. He drew the moral that if, like Lincoln, you treat the Confederates with kid gloves, forgiving them their trespasses, they'll repay your weakness with a gunshot to the back of the head. Lincoln hadn't quite caused his own murder, but he'd forced God's hand. He'd given the Almighty no choice but to sign off on assassination, saving the Republic by letting the tough-minded Andrew Johnson take command.

Speaking after Butler, Republican James Garfield of Ohio, the "praying colonel" who, before being elected to the House of Representatives, had preached in Disciples of Christ churches, extended Butler's religious construal of the assassination. He, too, provoked rapturous applause. Lincoln, said Garfield, "the kindest, gentlest . . . friend the people of the South could find among the rulers of the nation," had followed the path of Jesus: he "forgave" his enemies "all they had done . . . dying with words of tenderness and magnanimity on his lips."

Since the rebels had spurned the president's doctrine of love, "justice, with hood-winked eyes, and with sword and scales," was now prepared to lower the boom on them. Garfield tapped the Gospel according to Matthew and the book of Joshua for some heavy scriptural artillery: "From every gaping wound of our dead chief, from every stab upon the Secretary of State, let a voice go up as of the people in their majesty, 'let this, my house be swept and garnished—let it be purged of this accursed thing.' [Great applause.]" Thankfully, God had taken Lincoln back to his bosom before the president could dilute justice with too much love. The saintly rail-splitter was ultimately too good for the nasty work of Reconstruction.[16]

Summing up Garfield and Butler's interpretation of God's doings, Lucius Chittenden, a former Lincoln appointee at the Treasury Department, asked the crowd two loaded questions: "Would God, in his mercy, permit such a good and great man as Abraham Lincoln to be assassinated, unless it was for a purpose? Was it not that he should be prevented from pardoning these traitors who have caused this dreadful war? ['Yes, yes.']" The rebels, who had not hesitated to starve Union prisoners, would now pay for their crimes. (Great applause.) "I can now understand it," declared Chittenden. "Abraham Lincoln was not the man to do this."

Butler, Garfield, and Chittenden—and scores of other Republican speakers at Saturday assemblies across the North—concurred that during the war, God had entrusted Lincoln to save the Union. But with the postwar rebirth of the Republic in mind, God had now saved the nation from Lincoln, ironically enlisting his own saintliness to remove him. The president had evolved at the end of the war into an imitator of the sweet and loving Christ. God had let Lincoln be sacrificed for too closely resembling the greatest martyr of them all. Oddly enough, it's these secular Republican orators, speaking within hours of Lincoln's death, who first insisted on grafting a religious interpretation of his greatness onto the well-grooved "republican" one. The Radicals couldn't resist sanctifying the president, since that move supplied rhetorical firepower for discrediting him and his policies.

FOR BUTLER, Garfield, and Chittenden, God had stepped in to rescue the Republic. Lincoln had shown himself unfit for postwar politics; the soft saint had body-snatched the virile leader of the war years. Many northerners wanted desperately to take these gentlemen's word for it, and to believe that Lincoln's death could be fitted smoothly into God's plan. But they wanted more than verbal assurances from public officials. They grasped at whatever additional straws they could find to suggest that Lincoln, like Jesus, *knew* he'd been chosen by God for special service.

Within days of Lincoln's death they received some sketchy evidence to support that supposition—enough to persuade some of them that he had sensed his death was coming, and was perhaps even in contact with God. It all started when they got wind of what had happened at his last cabinet meeting on April 14, the morning of the assassination. Naturally, the president and his colleagues—including their special guest General Grant, fresh from Appomattox—were feeling chipper that day, still reveling over all the good news received from the Virginia front since the fall of Richmond on April 3. Those present remarked later on Lincoln's unusually high spirits. Secretary of War Stanton found him "more cheerful and happy than I had ever seen [him]."[17]

Lincoln took advantage of the relaxed atmosphere to tell the group about a dream he'd had the night before—and to disclose that he'd had the same dream many times before during the war. He'd simply never seen fit to mention it. Within a few days, Secretary of the Navy Gideon Welles recorded in his diary what he remembered Lincoln saying about the dream: he was riding along on a body of water in "some singular, indescribable vessel," and "moving with great rapidity." That was it. Lincoln reported nothing more about the content of the dream, but he did add a crucial detail about its frequency. Every time he'd had the dream in the past, some "great and important event of the War" had taken place at about the same time—including, among others, the battles of Sumter, Bull Run, Antietam, Gettysburg, Stones River, Vicksburg, and Wilmington.

Usually the dream presaged some sort of victory for the Union, said Lincoln, but not always, as the mention of Bull Run and Fort Sumter revealed. In this case, he thought his dream indicated they'd likely be getting good news from General William Sherman, still locked in hostilities in North Carolina with the outnumbered Confederate general Joe Johnston. Good or bad, and from Sherman or not, the news would surely "come soon" and qualify as "great"—that is, of major moment. Every one of the earlier events following the dream had measured up to that high standard.[18]

The cabinet members bantered back and forth, caught up in the challenge of interpreting the dream. Acting Secretary of State Frederick Seward (his father, Secretary of State William Seward, was at home recovering from a carriage accident) later wrote that one listener scoffed at probing the dream for meaning: it was nothing, he said, but a string of coincidences. Another man pooh-poohed Lincoln's idea too, observing that with the war's outcome already decided, no dream could now presage victory or defeat. A third person listened more sympathetically, attempting a psychological reading of the dream, based on its regularity. Every time the dream had come to him, Lincoln had been feeling "uncertainty" in the face of "great change or disaster." Perhaps this underlying tension had provoked "the dim vision in sleep."

Undeterred by the three doubting Thomases, the president reaffirmed the predictive value of his speeding vessel, assuring the group that some momentous event would soon take place. This is a rare instance of Lincoln's commenting directly on the way his mind worked: here he saw himself not as the analytical powerhouse of the law courts and halls of government, but as a man strangely in touch with an external force. A few men in the room were rolling their eyes at his superstitious streak, just as some had regularly cringed at his folksy stories and his lowbrow humor.[19]

It didn't take long for the entire nation to get news of the ship dream, and for many to conclude that Lincoln had been given a premonition of his death. It comforted some people after April 15 to remember the president's joy on the morning of his assassination. Others clung to the dream story for solace: Lincoln had been allowed some inkling of his fate. Before giving up his life, he'd made contact, yet again, with a hidden power. Maybe, on the morning of his death, he'd contemplated his end. At the very least, he'd revealed his belief that he could penetrate the veil separating humanity from an invisible realm of mental or spiritual reality.

The *New York Herald* soon got wind of the dream report and printed a short item about it on April 18. This bit spread quickly to other papers, and the tale turned up in the diary of the ever-attentive George Templeton Strong on April 21. Strong had gotten his account from Dr. Robert Stone, Lincoln's personal physician, a source solid enough to convince the skeptical Strong that "the story of his dream the night before his death, as retailed in the newspapers, is true."[20]

Less than half a day after invoking his swift, shadowy vessel, Lincoln lay dying in Ford's Theatre, and within days masses of people were nodding ruefully at the premonitory power of his dream. The account of Lincoln's singular and swiftly moving ship had embarked on a voyage of its own through the postassassination waters of American culture, passing from newspaper to newspaper and mouth to mouth. New story details were picked up along the way, the embellishment reflecting Lincoln's rapidly expanding place as the nation's divinely and popularly designated martyr.

By the time Strong heard the story (within a week of the assassination),

Welles's "indescribable" vessel skimming across the water had received a description and a destination: a "fine ship entering harbor under full sail." Perhaps trying to correct the "harbor" distortion, Secretary Welles soon supplied a mistier end point, adding yet another adjective that has long proved irresistible to Lincoln biographers: the ship was now speeding toward "a *dark* and indefinite shore." From that kind of shore there was no hope of return; the president had dimly but surely anticipated his final voyage. Lincoln the dreamer had morphed into Lincoln the seer. The saintly republican martyr possessed mystical powers to match his ethical genius. Many hoped and some believed that this ordinary man with extraordinary gifts had been prepared for his rendezvous with God.[21]

AFTER THE ASSASSINATION, most northern Protestants were enamored of Lincoln's saintliness—Democrats and Republicans alike. Only the roughly three million northern Roman Catholics sat out the sanctifying campaign as a group, objecting to the entire program of making a martyr out of Lincoln. Many Catholics objected to the war, and many more had bemoaned Lincoln's evident solicitude toward African Americans. But political differences alone don't account for the animus that many Catholics directed at Lincoln even after his death. They were expressing their insular religious beliefs—martyrs and saints were Catholics, not Protestants—and their anger at Protestant America for decades of belittling them as credulous primitives with a prior loyalty to Rome.[22]

The majority of Protestant Democrats hailed Lincoln's saintliness because they thought his tenderhearted, love-your-enemies convictions made good policy sense for Reconstruction. By and large, they'd opposed the president when he made emancipation an essential component of saving the Union. But in the early spring of 1865, with slavery destined for legal extinction as soon as enough states ratified the Thirteenth Amendment (that happened in December 1865), Democrats believed Lincoln was sidling up to them by seeking "conciliation" with the former slaveholders.

Democratic or Republican, northern Protestants found it easy to turn Lincoln into a religious exemplar. It gave them a way to unite emotionally around their fallen chief without having to surrender their policy differences. While not averse to describing their hero as "saintly," they rarely labeled him a "saint." In their eyes that term had been tarnished for centuries by gullible Roman Catholics, who supposedly worshipped their saints instead of Jesus. Protestants faulted Catholics for adoring not just their saints, but their saints' holy relics too—further proof of their spiritual vacuity.

Yet no one told northern Protestants there was anything wrong with prizing the blood, brains, hair, and bones of the republican martyr Abraham Lincoln. No sooner had Lincoln's body, wrapped in blankets and placed in a quickly assembled pine casket, left Tenth Street on the morning of April 15 than the young male residents began making off with whatever treasures they could find. Albert Daggett, a nineteen-year-old State Department clerk, picked up "several relics of the awful event," as he told his mother: torn-off pieces of Lincoln's collar, sheet, and pillowcase, all "stained with his blood." William Clark claimed to have found "a lock of Mr. Lincoln's hair," and he squirreled away "a piece of linen with a portion of his brain." It was Clark's bed that Lincoln had died on, and Clark told his sister he'd kept "the pillow and case" from the moment of death. Five days after assassination, he was still sleeping on the deathbed and using "the same coverlid . . . that covered him while dying."[23]

At 11:00 a.m. on Saturday, April 15, a team of physicians and surgeons arrived at the White House to perform the autopsy, and they soon revealed the same appetite for presidential relics shown by the young clerks at Petersen's. First they removed Lincoln's whole brain and sliced it open, tracking the derringer ball's trajectory through "the left posterior lobe of the cerebrum," into "the left lateral ventricle," and into "the white matter of the cerebrum just above the anterior portion of the left corpus striatum," as Dr. Joseph Woodward put it in his official report.[24]

They couldn't tell with certainty where the ball had ended up, for it fell out of the brain as they were handling it, tumbling with a clatter into a metal bowl. It had lodged behind one of Lincoln's eyes, both of which, according to the *New York Times*, now exhibited a "deep black stain"— the result of a "comminuted fracture" of both orbital plates caused by "contre coup." Otherwise, his face looked "very natural." The *Times* and other papers went on to divulge that "a few locks of hair were removed from the President's head for the family," but they didn't disclose the doctors' own eagerness for bodily relics.[25]

That news, unfit to print in 1865, apparently remained off the record until thirty years later, when Dr. Charles Taft—the only physician to attend to Lincoln in the Ford's Theatre box, at the deathbed, *and* at the autopsy—related the story. After Lincoln family physician Robert Stone clipped some of the president's hair for Mrs. Lincoln, Taft reached out his hand "in mute appeal, and received a lock stained with blood, and other surgeons also received one." The previous evening, in the box at Ford's Theatre, Taft had already taken possession of "a gold-and-onyx initial sleeve-button," lifting it from "Mr. Lincoln's cuff when his shirt was hastily removed in searching for the wound." Taft claimed to have returned the button to Mary Lincoln, who later gave it back to him (she died a decade before he spoke of this).[26]

The lucky recipients of the martyr's relics included Surgeon General Joseph Barnes and Dr. Edward Curtis, a twenty-seven-year-old surgeon who went on to a distinguished career as a developer of microscopic photography at the Army Medical Museum and as professor of medicine at Columbia University. Barnes obtained some of the highly sought strands of hair snipped from around the wound—hence, hair carrying some of the president's blood and perhaps dabs of the cherished brain matter.

But young Dr. Curtis, passed over when the hair was doled out, left the White House carrying a unique martyr's relic, as well as some of Lincoln's blood. At least, he carried off those relics if we can believe an affidavit prepared in 1926, fourteen years after Dr. Curtis's death, by his widow, Augusta. She declared that her husband, upon returning home from the autopsy to their boardinghouse apartment (on Vermont Avenue, just north of Lafayette Square), had discovered that "a few drops of the President's blood had stained the cuffs of his shirt." Immediately, Augusta cut the cuffs from the shirts and placed them in an envelope for safekeeping.

As she did so, Dr. Curtis began cleaning his surgical instruments. He soon found "a tiny splinter of bone from President Lincoln's head," which "had evidently been driven into the brain by the bullet." He wrapped this little treasure in a piece of writing paper, put the words "splinter of bone from the skull of Abraham Lincoln" on the paper, and mailed the package to his mother. She became the proud possessor of the most eagerly pursued type of bodily relic in the Christian West since the fourth century: a sliver of a martyr's bone. After his mother's death, Curtis and his wife reclaimed the fragment of bone, and their descendants donated it to the Army Medical Museum (now called the National Museum of Health and Medicine), where Curtis had worked after the war. To this day the bone fragment shares pride of place with the lock of hair taken by Surgeon General Barnes.[27]

AT 3:00 P.M. on Saturday, April 15, the embalmers from the Washington firm of Brown and Alexander took over from the doctors, fixing Lincoln's face in the final look of contentment that deathbed observers had reported seeing at the Petersen house. Thanks to Charles Brown, whose team had also prepared the body of Lincoln's eleven-year-old son Willie for viewing after he died of an infection in 1862, the *New York Herald* could tell readers a few days later that "the muscles about the mouth still retained that pleasant and happy expression which we saw settle upon his face as his spirit took its flight on Saturday morning."[28]

The practice of embalming human remains went back to the ancient Egyptians, but Americans had only recently begun to embrace a modern version of it, as they coped with the deaths of hundreds of thousands of young men in Civil War battles and camps (many more soldiers died from disease than from enemy fire). Traveling to the war zone after the battle, and bringing home a loved one's embalmed remains, permitted families to gather for what amounted to a deferred deathbed ritual.

Tens of thousands of northern soldiers—mostly officers—were embalmed, beginning with Lincoln's own young friend Colonel E. E. Ellsworth, killed in Virginia in May 1861. As historian Drew Gilpin Faust has shown, relatives of the dead had to perform these tasks (including procuring the metallic coffin required for transport) because the armies on both sides lacked the resources even to identify the dead and bury them where they had fallen, much less collect them and send them home.[29]

Embalmers did their best to spread the practice to the civilian population through advertising. "Bodies embalmed by me never turn black," announced "Dr. Hutton" (one of Brown and Alexander's two competitors in Washington) in his full-page 1864 city directory advertisement. Guaranteeing his customers the undistracted "contemplation of the person embalmed, with the countenance of one asleep," Hutton invited families to stop by his establishment on Louisiana Avenue to "examine specimens" of his "beautiful art." Hutton pledged to exhume interred corpses at any time in the future to confirm that a loved one had not decomposed beyond recognition.[30]

Brown and Alexander placed no ads in the Washington directory during the war. Having procured the Lincoln family as a client in 1862, the firm may have gotten all the endorsement it needed. But Charles Brown gladly touted his skill to the press in 1865. He wouldn't identify the chemical fluid pumped into carotid artery, but he claimed (as the *Chicago Tribune* paraphrased him) that his process managed "absolutely to arrest the process of dissolution," while leaving "the brain and viscera" intact.

True, he could not "restore a body to its life-like appearance before death." He could, however, preserve a body in "just the condition in which he receives it"; in the case at hand, "the body of the President will never know decay." In the long run, Lincoln's corpse would lose its marble-like veneer and acquire a "mummy-ized" look. But Brown assured the public that no perceptible change would take place until several months after the president's burial in early May.[31]

Brown's admission that embalming could not produce a "life-like appearance" did not stop journalists and other observers from detecting signs of life in Lincoln's body. The "countenance of one asleep," guaranteed by Dr. Hutton's art, did not suffice for many who loved Lincoln. George Alfred Townsend, soon to become, at age twenty-four, one of the most famous and brashest newspaper writers and authors of the day, studied the president's corpse during the public White House viewing on Tuesday, April 18. He saw continued moral and physical vitality, not slumber. "His face wore that benignant, half-thoughtful, half-tender expression which distinguished it through life . . . The scalp was readjusted over the skull so tastefully that it seemed never to have been removed." Only "a dark discoloration" below his eyes indicated "life departed." Otherwise "mortality was a perfect counter part of life."[32]

In this era, many people believed a dying person's equanimity or distress carried over into the afterlife, and for the next week or two journalists told them that in Lincoln's case, all physical signs pointed to his final contentment. Victorian sentimentality thus added a new twist to the long annals of martyrdom: Lincoln had given up his life, but his offering had entailed neither bodily suffering nor physical disfigurement. The "dark discoloration" under Lincoln's eyes had resulted entirely from postgunshot trauma; it indicated no conscious pain on the victim's part.

Thanks to the embalmer's art, the president's corpse resembled a motionless living Lincoln. People could picture him at peace, spiritually and physically, suspended in the moment *between* life and death. Keeping him in that transitional state for three weeks allowed a mass of northerners to bid him farewell face-to-face. Peering down at his face and chest, they could imagine he had not quite departed. For four years he had flung his door open to all who entered the White House, and here, at the very end, he was still welcoming the common people to his side.

ON THE WEEKEND of the assassination, the Radical Republican story of Lincoln's martyrdom took hold, and it dominated northern public opinion for weeks. The president had surrendered his body for the nation, and God had seen to it that the sacrifice happened at just the right moment: *after* Lincoln had ensured the Union victory and freed the slaves, but *before* he could let the ex-Confederates off scot-free and botch the chance to remake southern society.

Hundreds of Protestant sermons took the same Radical line on Easter Sunday, mixing politics and religion just as Butler, Garfield, and Chittenden had mixed them the day before at their secular gathering on Wall Street (which nevertheless began with a mass recitation of the Lord's Prayer). In a spectacular, ironic, and providential act, God had used Booth and his Confederate backers as divine instruments. Martyrs' blood had always replenished the church, and Lincoln's would now revivify the nation. "May we not have needed this loss," the prominent Unitarian Henry Bellows asked his Manhattan congregation, "in which we gain a national martyr and an ascended leader, to inspire us from his heavenly seat?"[33]

The young Philadelphia Baptist minister George Dana Boardman, years later a leading Social Gospeler, praised God for taking Lincoln at the very moment his inspired service had peaked. "A green old age . . . amidst the tranquilities of his Illinois home" would have consigned him to a gradual petering out of his energies—a fate resembling that of the kernel of wheat in John 12:24, which "abideth alone," rotting as it lay on the ground, and bearing no fruit. God had permitted Lincoln to exit in his prime, when his death could still "bring forth much fruit."

Two such fruits occurred to Republican preachers on Easter Sunday, just as they had to public officials on Saturday: Andrew Johnson had come forward to make southern traitors pay, and representative government had manifested its mettle, showing it could survive an assassination. Of course, Lincoln had proved himself a gifted leader, but the genius of a republic lay in its renewable supply of chief magistrates. "No one man is great enough to do this mighty work," said Episcopal priest A. D. Mayo in Cincinnati, and "neither is any one man indispensable."[34]

The Union's roughly 150,000 Jews hadn't had time to absorb the news of assassination before heading to their synagogues for Passover services on Saturday morning, April 15, but their rabbis were soon speaking out in support of the Radical Republican viewpoint. Jews took Lincoln's killing hard, since he had gone out of his way as president to ensure their fair treatment. He had appointed Jewish chaplains to serve the troops, and shielded Jewish employees in the federal government against discrimination. He "recognized in full our claims to an equality before the law," said a tearful Rabbi Isaac Leeser at Philadelphia's Beth-el-Emeth Synagogue.

Rabbi Leeser, a major Jewish publisher and editor, and a translator of the Hebrew scriptures into English, had gotten the initial assassination report from the morning papers as he left home for temple worship. News of Lincoln's death was handed to him during the service, and Leeser thought immediately of the irony that the president had come safely through the April 4 trip to Richmond, the enemy's capital, only to be "stricken down unawares, unprepared," in his own.[35]

Within days, rabbis around the North had embraced the Republican Party consensus and given it a Jewish inflection. At Manhattan's Broadway Temple, Rabbi Samuel Isaacs told his audience to weep for their martyred president, as their ancestors had wept for Moses, but to take heart from the proven rhythm of history: the sun of Moses had barely sunk before the sun of Joshua burst through the gloom. Now Andrew Johnson's "resplendent light" flooded into the darkness left by the "lost chief," betokening "the cessation of [Lincoln's] conciliatory policy towards treason and traitors" and a "more vigorous course of action at the hands of his successor."[36]

The personal affection that northern Jews felt for Lincoln came through in a heartfelt but mistaken claim made by Rabbi Isaac Wise of Cincinnati's Lodge Street Temple: he told his congregation that Lincoln "believed himself to be bone from our bone and flesh from our flesh. He supposed himself to be a descendant of Hebrew parentage. He said so in my presence. And, indeed, he preserved numerous features of the Hebrew race, both in countenance and character."

Historian Bertram Wallace Korn, in his study of American Jewry during the Civil War, speculates that Wise misconstrued a jocular comment Lincoln may have made about having descended from common parents, meaning Adam and Eve. Lincoln did not spring from Jewish ancestors, and Wise was apparently alone in publicly attributing "Hebrew" characteristics to him. Had Wise settled for pointing out Lincoln's profound attachment to the Hebrew scriptures, he'd have conveyed an important truth about Lincoln's religious sensibility.[37]

Though he cherished the Bible and often attended New York Avenue Presbyterian Church with Mary, the president showed little or no interest in a divine Jesus or personal redemption. During the war, his belief in God's active role in history deepened, but he came no closer to professing faith in a savior from sin. In one of the biggest ironies of the postassassination period, the religious convictions of the nation's martyred chief—constantly likened to, but not ranked with, Jesus by African Americans and northern whites—drew as much or more on the Old Testament (the Hebrew scriptures) as they did on the Christians' New Testament.

A MASS of northern Protestant Democrats, and many Republican moderates, reviled the Radicals' views, but in late April 1865, neither group could confront them directly. Capitalizing on northern revulsion against the Confederates and their supposed puppet John Wilkes Booth, the Radicals were temporarily untouchable. And in any case, the Democrats were preoccupied with proving how much they truly loved Lincoln. They were forced to assume a tail-between-the-legs position: Please forget all the nasty things we said about him and his policies during the war. We adore the saintly man of peace who lately wished to let bygones be bygones, welcoming the secessionists back to the national fold if they would kindly sign off on the abolition of slavery and affirm their loyalty to the Union.

For the moment, all that Democratic editors could do was to glorify Lincoln while defending the free-speech rights of those vilified or assaulted by Republican enforcers. Democratic papers sprang to the

defense of ex-presidents Franklin Pierce and Millard Fillmore after
mobs confronted them in Concord, New Hampshire, and Buffalo, New
York, demanding that they drape their homes in signs of mourning. And
they stuck up for the public advocate of secession Julia Tyler, widow of
ex-president John Tyler, whose home on Staten Island was invaded by
Republican ruffians looking for her Confederate flag.

Democrats did dare to accuse the Radical Republicans of inconsis-
tency. Here they were praising God for removing Lincoln, yet they were
still condemning Democrats for having hoped, during his presidency,
that God would do just that. Republicans now approved of assassination, said the *Cincinnati Enquirer*—a conviction "which, in us, would be
counted treasonable." Many Democratic papers pointed to a Republican
speech given by one Reverend Motly in Lima, Ohio, on the day of Lincoln's death. "For a week or ten days prior to the assassination," declared
Motly, Lincoln was aiming to "bring those scoundrels down South back,
and give them the right of suffrage and when I heard of the assassination,
I just thought to myself that God, in His inscrutable Providence, had
taken him off just about the right time."[38]

While northern Protestant Democrats actively defended their integ-
rity with professions of love for Lincoln, Republican Party moderates sat
back and bided their time, knowing it was too soon to challenge the Radicals' position on Reconstruction. As they waited, they joined the Radicals in blasting away at every northern Republican's favorite target: the
conspirators who had taken down Lincoln. Ten days after the assassination, moderate party insider Henry Raymond's *New York Times* voiced
the general sentiment of moderates and Radicals alike: capturing John
Wilkes Booth had not put an end to the likely larger plot against the
Union. Andrew Johnson remained vulnerable to perhaps dozens of nefar-
ious operatives, a group "as secret, as much enveloped in mystery, and as
powerful as ever."[39]

But the *Times* identified an additional target for its scorn. John Wilkes
Booth had had another helper besides the pro-Confederate agents. The
Times identified this man on the very day, Monday, April 24, when Lin-

coln's body arrived in New York City for his lying-in-state. The funeral train had left Washington, DC, on April 21, and news accounts of the two public viewings in the capital—and those in Baltimore, Harrisburg, and Philadelphia—had sparked a frenzy of anticipation in New York.

Twenty thousand people were already waiting at City Hall when Lincoln's hearse arrived, and a chorus of nine hundred German Americans chilled everyone's spines with the "Pilgrims' Chorus" from Wagner's *Tannhäuser*. Its stately echoes could be heard blocks away, just like the booming reports of cannons and the somber pealing of bells all around the city. Two hours later, the twenty-three-hour viewing began. At least a hundred thousand mourners—men, women, and children, black and white—shuffled past Lincoln's open coffin before the doors were closed at noon on Tuesday.

Those clutching copies of the *Times* as they waited endlessly in line that afternoon could read on the editorial page that the additional guilty party had failed to perceive the proper responsibility of a president to the body politic. He had put "personal convenience" and "personal feeling" ahead of "public duty." The *Times* was positively incensed, and would not let the malefactor off the hook. "In this matter," said the editorial, "we have no hesitation in saying that President LINCOLN has been culpably remiss."

In all likelihood, editor Henry Raymond wrote this editorial himself, since it perfectly reflected his views and contains some of the very language he had used in 1861 when he praised Lincoln for putting personal preference aside and letting himself be slipped secretly through Baltimore in the middle of the night to avoid an assassination plot. Raymond had known Lincoln well. He'd written a campaign biography of him in 1864, praising him as a moderate who placed "facts" above "theory." Lincoln knew how to abolish slavery in the real world—by "awaiting the development of public sentiment" rather than imposing emancipation on an unprepared public, as recommended by the abolitionists.[40]

Now Raymond, still a devoted Lincoln man, couldn't contain his ire. The president had concealed headstrong selfishness under a guise of affable insouciance. Like anyone else, the president had preferred "perfect freedom in his public movements" to placing "a guard about his person in his intercourse with the people." But he had forgotten what he'd learned in Baltimore in 1861: this decision wasn't up to him. Then, as president-elect, he had recognized the higher need of the nation to preserve his life. As president, he had turned around and "placed his life at the command of any man who might choose to take it." Raymond was "far more surprised that he was not assassinated months or years ago, than that he did at last perish by the hand" of John Wilkes Booth.[41]

The editorial presented a jaundiced view of Lincoln's position, but it did so with befuddlement, not malice. Henry Raymond couldn't believe that Lincoln had proved so immovably negligent, so blind to the obvious necessities of the modern-day presidency. But Raymond was just as blind as Lincoln. The editor, like Edwin Stanton before him, couldn't see that Lincoln subscribed to a plausible vision of the public good that differed from his own. For the president, "intercourse with the people" qualified as both a public duty and a personal predilection.[42]

IF ANYONE were going to resist the sanctification of the martyr in April 1865, it would be a Republican moderate such as Henry Raymond. His treatment of the president in his August 1865 biography—an expansion of his 1864 campaign book, with the addition of many Lincoln speeches and letters—shows how the president's martyrdom might have looked if God had been left out of it. The book's title, *The Life and Public Services of Abraham Lincoln*, gives away Raymond's approach. Lincoln's private life, including his religious beliefs, is irrelevant. As for the Almighty's purposes, they're irrelevant too.

Raymond's Lincoln was a republican with no religious veneer. Providence had ordained Lincoln's death, Raymond said, but only in the sense that death waits for no one. People die at their appointed time. He refrained from describing Lincoln as saintly, giving him instead a wholly secular ardor and simplicity. He had achieved immortality—as Lincoln had said of President Taylor in 1850—in the retrospective judgment of his fellow citizens. They found his public virtue impeccable, as he had never corrupted his office by pursuing private gain. Lincoln had possessed but one literally fatal flaw: unable to imagine doing harm to any individual, he couldn't imagine any individual doing harm to him.

In his own way, Henry Raymond politicized the death of Lincoln as much as the Radical Republicans and Democrats did. He wanted to make the loss of Lincoln "serviceable to his country," as Ben Butler had said on April 15. But the way to do that, in Raymond's eyes, was not to revel in Lincoln's ascension to a special companionship with God. Lincoln had given up his body for the people. Much as Raymond disliked Lincoln's incessant mingling with the citizenry, he cherished his public probity. His lasting significance lay not in his having been chosen by God, but in his having been chosen by the people for their highest accolades. "The Chief Magistrate," Raymond concluded, "found his reward in the martyrdom which came to round his life and set the final seal upon his renown."[43]

Of course Henry Raymond, the disciple of "facts" rather than "theories," knew that by laying himself open to attack, Lincoln had inadvertently prepared the way for his religious apotheosis. The martyred chief [magistrate] was already being squeezed out of public discussion by the sacred martyr. No straightforward republican assessment of Lincoln's death could capture how deeply most African Americans and northern whites now loved him. Meanwhile, four and a half million African Americans—four million of them newly freed in 1865—were embarking on their own track of mourning. They would try to preserve Lincoln's republican essence even as they sanctified him.

CHAPTER FOUR

African Americans and Their Emancipator

We have lost our Moses.

—A BLACK MOURNER OUTSIDE
THE WHITE HOUSE, APRIL 19, 1865

O N APRIL 15, 1865, white Republicans could comfort themselves with the thought that Lincoln had completed his work. They found solace in the idea that the American Republic could replace anyone. They allayed their anger by asserting that God was now angry and would smite the secessionists by turning them over to a no-nonsense dispenser of justice from Tennessee.

Few African Americans found consolation in any of these stratagems. Most free blacks in the North and South (about half a million in all, a slight majority in the South) and most of the four million slaves believed that Lincoln had stepped off with them, years before, on a march toward freedom. He was in midstride when the derringer went off. Some of them surely knew that the Lincoln in their minds surpassed the actual man in his beneficence, but his Emancipation Proclamation—announced in September 1862 and enacted on January 1, 1863—had given them all the evidence they needed that this republican leader could not be replaced. The presidents before him had done little or nothing about black people's exclusion from the body politic.

After the proclamation came out, many white northerners took to calling Lincoln another George Washington. Black people placed him beyond comparison to any other republican hero by exalting him, in the words of the *Colored Citizen* in Cincinnati, as "our modern Moses." Placing such grand hopes in Lincoln's power promised substantial benefits, but it also set up a risky double dependency: tying their fortunes to a single mortal man, and embracing an ancient biblical hero whose symbolic aura no longer quite matched the American situation. When they lost Lincoln in 1865, their devastation was complete: the man was gone, and the symbol was teetering.[1]

AFRICAN AMERICANS had begun building up their mythic Lincoln about the same time that northern Republicans converted their Honest Old Abe into the rail-splitter—during the election campaign of 1860. In that year, slaves could perceive no immediate prospect of freedom, but many could already tell that Abraham Lincoln, the presidential prospect reviled by most white southerners, deserved their allegiance. After his inauguration in March 1861, and the start of the war in April, thousands of slaves began making plans to leave their owners. In effect, over the next year and a half they freed themselves, most often by making a beeline for Union army camps. But they freed themselves in full confidence that *their* Lincoln was furnishing enthusiastic support.

In fact, for the first seventeen months of the war, the actual Lincoln— fearful that encouraging fugitive slaves might harm the Union cause— actively resisted his army commanders John Frémont and David Hunter, who decided not to return runaway slaves to their masters. Two Lincolns existed side by side before September 1862: the flesh-and-blood politician who worried about pushing too fast, and the heroic beacon of freedom conjured up by thousands of slaves. When the proclamation took effect on January 1, 1863, it didn't free many slaves outright, but it sparked further momentum for liberty. "The year of jubilee has come," said (Frederick) *Douglass' Monthly*, which called for "one long, loud,

An African American family arriving at Union lines,
January 1, 1863. This family left home before the Emancipation
Proclamation took effect, and had decided to leave home well
before that. On January 31, 1863, Harper's Weekly *commented*
on the family ("Contrabands Coming In," p. 78) and ran a drawing
(p. 68) based on this photograph by David B. Woodbury.

hearty Hallelujah that shall rend the heavens and thrill the inmates of every slave-hut in America."[2]

Former inmates of those huts, interviewed in the 1930s, testified repeatedly (encouraged by New Deal questioners instructed to ask them about Lincoln) to his vital presence in the slave culture of their youth. Many former slaves depicted Lincoln as a wily trickster, outsmarting their owners by sneaking into slave communities before issuing his proclamation. "Dis heah old Abe Lincoln come through our town," said Mrs. Lou Griffin, born in the 1840s. "He just come 'round to see how de Rebs do de slaves. I gets so full thinkin' how de good Lawd fix it for us. He [Lincoln] come 'round when nobody's lookin' for him. Bye and bye he says, fight for your freedom in de Yankee army instead of standing 'round here being sold and treated like beasts."[3]

Charlie Davenport remembered being about fifteen years old "when hones' Abe Lincoln what called hisself a rail-splitter come here to talk wid us":

He went all th'ough de country jus' a-rantin' an' a-preachin' 'bout us bein' his black brothers. De marster didn' know nothin' 'bout it, 'cause it was sorta secret-lak. It sho' riled de Niggers up an' lots of 'em run away. I sho' hear'd him [Lincoln], but I didn' pay 'im no min'.[4]

One former slave showed in the 1930s that white Americans were not the only ones captivated by Lincoln's appearance. "He was de uglies' man I ever seed," said eighty-one-year-old Mary Wallace Bow to her interviewer. "He was tall an' bony wid black whiskers an' black bushy hair an' curious eyes dat set way back in his head. Dey was dark an' look like a dog's eyes after you done hit him." Posing as a peddler, Lincoln had stopped off at Mary's North Carolina plantation to collect intelligence. He made up in caginess what he lacked in looks. He got her owner's sister "Miss Fanny" so interested in buying his wares that she didn't notice she was answering his queries about Confederate war strategy.[5]

Some slaves found ways of letting their masters know where they stood on Lincoln. In the 1930s, Susan Snow, born into slavery in Alabama in 1850, recalled the white children on her place singing a song about Lincoln and Jefferson Davis (many former slaves recalled other versions of the same song):

> *Jeff Davis, long an' slim,*
> *Whupped old Abe wid a hick'ry limb.*
> *Jeff Davis is a wise man, Lincoln is a fool,*
> *Jeff Davis rides a gray, an' Lincoln rides a mule.*

One day, as her white mistress stood within hearing distance, she "hopped up an' sung" to the white kids a song she'd learned in the slave quarters:

> *Old [Union] Gen'l Pope had a shot gun,*
> *Filled it full o' gum,*
> *Killed 'em as dey come.*
> *Called a Union band,*

Make de Rebels un'erstan'
To leave de lan',
Submit to Abraham.

"Old Mis' was a-standin' right b'hin' me," Snow recollected. "She grabbed up de broom an' laid it on me. She made *me* submit. I caught de feathers, don't you forgit it."[6]

Former slaves' recollections from the 1930s are matched by published accounts from the 1860s. Young Mattie Jackson's story of her Missouri enslavement was printed in 1866, and she recorded that her mother had displayed a picture of Lincoln in their quarters. Their master once "searched my mother's room and found a picture of President Lincoln, cut from a newspaper, hanging in her room. He asked her what she was doing with old Lincoln's picture. She replied it was there because she liked it. He then knocked her down three times, and sent her to the trader's yard for a month as punishment."[7]

The common tales of slaves encountering a disguised Lincoln in the South during the war were only slightly more fantastic than the actual experience of thousands of blacks in Petersburg and Richmond on April 3 and 4, 1865, when they got to see and (at least in Richmond) touch him on the day after the Union army took control. In both cities, African Americans were busy celebrating the new regime when who should materialize among them to fulfill their deepest mythic longings but their flesh-and-blood liberator![8]

That real-life encounter can only have confirmed, for some African Americans, the validity of the earlier imagined meetings. Lincoln had evidently made a practice of suddenly showing up physically in the lives of his people, proving his unshakable dedication to their well-being. He proved it to Frederick Douglass in reverse fashion, by welcoming him to the White House. A month before Lincoln's march through Richmond, Douglass showed up in the reception line at the executive mansion after the second inaugural address. Doormen tried to keep him out, but Lincoln waved them aside and greeted him warmly. Shaking the president's hand, Douglass marveled at his forthright display of fellow feeling.

He'd had the same experience in 1863 when he met Lincoln at the White House to discuss the recruitment and fair treatment of black troops. Douglass was used to the acclaim of some white people, but not to being treated, without fanfare, as their equal. Lincoln gave him the ultimate compliment of not noticing his race. "Long lines of care were already deeply written on Mr. Lincoln's brow," Douglass wrote decades later, "and his strong face, full of earnestness, lighted up as soon as my name was mentioned . . . he arose and extended his hand, and bade me welcome. I at once felt myself in the presence of an honest man—one whom I could love, honor, and trust without reserve or doubt."

Like the hundreds of whites who published their recollections of Lincoln in the late nineteenth century, Douglass joined the president's appearance to his character: "The expression of his face was a blending of suffering with patience and fortitude. Men called him homely, and homely he was, but it was manifestly a human homeliness . . . His eyes had in them the tenderness of motherhood, and his mouth and other features the highest perfection of a genuine manhood."[9]

AFTER LINCOLN announced the Emancipation Proclamation in September 1862 (to take effect in January 1863), white antislavery northerners began likening his future fame to that of George Washington. "The *'year of Jubilee'* has indeed come to the poor slave," Lieutenant John P. Jones of the Forty-Fifth Illinois Regiment wrote to his wife from Tennessee in October. The president's name, "handed down to posterity," would "not [be] surpassed by the immortal Washington himself."[10]

This act of comparing the two presidents' postmortem reputations—with the second one not even two years into his first term—reveals the republican mind-set at work. Lieutenant Jones could imagine no greater accolade for Lincoln than his eventual enshrinement with Washington. Self-denying public service, as Lincoln had said in eulogizing Zachary Taylor in 1850, ranked as the highest virtue in a republic. Lieutenant Jones and many others performed the people's task of designating the best leaders for the ultimate distinction.

Putting Lincoln and Washington side by side became so common as to seem self-evident. By October 1864, Republican Party stalwart Carl Schurz, a German immigrant and a veteran of the 1848 armed republican uprising in Prussia, was letting a German friend in on what appeared obvious in the US North: "In fifty years, perhaps much sooner, Lincoln's name will stand written upon the honor roll of the American Republic next to that of Washington, and there it will remain for all time. The children of those who now disparage him will bless him." Of course, Schurz's prediction erred in its estimate of how long the turn-around would take. Just five months later, northern Democrats began blessing the president, hailing him for apparently planning to go easy on the Union's enemies.[11]

To most black people in 1863, the notion of likening Lincoln to Washington would have made little sense. With his Emancipation Proclamation, Lincoln had left Washington in the dust as a proponent of freedom for all. In a jubilant speech on the proclamation at New York City's Cooper Institute on February 6, 1863, Frederick Douglass did praise Washington and Jefferson, slave owners both, for having "desired to see Slavery abolished" someday. But Lincoln, he said, had finally broken with the founders' head-in-the-sand system of cruel deception: freedom for all—except for those who weren't free.

Engineering "the greatest event of our nation's history if not the greatest event of the century," Lincoln had "dared, in this dark hour of national peril, to apply . . . the sacred truth of human liberty" to a mass of enchained Americans. Slaves under rebel control, Douglass proclaimed, were no longer being legally held. "At last the out-spread wings of the American Eagle afford shelter and protection" to everyone.[12]

Douglass's secular and republican version of Lincoln—already, in his eyes, an international leader in the onward march of liberty—flew in the face of the common African American understanding of Lincoln as another Moses. Appealing to the Moses figure had made perfect sense when Lincoln was first elected in 1860. For decades the biblical account of the ancient Hebrews' exodus from Egyptian slavery had been embedded in black culture, as the spirituals made plain: "When Israel was in Egypt land / Let my people go / Oppressed so hard they could not stand / Let my people go."

Like the ancient Jews, many American slaves had dreamed of deliverance to a *place* beyond the reach of their oppressors. In 1838, Douglass himself had escaped by train from Maryland to Massachusetts (carrying the papers of a black seaman), and he assumed the biblical exodus story could help spark hope in others, too, of a new life in the North or in Canada. But by 1863, he realized the Moses story needed updating. After Lincoln's proclamation, it was not just unnecessary, but dangerous, to suggest that African Americans were a captive people in need of deliverance to some other place.

Douglass knew that until August 1862, Lincoln himself had publicly subscribed to precisely that view, dreaming of the day when black Americans would decamp for a foreign land. A decade before that, in his 1852 eulogy for Henry Clay, Lincoln had directly applied the Exodus tale to the African American experience, quipping that he hoped the United States could escape the fate that befell "Pharaoh's country . . . cursed with plagues, and his hosts . . . drowned in the Red Sea for striving to retain a captive people." As Lincoln told a small group of free black men invited to the White House on August 14, 1862, any white or black person who truly cared about American slaves' liberty should help them relocate to a land untouched by white racism.[13]

Douglass detested the words Lincoln spoke on that August day. African Americans didn't need to be told to leave the only home they'd ever known. They needed to be defended as Americans possessing the same right to the pursuit of happiness enjoyed by everyone else. In 1863, Douglass embarked on a mission to save African Americans *and* Abraham Lincoln from the idea that freedom was waiting for blacks in some better place. Douglass pushed to get all Americans, white and black, to modernize the Moses story and make it serve republican ends. Emancipation now meant deliverance to full freedom for blacks wherever they lived.

In 1879 he was still at it, objecting to a black-organized push for resettlement to Kansas. While begrudging no one the chance to escape southern-white intimidation and violence, he cautioned against a general departure. "Exodus" by *choice* rather than out of physical *necessity* tied "freedom and free institutions" to "flight," not "right," handing victory to the southern enemies of liberty.[14]

AT FIRST LIGHT on April 15, with an unconscious Lincoln still gasping for air on his deathbed, clumps of mourners hovered on sidewalks near the Petersen house. Secretary of the Navy Gideon Welles encountered several of them when he left the deathbed at 6:00 a.m. to get some fresh air. Every fifteen or twenty feet, he ran into another little circle, and he saw that most of those gathered in the light rain were African Americans—not because this was their local neighborhood, but because they had come here. Someone in each group would ask him if any hope remained. When he replied that Lincoln would die shortly, the black people "especially . . . were painfully affected."

A few hours later, under still gloomy skies, Welles made his way to the White House, where his wife Mary Jane was tending to her friend Mary Lincoln, mired in her misery. Approaching the gate on Pennsylvania Avenue, he saw several hundred African Americans—mostly women and children—"weeping and wailing their loss," unsure "what was to be their fate since their great benefactor was dead." Their numbers held steady "through the whole of that cold, wet day," and their "hopeless grief" stayed with him as an unsettling memory of that Washington morning.[15]

In Vicksburg, Mississippi, news of the assassination reached the populace sometime in late April, and a crowd of African Americans converged each day outside a store window that displayed a portrait of Lincoln. A white correspondent of the *New York Tribune* wrote that many of them stood "gazing with tearful eyes upon the shadow of him . . . afraid that Mr. Johnson, being a southerner," would abandon the martyr's proven dedication to their advancement. The *Tribune* editorial page scoffed at their anxiety, assuring them that Johnson would honor his pledge, the previous winter, "to do every thing in his power to secure them right and justice."[16]

Black Americans were happy to hear that powerful whites might now battle for justice in the South, especially if that meant voting rights for some of their men, as Lincoln had publicly proposed on April 11. But the fallen president, as Douglass had stated repeatedly since 1863, had built up a track record of intensifying resolve for black freedom. Andrew Johnson had done nothing of the kind. True, Johnson had likened himself to Moses in the fall of 1864 when, as governor of Tennessee, he declared an end to slavery in his state. He promised to lead black Tennesseans through "the Red Sea of war and bondage" into "a fairer future of liberty and peace." But of citizenship or voting rights he said nothing. By the spring of 1865, African Americans had good reason to believe that Lincoln's successor wasn't thinking about them when he thought about justice. Johnson's recent rhetorical blasts had targeted the treason of white rebels, not the deprivations and humiliations suffered by blacks.[17]

On April 15, Frederick Douglass tried to get blacks as well as whites to see a silver lining in the disaster. That afternoon, he sat in the audience at a hastily called public meeting in Rochester, New York. Fellow mourners clamored for him to speak. "On account of the race to which I belong," he said, "and the deep interest which that good man ever took in its elevation," he felt the murder "as a personal as well as national calamity."

But the "national" side of Douglass already found reason to hope. Only days before, in the general euphoria over Appomattox, northerners had appeared to be letting bygones be bygones. "It seemed to me that General Lee was about the most popular man in America. [Applause and laughter.]" Now, with "this drawing of the Nation's most precious heart's blood" at Ford's Theatre, northerners would cease "growing weak" and regain "a just appreciation of the awful crimes of this rebellion." Just like Generals Butler and Garfield at the tumultuous Wall Street event that afternoon, Douglass used Lincoln's death to stiffen Republican spines for Reconstruction struggles ahead.[18]

STARTLING ERUPTIONS of northern racism on the weekend of the assassination only strengthened African Americans' attachment to Lincoln and confirmed their trepidation about the future without him. On April 15 and 16, most of the Lincoln detractors who voiced pleasure at his passing—incurring the instant wrath of other citizens—simply bad-mouthed Lincoln, claiming he deserved what he got. Sometimes they "ventured a shout for Jeff. Davis," as Charles Taft witnessed during the procession of Lincoln's hearse back to the White House on April 15.

But other comments took on a racial tinge. The African Americans still present in New York City in 1865—because of the attacks on them during the 1863 draft riots, their numbers had dropped to perhaps 10,000, compared to 12,500 in 1861—recoiled when they found out that a white man had chosen the day of Lincoln's death to call him "a damned

nigger" who "ought to have been shot long before."[19]

Anti-Lincoln outbursts quickly evaporated after the weekend of April 15–16, as more and more Democratic newspapers voiced horror at Booth's act, and rued the aid the president's killing had rendered to the Radical Republicans,

This 1863 carte de visite attacks Lincoln's emancipation policy, promoting opposition to it by deriding him and two other Republican stalwarts (Horace Greeley and Henry Ward Beecher) as deranged by their devotion to black freedom.

bent on imposing harsh measures on the South, including suffrage for black men. Even the rabidly anti-Lincoln *New York Freeman and Catholic Register*, edited by Copperhead loyalist James McMaster, called the assassination "an act of *frenzied madness*," of benefit only to "the most fanatical faction of the Puritan party [the Radical Republicans]." With leading Democrats now attesting to Lincoln's pure and forgiving character, and deploring his removal as a disaster for the whole nation, individual Lincoln haters stopped testing the tolerance of police and citizens for their anti-Lincoln speech.[20]

Yet many African Americans still harbored the sinking feeling that the assassination had left them dangerously exposed. Like Douglass, they believed that President Lincoln would have kept taking steps to push their equality. Within weeks, Andrew Johnson was being praised in the northern Democratic press for his erstwhile white-supremacist racial views. The Columbus, Ohio, *Crisis*, an anti-Lincoln paper with a national following, contentedly reminded everyone that in 1859, Johnson had said that the preamble of the Declaration of Independence—"all men are created equal"—did not apply to blacks.[21]

LINCOLN'S MARTYRDOM ten days after the momentous Richmond walk compounded his religious significance for many blacks, as elements of their personal savior—Jesus the sacrificial lamb—were fused with Moses the law-giving liberator. As for northern white Protestants, so also for black Protestants north and south: God had chosen Lincoln for the ultimate act of self-surrender. "He was crucified for us," a black mourner was overheard saying in York, Pennsylvania, when Lincoln's funeral train passed through.[22]

Yet, many black writers and preachers joined the chorus of white voices making sure they weren't succumbing to Catholic-style idolatry: they specified that Jesus alone was divine. As the San Francisco *Elevator*'s editor Philip A. Bell—a quarter-century veteran of African American journalism going back to the *Colored American* in Manhattan in the

1830s—wrote, Lincoln's "memory [will] be held in adoration, but one degree inferior, to that which we bestow on the Savior of all mankind."[23]

Many Jews and white Protestants also hailed Lincoln as another Moses. Some of them echoed the African American conviction that Lincoln had been called, like Moses, to lead black people to freedom. Henry Ward Beecher of Brooklyn's Plymouth Church spent Easter Sunday preaching to a throng of black worshippers in Charleston, South Carolina. Returning to his home pulpit a week later, he said he could easily give comfort to grieving whites, since *their* martyr had completed his work and gone to his rest. But there could be no relief from any human source for the "wailing" blacks "in hamlet and cottage, in woods and wilds and the fields of the South," since they saw him as "a Moses come to lead them out from the land of bondage."[24]

Yet most white rabbis and ministers used Moses simply to reassure their white flocks: God had blessed the transfer of leadership from Moses to Joshua in biblical times, and now God had blessed the succession from Lincoln to Johnson. Their fallen leader was giving way to a providentially chosen successor. As much as losing Lincoln might hurt, the Republic was safely in God's hands.

AFRICAN AMERICANS turned out in large numbers for most of the twelve major funeral processions and thirteen viewings of his corpse (two in Washington, DC). Of course, like the white mourners, black people wanted to say goodbye to Lincoln in person. But they also wished to signify their inclusion in the nation—to participate in public gatherings where they were welcomed and protected. The mourning events doubled as republican assemblies, this time—in principle at least—with full representation for those who the infamous Dred Scott decision of 1857 had declared could never qualify as citizens of the United States.

White reporters covering the Washington rituals—the lyings-in-state on Tuesday and Thursday, April 18 and 20, and the White House funeral and procession to the Capitol on Wednesday, April 19—discovered how keenly African Americans felt their loss. With black men given a place in the official parade, and black women lining up on the sidewalks to watch, African Americans earned special attention in Republican newspapers. When the journalists asked the black women to comment on Lincoln's death, they spoke of their love for him and of their fear for the future.

At the first lying-in-state in Washington, a reporter found "an old gray-haired negress" waiting patiently in line outside the White House in the midday heat, "holding her little grandchild above the heads of people to prevent it from being smothered." She told the writer, "I wants dis little chile to see de man who made her free."[25]

During the funeral procession to the Capitol the next day, the *New York Tribune's* Charles Page, recently returned from duty in Virginia as a war correspondent, took a particular interest in the black mourners. "All the fifteen thousand that live in this city," he wrote, were "dressed in their best, and all, even children in arms, wearing badges of mourning." Page heard African Americans talking "in low tones of him that was gone as the savior of their race, their liberator." One woman made a stark Washington-Lincoln contrast, saying of the first president that "he went in for liberty" and they "love him for it." But Washington "didn't see things as clear through 'em as Lincoln did. Lincoln didn't stop with white folks, but kept straight ahead, and took all us too."[26]

Hours before the procession, Leonard A. Grimes, a freeborn black Baptist minister from Boston, approached the White House and saw that African Americans had arrived first and stationed themselves along the fence on all sides of the building. At the main gate in front of the North Portico, he noticed "a poor old contraband [fugitive slave] woman . . . weeping like a broken-hearted mother" over Lincoln's death. Grimes tried to reassure her by sharing his belief that "God would raise up another Moses for them." "Ah," she replied, "but we *had* him."

Frederick Douglass read about this encounter in the New York anti-slavery weekly *Independent*, and on June 1 he amplified the story in his national Fast Day speech at New York City's Cooper Institute. Reprinted in the *National Anti-Slavery Standard*, Douglass's oration gave the nameless woman's words an international audience. Calling her response to Grimes "the most affecting incident he had heard" since the assassination six weeks earlier, Douglass ramped the story up by having the old woman offer the name of Moses with no prompting from Grimes. "When asked why she wept," said Douglass, the woman answered, "We have lost our Moses." Told that "God will send you another," the woman responded, "I know that, but we had him already."[27]

IN THE WASHINGTON, Baltimore, and Philadelphia funeral processions, free African Americans marched in huge numbers, corresponding to their relatively large shares of the local populations. At the invitation of Secretary Stanton, members of the Twenty-Second Regiment US Colored Troops traveled all the way from City Point, Virginia, to join in the Washington parade. Arriving late at the Washington Navy Yard, they proceeded up Seventh Street to Pennsylvania Avenue, only to see the head of the line already approaching them from the west.

Rather than backtracking to the staging area, they simply took over the front position, leading the way to the Capitol. African American men thus occupied the first and last ranks of the procession, for the planners had assigned several black organizations—Harmony Lodge No. 18, Grand United Order Odd Fellows of Colored Men, King Hazekiah's Pasture No. 3, the Union Grand Lodge of Masons, and the Benevolent Association of Colored People—to the end of the parade.

In Baltimore on April 21, Charles Page of the *New York Tribune* estimated the turnout of black marchers and spectators at thirty thousand, including a group of wounded soldiers positioned in the military ranks and a variety of civilian units bringing up the rear of the procession. Some of these religious and fraternal organizations—the African Methodist Episcopal Church, the Grand Order of Nazarites, and assorted lodges of Good Samaritans, Odd Fellows, and Masons—had traveled to Washington on April 19 to appear in that procession too. A special train of fourteen cars had brought them and the instruments for their two marching bands to the capital (in all, twelve musical groups appeared in the Washington march, including Lincoln's favorite, the United States Marine Band, of thirty-five pieces).[28]

Page was not surprised by the size of the black turnout in Baltimore, but by the display of unforced racial mixing among the spectators. "Let not the reader imagine this an overdrawn picture," he solemnly began.

White and black side by side in the rain and the mud, with eyes strained upon that coffin, with eyes running over, and with clasped hands, and with faces all drawn and distorted, or set in marble fixedness. White and black leaned forth from the same windows . . . and there seemed to be no consciousness of any difference of color.

Page found it stunning that in Baltimore, where in 1861 whites "would have stoned [Lincoln] to death" during his inaugural train trip, blacks and whites were being welded together "in the white heat of a common sympathy and common sorrow."[29]

Philadelphia's gigantic procession on April 23—about a hundred thousand marchers and three hundred thousand spectators, perhaps half of whom got to see Lincoln's body during a marathon twenty-hour viewing—featured soldiers from the Twenty-Fourth Regiment US Colored in the military ranks at the front of the parade, and the usual black civilian groups at the end of it. As always, the white press took special note of voluble African American mourners.

Reporting from the darkened, candlelit interior of Independence Hall, where Lincoln was lying in state, the Associated Press writer featured "an old colored woman, 65 or 70 years of age," who "thrilled [chilled] the spectators with her open expressions of grief. Gazing for a few moments on the face of the dead, she exclaimed, clasping her hands, while tears coursed down her withered cheeks: 'Oh Abraham Lincoln! Oh, he is dead! He is dead.' The sympathy and love expressed by this poor woman found a response in every heart, and seemed to increase, if possible, the general grief."[30]

A nearly identical scene unfolded in Albany on April 26. Louise Coffin Smith, who had been sitting in her uncle's garden outside Troy on the morning of April 15 when a rider galloped by announcing the assassination, paced by the coffin and observed "the tired worn face of our President," which "had a look of peace." She added that a black female mourner had spoken out the feelings that others kept to themselves. "An old colored woman just ahead of us attempted to kiss him, saying between her sobs, 'we have lost our best friend.' Soldiers hurried her on."[31]

THE WELL-PUBLICIZED presence of African American units, military and civilian, in Washington, Baltimore, and Philadelphia heartened many black and white observers, but the gargantuan event in heavily Democratic Manhattan on April 25 delivered a serious wake-up call to advocates of black inclusion. As late as April 24, with Lincoln already lying in state at City Hall, the Common Council had taken no steps to include black marchers in the New York procession. For days, J. Sella Martin, pastor of the First Colored Presbyterian Church, had tried to persuade the council to permit a group of African Americans to join the ranks. He had gotten nowhere.

On the twenty-fourth, the council claimed the black marchers' application had missed an unbendable deadline. Getting wind of the exclusion from a Washington newspaper, Edwin Stanton sent word that the deadline didn't matter: in the funeral procession honoring the emancipator, "no discrimination respecting color should be exercised." The council duly reversed itself, but only about two hundred African Americans assembled to march as the final unit in the parade. Some black men remained wary about possible violence against them, despite police protection.[32]

The Reverend James Pennington, a leader in the black community, had inadvertently increased their concern, for his letter warning of renewed racial tumult in the city appeared in the morning *New York Tribune* of April 25, the same issue that carried his appeal for African Americans to join the day's procession. On April 19, he reported, three white men had accosted him after noticing his mourning badge. "Ain't you sorry your father Abe Lincoln is dead?" said one. "I will shoot you," said another. Other blacks, said Pennington, were being assaulted or taunted as "Old Abe Lincoln's black orphans." "If not checked," he claimed, the "intensified feeling of barbarism" toward blacks in New York "will result as heretofore," referring to the draft riots of July 1863, when white mobs killed at least a dozen African Americans and beat or stoned many more.[33]

The black men who decided to march on April 25 gathered at Reade Street, a block north of City Hall Park, and took up their place in the rear. Carrying a banner reading "Abraham Lincoln Our Emancipator" on the front and "To Millions of Bondmen he Liberty Gave" on the back, they met no violence (two platoons of city police protected the front of their lines, and another two platoons watched their back). They doffed their hats to the white spectators who expressed their support. "There could be no cheering of course," George Templeton Strong wrote in his diary, but "the crowded sidewalks and windows all along the route were white with waving handkerchiefs. Times have changed since July/63!"[34]

The assassination might have prevented Democratic newspapers from pummeling Lincoln, but it didn't stop some of them, like the *New York Weekly Day-Book*, from directing their rage at a safer target: black people. In March 1865 the *Day-Book* had judged the president "contemptible" for having claimed to love the Union "as it was" while actually pushing a policy of "nigger freedom." After the assassination, the *Day-Book* let up on Lincoln—he was "naturally disposed to clemency and kindness," and had just been pushing his party toward "conciliation and magnanimity"—but spewed contempt for African Americans. The Common Council's opposition to black men marching in the Manhattan procession reflected the sure "instincts of the people," who knew that "the Constitution was made by white men, for white men . . . and [that] the 'Union' is the creature, body or organism of the former."[35]

On the very day that Lincoln's body was put on view in Harrisburg,

Pennsylvania, the weekly *Democratic Standard* appeared in Pottsville, fifty miles to the east. Its War Democrat editor N. C. Barclay had always endorsed Lincoln's "efforts to crush the insurrection," opposing only his "policy of changing the war for the Union into a crusade for the uncertain experiment of negro emancipation." Unable now to assail Lincoln, the *Standard* went after the racial mixing that the paper claimed would follow black freedom. A racially mixed dance had just taken place in Michigan, said the *Standard*, where whites were affronted by "that odor peculiar to the African in too powerful a degree to be indured [*sic*] by the nasal organs of the whites."[36]

This venomous passage helps one grasp the urgency of Lincoln's contrast, in his 1857 speech on the Dred Scott decision, between Republicans and Democrats. Though few Republicans at the time could imagine pushing *social* equality between whites and blacks, most agreed with Lincoln about everyone deserving basic protection and respect as they climbed the ladder of opportunity. Republicans, Lincoln said, believe "the negro is a man," while "the Democrats deny his manhood; deny, or dwarf to insignificance, the wrong of his bondage; so far as possible, crush all sympathy for him, and cultivate and excite hatred and disgust against him."[37]

The Democratic *New York World*, edited by the elegantly articulate Manton Marble, revealed that African Americans in New York City and elsewhere in the North faced a subtle barrier to equality along with the overt violence, daily intimidation in the streets, and racist fulminations. Marble laughed off the entire issue of whether blacks should have been included in the Manhattan procession, treating it as the odd fixation of the local reformer class. "A queer city is New-York. Less than two years since, for one entire week [during the draft riots] it was as much as a negro's life was worth to be seen in the streets, while now they are on the very topmost wave of fashionable favor! What next, we wonder." Marble's editorials after the assassination eloquently praised Lincoln as savior of the union, but they remained unmoved by Lincoln as martyr to liberty.[38]

IN OHIO, Indiana, and Illinois, funeral-event organizers, well aware of what had transpired in New York, went out of their way to make black participants feel welcome. And in some midwestern cities, a wave of white outreach toward African Americans seems to have preceded—just barely—Lincoln's assassination. According to the Indiana correspondent ("M") of the weekly *Christian Recorder* of the African Methodist Episcopal Church, a new tolerance was on display at civic processions held on April 14 across the region to celebrate the Appomattox surrender.

In M's hometown of New Albany, Indiana, a city of about fourteen thousand, the local evening paper made a point of announcing "*all are invited*" to Friday's "great demonstration." M decided to risk the "broken head" commonly meted out to black men who showed up for public events. To reduce the risk, he got his "respectable"-looking landlady to come along. The procession was already moving forward when the pair arrived at the public square, "a living mass of people, all joyful and happy." No one paid him any mind, since all were so entranced by the "nearly one hundred colored soldiers with their guns and bayonets gleaming in the sun, and one of their number carrying the American Flag! And all this in [New] Albany."

It took some time for M to get over his shock at the sudden inclusion of African Americans in the body politic. "I could hardly realize I was in the same city where only a few months ago, the colored people were mobbed and persecuted indiscriminately, and even now are insulted at every opportunity." He soon learned that New Albany's integrated parade was no fluke. African Americans had also been "invited to join" the processions in the two biggest metropolises of the Midwest: Cincinnati (over 160,000 residents) and Chicago (over 115,000). In neither city had any black marchers been "molested."[39]

In Columbus, Ohio, a small city of about twenty thousand, African Americans were welcomed to the April 14 "Jubilee," a torchlight procession celebrating Grant's victory over Lee. At the exact moment of the

Ford's Theatre shooting, the *Columbus Gazette* calculated, the ecstatic Columbus crowd of whites and blacks had been singing "The Battle Hymn of the Republic."[40]

After the Chicago funeral procession on May 1, a correspondent for the *Christian Recorder* ("Ruth") voiced her euphoria at the reception accorded the five hundred African American marchers. A few blacks had stayed away for fear of being "laughed at by some outside loafers, but every thing passed off without any insults, the colored citizens being cheered at every corner."

White Chicagoans seemed determined to do "justice to loyal mankind, white or black." Ruth applauded the Chicago Citizens' Committee for insisting that an African American man be included in the delegation accompanying Lincoln's body to Springfield. The committee selected longtime antislavery and civil-rights activist John Jones, a freeborn tailor who had come to Chicago in 1845. He'd also gone with the committee's delegation when it met Lincoln's body in Michigan City, Indiana, on its way to Chicago. It appeared to Ruth that a new day had arrived for blacks. "We can only look on in breathless silence, and think of the great change."[41]

The approaching end of the war, and the death of Lincoln, had sparked a measure of unaccustomed fellow feeling among midwestern blacks and whites. Perhaps the new white goodwill was restricted to "respectable" blacks like M and his landlady in New Albany, and Ruth in Chicago; and in 1865, mere inclusion in a public event probably would not have registered with African Americans in Washington, Baltimore, or Philadelphia as a major advance in race relations. But in some cities and towns of the Midwest it counted for a great deal.

MOST OF the quarter million African Americans in the North knew that their love for Lincoln and for the Union—which 180,000 black men had taken up arms to defend—had given them a new badge of honor as members of the postwar nation. They realized that this hard-earned status might provoke a rebirth of race prejudice among disgruntled whites, and that loyalty to Lincoln could offer blacks a measure of protection.

Into the mid-twentieth century it would not occur to many African Americans, north or south, to doubt that "Lincoln freed the slaves." Most believed that he'd done much more than that. He had died for them, and his sacrifice would help shield them and keep alive their claim on equality.

The members of the Hamilton Street African Methodist Episcopal Church in Albany, New York, captured this dynamic in one of their mourning resolutions, published on April 26, the day that Lincoln's body lay in state in the city. They didn't mean to diminish "the magnitude of the calamity" for others "over the whole land." Nevertheless, "we deem it our right to claim his death as our more peculiar loss and affliction, because he has been the instrument of good in striking off the chains from so many millions of our brethren, and because he has ever stood forth as our peculiar friend and benefactor, whose memory will be cherished by us and our children for generations to come."[42]

A southern newspaper concurred. "Hereafter, through all time," declared the New Orleans *Black Republican*, edited by former slave S. W. Rogers, "wherever the Black Race may be known in the world; whenever and wherever it shall lay the foundations of its power; build its cities and rear its temples, it will sacredly preserve if not deify the name of '*Abraham, the Martyr.*' "[43]

In 1865, African Americans created a time-transcending, Moses-and-Jesus-inflected Lincoln that helped in the long run to preserve the historical Lincoln's republican vision. For a century to come, this biblically framed Lincoln icon offered protective cover for Lincoln the emancipator—the antislavery president who had begun, by the time of his death, to imagine opening the body politic to black citizenship.

FITTINGLY, as Lincoln's remains left the Washington, DC, train depot on the first leg of his twelve-day funeral journey, the honor guard standing by the tracks was drawn from the Eighth Regiment US Colored Artillery, recently back from Virginia. The Eighth Regiment had fought at Olustee, Florida, in 1864, and had sustained heavy casualties. Later that year, Lincoln publicly repudiated those "men base enough to propose to me to return to slavery the black warriors of Port Hudson [Louisiana] and Olustee [Florida], and thus win the respect of the masters they fought. Should I do so, I should deserve to be damned in time and eternity."[44]

CHAPTER FIVE

Rolling Funeral, Living Corpse

Death . . . has not changed one line of his grave, grotesque
countenance.[1]

—GEORGE A. TOWNSEND, APRIL 20, 1865

D URING THE CENTURY of what David Donald dubbed the
"Lincoln cult"—from the 1860s to the 1960s—his biographers
generally ended his life story not with his death on April 15,
but with his Springfield funeral on May 4. That's because they took for
granted the momentousness of his body in making sense of his life. The
last great deed of his life was his dying—so great an act that it prompted
a three-week outpouring of love, grieving, and recollection. As long as his
body was still being viewed, his life story was still being written.[2]

During the funeral period, northerners kept saying that Lincoln
looked alive. Some thought he looked *more* alive during the first week
after his death than he had right after the embalming on April 15. By the
second and third weeks, he was plainly fading. Thus the funeral weeks
recapitulated his actual life cycle: "a vapor that appeareth for a little time
and then vanisheth away." The Lincolns' minister, Phineas Gurley, read
those words from the Episcopal burial service as the martyred chief lay
in state at the US Capitol on April 19. Further on came the words "earth
to earth, ashes to ashes, dust to dust." Mourners never got last words

from Lincoln's lips, but they got to experience a three-week encapsula-tion of his life.[3]

Most biographers before the 1960s aimed to contribute to the Lin-coln cult, and recounting the postmortem events served that purpose. Millions of northerners assembling in 1865—gathering by the tracks for a glimpse of the train, lining up to gaze at his body, marching in proces-sion behind the hearse, squeezing onto sidewalks to watch it roll by—could kindle devotion to Lincoln among the readers of any era. In 1939, Carl Sandburg's *Abraham Lincoln: The War Years* finished with a thirty-three-page, city-by-city, wreath-by-wreath encomium to the heroes who put on the "vast pageant." In 1995, by contrast, David Donald's *Lincoln* stopped dead with Stanton's alleged words in the Petersen house bed-room: "Now he belongs to the ages."[4]

When the official mourning period ended on June 1, 1865, Josiah Holland put pen to paper and completed his *Life of Abraham Lincoln* in five months. The first full-scale biography, it showered the president with praise as a political genius and moral exemplar, and heaped more hosannas on the northern populace for coming together in harmonious union around their fallen hero. "A whole nation mourned its dead. One thought enthralled every heart—the thought of a great, good man . . . all animosities were overwhelmed in the general grief." Published in early 1866, Holland's *Life* breathed the cult of Lincoln on every page.[5]

In his last chapter, Holland summed up the slow trek of the funeral train, still fresh in readers' minds. But as his prose trudged from one city's "minute-guns, tolling bells, requiems by choirs of singers, dirges by bands of musicians, military and civic displays, suspended business, draped flags, and shrouded private and public buildings" to another's, he knew his narrative was losing steam. "Why repeat the same story again, and again?" he asked his readers, begging their indulgence to let him skip over the ceremonies in Columbus, Indianapolis, and Chicago. A writer of fiction as well as nonfiction, he believed that a gripping story would do more for the appreciation—and enshrinement—of Lincoln than a procession-by-procession chronicle.[6]

Holland was too close to the funeral events to see that the observances were *designed* to be repetitive, with each town trying to match
the others in mounting proper mourning rites—traditional and majestic. Civic pride and honoring Lincoln were both at stake. Telegraphic
reports detailing each city's observances made organizers at upcoming
stops intensify their preparations. Everywhere, newspapers posted the
latest accounts on their bulletin boards.

This real-time information created a ripple effect, as citizen interest in
Albany or Buffalo swelled in response to events in Philadelphia or Manhattan. Local events combined in citizens' minds to create a rolling national
extravaganza. "Cities and states are his pallbearers," intoned preacher
Henry Ward Beecher, and the "nation rises up at every stage of his coming." "A unity of feeling pervades the entire North," said the *Philadelphia
Press*, "which has sprung directly from the blood of the great victim."[7]

The funeral train contributed an aura of national unity all by itself.
The elegant and imposing "United States," the car carrying the corpses
of Lincoln and his son Willie, voyaged all the way from Washington,
and silently advertised the glory of the nation. (Willie's body had been
removed from its aboveground vault in Georgetown and placed in a small
black-and-silver coffin to match his father's.) Painted a reddish chocolate
brown with red edging and gilded bolt heads and knobs, the car had
been put into service in February 1865 as the president's private coach,
but he'd never gotten to use it.

The train's flawless passage (under federal military control) gave
northerners a firsthand experience of the clockwork planning produced
by an integrated rail and telegraph system—the same network that would
drive the dramatic economic expansion of the postwar years. Passing
along an almost uninterrupted seventeen-hundred-mile rail line—the
funeral car was twice floated across the Hudson River, at New York City
and Albany—Lincoln's body baptized the burgeoning national infra-
structure of the industrial age.

Spectators along the route could sense that the president's body had
come directly to *them*, originating in the seat of national power and exalt-

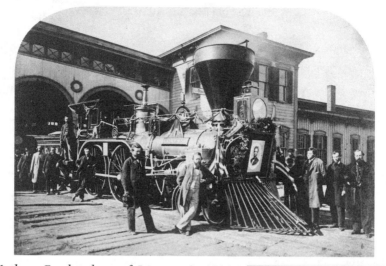

A Mathew Brady photo of January 8, 1864, appears to be the one mounted on the "Nashville" locomotive, which pulled the train from Cleveland to Columbus in the wee hours of April 29, 1865. If the portrait remained in position during the chilly night's heavy rains, crowds of mourners along the tracks—armed with water-resistant torches and lanterns, and warmed by bonfires—would have had no trouble seeing it.

ing each of the hundreds of towns it passed on its path to Springfield. The presidential coach offered northerners a moving shrine they could approach as pilgrims. They came on foot, in wagons, and on the trains (comprising up to twenty cars) that brought them from distant towns to one or another depot along the funeral itinerary.

In the stately movement of his body across the North, Lincoln could be seen as a kind of pilgrim himself, retracing most of the path he had taken in 1861 on his way to Washington, acknowledging in his postmortem westward journey that he had emerged from the heartland and was now going home. On many of the regional locomotives that pulled the train, a large, framed Lincoln photograph was prominently placed just above the cowcatcher. Lincoln's face crossed the North and Midwest looking out at the people waiting to glimpse it.

By skipping the last part of the funeral trip, Holland's *Life of Lincoln* spared readers the boring repetition, but it also avoided the most wrenching development of the entire affair. Northerners in mid-April 1865 believed they were honoring the martyr by parading his body across the land. But as his trip neared its end, some worried that they had dishonored him by putting his body through such a punishing ordeal. They'd thought only of what *they* needed, not what *he* needed. Perhaps Mary Lincoln had been right to entreat Edwin Stanton for a shorter funeral journey.

WHEN LINCOLN breathed his last on Saturday morning, April 15, his wife was ensconced in the front parlor of the Petersen house. Stanton had invited her to the deathbed for a brief visit about twenty minutes before the end, and that may have been the last time she saw her husband's body. Stricken widows commonly avoided their spouse's funerals in those days, but her apparent avoidance of all contact with the corpse prior to burial struck her contemporaries as unusual, a sign of her excessively nervous temperament.

When she departed from the Petersen house, descending the front steps and gripping the curved metal railing still in place to this day, she looked up at Ford's Theatre, cursed it, and then climbed into her closed carriage alongside her son Robert and her friend Elizabeth Dixon. Back at the White House, she ascended to the second-floor living quarters and stayed there for five straight weeks.

Yet choosing distance from her husband's body did not mean choosing distance from *him*. She called in Dr. Anson Henry—the Lincolns' old friend and family physician from Springfield—and they spent several hours together every day musing about the proximity of Lincoln's soul. She almost "refused to be comforted," he reported to his wife back in Illinois, but he got through to her with what he called his "halfway" spiritualism—his belief that "our departed friends hover over and around us, and are fully cognizant of all that transpires, while we are not sensible of their presence."[8]

Mrs. Lincoln confirmed Dr. Henry's influence by repeating his views to others once she had emerged from her seclusion. "Death is only a blessed transition to the 'pure in heart,'" she wrote on July 4 to Charles Sumner, long a personal friend. "A very slight veil separates us from the 'loved & lost,' and to me there is comfort in the thought that though unseen by us, they are very near."[9]

Mary's lengthy White House isolation gave northern mourners a chilling crystallization of their own suffering. Until April 20, she did not even sit up in bed. Having been denied any semblance of a family deathbed scene at the Petersen house—Edwin Stanton refusing to let her bring in young Tad, or to let her mourn as inconsolably as she had wished—she settled into a deafening public silence.[10]

In doing so, she unintentionally bestowed a great gift on the American people. She handed her husband's body over to the body politic. The people's grief, and the people's martyr, would take precedence over the family's mourning and family's loved one. Of course, family metaphors shaped the people's perception of Lincoln during the war and after his death. The Union's soldiers especially called him Father Abraham, but many others insisted that losing him felt exactly like losing a member of their family.

ON SATURDAY morning the corpse arrived at the White House and was lifted out of its pine box, "all limp and warm," observed Benjamin Brown French, the commissioner of public buildings. It was "laid upon the floor, and then stretched upon the cooling board." On Sunday the cooling board was perched on two stools, draped with black velvet. A delicate cambric handkerchief protected Lincoln's face, and he was dressed in the same black Brooks Brothers suit he had worn at his second inaugural ceremony.

White flowers and green leaves—"offerings of affection"—were spread around his pillow and his chest, and a white cloth was stretched over his clothes to catch the dust. One or another army general, along with junior officers, had stood by his side ever since the autopsy. On Sunday, Brown found the remains "growing more and more natural." The embalming had achieved its goal of verisimilitude: the limp corpse of Saturday had come to look properly lifelike.[11]

Mrs. Lincoln's withdrawal from the physical body created a vacuum that Secretary of War Stanton gladly filled. Having failed to protect his friend in life, he would now micromanage him in death, surrounding the corpse with the military guard that the living president had so often eluded, and keeping track of which individuals were permitted to touch him or his coffin. For all he knew, Confederate sympathizers might attempt to desecrate the remains.

Stanton left no detail to chance. Only hours after Lincoln's death, it was apparently he who decided what to do about the ugly bruises under Lincoln's eyes. The embalmers' impulse was to make him look "natural," said the *New York Herald*, just as he looked in "the portraits of the late president, so familiar to the people": a "broad brow and firm jaw" and "a placid smile upon the lips." That would require them "to remove the discoloration from the face by chemical process." But the secretary of war insisted on preserving the purple splotches as "part of the history of the event . . . an evidence to the thousands who would view the body when it shall be laid in state, of the death which this martyr to his ideas of justice and right had suffered."[12]

This noteworthy Easter dispatch, reprinted across the North, colored the public experience of the funeral events over the next two and a half weeks. Wherever Lincoln's face was put on public view, from the White House on April 18 to Springfield, Illinois, on May 3–4, people passing by Lincoln's coffin sought out the graphic mark that signaled Booth's malice, the Confederates' perfidy, and the president's exemplary death.

Lincoln's embalmed body, discoloration and all, thus conveyed his heroic sacrifice along with his natural vitality. His body didn't just *symbolize* his virtues: his service to the people, his willingness to die for them. His body didn't simply stand for something else. His body was his actual, material offering to the Republic. It was the gift itself, carrying on his flesh the sign of his enemies' treachery.

ALL MANNER of humanity, rich and poor, young and old, streamed into the White House for the eight-hour lying-in-state on Tuesday, April 18. Many never made it to the front of the line. They would get another chance; a second viewing was scheduled for the Capitol rotunda on Thursday, April 20. Like many other people, Leigh Huntley, a member of the Veteran Reserve Corps, took advantage of both events. Having seen the corpse on Tuesday—"he looked natural as life," Huntley wrote in his diary—he also joined the Capitol throng two days later.[13]

At the White House viewing, the crowd filed in from Pennsylvania Avenue through the North Portico, crossed the main hallway to the Green Room, and turned left into the south end of the vast East Room, which measured about eighty by forty feet. As they entered, they saw Lincoln's $2,000 coffin—black mahogany with assorted silver bullion fixtures and flourishes—looming across the floor to their left, placed within a four-posted catafalque whose canopy rose eleven feet in the air. They knew the coffin's lid would be open, exposing his upper chest and head. "He lay in simple, artistic state, not gaudily, but tastefully enshrined," said the *New York World*.

A central dais supported the coffin three feet above the floor, and an additional two-foot-wide platform, built all the way around the base of the dais, was elevated eighteen inches off the floor. Stepping onto this platform, mourners skirted the coffin in two lines, one on each side of the body. They were granted just enough time to glance at Lincoln's turned-down collar and black cravat, the tuft of hair protruding from his chin, his large mouth "firmly and pleasantly shut," and the "dark discoloration" beneath his eyes. They exited to the north through two East Room windows temporarily equipped with steps.[14]

Just before noon on Wednesday, April 19, a gathering of six hundred politicians, generals, diplomats, clergymen, and other ticketed guests squeezed into the East Room, replacing the plebeian mourners of the previous day and lending an august and masculine air to the official state funeral. Only six women attended: four wives of cabinet members and two daughters of Supreme Court Chief Justice Salmon P. Chase. Like the deathbed vigil four days earlier, this ritual featured a minimal family presence: twenty-one-year-old Robert Todd Lincoln, dressed in his blue colonel's uniform, was joined by two Todd in-laws, while Mary and twelve-year-old Tad remained sequestered upstairs.[15]

ALL ACROSS the north, at Secretary Stanton's request, civic and religious officials organized processions, services, and speeches to coincide with the White House funeral. At noon local time in San Francisco (a city of sixty thousand inhabitants), fifteen to twenty thousand military and civilian marchers set off through the downtown streets, following an empty hearse. Last in the announced order of march were not the African Americans—the usual group chosen to bring up the rear—but "a long line of carriages containing the principal Chinese merchants of the city."[16]

In Concord, Massachusetts, the citizenry preferred to honor Lincoln with intellection rather than locomotion. They gathered at noon in the Unitarian church to hear Ralph Waldo Emerson eulogize the man whose election in 1860, he told them, had proved a triumph of "good sense": "This middle-class country had got a middle-class president, at last"— one who "had what farmers call a long head, was excellent in working out the sum for himself." Middle-class in "manners and sympathies," yes, "but not in powers, for his powers were superior."

Immediately, the funeral-day oration of this celebrated wise man was published in papers throughout the North. Internationally known for two decades as the most original of American thinkers, Emerson had authored such renowned essays as "Self Reliance," "The Over-Soul," and "Experience." He had made stylistic innovation central to the radicalism of his ideas. Everyone knew Emerson possessed unmatched verbal gifts.

Speaking of the murdered president, the "Sage of Concord" said he had beheld a kindred spirit in Lincoln.

> He is the author of a multitude of good sayings, so disguised as pleasantries that it is certain they had no reputation at first but as jests; and only later, by the very acceptance and adoption they find in the mouths of millions, turn out to be the wisdom of the hour.

In Emerson's eyes, Lincoln's dedicatory remarks at Gettysburg in 1863 faced only one rival for the best speech ever delivered by an American orator: the words uttered by militant abolitionist John Brown, speaking to the Virginia court that sentenced him to death in 1859. But Emerson saw that Lincoln would rise to heights of cultural adoration unmatched by any other American. The martyred president would one day achieve mythic status in the literal sense of the word.

> I am sure if this man had ruled in a period of less facility of printing, he would have become mythological in a very few years, like Aesop or Pilpay, or one of the Seven Wise Masters, by his fables and proverbs. But the weight and penetration of many passages in his letters, messages, and speeches, hidden now by the very closeness of their application to the moment, are destined hereafter to a wide fame. What pregnant definitions; what unerring common sense; what foresight; and, on great occasion, what lofty, and more than national, what humane tone!

Emerson concurred with the current Republican line that Lincoln's death was good for him: "far happier this fate than to have lived to be wished away, to have watched the decay of his own faculties." And his removal was good for the country: the times called for toughness, so this "completed benefactor" might now "serve his country even more by his death than by his life . . . who does not see, even in this tragedy so recent, how fast the terror and ruin of the massacre are already burning into glory around the victim?"

Yet Emerson highlighted the broad republican meaning of the martyrdom, not its beneficial political effects. Lincoln had died at the peak of
his power to represent the people, culturally as much as politically. "Step
by step he walked before them; slow with their slowness, quickening his
march by theirs . . . an entirely public man." He summed up their way
of life and stood for their deepest aspirations. People all over the world
looked at him and saw America, listened to him and heard America.[17]

Only four days after Lincoln's death, Emerson's noontime eulogy
in Concord announced the scope of Lincoln's apotheosis to come. His
words were being engraved in Americans' minds along with his deeds
and his person. He might be replaceable as republican leader, but not as
republican exemplar: his face, his body, his style had become emblematic
of American manners, thoughts, and ideals.

As Emerson was speaking in Concord, Josiah Holland was delivering
his funeral-day eulogy, ninety miles to the west, in Springfield, Massachusetts. Like Emerson, he presented a unified vision of Lincoln's body,
mind, and character—beginning, strange as it may seem 150 years later,
with his off-putting looks. "Unattractive in person, awkward in deport-
ment," Lincoln had been initially greeted on the national stage with
"ill-disguised contempt."

Lincoln's unlovely appearance was bad enough. His curious temperament—"this homely simplicity, this artlessness, this direct out-speaking
of his simple nature"—made things worse, raising doubts about his seri-
ousness. Over time, "we did learn . . . to love him for these eccentrici-
ties, because they proved to us that he was not controlled by convention
and precedent, but was a law unto himself . . . nature's nobleman." His
bizarre physiognomy and comportment became familiar indicators of his
originality.

What would Lincoln say now, Holland asked, "if he could speak to me
from that other shore"? "My death was necessary to the perfection of my
mission," he would affirm, "and was only one sacrifice among hundreds
of thousands of others made for the same end." The secret of Lincoln's
authority lay in its joining of elemental power and unforced humility. His
contribution was no greater, in his eyes, than that of his soldiers.[18]

———

A WEEK to the day after the assassination, the funeral train was ready to depart. Secretary Stanton's team of planners had mobilized manpower and equipment with military efficiency. They wasted no time wondering how to honor a departed leader or conduct him to his place of burial. It had all been done before, just not on Lincoln's scale.

As early as 1841, a black-draped railway car had conveyed the body of William Henry Harrison, hermetically sealed in a lead-lined coffin, to Baltimore, where he lay in state at the City Hotel. A second train took him a few miles west to Columbia. From there he was transported overland to the Ohio River, and a steamer took his body on to North Bend, Ohio, for interment.

Henry Clay's funeral journey in July 1852 laid down a city-by-city model for honoring Lincoln's remains in the major metropolises of the East. In that year, Lincoln was a recently retired one-term congressman at home lawyering in Springfield, where on July 6 he marched in the town's procession honoring Clay. After the marchers reached the Hall of Representatives—the same place where thirteen years later Lincoln would lie in state—he delivered the city's eulogy for his Whig political hero.

Clay's nine-day, twelve-hundred-mile funeral journey to Lexington, Kentucky—with major stops at Baltimore, Philadelphia, New York, Albany, Buffalo, Cleveland, Cincinnati, and Louisville—unfolded on a succession of steamboats and trains. Large crowds assembled everywhere to honor him, though only the citizens of Baltimore, like those in the Capitol rotunda the day before, got to look through the coffin's glass lid to see his face. Without embalming, his body decayed too rapidly in the summer heat to allow more viewings. Officials noticed a change in the appearance of his corpse even between Washington and Baltimore, forcing the cancellation of the open-coffin plan for Philadelphia and points north. Thirty thousand disappointed New Yorkers filed past Clay's firmly fastened coffin in Manhattan's City Hall.

Secretary Stanton completed Lincoln's funeral itinerary on April 19, two days before the train's departure. He had obtained Mary Lincoln's proxy for handling the body and planning the funeral events—except for the choice of burial site. From the start, despite press speculation about a Washington or even a Mount Vernon burial (the two national fathers lying side by side!), Mary opted for Illinois. She kept Springfield residents guessing by briefly broaching Chicago (Lincoln and Douglas reconciled, gushed the Chicago press), but she soon settled on the state capital. Everyone in 1865 agreed on a widow's right to do with her spouse's remains as she saw fit, even in this special case of national martyrdom. Mary never wavered in asserting her control over the burial place, and Stanton never challenged it.

Mary beseeched Stanton to send Lincoln home by the most direct path—west across Pennsylvania from Philadelphia to Pittsburgh and on to the Midwest—thus avoiding the lengthy northern trek through New Jersey and New York. But Stanton held out for the Henry Clay model, taking the body all the way north to Albany (where thousands of New Englanders could cross over the Hudson to see the sacred martyr) and then west through Buffalo and Cleveland. On April 19, Mary gave Stanton and the five million residents of New Jersey and New York (one-fifth of the northern population) what they desired. The funeral journey would qualify as a truly Union experience. The train carrying Lincoln's body would pass through all five of the most populous northern states—Pennsylvania, New York, Ohio, Indiana, and Illinois—and would miss only one state (Massachusetts) containing more than a million inhabitants.[19]

Mrs. Lincoln fought tooth and nail for just one thing: the particular burial plot in Springfield that would receive her husband's and Willie's remains. She took umbrage at the unilateral decision of Lincoln's old political friends in the Illinois state capital to build him a downtown tomb within walking distance of the train depot. They had already purchased a site. She ordered instead that her husband's body be placed in the bucolic Oak Ridge Cemetery, two miles outside of Springfield. This battle over the burial site awakened in her a renewed sense of purpose.

She claimed to be defending her husband's desire (expressed before his death only to her) that he be put to rest in a "rural" cemetery.

The path of Lincoln's funeral train nearly duplicated, in reverse, that of his inaugural trip in February 1861, dropping the original side trips to Cincinnati and Pittsburgh but adding a two-day stopover in Chicago. Many of the same people who had crowded the depots in 1861 gazed at him again four years later lying in his coffin. Wherever possible, planners put locomotives in the hands of the same local engineers who had conducted Lincoln eastward in 1861.

The additional train cars accommodated the men approved by Secretary Stanton (no women were invited): thirty US senators and representatives, another thirty Illinois officials, a contingent of official "mourners" (old friends of Lincoln plus Todd family in-laws), an honor guard of nine senior military officers, two dozen soldiers, half a dozen journalists, the ever-faithful Reverend Phineas Gurley, and the all-important embalmer Charles Brown and undertaker Frank Sands—the two men charged with keeping the president's remains presentable.

Not all of the invited civilians ended up making the trip, and some came along for only part of the journey. One of the many no-shows, Radical Republican congressman George Julian of Indiana, wrote on April 17 of getting his appointment to "the committee of escort," but claimed he couldn't spare the time. During the trip the passenger list would keep changing, as would the number of coaches. Local and state delegations would climb aboard for short rides within their domains, while some long-term riders either dropped out before the end or took a break, catching up with the funeral cortege by riding an express. As the train left for Baltimore, fewer than 150 people were on board, and some cars were almost empty. Only the military personnel and perhaps two dozen civilians stuck it out for the whole two weeks.[20]

LINCOLN'S BODY held up well through the first stops of the funeral train: Baltimore, Harrisburg, and Philadelphia. During the twenty-hour marathon viewing in Philadelphia, perhaps 150,000 people passed by his coffin after waiting for up to five hours. Lincoln's old Springfield friend Ozias Hatch, riding on the train as part of the Illinois delegation, noted the facial splotches but found him looking "quite natural." So did the *Philadelphia Inquirer*, which observed "a natural, placid, peaceful expression." The *New York Tribune*'s Charles Page went further: Lincoln's face appeared "more natural, more *his*, than when seen four days ago at Washington." A young woman from New Jersey thought he still looked just like his "pictures." "Our last President was certainly a very homely man," she wrote to her husband, "yet there is certainly something more than ordinary in every line of his care worn looking face."[21]

The tide began turning for Lincoln's corpse after the marathon viewing in Manhattan, hard on the heels of the first one in Philadelphia. In New York City the body was exposed to the air for twenty-three straight hours—from 1:00 p.m. on Monday, April 24, to noon the next day. Among the thousands, black and white, who shuffled past the bier, seeking to soak in Lincoln's face and upper torso, was seventeen-year-old Augustus Saint-Gaudens, the future sculptor. Having gazed at the president's flesh, the teenager walked out of City Hall and got back in line, waiting hours more to see the corpse a second time.

As the train left New York City for Albany on Tuesday afternoon, newspaper readers got alarming reports about the condition of the body. The *New York Times* claimed the body "had very materially altered" while on view in the city. "Dark as was the face before, and unearthly, it was, at 11 o'clock [Monday night], nearly five shades darker. The dust had gathered upon the features, the lower jaw somewhat dropped, the lips slightly parted, and the teeth visible. It was not a pleasant sight." The condition of the body made it "doubtful," said the *Times*, that additional public viewings could take place.

Poet and editor William Cullen Bryant's *New York Evening Post* went further, declaring, "It is not the genial, kindly face of Abraham Lincoln; it is but a ghastly shadow." Those seeing "our martyred president for the first time" would get "but a poor idea of his homely, kind, intelligent countenance." His now "sunken, shrunken features," in Bryant's estimation, meant that New Yorkers would surely be the last to "gaze upon the upturned face of President Lincoln."[22]

When the train reached Albany late Tuesday night, embalmer Charles Brown and undertaker Frank Sands handed a firm denial to the press: "No perceptible change has taken place in the body of the late President since it left Washington" (the word "perceptible" appeared to concede that some change might have occurred, but that skilled hands could obscure it with powder). Citizens in Ohio, Indiana, and Illinois could breathe easier; they would get to see Lincoln's remains after all.[23]

But dueling claims about the condition of the corpse now colored the rest of the journey. Who was right—Brown and Sands or the New York City papers? Had no perceptible change taken place, or had "the embalmer's labors," as the *New York World* contended, been "set at naught by the organic forces with which the King of Terrors completes the sentence [of] 'Dust to dust' "? Reporters on the scene in Albany added support to the *World*'s vivid speculation by noting that Lincoln's face was "evidently growing yet darker in spite of the chemicals used as preservatives"; "the kindly face is discoloring."[24]

Intensifying alarm about the body's state gave the last week of the funeral journey a very different feel from that of its first five days. From April 21 to 25, officials debated how to maximize spectatorship and maintain order. Now, as they managed a public still desperate to lay eyes on Lincoln, they fretted about keeping spectators locked into a proper posture of mourning. Journalists began wondering whether the corpse's decay was altering the makeup of the crowds. Charles Page soon decided that it was: some mourners were now lining up out of "morbid curiosity" alone.[25]

Once the train made it to Buffalo, after a grueling fifteen-hour trek covering three hundred miles, the *Chicago Tribune* reporter on board tried to reassure Illinois readers about the appearance of the corpse: death had simply "softened and mellowed" the "strong outlines" of his face. But the Illinois delegates aboard the train, including Governor

Richard Oglesby, were taking no chances. Before leaving Albany, they had already cabled Springfield organizers, warning them to move up the funeral ceremony from May 6 to May 4.[26]

Embalmer Charles Brown had said from the beginning that the corpse would eventually take on a mummified look, but he'd promised that for months it would look as "natural" as it did on the day of Lincoln's death. Ten days of exposure to air and dust, and six days of jiggling on the train, had provoked a rapid erosion. More and more observers thought the president's remains belonged in their burial place, not on display. With a week to go before the Springfield funeral, many citizens faced a dilemma: how to walk past the coffin to honor Lincoln while sensing that the display of his body amounted to disrespect.

UPON ARRIVAL in Buffalo on Thursday morning, April 27, the funeral party found out that John Wilkes Booth had been captured and killed at Garrett's Farm in Virginia the day before. The politicians in the group regretted the killing, as they told Charles Page, since Booth deserved "a worse fate than to die suddenly without torture of soul." They also thought that if captured alive, Booth might have blown the whistle on "the masters, inciters and approvers" of the assassination plot.[27]

An army of hawkers was already furnished with pictures of Booth, selling them, along with images of Lincoln, to the long line of men waiting for admission to the Buffalo lying-in-state. (In Buffalo, unlike any other city, men and women lined up separately, and the women had to peer at the coffin from a greater remove than the men—to prevent them from lingering unduly beside the corpse.) The next day, Rochester's *Semi-weekly Union and Advertiser* ran a two-inch-high advertisement for a local distributor offering "10,000 Photographs of John Wilkes Booth, the Assassin. The trade supplied."[28]

The spike in press attention to Booth helped push funeral-journey news off the front pages of East Coast papers that had reported on little else for a solid week. The eastern press might have demoted the story anyway, since for them Lincoln's body had come and gone. The Booth story may actually have prolonged rather than diminished national newspapers' interest in following the voyage of Lincoln's body. From the beginning—April 15—Booth's saga had worked in tandem with the funeral coverage, heightening people's attention to the last voyage of their martyred chief. The Maryland-born assassin supplied a symbol of vice that further magnified Lincoln's virtue, and it only widened the moral gap between the two men when newspapers publicized Booth's good looks and athletic physique.

"Nature had done much for him," wrote the *New York World*. True, his legs "were inclined to bow," but "from the waist up he was a perfect man." Full chest, shoulders slightly sloping, arms of alabaster white and hard as marble, and it only got better from there: "Over these, upon a neck which was its proper column, rose the cornice of a fine Doric face, spare at the jaws, and not anywhere over ripe, and seamed with a nose of Roman model." Two "direct, dark eyes" and a "lofty square forehead" were "crowned with a weight of curling, jetty hair, like a rich Corinthian capital." Yet Booth had dishonored himself and his maker by throwing away his bodily assets. "In this beautiful palace an outlaw had builded his fire, and slept, and plotted, and dreamed." Booth had spiraled down-ward, pursuing the private vanity of stagecraft, while Lincoln had risen steadily in the public discipline of statecraft.[29]

As a lover of the theater, Lincoln would have scoffed at any contrast between moral public service and immoral theatricality. He may even have admired the acting of John Wilkes Booth, who, like his father and brothers, had helped keep Lincoln's beloved Shakespeare thriving on the American stage. Booth had performed seven leading Shakespearean roles, along with many non-Shakespearean parts. His acrobatic and mus-cular feats had made him a popular and recognizable "star."[30]

All the press coverage showered on the display of Lincoln's body since April 18—when citizens had first filed by his exposed remains in the East Room of the White House—helped magnify the mass fascina-tion with the fate of Booth's body. Fearing that some northerners might take Booth as a martyr in his own right, the secretary of war insisted on concealing his corpse. Stanton was now monitoring two bodies at once, hiding one and hallowing the other. He was protecting Lincoln's remains twice over, from possible physical accident or foul play, and from any competing interest northerners might take in looking at Booth's corpse or in congregating at his burial place, which Stanton refused to divulge.

Perhaps the secretary's strategy of concealment backfired by adding to the aura of mystery about the assassin's body. Even Republican newspapers suspected that his corpse had been mutilated, not just hidden away. Many witnesses had watched as Surgeon General Joseph Barnes and Dr. Joseph Woodward performed an autopsy on April 27 (they had also helped conduct Lincoln's on April 15). Then Booth's remains were sewn into a common gray army blanket and clandestinely buried at the Washington Arsenal. A newpaperman sniffed out the general location of the grave but said it was "smoothed and carefully sodded over" so that "no one will ever be able to distinguish the place."[31]

Rumors flew claiming that Booth's head and heart had been removed and sent to the Army Medical Museum, causing Republican as well as Democratic papers to air misgivings about the government's moral compass. In fact, several vertebrae, but not his head and heart, were removed during the autopsy and taken to the museum. But Democratic editors had been handed a volatile story with which to whip Stanton. Unable any longer to attack their old nemesis Abraham Lincoln, they would soon turn their fire on his friend and collaborator, the secretary of war.

One daring Democratic editor, S. A. Medary—son of famous Copperhead journalist Samuel Medary, a perpetual thorn in the side of Unionists until his death in 1864—may have been the first writer in 1865 to turn the condition of the president's corpse into an attack on Edwin Stanton's management of the funeral. Peering into Lincoln's coffin at the Columbus, Ohio, State House on Saturday, April 29—two weeks after the president's death—the *Columbus Crisis* editor beheld "a dark, unnatural face whose features were plaintive and pinched and sharp, piteously like death."

In its current condition, grumbled Medary, "the face of the corpse should not have been exhibited." Displaying it "gratified curiosity and awakened pity, but it revealed nothing of ABRAHAM LINCOLN." Lincoln himself, announced Medary, would have objected to "making a show of all that was mortal of a fellow-man." By overruling Mary Lincoln "in her desire that the body of her husband should be entombed within a more appropriate period after death," Stanton had desecrated his remains.[32]

IF ANYONE could have been counted on not to mind that his corpse was being exposed beyond all reasonable limits, it would probably have been Abraham Lincoln himself. He would have been reminded of some story (a feeding frenzy of farm animals at the trough?) that tweaked the millions of people who pressed forward to feast on his body. The champion of people's access to their representatives might quite seriously have carried approachability to its logical conclusion: let the people have his body as long as they could stand having it.

This lengthy event made eminent republican sense. A repetitive national farewell—a vast coordination of military and civilian officialdom, and of elected officials at federal, state, and local levels—it celebrated Lincoln's love for the people and their love for him. "Love is a rare attribute in the chief magistrate of a great people," said P. D. Day, a Protestant preacher in Hollis, New Hampshire, in his address at the end of the funeral period. "We have so long regarded an iron will . . . as the first requisite for a ruler, that we have thought tenderness and love a weakness. But MR. LINCOLN has changed our views . . . he was *beloved* by the nation, and they loved him because he first loved them."[33]

Once the funeral train reached Illinois on May 1, the press lost interest in analyzing the condition of the corpse. The *Chicago Tribune* reverted to boilerplate reverence: "an extremely natural and life-like appearance, more as if calmly slumbering, than in the cold embrace of death." The corpse hadn't suddenly become lifelike again. The *Tribune's* self-conscious diversion connoted that Lincoln was now finally resting among his Illinois intimates, those who could approach his body as if they were friends and family. The civic body had become the domestic body. The state of decay didn't matter to those who cared. They could see only their beloved boy and man.

The Republican *Tribune* and Democratic *Chicago Times*—long a Copperhead antagonist to Lincoln the president—now joined forces in exalting him and heralding Chicago's preeminent standing in his life. This hero didn't hail only from Springfield. Having "nurtured him in life," said the *Times*, Chicago was feeling authentic bereavement for "a brother, a son."

Finally the routinized rituals of mourning had met their match: in this city the observances went beyond "mere semblance" or "empty ceremonial" to become "emblems of an actual grief, everything external . . . [was now] the interpreter of a genuine feeling." Lincoln's "every trait and habit," the *Tribune* added, "were as familiar to us as household words." Loyal citizens in the East "admired and respected him"; Chicagoans "loved him as a friend and neighbor who had grown up amongst us."[34]

FOR THE FINAL public viewing in Springfield on May 3–4, thousands of outsiders streamed into town. A fast-growing and politically split city of fifteen thousand, Springfield attracted eighty to ninety thousand visitors for the funeral, thousands of them wandering the streets all night long in the warm spring air. As in Chicago, Democrats and Republicans outdid one another in professions of love for Lincoln. The Democratic *State Register* and Republican *State Journal* felt no need to justify their claims that Lincoln belonged distinctively to them. They let Lincoln make the case for them. They simply reprinted his 1861 "farewell address," delivered extemporaneously from the rear platform of his inaugural train.

"Here I have lived a quarter of a century," said Lincoln as his friends' and neighbors' eyes welled up, "and have passed from a young to an old man [he would turn fifty-two the next day]. Here my children have been born, and one [Edward] is buried. I now leave, not knowing when, or whether ever, I may return, with a task before me greater than that which rested upon Washington." He finished by invoking God's assistance and bidding his neighbors "an affectionate farewell."[35]

In the rotunda of the Hall of Representatives, where Lincoln had delivered his Dred Scott speech in 1857 and his "house divided" speech in 1858, the lying-in-state began at 10:00 a.m. on May 3 and continued for twenty-four hours. The motto "Sooner than surrender this principle, I would be assassinated on this spot" was inscribed in a circle around the higher reaches of the rotunda. Some seventy-five thousand mourners filed by Lincoln's body. Lincoln's friends and neighbors could hardly recognize "the poor, chilled, shrunken features for his," wrote Charles Page; "the beautiful soul that transfigured them into all loveliness no longer illumines this bit of clay."[36]

Not all of the journalists covering the final funeral event subscribed to Page's realism. Veteran reporter Lawrence Gobright of the Associated Press preferred euphemism to exposure. All he would tell the nation's readers was that the president's remains had "very much changed" since Washington. Four years later, in his memoirs, he opened up, conceding that Lincoln's "face had considerably withered" by the time the train reached Springfield, "the flesh adhering closely to the bones, and the skin had turned dark." In 1900, popular writer Ida Tarbell may have been the first Lincoln biographer to repeat for her audience the gist of what Page had conveyed several times to *New York Tribune* readers in 1865: "By the time Springfield was reached," she wrote, Lincoln's face "was black and shrunken almost beyond recognition."[37]

A few days after the Springfield funeral, town resident Anna Ridgely explained in her journal why she hadn't joined the crowds of men, women, and children at the viewing. The twenty-three-year-old didn't want the "image" of the "decaying corpse" to get stuck in her mind. She was even happier she hadn't gone to see Lincoln's body when her sister, a singer with the Philharmonic Society, returned from sitting near the open coffin for a solid hour. Her sister "came near fainting" from the mixture of smells in the gaslit, "close" room.[38]

At 10:00 a.m. on a sweltering Thursday, May 4, the coffin was closed while 250 singers, accompanied by the twenty-piece Lebrun's Washington Band from St. Louis, sang "Peace, Troubled Soul," the same hymn that had welcomed Lincoln's body to the first lying-in-state in Baltimore on April 21. The regionally famous St. Louis Silver Cornet Band struck up the newly published "Lincoln's Funeral March," and the procession moved off toward Oak Ridge Cemetery at 11:30 a.m.[39]

Robert Lincoln and several Todd relatives rode in carriages for the family, and William Herndon, Lincoln's law partner, served as marshal for the march's sixth division. Representing the nation were General Joseph Hooker, commander of the Northern Department of the army, Secretary Stanton's aide General E. D. Townsend, and the other military men appointed by Stanton to guard the coffin. Following the white "Citizens at Large," at the very end of the eighth and last division, came the "Colored Persons" (except for the two black "grooms," ministers Henry Brown and William C. Trevan, who pulled "Old Bob" along right behind the majestic hearse). According to the *Bloomington Pantagraph*, "the colored societies of Odd Fellows and Masons . . . demeaned [that is, acquitted] themselves in a most creditable manner."[40]

In 1909, Colonel Robert McClaughry, one of the officers in the Springfield procession, recalled "the intense grief" of the black spectators, "thousands of whom had journeyed for days" to attend the funeral. They were given a separate stretch of their own along the route to the Oak Ridge Cemetery, and as the cortege went by "almost every one of them knelt or prostrated" themselves on the ground. "They well knew that their greatest friend was passing to his rest and the future seemed dark to their vision."[41]

About a hundred thousand people stood along the road, and several thousand of them continued to the cemetery, where the trusty Phineas Gurley recited the last of his many prayers over Lincoln's body, the first having come three weeks earlier at the Petersen house on the morning of April 15. After a local Baptist minister, the Reverend Andrew Hubbard, read Lincoln's second inaugural address, Methodist bishop Matthew Simpson delivered an hour-long eulogy surveying Lincoln's career and highlighting its republican significance.

"A republic," said Simpson, was "declared by [European] mon-

Guards stationed outside the Oak Ridge public vault
after Lincoln's funeral service on May 4, 1865.

archists too weak to endure a civil war," yet the Union had "come out unharmed"—indeed, "stronger for the trial." With a majestic success like this, "republics will spread, in spite of monarchs, all over this earth." Mourning Lincoln meant celebrating his world-transforming leadership. Sorrow could now cede the ground to gratitude. "His fame was full," Simpson concluded, "his work was done, and he sealed his glory by becoming the nation's great martyr for liberty."

Simpson invoked Lincoln's Gettysburg principle: the work of the dead was all in vain unless confirmed by the labor of the living. The bishop recommended quick punishment for the rebel leaders, including "a traitor's death" for every Confederate officer who had "turned his sword against the vitals of his country." They had aimed their weapons at the national life, just as Booth had pointed his pistol at the head of the body politic. A clear-sighted meting out of justice met Lincoln's standard of "malice toward none," said Simpson, since it forswore vengeance and sought only legal and impersonal punishment.[42]

In the bright midday sun, Robert Lincoln, John Nicolay, and thousands of others watched silently as Abraham and Willie Lincoln's coffins were placed on a marble slab inside Oak Ridge's fifteen-foot-high, fifteen-foot-wide limestone public vault, located at the base of a sparsely wooded, steep incline. Black velvet adorned the vault's interior, along with evergreen branches. As a choir of 350 voices sang the "Dead March" from Handel's oratorio *Saul*, the thick doors and iron grating were closed.

A military guard took up positions outside the tomb, and in the days that followed, an entire company of soldiers was stationed at the vault to guard against the depredations of souvenir hunters, who were removing "everything, living or dead, near the tomb . . . as mementoes of the visit." If Abraham Lincoln had ever been told that one day his body would lie in an aboveground tomb with a guard posted at the door—like the body of Jesus eighteen hundred years earlier—his first words, spoken through a broad grin, would surely have been, "That reminds me of a story."[43]

BY THE TIME Lincoln was placed in his vault on May 4, citizens were busy raising money for bronze and marble statues that would enshrine his body in cities across the North. But one tiny monument had already attracted attention while rocking and swaying atop the hearse that carried Lincoln's body up Broadway in the Manhattan procession of April 25. The elaborate funeral car, accompanied by soldiers of the Seventh Regiment, was drawn by sixteen gray horses, themselves draped in black cloth with silver-bullion borders to mirror the color scheme of the president's coffin. In its intricate symbolism, this hearse outdid the others that carried Lincoln's remains along the funeral route.

The Manhattan "funeral car"—coffin below, Temple of Liberty on top.

Just above the coffin, hanging from the black canopy, hovered a large eagle, wings outspread, clutching laurel sprigs in its talons. And atop the canopy, fifteen feet off the ground and easily seen by thousands in the crowd, stood a circular temple, with no walls and empty inside. As the *New York Times* explained, this structure symbolically tied Lincoln's physical being to the body politic. On the one hand, the temple stood for the president's own body, "the temple of life . . . empty of its former tenant." On the other, it stood for the Republic's "home of freedom, bereft of its representative man."[44]

The empty temple captured the main theme of the final week of the funeral journey. Lincoln's vitality on the deathbed, and the "natural" look of his corpse in Washington, DC, Maryland, and Pennsylvania, had given way, beginning in New York, to ever more evident decay. As they beheld his body in Ohio, Indiana, and Illinois, more and more people registered his absence. His body was missing its former tenant. Many vowed to keep him present through the work of memory.

PART TWO

The Enshrined Body
(1865–1909)

Thomas Ball's 1876 Emancipation *statue in
Washington, DC, photographed in 2010.*

CHAPTER SIX

The First Lincoln Memorials

I love the President personally.
— WALT WHITMAN, NOVEMBER 1, 1863

T HE FIRST Lincoln memorials were verbal, not sculptural, and
they began appearing as the funeral train rolled toward Springfield. Local officials commissioned many memorial poems, but
thousands more bubbled up from the ranks of amateur writers, and hundreds of both sorts found their way into newspapers. In 1865, people
turned to well-chiseled verses for comfort, knowing they would help preserve Lincoln in public memory. Especially choice words could immor-
talize a hero's name.

Today Walt Whitman's two main poetic tributes to Lincoln—"O Captain, My Captain" and "When Lilacs Last in the Dooryard Bloom'd"—
are by far the best-known memorials to him, and they were well liked
when they first came out in the fall of 1865. A decade earlier, Whitman's *Leaves of Grass* had shocked and bewildered respectable opinion
for its frank attention to bodily desire, but his loving lines on Lincoln
enchanted a mass of readers—thousands of whom had already tried to
compose such verse themselves.

The Republican *New York Evening Post* editor William Cullen Bryant read sixteen untitled lines to a large Union Square crowd on April
25, just after Lincoln's body had departed for Albany, and these became

the most popular rhyming words of the official mourning period, which ended on June 1. The president was a reluctant warrior ("slow to smite, and swift to spare"); the people were stricken ("in sorrow by thy bier we stand"); and Lincoln's most momentous work was accomplished.

> *Thy task is done; the bond are free:*
> *We bear thee to an honored grave,*
> *Whose proudest monument shall be*
> *The broken fetters of the slave.* [1]

While Bryant was declaiming in Manhattan, the residents of Schenectady, New York, were reading the seven stanzas on Lincoln composed by one "Emma D.," which stand up very well against Bryant's verses. The last stanza:

> *O thus be forever*
> *Our feelings outpoured*
> *To him who is worthy—*
> *The patriot's reward!*
> *In that nation which rises*
> *Such men to revere,*
> *O who can Disunion*
> *Or Slavery's curse fear!* [2]

To the flood of popular poetry, orators in 1865 added hundreds of memorial addresses, many of them printed in newspapers and published as pamphlets. Four of the most significant were delivered by historian George Bancroft, US Senator Charles Sumner, US Representative and Speaker of the House Schuyler Colfax, and Springfield lawyer William Herndon. Sumner, Colfax, and Herndon, Lincoln's former law partner, spoke with special authority because they had known Lincoln personally. Yet Whitman and Bancroft claimed unique placement too—Whitman as a close observer of Lincoln on the streets of New York City and

Washington, DC, and Bancroft as a student of American history and politics.

This was a high-stakes interpretive battle, with substantial cultural or political clout awaiting those who managed to stake a claim to Lincoln's meaning. His body carried within its symbolic scope the hundreds of thousands of other bodies lost in the war. Thanks to him, families across the North could feel their personal agony as national pain and national purpose. Whoever could mobilize feelings about Lincoln with original and inspiring language could shape the country for generations to come. It's as if all five of these major memorialists—Bancroft, Sumner, Colfax, Whitman, and Herndon—were repeating to themselves the words of Episcopalian priest Libertus Van Bokkelen, who said to his St. Stephen's parishioners in Baltimore on Easter Sunday, "We see in thy mangled form not [just] a tender father, an ardent friend, a patriot citizen, but our country bleeding at every pore."[3]

Bancroft and Sumner, both of them accomplished men of letters and public affairs, used their addresses to make Lincoln's death serviceable for politics, tying the martyr to the policies they claimed he would have pushed during Reconstruction. Colfax and Whitman left current politics aside, highlighting their personal love for Lincoln, and Lincoln's love for the people. They hoped everyone would join them in creating an intimate bond with Lincoln, making his national enshrinement all the more deeply rooted, and all the more readily passed down from parents to children.

With Bancroft and Sumner pushing an impersonal republic keyed to the proper Lincolnian principles, and Colfax and Whitman preaching a personal republic of citizens united by their attachment to the fallen father, Herndon threw up his arms at all the ways Lincoln was being *used*. Everyone wanted a piece of him—and their piece would be all the more precious if they buried the man himself and glorified him as superhuman. Their pure, saintly, imperturbable Lincoln had little in common with the man he had lawyered with in Springfield, or with the young man from New Salem who had experienced a frontier life like any other. Herndon would liberate his old friend from the albatross of his postmortem image. He would introduce a new kind of "memorial," bringing Lincoln down to earth by assessing his unique flaws and gifts.

GEORGE BANCROFT had disliked Lincoln for years before he took a shine to him in 1863. A German-educated scholar of immense learning and elegant pedigree—Puritan roots in early Massachusetts and a Harvard degree—he had been a longtime fixture in the Democratic Party, serving as secretary of the navy and minister to England in the 1840s. In 1860, he backed Stephen Douglas for president, and he belittled the victor in that contest as an untested ignoramus.

"We have a president without brains," he wrote of Lincoln in 1861. After the Emancipation Proclamation, however, the antislavery Bancroft (an unusual stance for a Democrat) changed his mind. In 1864, with the Democratic Party platform controlled by antiwar Copperheads, and with Lincoln on board for a Thirteenth Amendment abolishing slavery, Bancroft avidly supported him for reelection. In the 1864 campaign, Republicans counted him an important War Democrat ally.[4]

Bancroft delivered his memorial oration in Manhattan on April 25, only minutes after the funeral train's departure for Albany. One of the most renowned historians in the United States (though unattached to any college), he rose on a temporary platform in Union Square to deliver the city's official discourse on "the illustrious dead." The sixty-four-year-old eminence came as close as anyone could to speaking for all Lincoln-loving northerners, Republicans and Democrats alike.

His multivolume *History of the United States*, a valedictory to American nationalism as a divine instrument in the progressive march of liberty, had made him a popular public figure since the 1830s. Whigs and their Republican successors gagged on his enthusiasm for Andrew Jackson, his zeal for territorial expansion in the 1840s, and his knee-jerk preference for "state rights" over federal initiatives, but many loved his soaring rhapsodies on the advance of freedom. And they enjoyed watching his fellow northern Democrats squirm when Bancroft assaulted slavery as an antiquated system of labor.

As Bancroft stood to speak at Union Square on April 25, a line of soldiers streamed by on Broadway in quickstep formation, returning to lower Manhattan from the completed funeral procession. A reporter noted the slanting sun illuminating their "long polished lines of steel," and shimmering in the folds of "the gay pennons of the troops of lancers." An audience of two thousand people cupped their ears to make out Bancroft's words, as hundreds more jammed the windows of surrounding buildings. Six-year-old Teddy Roosevelt—himself a future historian and assistant secretary of the navy—may well have witnessed this scene unfolding around the corner from his grandfather's town house.[5]

Standing beside an appropriate classical prop—a mock-up of a broken column, its base draped in black crepe—Bancroft heaped praise on Lincoln's Emancipation Proclamation of 1863 as a historic breakthrough in the global development of liberty. No longer would Americans face the impossible task of reconciling "a caste of hereditary bondmen through endless generations" with "the existence of republican institutions."

Some Democrats in the audience winced: though they now loved Lincoln for his apparent leniency toward the Confederates, many still detested his decision to turn a war for union into a war for freedom. Some whites thought Lincoln had purposely prolonged the battle, needlessly taking northern and southern white lives, for the sole aim of destroying slavery. Some blacks agreed he'd prolonged the battle for their sake— following a mandate of heaven, as the *Cincinnati Colored Citizen* put it, to establish "the *black man's* rights" and to raise his "status" by letting him fight for his freedom.[6]

But Bancroft gave Democrats something to cheer about too. He made no mention of extending emancipation by giving the vote to freedmen. Instead, he called for rear-guard vigilance: blocking the possible return of chattel slavery to the South. The politically crafty Bancroft was showing northern Democrats how to seize the middle ground for the postwar period: renounce their nostalgia for the days of slavery and praise the savior of the Union for wiping it out, while consigning the president's emancipation policy to the past.

For Bancroft, the future would feature a national marketplace of free laborers, but not a national campaign for equal citizenship. Democrats could salvage the principle of state rights by decoupling it from the historical anachronism of slavery. In an obvious knock on Radical Republicans, the orator observed that Lincoln had possessed the sureness of vision, and magnanimity of spirit, to hate slavery, and to help abolish it, without hating the slave owners. He was incapable of "harboring one vengeful feeling."[7]

While the Republicans hailed his sacrifice for both liberty and union, and praised God for removing him just in time to let justice prevail over mercy, Democrats could position him as the historic herald of freedom— especially the freedom of individuals and states from federal control. If anything, the champion of "malice toward none" could more easily be pressed into partisan service on the Democratic side of Reconstruction debates: the man of charity could certify the smooth and speedy return of eleven rebellious states.

With his Union Square performance of 1865, Bancroft was not done memorializing Lincoln. Less than a year later, on what would have been Lincoln's fifty-seventh birthday, he delivered the Union's official memorial address before a joint session of Congress. Speaking in front of President Johnson, General Grant, cabinet members, Supreme Court justices, and the diplomatic corps, he slapped the Radicals once more by asserting each state's right to decide on who could vote.

Lincoln would surely have agreed with him, he said. When the president announced from the White House window ten months earlier that he thought some black men deserved the vote, he plainly "wished it done by the States themselves." Lincoln "never harbored the thought" that federal officials would impose black suffrage on a new state government "as a condition of its recognition."[8]

WELL-KNOWN Republicans answered Bancroft's Union Square speech, and his joint-session oration, many times over in speeches celebrating Lincoln as the "martyr to liberty." None rivaled Senator Charles

Sumner in taking Lincoln's entire career as proof that had he lived, he'd have backed the voting rights of African American men.

A long-standing abolitionist star, and a graduate of Harvard College and Law School, Sumner had known Lincoln well. Despite their policy differences, he'd been a frequent guest at the White House, drawn there as much by Mary Lincoln's conversational talents, and her respect for his learning, as by the singular republican bearing of a man whose "simple presence was like a proclamation of the equality of all men." At the Petersen house during the all-night deathwatch of April 14–15, 1865, Sumner had stood in as a virtual family member. For a portion of that grueling night, young Robert Lincoln's head had rested on his shoulder as they stood at the foot of the bed.[9]

By mid-May, Sumner realized that President Johnson was stringing the Radical Republicans along: his calls for justice in the South had been meant to throw them off track. The former Democratic governor of Tennessee didn't care about equality for the freedmen. "Johnson will insist that he is in favor of the colored suffrage," Sumner wrote to English Radical John Bright, "but [also will insist] that he must leave the decision to the States. Here again we have State Rights [getting] in the way of Equality, as they were in the way of Liberty."[10]

Sumner spoke virtually the same words in his two-hour-plus memorial address for Lincoln on June 1, 1865, at the Boston Music Hall. This was the day chosen by President Johnson for "national mourning and humiliation" in his predecessor's honor. Hundreds of memorial speeches were given around the country, often delivered by the same orators who'd preached or spoken on Easter Sunday and again on the national funeral day of Wednesday, April 19.

After a long sequence of prayers, scripture readings, and choral selections, including the dirge "Mourn, Ye Afflicted People" performed by the six hundred singers from the Handel and Haydn Society, Sumner spoke eloquently of the president's republican leadership and postmortem influence. "Liberty has been won," but "the battle for equality is still pending." Andrew Johnson was preparing "a new compromise": "colored

persons are to be sacrificed in the name of State Rights." Forced to surrender its slave system, the white South now intended to "perpetuate an
oligarchy of the skin"—a plan that stained Lincoln's legacy.[11]

For Sumner, Lincoln's "speech uttered at the field of Gettysburg" in
1863 mattered more in the postwar era than his beloved second inaugural address. Too much focus on the second inaugural—dwelling on
the sins of the North as well as the South, and stressing the forgiveness
of enemies—had sown confusion about the proper path forward. The
Gettysburg speech applied the proper corrective, asserting that "all men
are created equal" and calling for dedication to the "great task remaining
before us": a "new birth of freedom."[12]

NEITHER Bancroft nor Sumner showed much interest in Lincoln's
martyrdom as such. It was Schuyler Colfax who put the president's
bodily sacrifice at the heart of his memorial address, and who showed
that remembering Lincoln's body carried broader political significance
than either Bancroft or Sumner perceived. Lincoln's republicanism had
entailed a physical commitment: putting his body at the people's disposal. And Colfax, one of the very last officials to see the president alive
and conscious, could now send up a cri de coeur over the republican
world that John Wilkes Booth had destroyed.

Colfax spoke in Chicago on April 30, the day before the funeral
train arrived. Bryan Hall, the largest venue in the Midwest, was filled to
bursting. In stark contrast to Sumner, who would make no reference to
his intimate ties with the Lincoln family, Colfax shared his aching grief
at the loss of a close collaborator. "How much I loved him personally,"
he said, "I cannot express to you." He chastised himself for not having
accepted Lincoln's invitation to go along with him to Ford's Theatre. "My
mind has since been tortured with regrets that I had not accompanied
him." He kept playing out scenarios that might have saved the savior
of the country: he could have warned Lincoln of Booth's approach; he
could have put himself in the line of fire.

Sumner would note Lincoln's simple republican character, but Colfax saw republicanism as his chosen way of life. "Easier of access to the public at large than had been any of his predecessors," he "could not be persuaded that he ran any risk whatever." He welcomed his "bitterest enemies" to his reception room, with no guard to protect him. He had "walked fearlessly and carelessly through the streets" of Richmond on April 4. With his death, said Colfax, thousands of "bereaved circles" whose dining tables already featured a "vacant chair" left for a lost soldier would add one, figuratively, for Lincoln.[13]

Into the 1880s, Colfax spoke publicly of the love he felt for Lincoln. The president's saintliness stemmed from his sacrificial bearing, not just from his forgiving nature. His demeanor as he delivered his second inaugural address suggested he was prepared to give himself up: "he seemed to feel as if he were standing on the edge of the grave."[14]

THE FINEST literary memorial of all, Walt Whitman's "When Lilacs Last in the Dooryard Bloom'd," came out in October 1865. As he began imagining this intricate elegy in the spring, Whitman noted that Lincoln alone among the presidents, "in life and death," had "touch'd the popular heart to its deepest. For this one alone, through every City, every Country farm, the untouch'd meal, the heavy heart & moisten'd eye and the sob in private chambers."[15]

To do justice to his own and other people's disorienting pain over Lincoln's death, Whitman broke the mold of the classic memorial: rather than summing up the hero's character and achievements, he conveyed the actual experience of the people's weeping for their "martyr chief." Any idea of what we now call "closure," getting over the grief, made no sense to him. In "Lilacs," Whitman made the stab of loss perennial—a seasonal growth in the mourner's heart:

> *When lilacs last in the dooryard bloom'd,*
> *And the great star early droop'd in the western sky in the night,*

I mourn'd—and yet shall mourn with ever-returning spring.
O ever-returning spring! trinity sure to me you bring;
Lilac blooming perennial, and drooping star in the west,
And thought of him I love.[16]

Ever since 1865, the poem's sixteen cantos have met with popular enthusiasm and critical acclaim. The countless amateur poets of the North and Midwest loved it. So did the critics. In 1866 the *New York Times* "Current Literature" column was already calling it "that noble, almost unrivalled hymn on the funeral procession of Lincoln," containing "some of the loftiest and most beautifully majestic strains ever sounded by human meditation." "Hymn" and "strains" were apt labels for an elegy designed to sound like "the mournful voices of the dirges pour'd around the coffin" for "the dead one there I loved."[17]

Whitman had caught many glimpses of Lincoln in Washington, where the poet landed a part-time job in the paymaster's office in early 1863. A longtime antislavery Democrat, Whitman found himself drawn, like Bancroft, to the president's resolute Unionism and, unlike Bancroft, to his provincial, unpolished style. Lincoln's body fascinated him, for it confounded expectations. "I think well of the President," he wrote in March of that year. His "awful" physical ugliness had come, in Whitman's eyes, to stand for an utterly original perception and an unrivaled ability to command.

"Underneath his outside smutched [smudged] mannerism, and stories from third-class county bar-rooms . . . Mr. Lincoln keeps a fountain of first-class practical telling wisdom." Somehow he had not just kept the ship of state "afloat" in the first two years of the war, but had kept the "flag flying in sight of the world, menacing and high as ever . . . I more and more rely upon his idiomatic western genius, careless of court dress[,] of court decorums."

"I see the President often," Whitman added in 1864. "I think better of him than many do. He has conscience & homely shrewdness— conceals an enormous tenacity under his mild, gawky western manner.

The difficulties of his situation have been unprecedented in the history of statesmanship. That he has conserved the government so far is a miracle itself."[18]

Whitman never met or spoke to Lincoln, but he did meet John Hay, Lincoln's secretary. While conversing with him at the White House in late 1863, he "saw Mr. Lincoln standing, talking with a gentleman, apparently a dear friend . . . his face & manner have an expression & are inexpressibly sweet—one hand on his friends [sic] shoulder the other holding his hand. I love the President personally."[19]

"Lilacs" gripped many readers from Whitman's day forward because it caught the special distress of the multitudes of men and women who felt the loss of Lincoln as that of a dear friend or relative. They wanted to remember him, and they wanted to remember the intensity of their shock at his death. Whitman showed them how to keep those memories alive in their immensity: by connecting Lincoln's corpse to the bodies of the fallen soldiers, "the battle-corpses, myriads of them, the white skeletons of young men." Let one approachable coffin—"With the show of the States themselves, as of crape-vail'd women, standing / With processions long and winding, and the flambeaus of the night"—stand for all.[20]

Memory in this instance went beyond a reflective act of mind. Remembering meant reexperiencing the pain of bereavement. With the exemplary death of Lincoln—"the lustrous and drooping star with the countenance full of woe"—mourners could take solace in knowing that the victim did not suffer, and in realizing that he, "the sweetest, wisest soul of all my days and land," rose to a symbolic greatness all his own by encompassing the entirety of the war dead.[21]

WHITMAN'S most famous Lincoln poem, "O Captain! My Captain!," also came out in October 1865. The ship of state is returning to port in victory, "the people all exulting" to the sounds of bells and bugles as they crowd the shore to greet their "Captain! dear father!" They don't realize he has collapsed on the deck amid "bleeding drops of red," or that a ship's mate, pleading with him to "rise up and hear the bells," has been unable to rouse him. The mate places his arm beneath the motionless head, but the captain's "lips are pale and still."[22]

"O Captain" dwells more on Lincoln's actual dying than does "When Lilacs Last in the Dooryard Bloom'd," but neither poem directly invokes its sacrificial meaning. Lincoln had not died *for* his friends; he had been stolen from them, leaving them desolate. They managed their loss by adding perpetual mourning to the seasonal cycle of their lives. Some warriors lived, others died; the majesty of Lincoln was to embody the memory of lost legions.

Whitman lectured on Lincoln up and down the East Coast for several years in the late 1870s and early 1880s, always choosing April 14 as the date for his talk titled "The Death of Lincoln." The significance of his speech, he told the audience as he began, lay not in what he would say, but in their all joining together for a "tragic reminiscence" on this day. "Oft as the rolling years bring back this hour, let it again, however briefly, be dwelt upon."

What Whitman actually said was well worth hearing. He dramatized the jolt he'd received from Lincoln when he got his first glimpse of him as president-elect in February 1861. Whitman was watching from the top of a stationary Manhattan omnibus on Broadway as Lincoln—no favorite in predominantly Democratic New York City—arrived at the Astor House, near City Hall. He'd been on the road from Springfield for more than a week, and as he stepped out of his "shabby hack barouche" (an open carriage) on "rather a pleasant afternoon," he stretched his arms and legs and "paus'd leisurely on the sidewalk." He looked up to absorb the "granite walls and looming architecture" of the Astor House, and then gazed "slowly and good-humoredly" at the crowd of thirty or forty thousand people.

All vehicular traffic had been stopped, "leaving an unusual hush in that busy part of the city." Even more unusual was the absolute silence of the crowd. For thirty-five years Whitman had witnessed the visits of famous men (Lafayette, Jackson, Clay, Webster, Kossuth, William

["Filibuster"] Walker, and the Prince of Wales), and always he had been enveloped by a "human roar and magnetism, unlike any other sound in the universe—the glad exulting thundershouts of countless unloos'd throats of men!"

In Lincoln's case, the people and president-elect were sizing each other up. Lincoln "look'd with curiosity upon that immense sea of faces, and the sea of faces returned the look with similar curiosity. In both there was a dash of comedy, almost farce, such as Shakspere [*sic*] puts in his blackest tragedies." From his lofty perch, Whitman got a good view of the visitor: "his perfect composure and coolness, his unusual and uncouth height, his dress of complete black, stovepipe hat push'd back on the head, dark-brown complexion, seam'd and wrinkled yet canny-looking face, black bushy head of hair, disproportionately long neck, and his hands held behind as he stood observing the people."

Unbeknownst to Whitman, Lincoln did address a few words to the people at the front of the crowd. He gave them his usual quip for an occasion like this, along the lines of "I stand before you just to say hello, not to make a speech, which is a lucky thing, for I have nothing to say right now that would be worth hearing." The *New York Herald* reporter on the scene said the people outside the Astor House "greeted him with considerable enthusiasm, the flourishing of hats and other demonstrations of applause," throwing some doubt on Whitman's late-1870s memory of a "sulky, unbroken silence."[23]

Whitman needed the silent scene to convey the anxiety he'd felt during this brief standoff between Lincoln and the New York masses. He was sure that "many an assassin's knife and pistol lurk'd" in many a "hip or breast-pocket." With an actual assassination plot taking shape in Baltimore, and scheduled for the president's arrival there two days later, Whitman may well have been right. As he looked back at the Astor House almost two decades later, Whitman drew a profile in composure, the lone hero standing tall against a mutely staring, if not glowering, horde. This stalwart did not fret about his fate. He "gave another relieving stretch or two of arms and legs," turned, and quietly entered the Astor House.

In Whitman's retrospective view, Lincoln had been saved from danger in 1861 by his own courage. And in 1865, he saved the nation not so much by reuniting it, but by offering "a heroic-eminent death" that the nation could absorb into its very identity. This martyr to union was not simply bringing the states back into a uniform polity. He was giving "a cement to the whole people, subtler, more underlying than a written constitution, or courts or armies—namely, the cement of a death identified thoroughly with that people at its head, and for its sake."[24]

NO ONE was ready for William Herndon's memorial oration on Lincoln in December 1865. He had worked side by side with Lincoln for seventeen years—until the president-elect departed for Washington in 1861—and could have been expected to gush forth on his friend's unparalleled grandeur. But soon after the assassination he had grown uneasy about the mounting wave of Lincoln sanctification. The people's love for the president was obscuring the actual man Herndon had known in Springfield. Herndon decided to rescue Lincoln's quirky individuality from the hero-worshippers. He set off on a hunt for recollections from those who'd known Lincoln in New Salem in his twenties.

With out-of-town journalists such as Josiah Holland already seeking him out as the must-see expert on Lincoln's Springfield years, Herndon soon realized he could do more than collect information. He could produce a biography himself, shaping the memory of his friend for all time. Holland had never met Lincoln and was likely, Herndon thought, to thicken the fog of beatification around him. Herndon described his own approach in a letter to Holland himself: to capture Lincoln "*just as he lived, breathed—ate & laughed in this world, clothed in flesh and sinew—bones & nerve.*"[25]

On December 12, a bundled-up Springfield crowd, "large and highly intelligent" in the estimate of the town's Republican paper, shuffled up the stairs and into the second-floor auditorium of Rutledge & Davidson's Practical Business College to hear the first installment of Herndon's work, centering on Lincoln's character. Excerpts of his address, like a two-thousand-word selection in the *New York Times*, whetted readers' and publishers' appetites for a gripping volume that would scrutinize Lincoln's "inner life." Herndon adopted a detached posture and a chatty tone; he proved a meticulous observer.[26]

Nineteenth-century Americans took for granted that what was etched on a person's body gave a good inkling of what lay grooved within. A sharp analyst of the surface got access to the depths. Herndon's audience nodded approvingly when he told them Lincoln's body and mind operated together, lumbering forward in tandem. Deftly he put the president in motion, nine months after his death, making him stride once more down the wooden sidewalks of Springfield. Lincoln's cumbersome physical movements pointed to fundamental features of mind and heart.[27]

"He was [a] thin—tall—wiry—sinewy, grisly—raw boned man," Herndon wrote, "thin through the breast to the back—and narrow across the shoulders."

His blood had to run a long distance from the heart to the tips of his frame, and his nerve force—mind force had to travel through dry ground a long distance before the muscles & nerves were obedient to his will. His structure—his build was loose and leathery . . . The whole man—body & mind worked slowly—creakingly, as if it wanted oiling . . . When Mr. Lincoln walked he moved cautiously, but firmly, his long arms—his hands on them hanging like giants' hands, swung down by his side. He walked with even tread . . . did not walk cunningly—Indian like, but cautiously & firmly . . . Mr. Lincoln put the whole foot flat down on the ground at once, not landing on the heel. He lifted his foot all at once—not lifting himself from the toes, and hence had no spring or snap . . . In sitting down on common chairs he was no taller than ordinary men from the chair to the crown of his head. A marble placed on his knee thus sitting would roll hipward, down an inclined plane. His legs & arms were abnormally—unnaturally long, & hence in undue proportions to the balance of his body. It was only when he stood up that he loomed above other men.[28]

Herndon followed that dynamic portrait with an animated description of Lincoln's head and face. "His head ran backward, his forehead rising as it ran back at a low angle like Clay's and unlike Webster's—almost perpendicular."

His eyebrows cropped out like a huge rock on the brow of a hill. His face was long—sallow—cadaverous—shrunk—shriveled—wrinkled and dry, having here and there a hair on the surface. His cheeks were leathery and flabby, falling in loose folds at places, looking sorrowful and sad. Mr. Lincoln's ears were extremely large—and ran out almost at right angles from his head—caused by heavy hats and partly by nature. His lower lip was thick . . . hanging undercurved while his chin reached for the lip up curved. Mr. Lincoln's neck was neat and trim, his head being well balanced on it.

The bodily features pointed to a stalwart republican core. This "homely looking man . . . was careless of his looks—was simple in dress and plain looking and plain acting. He had no pomp—display and dignity so called. He appeared simple in his carriage & bearing."

Lincoln's plodding physical movement was matched by his slow mental labor. He lacked "the soul's quick, bright flash over scattered and unarranged facts." But his "cold, precise and exact" buildup of perceptions yielded "power of thought in an eminent degree . . . All opponents dreaded him in his originality of ideas—condensation—definitions & force of expression . . . and woe be to the man who hugged to his bosom a sacred error, if Mr. Lincoln got on the chase."

Audiences had become accustomed to glazing over when speakers on Lincoln piled up the plaudits. Herndon knew that well-placed criticism could open up space for praise that would stick. The analytical and logical capacities had colonized Lincoln's character, he asserted, squeezing out the imagination. So busy thinking, Lincoln didn't have time to read anything but newspapers, Shakespeare, and the Bible—a capital short-coming in the bookish Herndon's eyes. He "read *less* and thought *more* than any man in America. No man in this audience—no woman here . . . can put his or her finger on any great book written in the last or this century that he read."

Lincoln's practical, methodical striving left no time for exploring modern books, and worse still, said Herndon, it left no place for the passions of love. Tender and kind as Lincoln could be, his coolness of mind and body corresponded to a decided coolness of heart. He could love "abstract humanity *when it was* oppressed," but he could not love concrete individuals.

His famous phrase "with malice toward none, with charity for all" inadvertently supplied the key to his private life: "Lincoln had no intense loves & hence no hates & no malice." Anyone who supposed "that his heart led him out of himself and compelled him to go in search of the objects of his love, for their sake," were projecting onto him a romantic hero or selfless saint of their own devising. Lincoln could give himself passionately to people in groups, but not to a single beckoning heart.

Herndon sensed that Lincoln's constricted capacity for love lay behind the sagging spirit revealed on his cheeks, and the darkness that periodically engulfed his entire body. Lincoln "was a sad looking man: his melancholy dripped from him as he walked. His terrible gloom struck his friends and created a sympathy for him—*one means of his success.* He was gloomy . . . humorous by turns. I do not think he knew what joy was—nor happiness for more than 23 years."

Why did Herndon specify twenty-three years? He didn't let on, coyly hinting that he possessed information he couldn't divulge. Some people in the Springfield audience, and the newspaper readership, knew Lincoln well enough to do the math: twenty-three years was the length of his marriage to Mary Lincoln. For them the meaning of Herndon's words was unmistakable. He thought Abraham, after uniting with Mary, had known neither delight nor contentment. Herndon seemed also to be hinting that something or someone might have made Lincoln very happy before 1842. Herndon said nothing more about the Lincolns' relationship, or about his friend's emotional life before his marriage.[29]

FOR ALMOST A YEAR, Herndon basked in the acclaim accorded to his "very striking analysis of [Lincoln's] intellectual and moral qualities," as the *Chicago Tribune* and other papers described his "character" lecture. That speech showed "a very remarkable knowledge of the man." He had memorialized Lincoln through a rigorous and sympathetic evocation of his person, physical and mental. Readers were captivated by Herndon's grasp of his friend's particularities.

Yet Herndon had barely gotten started on what the *Tribune* called the president's "moral qualities." On that score, the tireless researcher cast about gathering more opinions from those who'd known the young adult Lincoln. Herndon's home and office drawers filled up with letters, notes, and newspaper clippings. The more information he collected, the more it eluded easy interpretation, especially when one witness contradicted another.[30]

By the fall of 1866, Herndon nevertheless felt compelled to spell out for a national audience some of what he'd left concealed in his lecture the year before. It turned out that Lincoln had "had more, much more, emotion, fancy and imagination, in 1835, when he was 26 years of age," than he had in his maturity. And it turned out that he *had* responded, in that early era of his romantic longing, to a beckoning female heart. Herndon believed his evidence (most of it supplied by his informants thirty years after the fact) pointed to a clear conclusion: Lincoln had fallen in love with—and become "conditionally engaged to"—the "beautiful, amiable, and lovely" Ann Rutledge, and he loved her "with all his soul, mind and strength. She loved him as dearly, tenderly and affectionately. They seemed made in heaven for each other, though opposite in many things."[31]

A match made in heaven, perhaps, but not one meant to be. Ann died of "a raging fever" in August 1835, and Abraham, as many sources attested, fell into a perilous pit of despond. Having supposedly contemplated a fully realized love with Ann—physical, emotional, and spiritual—he now wanted only to join her in the grave. Herndon claimed to know that Lincoln had said at the time "his heart, sad and broken, was buried there" with Ann in the cemetery.

The upshot of this purported remark was obvious to a mass of readers: Herndon believed Lincoln had never found true happiness after his 1842 marriage to Mary Lincoln because he had years earlier given his heart once and for all to Ann. Crushed by her death, Abraham worked his way back, little by little, from the "dethronement of his reason," and returned to New Salem "a radically changed man"—one prepared to turn to politics as a perpetual substitute for love.

The *Chicago Tribune, New York Times,* and other papers declined to print that final reflection on politics as psychic compensation, but in his own printing of the address, Herndon wrote, "If Lincoln had married Ann Rutledge, the sweet, tender and loving girl, he would have gravitated insensibly into a purely domestic man." To Herndon it seemed likely that as Abraham regained his will to live, he "leaped wildly into the political arena as a refuge from his despair."

HERNDON'S Ann Rutledge lecture disappointed many of those who heard or read it. The resourceful analyst of the 1865 "character" lecture had delivered a disorganized ramble. Yet adverse reactions to the 1866 effort did nothing to stop Herndon's tale of Ann Rutledge from eventually catching fire in American culture, where it remained ensconced through most of the twentieth century. As a tale of Lincoln's youthful passion, depression, and recovery, the Ann Rutledge story may have exerted the humanizing effect Herndon desired, marking Lincoln as a man in touch with raw reversal and hard-won restoration.

But having humanized Lincoln with an exacting "character" lecture in 1865, Herndon had now enveloped Lincoln in sentimental speculation.

He had come close to creating a stoical, suffering servant—not unlike the icon of saintly public service already familiar to millions of northerners. He had jeopardized his quest to undermine pervasive mythologizing and to restore the actual man.

The real Lincoln had lived out a quarter-century-long, up-and-down relationship with Mary Lincoln, and Herndon had closed off that reality by conjuring up a perfect match between Abraham and Ann, one never tested in life. With Mary, Lincoln had given and received the imperfect love exchanged by many couples. They had fallen passionately for one another in part because they shared a love of politics. In Mary Todd, Abraham found a wife as devoted to his public success as he was. Their time together was turbulent, but it was also marked by passionate bonding. For the Lincolns, private love and public ambition intermingled in the delights and devastations of everyday life.

CHAPTER SEVEN

Monuments for the Ages

As near to life as art can render it.

—New York *Independent*, May 1865

T HE FUNERAL ceremonies wound down to their official end on
June 1, 1865, but the ritual engine of mourning rolled on, switch-
ing over to the track of commemoration. As with the funeral rites
and verbal memorials, northerners and southern blacks took for granted
that the best way to remember Lincoln was to follow well-grooved tradition: enshrine him with imposing statues in towns and cities across
the North. Lincoln would join George Washington and lesser lights in
presiding over public places, peering down to remind people of their
republican past and of their duty to sustain a republican future.

Just as William Herndon found fault with shining encomiums to the
great man's virtues, a few dissenting voices complained about the building of stately monuments. For a man comparable only to Washington,
and a hero that struck many as a fuller symbol of American virtue than
did the first president, erecting the usual edifices seemed lackluster, if
not trivial. Set aside "the mania for marble," urged the *New York Tribune*. Instead of stolid statuary, build "living" memorials, cutting-edge
structures "expressive of his practical character" and "the comprehensive
benevolence of his great heart."

Suggestions piled up for buildings that would carry on some vital work in Lincoln's name: a retreat for disabled soldiers, an orphanage for children left homeless by the war, a lecture hall for top-notch oratory. Why risk the "chronic mortification" of "a clumsy, awkward and unmeaning statue?" asked the *Tribune*. Mediocre public works of art were even worse than droning speeches, insipid rhyming verses, or repetitive pageants, for they would stain the visual landscape in perpetuity—"lasting testimonials," said the *New York Times*, "to national shame."[1]

The weekly New York *Independent* tried to quash the customary monuments too, but knowing that statues would be built anyway, this Radical Republican organ pleaded for keeping them "as near to life as art can render it." That meant sticking to the "life-size effigy, placed at just a sufficient height to be seen to advantage," not hoisted atop a lofty pedestal. Throw out the classical columns, the Roman fasces, the Egyptian obelisks, and other extraneous accessories that Lincoln monument committees were likely to inflict on the mourning public. A Lincoln statue, said Charles Sumner on the floor of the Senate, could be justified only if it attained the "truth and reality" of "art," depicting his "living features animated by living soul." No sculpture at all would be better than a formulaic likeness.[2]

As the *Independent* anticipated, dissenters couldn't halt the grinding wheels of cultural habit. In fact, harping on Lincoln's unmatched heroism as the reason for living memorials just reminded most people that they craved an inspiring marble or bronze to look at. They felt they owed him statues out of respect for his life and work, and they needed statues to help keep him vitally alive in their hearts.

Yet with monuments, as with funeral rites, Protestant America traced its familiar oscillation between planning correct observances and lamenting their lifelessness. The history of Lincoln statues adheres to the pattern: with a couple of notable exceptions, they were put up and then swiftly denounced for failing to achieve Sumner's standard of "living soul." Critics finding fault with physical monuments exerted the same effect as William Herndon cutting up sanctimonious oratory: all the naysayers spurred on other writers, speakers, and sculptors to try to capture him truly. Something about him seemed to defy accurate representation. The repeated failures only confirmed his transcendent greatness and reinvigorated the artistic quest.

IN SPRINGFIELD, Lincoln's old political friends moved quickly in late April 1865 to position their state capital as the chief site for enshrining the martyr. To them it was obvious that only Springfield could build a truly national Lincoln monument, for only the Illinois capital offered the holy foundation of his physical remains. The future looked dizzyingly bright: a town of fifteen thousand citizens would become a recognized site of national pilgrimage.

Soon enough the planners would find that possessing Lincoln's illustrious remains presented grave problems: raising the funds to build a tomb magnificent enough to match the man; protecting monument and body against vandalism or desecration; enabling visitors to feel Lincoln's presence without giving them undue access to the coffin (the decaying body would never again be seen by the general public after the May 4, 1865, Springfield funeral).

For now, Springfield organizers had to move fast to capitalize on the immediate outpouring of grief, and to fend off competition from other proposed "national" monuments. On April 24, 1865, with the president's corpse still on exhibit in New York City, the Springfield group formed the National Lincoln Monument Association and started collecting money from all over the North. Targeting churches, schools, military units, fraternal bodies, and "the colored population," the association helped make the raising of money for the monument an integral part of the springtime mourning. Thousands of dollars were collected from boxes placed in post offices, banks, and other public places. Military veterans donated the most of any group, contributing one-fifth of the $180,000 raised by the association. African American soldiers—no more than 10 percent of the Union forces—gave $8,000 of the $27,000 that came from military personnel.[3]

Right after the assassination, memorial committees swung into action in other cities too, and as they invited proposals from sculptors and architects, they faced the problem of deciding *which* Lincoln to favor in the statues to be cast or chiseled. Tiptoeing through charged ideological terrain, planners and sculptors were forced to choose: should they pick the martyr to liberty, the savior of the Union, or a combination of both? And if a sculpture depicted Lincoln's public achievements—placing a scroll of the Emancipation Proclamation in his hand, draping a cloak over his shoulders to suggest a link to his republican forebears—could it also do justice to his actual appearance, and to his one-of-a-kind character, at turns melancholic and elated, ruminative and decisive? Generic historical allegory might blot out the unique features of the flesh-and-blood man.

Lincoln sculptors confronted another difficulty that poets and orators were spared. William Cullen Bryant could highlight the "martyr to liberty" by simply announcing that Lincoln had broken the fetters of the slave. The best way to do that visually was to include at least one additional figure: the slave attaining freedom. Artists commonly proposed such a pairing, but they were usually turned down for financial and political reasons. Sculpting two figures increased costs dramatically, and in northern cities the Democratic masses—especially the Irish Catholics—might well voice their displeasure in acts of vandalism.

Artists and sponsors understood the risks of exposing controversial public art to the tender mercies of anti-Lincoln city dwellers. Raising money was already hard enough without alienating well-to-do Democrats likely to back statues of a stand-alone savior of the Union. As a result, the statues commissioned right after the war circumscribed the emancipation theme, just as George Bancroft did in his memorials of 1865 and 1866. Lincoln would stand alone as the farsighted leader who had indeed freed the slaves. But with that act, Lincoln had brought the era of liberation to an end. Public art praising emancipation would not imply an ongoing campaign for black civic equality.

In the single exception to this trend, former slaves—eager for a chance to show their love for Lincoln and their new standing as prospective citizens—were mobilized to finance a monument entirely on their own. In 1866 the talented Harriet Hosmer, an expatriate sculptor from Massachusetts then working in Rome, proposed an intricate emancipation statue for this second "national" monument. Her design was accepted, and she produced the model for a multitiered edifice with a martyred Lincoln at the summit, lying face up on a sarcophagus.

Below him, prominently placed on four pillars at the vertical midpoint of the structure, stood four African American male figures tracing the history of the freedmen: a partially clad slave put up for sale; a toiling slave resting on a hoe; a fugitive slave guiding Union troops; and a black Union soldier bearing his rifle. Critically acclaimed by many Republicans, Hosmer's conception grasped emancipation as "progressive stages of liberation," in her words. Lincoln's corpse reigned over the historic expansion of freedom, radiating power and inspiration to encourage African American achievement. His physical sacrifice offered the guarantee that true equality of opportunity was indeed meant for all.[4]

In a saga filled with irony, the Hosmer design proved far too expensive and was replaced by an utterly conventional layout: a kneeling slave about to be freed by the beneficent Father Abraham standing above him. In 1876, this creation by Thomas Ball, another expatriate sculptor, was dedicated in Washington's Lincoln Square (today's Lincoln Park), about a mile east of the Capitol. The freedmen's fund paid for the two statues, and Congress chipped in $3,000 for the pedestal engraved with the title "Emancipation."

Unlike Hosmer's design, this scene's kneeling slave and hovering liberator memorialized the single moment when Lincoln proclaimed an end to chattel slavery. Appropriately, the official unveiling of the statue took place at the very time when congressional Reconstruction—the effort to enact a measure of racial equality in the South—came grinding to a halt and federal troops were pulled out of the former Confederate states. *Emancipation* was unveiled just as the real-world campaign to extend black freedom was crumbling in the face of northern-white indifference and southern-white intimidation and violence.[5]

———

BRONZE AND GRANITE statues of Lincoln began rising in major
urban centers three years after his death: Washington, DC, in 1868;
Brooklyn in 1869; Manhattan in 1870; Philadelphia in 1871. All four of
these early sculptures remain on view to this day, sometimes relegated to
a site near the original one, and in the case of the statue now located in
Washington's Judiciary Square, brought down to earth (in 1919) from its
original perch atop a forty-foot column. Many other statues were put up
later in smaller cities and towns, with the pace of construction actually
accelerating in the early twentieth century.

As Lincoln's centenary approached in 1909, a virtual building boom
occurred, and it continued after World War I, when Lincoln settled into
his stature as symbolic face of the nation. The children of Lincoln's contemporaries—brought up, like Chicago reformer Jane Addams (born in
1860), on stories of the greatest man of the greatest generation—seem to
have craved new monuments to rejuvenate his memory and pass him on
to the next generation. They were trying to counteract "the silent artillery
of time," the phrase Lincoln had used in 1838 to capture his own cohort's
forgetfulness about the "living history" of the revolutionary era.[6]

In a useful compendium of public sculptures published in 1952, at
the height of the Lincoln cult, F. Lauriston Bullard counted eighty-seven
statues in all (including twenty replicas), fifteen of them in Illinois alone.
Fourteen of the eighty-seven were put up between 1866 and 1899, while
seventy-three appeared between 1900 and 1949—an overall average of
one every year. Others have been erected since 1952, but only a handful of them in urban centers (Detroit in 1956, Providence in 1958, Des
Moines in 1961, Indianapolis in 1963, Kansas City in 1986). Several others appeared in Kentucky and Illinois in the early 2000s, as Lincoln's
bicentenary approached. And in Richmond, Virginia, a pairing of Lincoln
and his son Tad was dedicated in 2003, to commemorate their historic
walk on April 4, 1865. This was the first Lincoln statue to be installed in
a city of the former Confederacy.[7]

In the twenty-first century, the original Lincoln sculptures attract scant attention from passersby, but their durability confirms the prediction of the Reverend Richard Storrs at the 1869 dedication of the standing statue of Lincoln in Brooklyn, where he spoke to fifteen thousand citizens assembled at the plaza entrance to Prospect Park. To Storrs, the nine-foot Lincoln spoke eloquently of his having removed "the shackles from the limbs of a race," and the bronze effigy would celebrate that achievement into the distant future.

> The men of other times shall see it. It connects us, as we stand here, to the coming generations. We cannot tell what great institutions shall have risen, and flourished, and turned to decay, before the figure upon this rock shall have yielded itself to rust and rot! [8]

The Brooklyn Monument Committee had been formed a week after Lincoln's death, just two days before his body arrived in New York City for the public viewing at Manhattan's City Hall. In 1866 the committee selected Henry Kirke Brown, the well-known sculptor whose equestrian statue of George Washington had been mounted in Manhattan's Union Square in 1856 to general acclaim. For his Brooklyn Lincoln, Brown wished to highlight the Emancipation Proclamation, and he chose the simple expedient of putting an open scroll of it in Lincoln's extended left hand. To make sure no one missed the political message, he had Lincoln point at the scroll with his right hand.

This wholly theatrical pose was made all the more artificial when Brown tied a cloak—an updating of a Roman toga—around Lincoln's neck and ballooned it over both shoulders. This enveloped emancipator is trumpeting his historic achievement but revealing nothing of himself as a distinctive man with his own character and form. The face looks like Lincoln, but the beefy body, balanced awkwardly in an almost demi-plié ballet pose, looks much more like Brooklyn's stocky preacher Henry Ward Beecher than the lanky and towering president.

Henry Kirke Brown was also selected to create a Lincoln statue for Union Square in Manhattan. The New York monument committee instructed him by letter to do something about Lincoln's ugliness: "As the person of Mr. Lincoln would not be graceful[,] it doubtless is desirable that a cloak or toga would hide much of the view." The committee also scratched Brown's bright idea of putting up an emancipation ensemble, with the presidential liberator pointing to the heavens while standing over a kneeling slave. The committee cited the obvious security risk, voicing the "fear that the figure of a negro in a public monument would arouse the resentment of the Irish citizens."

What New Yorkers got in 1870 was an eleven-foot bronze that almost duplicated Brown's nine-foot Brooklyn Lincoln. Only a minor tweaking separated the two: the gesticulating emancipator of Prospect Park now hung his left hand aimlessly by his side, while the bunched-up cloak now immobilized his right arm in what resembled a bulky sling. Lest any Irish Catholic viewers be offended by the words "forever free"—actually printed, though impossible to read from the ground, on the open scroll in his left hand in Brooklyn—the Manhattan scroll was carefully rolled up like a theater program.[9]

When the Union Square Lincoln was unveiled in 1870, the press deplored it. "The papers have tried to outdo each other in ridiculing the unhappy work," observed the *New York Tribune*. "It is ugly, ungraceful, undignified. The pantaloons are hideous. The cloak is an anachronism, wholly misplaced on his shoulders." The *Tribune* felt for poor Henry Kirke Brown. It wasn't his fault that Lincoln defied sculptural treatment. "A masterpiece of ungracefulness, long awkward, angular, and loose-jointed," Lincoln the man compensated for his physical flaws with "a grandeur of soul" that artists working in metal or stone could never capture.

In life, the charismatic Lincoln could make people forget his bizarre appearance by flashing his grin and telling a yarn. But "no sculptor can teach a bronze figure to do that." Brown's "rather grim-looking figure" burdened with a "knotty countenance" conveyed nothing of Lincoln's humanity to the multitudes traversing Fourteenth Street and pouring up and down Broadway. The sculptor's total failure did carry a thin silver lining: "that the public care enough about the statue to find fault with it."[10]

THE "NATIONAL" MONUMENT in Springfield, Illinois, was not dedicated until 1874, when a crowd of twenty-five thousand assembled on an overcast October day at the Oak Ridge Cemetery. An open competition in 1868 for the monument's design had yielded thirty-seven proposals, including Harriet Hosmer's much-traveled emancipation scheme and other designs depicting African American figures. Hosmer lobbied hard for the commission, collecting testimonials from such leading lights as Henry Bellows in the United States and William Gladstone and Henry Layard in England, who all received photos of her models before writing their excited (Bellows and Layard) or lukewarm (Gladstone) endorsements.

Embracing the path of least political resistance, the Springfield association rejected the elaborate and expensive emancipation ideas and chose a sky-high granite obelisk (initially 85 feet, later raised to 117 feet) and eleven-foot bronze Lincoln proposed by Larkin Mead, an accomplished student of Henry Kirke Brown. As *Harper's Weekly* described the statue in 1872, when the Ames Works in Chicopee, Massachusetts, had just finished casting it, Lincoln was depicted "in citizen's dress." His right hand was resting on the Roman fasces (with an American flag draped over it), and he was still grasping the pen he'd used to sign the Emancipation Proclamation. His left hand was gripping a scroll of the document. But the four Civil War bronzes positioned around the obelisk—battle scenes of the cavalry, infantry, artillery, and navy, with all of the soldiers depicted as white men—put the weight on Lincoln's wartime command, not his role in ending slavery, or his possible support, had he lived, for black civil and political rights.[11]

Critics in 1874 liked the obelisk more than the Lincoln statue (the battle ensembles formed part of the original design and were well publicized at the time, but for financial reasons they were mounted later). "The shaft of granite and bronze which rises above his dust is a fit emblem of his mental and moral solidity," said the *Chicago Tribune*. "Its massiveness,

its strong foundation, its permanent material, are typical of his fame."
But once again, said the *Tribune*, the statue got him wrong: "The proportions of the figure are much too muscular, and would be more apropos to
the rotund development of Long John Wentworth [a well-known three-
hundred-pound, six-foot-six Chicago politician] than to the meager form
of the martyr-President."[12]

The critics might carp, but within a decade, eighty thousand black
and white pilgrims were trekking to Oak Ridge Cemetery each year to
pay their respects at Lincoln's tomb. They weren't drawn to Springfield
by the statues or monument alone, but by the physical presence of Lincoln's body. Whatever their artistic worth, the obelisk and bronze mattered because they were perched atop the sacred remains.

Famous African American minister and publisher Henry McNeal
Turner, a Civil War chaplain and Georgia state representative during
Reconstruction, made the trip in 1877. "Every colored person that can
visit this monument ought to do it," he advised. "You must see it to appreciate and comprehend its grandeur." Visitors could climb a hundred feet
inside the tower to "take observations" of the surrounding countryside.
But the pièce de résistance, to be found in the (aboveground) "Catacomb," was "the marble stone coffin or sarcophagus that holds the body
of Mr. Lincoln."[13]

Henry Turner was wrong about the location of Lincoln's corpse, but
he came by his mistake honestly: the official custodian of the tomb—
amateur historian and all-purpose Lincoln aficionado John Carroll
Power—had been leading visitors to believe the body indeed lay inside
the sarcophagus. Nearby, the remains of Lincoln's sons Eddie, Willie,
and Tad (who had died of an illness in 1871 at age eighteen) lay in catacomb vaults. But in 1876, a year before Turner's visit, Power had helped
move Lincoln's body to a secret location elsewhere in the tomb. When
Turner meditated over the martyr in the sarcophagus, it was empty.

At that moment, Lincoln's remains were lying in their coffin in a dank
corridor beneath the monument, encased inside another wooden box and
covered with stray timbers. The loose lumber was supposed to shield

the coffin from drops of water that fell from the corridor's ceiling every time it rained. This inglorious arrangement followed the unsuccessful attempt of a gang of Chicago criminals to steal Lincoln's body and hold it for ransom. They didn't come anywhere near success. But they wreaked havoc on the nerves of John Power and the members of the Lincoln Monument Association, which was forced to pretend for the next decade that Lincoln's body was peacefully resting beside his three dead sons in the catacomb, when it was actually languishing in the dark, wet passageway.[14]

This much can be said for the clumsy body snatchers: they picked a good night for thievery. On the evening of November 7, 1876, ballots were being tallied across the nation in the historic Hayes-Tilden presidential election. Terrence Mullen and Jack Hughes, two Irish-immigrant members of a Chicago counterfeiting ring, arrived at the tomb accompanied by Lewis Swegles, a Secret Service informer who had gained their trust, and by a friend of Swegles assigned to drive the getaway wagon. Ordinarily quiet after dark, the streets of Springfield were busy with election night traffic; no one would notice a wagon slipping out of town lugging a well-covered load.[15]

Forewarned by the "roper" Swegles, government agents and private detectives were waiting inside the tomb for malefactors Mullen and Hughes to arrive. The lawmen proceeded to play their parts even more ineptly than the thieves. They sprang from their hiding places in the monument at the right moment, but as they ran silently (in stocking feet) a distance of forty yards to the catacomb to capture the criminals in the act, a fumbling detective accidentally discharged his sidearm. Upon hearing the shot, if not well before, Mullen and Hughes abandoned the coffin, which they had only partially extracted from the sarcophagus, and ran headlong out of the cemetery.

As the bad guys escaped into the night, the good guys gave chase, only to be separated and start shooting at each other. Their incompetence ended up not mattering, since the hooligans were easily captured ten days later when they blithely showed up at their favorite Chicago saloon. Outside of Illinois, little attention was paid to the whole affair.

———

IN THE WAKE of the ruckus, which counted as a serious criminal event in Illinois, the Lincoln Monument Association faced a dilemma: it couldn't permit another assault on the sarcophagus, but it couldn't afford to keep a permanent watch at the catacomb either. In 1876 the association could imagine only a single solution: hide the coffin somewhere in the bowels of the monument while letting custodian John Power inform visitors that the corpse still lay inside the sarcophagus. For a decade the shabby prevarication prevailed.

In 1887 the association renounced the subterfuge and built a theft-proof underground vault in the catacomb for the bodies of Abraham and Mary, who had died in 1882 and been secretly lying beside him for five years in the tomb's dingy corridor. (They had been put underground in shallow graves, in a portion of the corridor found to be dry.) Before the coffins of husband and wife were encased in concrete—with crushed stone tossed into the mix near ground level for good measure—Lincoln's face was exposed to the view of a few association members so they could certify that the body in the coffin was truly his. This was the fourth time since the funeral in 1865 that the association had confirmed the corpse's identity. Those members present, including Lincoln's old political collaborator Ozias Hatch (a veteran of the funeral train), recognized the corpse as that of "our former friend and fellow citizen"—an easy identification since "the features were quite natural," even if "somewhat shrunken."[16]

A *Chicago Tribune* dispatch dwelt on the unnatural aspects of the features: "The hair and whiskers have fallen off Lincoln's head and the face is very black." But, the *Tribune* added, "the contour is . . . still perfect." If more proof were needed that this was truly Lincoln, the *Tribune* added that for the Springfielders who'd been looking at their Larkin Mead statue for the last thirteen years, "the face [of the corpse] is said to strongly resemble that of the bronze statue on the monument." The *Tribune* had apparently forgotten its 1874 criticism of the statue for looking more like Long John Wentworth than Abraham Lincoln.[17]

The whole purpose of the monument association as incorporated in

1865 was to keep Lincoln's body forever in the hands of friends. Other monuments could celebrate the public Lincoln just as well as Springfield's could, but no other sculpture could embody Lincoln the local townsman. This was the man who had provoked tears among his shivering fellow citizens when he addressed them from the back of his departing train on February 11, 1861, reminding them that he'd "passed from a young to an old man" among them, and owed them "everything."

Newspapers across the North and South took note of the reburial in 1887, applauding the association for dispelling "all the mystery that has attached" to the body's location since 1876. The *Los Angeles Times* celebrated the reunion of Mary and Abraham Lincoln "in their final resting-place" beneath the marble slab floor of the catacomb, entombed within a cement mass that "will in time become as solid as rock." The *New York Tribune* considered the mass even more solid than that: "Hydraulic cement and pounded rock" made "a composition harder than stone." Evidently the Lincolns were set for eternity.[18]

And they would have been, had not the towering monument above the vault begun slowly to crumble. The private monument association couldn't handle the needed repairs, and pressure mounted in the 1890s for a state takeover of the tomb. Civil War veterans and civic leaders in Chicago lobbied the state legislature, claiming that the decrepit edifice dishonored the state's prime hero. Even the walls of the catacomb insulted his memory: the cheap red brick was eroding, and with no railing to guide them, visitors strode unknowingly across the holy spot directly above the president's and his wife's remains. The recently built Garfield monument in Cleveland, with its elegant masonry, mosaics, and stained glass, put the Lincoln shrine to shame.[19]

The state duly took over the shrine in 1895, but restoration required extensive rebuilding, and that job meant extricating the Lincolns from the tomb yet again. In March 1900, a heavy crane lifted the coffins of Abraham and Mary out of their concrete grave and deposited them in a double-decked temporary vault; a year later they were returned to the refurbished catacomb. This time Mary was placed in a crypt of her own, and her husband's coffin was deposited in the old marble sarcophagus manhandled and chipped by the grave robbers in 1876. A crowd of three hundred was permitted "to pass through the tomb and take a final look at the coffin," said the *Chicago Tribune*, "which, it is expected, will never again be exposed."[20]

The *Tribune* spoke too soon, for a few months later the martyr's coffin again saw the light of day. Robert Lincoln had grown alarmed at the decision to recommission the star-crossed sarcophagus. Doubting that it offered any more protection against theft in 1901 than it had in 1876, he came up with a plan to put his father's body once and for all beyond the reach of evildoers. A ten-foot grave was dug in the catacomb, and in September 1901, Abraham Lincoln—his coffin lodged within a steel cage— was covered with cement and committed to the earth once and for all.

Before the interment, a final viewing of his body—the fifth since May 1865—took place in the tomb's Memorial Hall. Roughly fifteen observers (two of them women) gazed at Lincoln's body, and five veterans of the 1887 viewing affirmed in writing that the remains "are in fact those of Abraham Lincoln." Local newspapers whipped up a minor tempest over the state of the remains. "The mephitic exhalations were so vile," said the *Bloomington Pantagraph*, "as to almost overcome those gathered about the scene. Even the features of the dead were shocking to the beholders." They were alarmed by the corpse's color as much as its missing hair and pitched-back head (the headrest holding it up had rotted away). Prepared for the black-faced Lincoln of 1887, they got a ghastly white one instead. His face was "as white as chalk," said the *Pantagraph*. His "extremely pallid" features, added the *Chicago Tribune*, were attributed "to a film that has crept over the face."[21]

OUTSIDE OF ILLINOIS, little attention was paid to the location or condition of Lincoln's body after the April 1887 burial of Mary and Abraham, side by side, in the Springfield catacomb. But the rest of the country did take note of a new statue of Lincoln unveiled in Chicago in October 1887. In an industrial age bedeviled by labor-capital conflict and enamored of, and disturbed by, the self-made and self-aggrandizing captains of industry and finance, many mourned a lost republican era of self-made but publicly spirited great men. In that charged environment, the installation of Augustus Saint-Gaudens's ten-foot bronze *Standing Lincoln* in Chicago's Lincoln Park was cheered by art critics and newspaper writers all over the nation. "Every lover of art," said the *Los Angeles Times*, would recognize Saint-Gaudens as "a prince among modern sculptors."[22]

Twenty-two years after his death, Lincoln the person had finally arrived in American sculpture, standing for Christian and republican self-giving as much as American self-making. This work captured the details of the man's appearance, much as Herndon had done in his "character" lecture, and presented him as the prepresidential lawyer-politician, the very image of small-town, midwestern virtue.

Depicting the up-and-coming Illinois figure rather than the Civil War president let Saint-Gaudens bypass the familiar accessories of the earlier statues—the scroll in the hand, the symbolic cloak over the shoulders— and concentrate on Lincoln's body and spirit. This president's main accomplishment had been to create a resoundingly independent self, in fulfillment of American myth, but one portrayed as self-possessed, not self-interested.

One simple accessory gave the sculpture movement and drama: Behind Lincoln himself sat a capacious chair of state—an eagle with outstretched wings carved on its back, and Roman fasces included on the sides of the seat—subtly linking the midwestern lawyer to his future position as chief magistrate. The empty chair also suggested that Lincoln had just risen and was preparing to speak. His left hand clutched his lapel, and his left leg pitched forward at the knee, with the toe of his left boot edging off the pedestal. His left side was tensed with impending action, but he remained at rest, looking gingerly down, his right arm pulled behind his back, as if pondering the words he was about to utter.[23]

The sculptor had delivered Lincoln in all particulars, wrote the *Chicago Tribune*, and embedded him in the masculine style of the prewar era: "The old-fashioned carelessly rolled collar falling in reversed furrow over the thick silk cravat . . . the medium low wrinkled vest, none too well fitted . . . the long round old-style black corded watchguard passing

A pre-1920 photo of the Saint-Gaudens bronze in Chicago's Lincoln Park.

about the neck and carrying the watch to the left pocket of the vest," and "the old frock coat" with "its slightly shirred sleeve tops, its loose, bagging sleeves, its buttons none too tight in their places, its collar showing the passing from the old high roll, like that on Byron and O'Connell, to the narrow fashionable flatness of the present day."

On the blustery fall afternoon of the statue's dedication, Robert Lincoln sat on the stage with Saint-Gaudens as five thousand chilled spectators looked on, enduring long speeches on the glories of self-making. In one of them, Leonard Swett, an old legal-circuit colleague of Lincoln, described his friend's vertical ascent from "the humblest citizen in the land" to "the most exalted." To move up from rail-splitter, flatboatman, and small-scale merchant to legislator, orator, and lawyer was common enough in the Midwest of the 1830s and '40s. But catapulting oneself from there to the presidency—and then rocketing into sacred memory—verged on the miraculous.[24]

With this *Standing Lincoln*, wrote the *Century* magazine's critic Mariana van Rensselaer, Saint-Gaudens had joined outward appearance and inward character, presenting the man in both his reality and his ideality. While artists had long considered Lincoln the perfect embodiment of "the sculpturally impossible," Saint-Gaudens had given him life without sentimental flourish or didactic distraction, producing "our finest work of monumental art." The November 1887 issue of the *Century* crowned Saint-Gaudens as the prospective savior of American sculpture and gave readers a striking full-page reproduction of the statue.[25]

SAINT-GAUDENS'S statue was unveiled just a year after the 1886 Haymarket Riot, which took place only two miles south of Chicago's Lincoln Park. In response to the large crowd of striking workers that had gathered outside the McCormick reaper factory, police moved in to break up the meeting, and someone threw a bomb, which killed one policeman and unleashed a battle that killed seven more, along with an unknown number of demonstrators. Immediately, Haymarket circulated through the North as a symbol of impending class warfare. Only weeks after the Lincoln statue dedication, four Chicago anarchists were hung at the Cook County jail for their alleged part in the police killings.

Right after the Haymarket explosion, journalist Edward Bellamy sat down to write his novel *Looking Backward*. Published at the end of 1887, it touched a nerve among northern readers reeling from the eruption of class conflict in American cities. An immediate breakaway best seller, the book found fault with the excessive individualism of anarchists and businessmen alike. Bellamy articulated a burgeoning consensus among many northern opinion makers—one that would drive the Progressive movement for the next thirty years: the split between rich and poor was growing permanent as "wage slavery" squeezed out Lincoln's beloved free-labor system.

The self-made-man idea, for Bellamy and his legions of "Nationalist" disciples, had stopped describing a real world of steady opportunity for diligent white boys and had become an ideological cover for the depredations of robber barons. In that ideological matrix, Saint-Gaudens's Lincoln could be seen as political after all. The simple pose of a reflective young republican helped inspire a generation of progressives in their call for public-minded service to bridge the gaps between poor and rich, labor and capital, immigrant and native, black and white.[26]

CHAPTER EIGHT

Black Emancipation, White Reunion

The hour and the man of our redemption.
—FREDERICK DOUGLASS, 1876

I N 1876, on the eleventh anniversary of Lincoln's assassination, Frederick Douglass spoke to the enduring significance of Lincoln in the battle for liberty throughout the nation. A huge crowd of citizens had assembled in Washington's Lincoln Park, ten blocks east of the Capitol, to hear Douglass dedicate Thomas Ball's long awaited *Emancipation* statue. It was a festive Friday afternoon, with the Marine Band offering up such rousing tunes as "La Marseillaise" and "Hail, Columbia," and the black community turned out in force.

A parade of African American groups, including soldiers, Knights Templars, Sons of Purity, Good Samaritans, and many others, marched into the park. On the speakers' stand sat President Grant, congressmen, foreign ministers, and members of the cabinet and Supreme Court—all saluting the emancipator at the very moment when northern white voters and politicians were growing weary of defending black people's rights in the South.

Before Douglass spoke, President Grant rose to unveil a twelve-foot bronze Lincoln standing above a muscular bronze slave, whose left knee was still touching the ground but whose right knee was lifted, poised in a ready-to-spring position. To call him a "crouching" or even "kneeling"

*Thomas Ball's slave figure stares forward, primed for action,
as the Emancipation Proclamation ripples in front of him.*

slave, as many critics did at the time and ever since, suggests a cowering or subservient attitude. Others saw power and determination in the figure, especially in the clenched right fist. This is a liberated slave "from whose limbs the shackles have just been freed," said the *New York Tribune*. Lincoln looks down at him to this day with solemn attention, extending his left arm over the man's body as if to bless him, and clutching a copy of the Emancipation Proclamation in his right hand. The slave is showing deference to the emancipator, as if waiting for him to wrap up his official duties so he can leap forward to freedom.[1]

In the twentieth century, this "group" of two figures continued to draw fire from critics such as art historian Freeman H. M. Murray, who believed that Ball (a white sculptor) had cast the slave in a demeaning posture. Murray also claimed that Douglass, who died in 1895, had felt the same way, and had said so from the platform, in full hearing of the crowd. But no one at the time reported hearing Douglass deprecate the depiction of the slave. It seems unlikely that the diplomatic

Douglass, in front of the president and other dignitaries, would have denigrated the very statue he was dedicating, a statue substantially paid for by the hard-earned wages of African Americans (and collected by the Western Sanitary Commission, a relief group in Missouri, and other organizations).[2]

The *Christian Recorder,* Philadelphia organ of the African Methodist Episcopal Church, showed how eagerly black Americans embraced the cause of building monuments for Lincoln. In June 1865, a white man in Natchez, Mississippi, knocked down an older black woman, Mrs. Agnes Fitzhugh, in the street. She appealed to the Union army's provost marshal for a response to this attack by a "notorious rebel deserter." The provost marshal gave her ten dollars as compensation, but she complained about the perpetrator's going free. "I don't want money," she said, "but justice!" She didn't want the money, but she didn't return it either. She handed it over to the Lincoln Monument Fund (probably for the Springfield memorial, also heavily supported by African Americans, especially soldiers).[3]

In his address, Douglass didn't disparage the statue, but he did criticize Lincoln, and those negative comments, quoted out of context, have led to widespread misunderstanding of the speech. "He was pre-eminently the white man's president," Douglass said, "entirely devoted to the welfare of white men . . . The race to which we belong were not the special objects of his consideration." Douglass pointed at the white members of the audience: "First, midst, and last, you and yours were the object of his deepest affection . . . You are the children of Abraham Lincoln. We are at best only his step-children, children by adoption, children by force of circumstances and necessity."

But this apparent rejection of Lincoln only prepared the way for Douglass's deeper embrace of him on behalf of all African Americans. He applauded his people for sticking with Lincoln despite the president's strong preference for his own kind. As fledgling citizens of the Republic, black Americans had wisely recognized that only an ordinary white man of Lincoln's ilk—someone who had "shared the prejudices common to his countrymen toward the colored race"—could have been elected and made emancipation happen in the real world of politics. Judged from a purely abolitionist standard, "Lincoln seemed tardy, cold, dull and indifferent." In the context of the reigning white sentiment about blacks, however, "a sentiment he was bound as a statesman to consult, he was swift, zealous, radical and determined."

In short, for all his limitations as "either our man or our model," Lincoln fully deserved the esteem that African Americans had lavished on him—and should continue lavishing on his memory. They had revealed their political maturity in holding fast to a figure capable of steady growth, and ultimately of putting principle above prejudice. "Our faith in him was often taxed and strained to the uttermost, but it never failed . . . We came to the conclusion that the hour and the man of our redemption had met in the person of Abraham Lincoln." Shaped by his human environment like everyone else—"in all his education and feeling . . . an American of the Americans"—Lincoln had risen to the occasion and materially advanced the cause of justice and equality.

Lincoln's death had given blacks in the North and South, educated and illiterate, a common hero to cherish. And raising the $17,000 for the statue from their own pockets had given them a practical way to show civic virtue as individuals and as a group. The *Emancipation* monument would keep reminding "our race," as Douglass said in closing, that "we have been fastening ourselves to a name and fame imperishable and immortal." Douglass could have added that his impassioned speech—featuring an epic battle between a 155-word sentence cataloguing Lincoln's early missteps on racial equality and a 360-word sentence listing the gains for blacks achieved "under his wise and beneficent rule"—created a verbal monument to go with the sculpted one. Douglass joined Thomas Ball in preserving the emancipator as the living symbol of equal protection under the law.[4]

ANYONE aspiring to leadership in the black community between the end of the Civil War and the early twentieth century learned not to skimp on Lincoln devotion. The image of an ever-attentive emancipator served as a lifeline for African Americans as the Reconstruction years of fragile hope were followed by decades of chilling violence and demeaning segregation. One former slave interviewed in the 1930s suggested the potency of the martyr's image well into the twentieth century. He disclosed his present-day feelings about him. "I think a lot of Abe Lincoln," he said. "I have often thought how hard it was to give up his life for de United States. But Christ died for to save de world an Lincoln died to save de United States. And Lincoln died more Christlike dan any other man dat ever lived."[5]

In his famous autobiography *Up from Freedom* (1901), Booker T. Washington, born in Virginia sometime in the late 1850s, said he first became aware of *being* a slave when he heard his mother, during the war, "fervently praying that Lincoln and his armies might be successful, and that one day she and her children might be free." By placing Lincoln at the origin of his self-consciousness, the principal of the Tuskegee Institute— and the nation's most famous and widely respected black leader at the turn of the century—was augmenting the respectability of his cause.

But in the context of other slaves' recollections, his story does ring true. Looking back at those years, he marveled at the slaves' knowledge of national politics, obtained via the "grapevine telegraph." He remembered "many late-at-night whispered discussions" spent poring over the latest news. Many slaves saw that the president possessed the military and political power to liberate them and their children.[6]

For most African Americans, the euphoria of dawning emancipation, followed within days by the liberator's sacrificial death, sealed Lincoln's place as a lasting symbol of deliverance. At a Republican Party rally in Charleston, South Carolina, in March 1867, Solon Robinson, a white northern writer with "silver beard and hair" reminded them of Lincoln's legacy, playfully asking his large black audience, "Where am I? I am dreaming. Will someone pinch me, pull my hair, knock me on the head? Can this be Charleston? When last I stood on this green it was to attend a great slave auction."

Robinson pretended to buy the crowd's freedom by selling them to the highest bidder.

Are you here to be sold? Well, I will sell you. I never separate families. I will not take a husband from his wife. I will not tear a child from its mother's arms; but I will put you all up together. Going— going . . . Look above for the bidder. It is the spirit of Abraham Lincoln! Oh bless God that he died for you—he has bought you all! And given you to yourselves!

Robinson's biblically savvy audience knew he meant Lincoln had bought their freedom from slavery the same way Jesus had bought their freedom from sin, through his atoning sacrifice.[7]

Holding on to Lincoln as their chief mythic support (among civic figures) didn't stop the lynching of black men, or prevent their disenfranchisement, or halt the daily humiliations of Jim Crow segregation. Still, the worse things got, the more tenaciously African Americans hung on to Lincoln as final arbiter of the nation's meaning: if all men were truly created equal, they all deserved an equal chance in life and equal treatment along the way. Well into the twentieth century, northern black newspapers were lashing out at any African American criticism of Lincoln, however slight.

For most African Americans, his name had become inviolable, and the offering of his body had become a central pivot of their consciousness. Blacks didn't much care about Lincoln's physical appearance. That mattered much more to the many whites who could identify with his early struggles to rise in the world without advantages of inherited wealth, beauty, or polish, or to those who enjoyed mocking his looks. Blacks cared about what Lincoln had done *with* his body. If they commented on his homeliness or ugliness, they did so, with few exceptions, in private.

Over the late nineteenth century, African Americans kept honoring the martyr's message of equality at annual Emancipation Day events and

A store at 2112 East Main Street, Richmond, Virginia, celebrating Emancipation Day in 1888.

Lincoln's birthday celebrations. Since most southern whites had accepted the end of slavery—as long as blacks were kept subordinate by other means—Emancipation Day gave African Americans a socially approved festival that they could sometimes use to call for true citizenship.

At Frederick, Maryland, fifty miles west of Baltimore, a large rally took place at the "Agricultural Fair Grounds" each August, bringing in thousands of blacks from across Frederick County. In 1881, a grand parade wound through the city streets, brass bands blaring and little girls representing each state of the union "arrayed in white and wearing sashes and turbans of the gayest colors." Men from a dozen religious, labor, and fraternal bodies carried banners reading "Give Us Recognition," "Equality Before the Law," and "Equal Chance in the Race for Life," among many others.[8]

At a January 1, 1892, Emancipation Day assembly at Metropolitan Hall in Raleigh, North Carolina, the Reverend Joshua Brockett of the

African Methodist Episcopal Church mentioned the recent spike in lynching and called on "the spirit of our martyr friend," living within "the hovering clouds," for solace. African Americans did not expect social equality, Brockett said, but they did want fair dealing. The hallowed Lincoln, "side by side with Moses," was watching over them—though Lincoln, having "offered up his life . . . not for his own, but a different race," shined with even greater glory than the "emancipator of Israel."

One can hear some of Martin Luther King's later appeal to mountain imagery in Brockett's rousing send-off to his listeners. Let their "praise ring out with joyous liberty," he bellowed, until the phrase "Lincoln and freedom!" echoed off "the western mountains" of North Carolina and was "hurled down to the embattled hills." "Lincoln and freedom," he proclaimed, "inseparable now and forever."[9]

IN THE LATE nineteenth century, while African Americans kept the emancipator fresh in memory, southern whites themselves warmed to Lincoln—as long as he was taken as the reunifier of the nation, not as

An Emancipation Day march in Richmond, Virginia, in 1905.

the champion of black rights. In April 1865, many whites, from Robert E. Lee down, had expressed dismay and sorrow at Booth's dishonorable deed, a murder committed in their name. Sneaking up on the president from behind and firing without warning disgusted them. Within days, the many southerners who initially believed Lincoln had gotten exactly what he deserved began having second thoughts: the belief settled in that the forgiving-by-nature Lincoln would have gone easy on the former slave owners.

A few southern towns in areas controlled by Union troops did put up perfunctory emblems of mourning for the president in April 1865, but like many northern Catholics, most white southerners couldn't begin to imagine Lincoln as a martyr. It was one thing to applaud the apparent moderation of his postwar vision, quite another to cherish his memory as such, much less elevate him to a place in the civic pantheon.

Besides, pro-Confederate white southerners had their own dead leaders to venerate. They hailed their "mighty chieftain" Stonewall Jackson after his death in 1863 as one of "the most renowned heroes and captains of all ages." For them, Lincoln loomed darkly in death, as he had in life, as a warmongering tyrant striking down the holy principle of state-rights republicanism, not to mention embracing the abolitionist assault on property in slaves. In a sense, the Confederate South itself qualified as the primary martyr to emerge from the war, and Lincoln, along with his secretary of war Edwin Stanton and his generals, had carried out the execution.[10]

Rising approval of Lincoln in the white South by the 1880s was reinforced by blue-gray (whites only) military reunions and, ironically, by the assassination of President James Garfield in 1881. A Civil War veteran himself, the scholarly and mild-mannered Ohioan had spent only six months in office, almost half of that time trying to recover from gunshot wounds inflicted by Charles Guiteau, a northerner who claimed, like John Wilkes Booth, to be protecting the purity of the Republic. To the crazed Guiteau, Garfield deserved death for having generally pledged to clean up the "spoils system" of government patronage, and for challenging New York senator Roscoe Conkling's informal control over federal appointments in the Empire State.

On hearing of Garfield's shooting, southern white opinion makers held their collective breath, fearful that Guiteau might claim, like Booth, to have acted somehow on behalf of the South. Relieved to learn that this assassination counted as a strictly northern affair, they seized the chance to affirm their national zeal—rebutting, retroactively, northern charges of complicity in Lincoln's death. "Innocent of the murder of Lincoln," said the *Augusta [Georgia] Chronicle*, "the South suffered long years of agony and persecution for another's [Booth's] crime. Innocent of the assassination of Garfield, the South . . . stands tearfully beside the relics of the President."[11]

In 1881, southern cities mounted mourning events and decorations indirectly meant for Lincoln too. In the midst of eulogizing Garfield, a North Carolina paper noted that "the troubles which afflicted the Southern States, and through them the whole country during and after the reconstruction period, were mainly attributable to the removal of Mr. Lincoln from the presidency by assassination." Most southern blacks believed Lincoln had saved them from bondage; many southern whites now supposed Lincoln would have saved them from Radical Reconstruction.[12]

White southerners generally balked at calling Garfield a "martyr," as northerners commonly did. Northerners knew very well, as the *New York Times* explained, that Garfield's death fell far short of Lincoln's sacrifice for "an exalted cause or a great principle." But Garfield made up in prolonged physical and mental suffering what he lacked in heroic self-offering. Lincoln's martyrdom occurred in an instant, while for eleven weeks Garfield endured a "slow martyrdom," as the *Times* put it, wasting away as the infection from the wound spread through his body. The prostrate president proved a moral giant on his sickbed, facing his physical erosion with self-deprecating grace.[13]

In North and South alike, people were awed by Garfield's spiritual strength. At the Raleigh City Hall, a series of speakers observed that the president's "long suffering" had "done much toward uniting the people into one common family of mourners." A reunion of white Civil War veterans acted out that solidarity at a requiem service on Cameron Hill in Chattanooga, Tennessee. The Confederate band played "Dixie" and the Union band played "The Star Spangled Banner" and "Nearer, My God, to Thee," while the soldiers joined thousands of onlookers in remembering Garfield along with those who had perished in the war.[14]

Celebrating Garfield's semimartyrdom carried with it a reminder of Lincoln's uniquely sacrificial death. By 1886, "New South" champion Henry Grady, editor of the *Atlanta Constitution*, could speak piously of Lincoln's actual martyrdom, not just of his imagined moderate approach to Reconstruction. Addressing the elite New England Society at its annual Founders' Day dinner in Manhattan, Grady lauded Lincoln as "the first typical American, the first who comprehended within himself all the strength and gentleness, all the majesty and grace of this Republic."

Seated at six long, rectangular tables in Delmonico's stately dining room on Twenty-Sixth Street, the assembled potentates polished off their plum pudding *au rhum* and applauded warmly as Grady reminded them that early America had featured Virginia Cavaliers as well as Massachusetts Puritans. Lincoln, the Kentucky-born northern transplant, had sprung from "the union of these colonists" and "the crossing of their blood."

> He was the sum of Puritan and Cavalier, for in his ardent nature were fused the virtues of both, and in the depths of his great soul the faults of both were lost. [Renewed applause.] He was greater than Puritan, greater than Cavalier, in that he was American [renewed applause]—and that in his homely form were first gathered the vast and thrilling forces of this ideal government—charging it with such tremendous meaning and so elevating it above human suffering that martyrdom, though infamously aimed, came as a fitting crown to a life consecrated from its cradle to human liberty. [Loud and prolonged cheering.]

Through his very blood, not just through his political strength and judgment, Lincoln had reconciled the warring sections. Grady was telling the northern white elite that white southerners could now take Lincoln the man and martyr as their hero too. His sacrifice had been safely depoliticized, turned into a character trait—an instinctive love of liberty imbibed with his mother's milk. The white South could embrace Lincoln as the symbolic unifier of the entire American people. All that the North had to do was stop telling white southerners how to manage their relations with African Americans. "The problem" of "the negro," warned Grady, was best "left to those among whom his lot is cast."

The Delmonico's diners gratefully took the deal, as did northern whites in general. Their indifference to full black citizenship underwrote the southern-white sidling up to Lincoln in the years to come. "Mr. Grady's glowing tribute to Abraham Lincoln brought every man to his feet," wrote the *New York Tribune* reporter in the hall. "At the close of this speech the band played 'Way Down South in Dixie,' and the entire company rose to their feet and gave three cheers for Mr. Grady and three more for the Empire State of the South [Georgia]."[15]

IN THE 1880s, Henry Grady safely embedded the spirit of liberty in Lincoln's body and blood, extricating it from the volatile world of politics and sectional differences. In the 1890s, moderate African American leader Booker T. Washington of Alabama's Tuskegee Institute made a similar move, traveling to New York to announce a "new emancipation" centered not on rights, but on individual "habits of thrift, skill, economy and substantial character." He identified Lincoln as the model, in his own "upward struggle," for young black individuals on the road to "self-improvement." "Emancipation" in Washington's updating meant being *like* Lincoln, not adopting a vision of civic equality in his name.[16]

Other African Americans, mostly in the North, invoked a rights-based Lincoln. The Colored Citizens League called "a mass meeting" at Cooper Union in Manhattan in October 1900, and lambasted the Democratic candidate, "Lung Expansionist Bryan," for allying himself with the very "enemies buried by Lincoln in 1865": the southern Democrats who had "risen again" to rule the South by "mob violence." The speakers called for military force to stop lynching and for new laws to affirm voting rights, and the racially mixed audience, protected by fifty policemen, eagerly endorsed President McKinley for a second term.[17]

The Republican Party may have appreciated the Colored Citizens League's support for McKinley, but few northern whites were listening when the gathering asked for renewed federal intervention in the South. They were happy to honor Lincoln for his long-ago achievement in putting an end to chattel slavery. But the emancipation he'd helped win bore little relation to their list of current civic concerns: immigration, labor-capital conflict, urban poverty, temperance, women's social and political roles, and the new status of the United States as a world power in the wake of the Spanish-American War.

The thousands of white liberals and radicals committed to pushing for social progress now found "class" issues much more salient than "racial" ones—except insofar as "race" now connoted immigrant groups in relation to the native-born, not blacks in relation to whites. Full citizenship for African Americans didn't register as a vital matter when the labor movement was fighting for higher wages and workplace rights, and when many in the white Protestant majority felt their Republic endangered by the arrival since the 1880s of millions of Jews and Catholics from southern and eastern Europe.

Defenders of the industrial working class and the labor movement— Eugene Debs, William Jennings Bryan, Samuel Gompers, and many others—often appealed to Lincoln's memory for support. The railsplitter, they observed, had stood for fairness and equality for all. But Lincoln posed a problem for the allies of "labor" in its battle with "capital." Those terms had meant something very different to him than they meant to them.

When Lincoln said, in 1859 and again in 1861, "Labor is the superior of capital," he didn't mean that the class of working people was superior to the class of capital owners, but that capital always derived from labor. In his experience, labor stood as the universally available springboard for white youth. He took for granted that any man, over the course of life's work, could progress from earning a wage to becoming an employer in his own right.[18]

The free-labor system allowed owners of capital to hire workers, said Lincoln, and it allowed workers to go out on strike. If their employer disregarded their grievances, they were free to take their skills elsewhere. That's how free labor differed from slave labor. Maybe, had he lived into the 1880s, Lincoln would have come to side with labor over capital—in their reconfigured meanings as two opposing social forces—but he never confronted that choice.

During the Pullman Strike in 1894, Chicago settlement worker Jane Addams revealed how difficult it was to draft Lincoln into service on the side of labor. He'd been her idol since childhood, thanks to her Republican father, an Illinois state senator. John Addams had known Lincoln well in the 1850s (Lincoln addressed him in letters as "Double D'd Addams"). In her autobiography, *Twenty Years at Hull-House* (1910), Jane Addams recalled her surprise in 1865, at age four, when two black-bordered flags appeared on her front gate in the small town of Cedarville, Illinois. She ran up the steps to ask her father what it meant, and found him sobbing. "The greatest man in the world" had died, he said.

For years, after finishing college, she had fretted about finding a career worthy of Lincoln's generation, those who'd struggled to save the nation and free the slaves. In 1889, when she was twenty-nine years old, it came to her. She founded Hull House, a "settlement" of college-educated women in a working-class neighborhood on Chicago's West Side. "Settlement" meant they were leaving their middle-class formations behind, seeking out new experiences on the urban frontier. The word also suggested they were looking for common ground—some kind of novel accord between the classes. Early on, she made sure immigrant children and adults alike learned about Lincoln, the most salient symbol of common ground in America.

When Chicago's streetcars were shut down during the grueling Pullman Strike in 1894, Addams walked the three miles from Hull House to Lincoln Park in search of illumination from her lifelong hero. She needed to sit with "the marvelous St. Gaudens statue . . . to look at and gain magnanimous counsel, if I could," from the nation's certified civic paragon. Meditating beside the likeness of Lincoln's body, she found a moment of spiritual calm in the midst of her anxieties, including a bedevilment, common to reformers of her ilk, over whether to embrace socialism.

On her trek to the park, Addams passed close to Haymarket Square, scene of the disastrous bombing eight years earlier. Once seated beside the bronze statue—depicting Lincoln, like herself, deep in thought—she received the sort of insight she craved. As she said on another occasion, "the memory of Lincoln" came to her "like a refreshing breeze from off the prairie." She realized he had nothing to offer her on "the industrial question" as such. But she found new wisdom in the words chiseled into the left edge of the pink granite bench that wrapped around the statue: "with malice toward none, with charity for all."

For Addams's generation, this was the most famous of all Lincoln phrases. It could help her avoid demonizing individual capitalists such as George Pullman, even as she stood personally with labor against capital. And it could spur her on in applying Lincoln's fair-mindedness to the conditions of her time. Lincoln modeled the patience she thought reformers would need. In the 1850s, he had pushed the founders' principle of equality for all, while going slow on the abolition of slavery and seeking an accommodation between free and slave states. In the 1890s, Addams pushed Lincoln's goal of equality for all, while pursuing an accommodation between labor and capital, and deeper bonds of understanding between immigrants and native-born Americans.

As Addams put it, Lincoln had been satisfied "to dig the channels through which the moral life of his countrymen might flow," biding his time as the people's sentiments evolved. Reformers would have to get used to partial successes and repeated reversals. "In the unceasing ebb and flow of justice and oppression," she wrote, "we must all dig channels as best we may, that at the propitious moment [something] of the swelling tide may be conducted to the barren places of life."[19]

ON SEPTEMBER 26, 1901, Abraham Lincoln was buried for the last time in Springfield, and at that very moment his assassination was again on many people's minds. Three weeks earlier, on September 6, President William McKinley had attended the Pan-American Exposition in Buffalo, and in a receiving line at the Temple of Music, closely supervised by security men, he shook hands with all comers.

Five years earlier, speaking in Chicago on Lincoln's birthday, McKinley had extolled his predecessor for his republican aversion to "the ceremonials of high official station," and for his habit of "permitting visitors to crowd upon him." He quoted Charles Sumner's perceptive comment— from his June 1, 1865, memorial—about Lincoln's body as the indicator of his political faith: "With him . . . the idea of republican institutions, where no place is too high for the humblest, was perpetually manifest, so that his simple presence was a proclamation of the equality of all men." "Nobody could keep the people away from him," McKinley concluded, "and when they came to him he would suffer no one to drive them back."[20]

McKinley took for granted that Lincoln's physical immersion in the ranks of the people could not be imitated in 1896, fifteen years after Garfield's assassination. The republican practice of politics had adjusted to the dangers of the modern world. Detectives were monitoring McKinley's receiving line at the Buffalo exposition in 1901 and, as Lincoln had always predicted, their efforts proved unavailing in the case of a determined killer.

Michigan-born Leon Czolgosz, the twenty-eight-year-old son of eastern European Catholic immigrants and a self-described anarchist, waited calmly for his turn to greet the president. The detectives thought nothing of the bandage wrapped around the right hand of this well-dressed, well-groomed citizen. When McKinley reached out his right hand to him,

Czolgosz took it with his left and got off two shots from the pistol concealed in his bandage.

As with Garfield in 1881, doctors thought McKinley might recover from his wounds, and he lingered for a week before taking a turn for the worse. He became the third president to be murdered in thirty-six years and, with Lincoln, the second cut down after his reelection.

To lend a measure of majesty to the deceased, writers and orators predictably turned to Lincoln. Secretary of State John Hay—forty years earlier Lincoln's own secretary—appeared at Delmonico's to address the New York City Chamber of Commerce, and he spoke with special authority as the living link between the two presidents. Hay doubted whether "any century of the glorious future" would produce two "lovers of the people" as "sincere" in their devotion as Abraham Lincoln and William McKinley."[21]

In his State of the Union message in December 1901, new president Theodore Roosevelt also used Lincoln to elevate McKinley. His predecessor, said Roosevelt, had "filled that political office for which the entire people vote, and no President—not even Lincoln himself—was ever more earnestly anxious to represent the well-thought-out wishes of the people." Draping Lincoln's prestige over the newly fallen president lent a note of solemnity to the mourning period, but it also called to mind the gap between them. Like Garfield, McKinley was often labeled a "martyr president," but the many who remembered 1865 knew that Lincoln, unlike them, had risen to the lofty heights of martyrdom by laying his life down for a cause.[22]

Garfield and McKinley were unfortunate victims, not self-sacrificial servants of the Republic. Writers had to strain to identify a cause that McKinley himself had represented, such as civilization against anarchism. South Carolina senator John McLaurin called McKinley a "martyr to envy and hate," showing how the term had slipped its tracks completely. Lincoln had been a martyr to what he believed in (liberty and union). McKinley was a martyr to whatever drove his enemies. By 1901, the phrase "martyred president" had been watered down to mean "beloved assassinated president."[23]

CULTIVATING the memory of Lincoln carried risks, President Roosevelt warned ten thousand listeners in Springfield, Illinois, in 1903, for it seeped easily into standpat nostalgia. It lent an aura of sanctity to old habits of mind. True loyalty to Lincoln meant abandoning antiquarianism and applying his "spirit" to the issues of the present. Above all, he could supply vital symbolic support to a new nationalism premised on American global engagement. "For weal or woe," said Roosevelt, still smarting from anti-imperialist attacks on the US annexation of the Philippines, "we are a great power, a great Nation. We cannot escape playing the part of a great nation. We can play it ill or well; but play it we must."[24]

An accomplished historical writer, and a youthful witness to the Lincoln funeral procession in Manhattan, Roosevelt claimed a tight bond with the sixteenth president. Yet over the seven and a half years of his presidency, which ended three weeks after Lincoln's one hundredth birthday, he kept repeating that Lincoln's preoccupations—emancipation and union—were now thankfully off the national table.

Roosevelt knew that African Americans were still seriously disadvantaged, and still being lynched in the South. He heartily endorsed "equal rights, and protection before the law," as he informed the thirteen hundred diners at the New York City Republican Club's Lincoln banquet in 1905. He bemoaned the "maltreatment of any man who, against crushing disadvantages, has by his own industry . . . struggled upward to a position which would entitle him to the respect of his fellows, if only his skin were of a different hue."[25]

But he also believed that conditions for blacks were steadily improving. And in any case, the national government could do nothing to change them. Standing on the dais at the 1905 banquet—beneath "an electrical sign" spelling out "with malice toward none, with charity for all"—Roosevelt urged "generosity" rather than "vindictiveness" toward "those [white southerners] who differ from us as to the method of attaining the right."

Like Henry Grady, who had exhorted the North in 1886 to let a loyal South solve its own labor problems, Roosevelt claimed race relations were best left to the people of each region. "If we are sincere friends of the negro[,] let us each in his own locality show it by his action therein." He made it easy for those white northerners troubled by racial injustice in the South to wring their hands and focus their attention elsewhere. He hoped they would join him in applying the memory of Lincoln to the building up of US power in the world.[26]

Like Jane Addams, Roosevelt was impressed by Lincoln's refusal to demonize his enemies, and his effort to see things from their point of view. Those traits had made Lincoln a better fighter. Roosevelt admired Lincoln's view that political and military battles concerned principles, not personalities. For too long, the sixteenth president had been praised as a self-abnegating conciliator. It was time to rescue Lincoln the warrior, and for modern leaders to absorb his vision and tenacity. He stood, for Roosevelt, as an exemplary instance of "the strenuous life"—a joining of "bodily vigor" with intellectual growth and personal fearlessness.[27]

In his nationally celebrated memorial address for Lincoln on February 12, 1909, Roosevelt took inspiration from his predecessor's body as well as mind. He told a crowd of six thousand assembled for the groundbreaking of Lincoln's birthplace monument near Hodgenville, Kentucky, that though his "gaunt shoulders were bowed," the Civil War president's "steel thews never faltered." It had often seemed Lincoln would give way entirely under the weight of "the task allotted him": "to pour out like water the life-blood of the young men, and to feel in his every fibre the sorrow of the women." His face grew cavernous from the burden of placing so many men, year after year, in the line of fire. But pushing himself to the limit of physical endurance only concentrated his perception and will.

Fascinated by the raw power of Lincoln's body, Roosevelt took little interest in his death, or in his elevation to a republican or religious pantheon. He granted that Lincoln became, in retrospect, "the man whose blood was shed for the union of his people and for the freedom of a race," but neither his willingness to die nor his body's postmortem power drew Roosevelt's attention. Dwelling on his death as some kind of victory—for Lincoln or for the nation—would only encourage the worship of him and of his Civil War cohort as a greater generation than their descendants. Better to focus on sparking new republican heroes than to make unapproachable icons out of old ones.[28]

Invited to the groundbreaking ceremony as an emissary of the South, Secretary of War Luke E. Wright, a Tennessee native who had fought for the rebellion, challenged Roosevelt's forward-looking thrust by embarking on a creative "effort of the memory," conjuring up the president's ancestors to exalt their racial purity. Lincoln had sprung from "hardy adventurers" who had crossed the Alleghenies, and they in turn had descended from colonial English, Scottish, and Irish who had "lived their lives in field and forest, uncorrupted by wealth, strengthened in body and mind by hardships and dangers endured and overcome, with imaginations quickened by the thought that a continent was theirs." Lincoln's distant kin, in this origin tale, had belonged to sinewy stock forged by natural vigor and republican virtue.[29]

Roosevelt shared Wright's enthusiasm for Lincoln's strength, which joined moral force and physical might. But in his speech, Roosevelt ignored Lincoln's racial roots. The president's stature had nothing to do with his bloodline. All that mattered was public performance. Roosevelt valued Lincoln's body as much as Wright did, but it never occurred to him to venerate Lincoln's unmixed blood—just as it never occurred to him to herald Lincoln's blood sacrifice for the people. Both of those fixations reeked of the past.

The white people in the racially mixed Kentucky crowd adored Wright's racial interpretation of Lincoln, and when the band immediately struck up "Dixie" at the end of the speech, "the rebel yell was heard on all sides," according to a local journalist. "The Union and Confederate veterans . . . sent up a chorus that set the blood on fire." On the speakers' platform, Theodore Roosevelt embraced the moment by jumping up on a chair and "keeping time with his hat."[30]

CHAPTER NINE

Celebrating the Centenary of 1909

Apparently I was Lincoln to them for a time.
— Benjamin C. Chapin, 1909

THE NATION'S press scarcely blinked when a few dozen activists, mostly in New York City, used the occasion of Lincoln's hundredth birthday, February 12, 1909, to launch a new campaign for black freedom. A precursor to the National Association for the Advancement of Colored People organized the following year, this loose network brought African Americans, led by scholar-editor W. E. B. Du Bois, into contact with such white radicals as socialist writer William English Walling, settlement worker Mary Ovington, and Oswald Garrison Villard, the grandson of abolitionist William Lloyd Garrison. Jane Addams, Ray Stannard Baker, John Dewey, Florence Kelley, Ida Wells-Barnett, and fifty other reformers added their names to Villard's "Call" for a "Lincoln Emancipation Conference."

If "the Great Emancipator" could "revisit this country in the flesh," Garrison wrote, he would be stunned to learn that southern black men had largely lost the vote they'd won under the Fifteenth Amendment. And he would be distressed to hear that black families now faced legalized segregation and in some places lived in fear of death or eviction at the hands of white mobs.[1]

In a striking historical coincidence, it was Walling's scathing story on the 1908 race riot in Lincoln's hometown of Springfield that helped lay the groundwork for Villard's 1909 "Call," and thus for the organizing of the NAACP in 1910. An expert on all the intricacies of class conflict, Walling kicked himself for not recognizing the urgency of the race question until the sultry Friday evening of August 14, 1908, when the deadly two-day riot erupted in the Illinois state capital. Events like this, thought northerners of Walling's progressive bent, were supposed to happen in the backward South, not the modern Midwest.[2]

In Springfield, eight people had perished, including two lynched black men—one of them the elderly William Donnegan, whose family said he had known Lincoln in the 1850s. Dozens if not hundreds had been injured, black homes and businesses had been torched, and perhaps two thousand blacks had fled the city after two nights of terror. Neighboring towns mobilized to block Springfield's black refugees from camping within their borders. "All niggers are warned out of town by Monday [August 17], 12 p.m., sharp," read a sign at Buffalo, Illinois, a village fifteen miles east of the state capital.[3]

The northern press paid little attention to the Villard group in February 1909, six months after the Springfield riot, but it gave extensive coverage to Booker T. Washington's upbeat Lincoln's birthday tribute at the annual banquet of the Manhattan Republican Club. Addressing eight hundred male diners—and their female relatives and friends seated in the balconies—at the Waldorf Astoria, the "Wizard of Tuskegee" heaped encomiums on "the brave and true white men of the South" who "have loyally accepted the results of the Civil War and are today working with a courage few people in the North can understand to uplift the Negro in the South and complete the emancipation that Lincoln began."[4]

Whites and many blacks in the North and South found this vision reassuring because it assumed that real progress for African Americans could occur within a segregated society. Talk of full citizenship or social equality could wait while blacks slowly built up their financial resources and occupational standing. It was easy to fit Lincoln's lifelong endorsement of individual self-making into this program, but only by suppressing something that he knew self-making depended on: free access to the social and political activities of the larger community.

Lincoln had learned firsthand that young men like him climbed ladders successfully when leading citizens—like the organizers of the Springfield Lyceum where he practiced eloquence—banded together to steady the ladders for them. Diligent striving for advancement had worked for him because he was welcomed into Illinois law offices and courtrooms, and into the apparatus of the Whig political party.

It made no sense to Du Bois, editor of the NAACP monthly *The Crisis* starting in 1910, to advise African Americans, derided and stymied at every turn, to embrace the rail-splitter's views on success through dogged labor. But he was not about to dispense with Lincoln. In the dire circumstances of 1909, the icon of self-making figured as a vital symbolic ally. For Lincoln had never equivocated on every person's right to fair treatment and respect as they pursued their place in "the race of life."

To those of Du Bois's persuasion, Springfield's one-hundredth-birthday celebration for the local hero revealed the dire situation facing proponents of equality. The city marked the occasion with a segregated banquet, and in his keynote address, British ambassador James Bryce inadvertently rubbed fresh salt in the black community's wounds. "To us in England," the author of *The American Commonwealth* (1888) told the seven hundred white diners, seated at seventy tables in the state armory, "he is one of the heroes of the race whence you and we spring."

Already booked into the Waldorf Astoria's event, Booker T. Washington couldn't attend the Springfield gathering, but he sent a letter to be read in his absence. Touting black uplift through self-improvement, he declared, "Every member of my race who does not work, who leads an immoral life, dishonors the name and memory of Lincoln." This advice poured on more salt: among the many blacks fleeing Springfield six months earlier, some had been dispatched from their jobs solely on grounds of race.

Springfield African American minister L. H. Magee, speaking at an alternative Lincoln dinner, told the audience he would rather be one of the "black devotees of Lincoln than toastmaster at a so-called Lincoln banquet at $25 a plate. Oh consistency, thou art a jewel! How can you play 'Hamlet' without the melancholy Dane?"[5]

IT'S HARDLY SURPRISING that on February 12, 1909, most white northerners were not thinking about racial justice. They were too busy trying to show their love for Lincoln, to transmit it to their children, to share it with new immigrants from Europe and Asia, and to exploit it for commercial gain. The day amounted to a grand Lincoln revival, featuring thousands of speeches, concerts, recitations, and department store promotions. State and city officials, the Grand Army of the Republic, and other patriotic groups were determined to pass their Lincoln ardor on to posterity.

Outside the South, Lincoln excitement prevailed from east to west, spurred on by the large metropolitan dailies, which spent months preparing special supplements about him. School districts took elaborate steps to instill Lincoln consciousness in the young. In San Francisco, all eighty-five public schools adopted the Grand Army's suggested program centering on the Gettysburg Address—including, as the *San Francisco Chronicle* reported, "the Oriental School, where many of the pupils are recently from China, and cannot speak or understand the English language." The immigrant children would pick up Lincoln's significance, said the paper, since the American-born Chinese pupils at the school displayed "the same enthusiasm" for him felt by every other student in the city.[6]

The number of Lincoln happenings in New York City dwarfed those of any other metropolis. "Over 600 Meetings Scheduled for Tomorrow's Celebration," said the *New York Times* on February 11 in listing the next day's goings-on. That number didn't count the readings of the Gettysburg Address due to take place at all theater matinees. It did count the more than 545 programs to be held in all New York City public schools during the morning, and the evening speeches to take place in each of the city's forty-six school districts. The schools accounted for the vast preponderance of nontheatrical Lincoln observances.

With nearly five million residents, New York City contained more than twice as many people as Chicago, the next largest American municipality. Nearly two million of these New Yorkers had been born overseas, including half a million eastern European and Russian Jews and a third of a million Italians. In 1909, public officials saw their chance: the centenary could serve their ongoing "Americanization" campaign by bringing Lincoln into the schools on this state holiday. Principals arranged visits from Civil War veterans, ministers, politicians, judges, journalists, and educators; at noon sharp, six hundred thousand pupils began a simultaneous recitation of the Gettysburg Address, and the distinguished guests then spoke of Lincoln's simple beginnings and sterling virtues.[7]

The evening events were swamped to overflowing. While thousands were turned away, an estimated seventy thousand people got to hear such luminaries as New York lieutenant governor Horace White, former mayor Seth Low, Columbia sociologist Franklin Giddings, and poet Edwin Markham, whose new verses "Lincoln, the Man of the People" had just been published that morning in the *Times* and other papers around the country.

One Grand Army official, speaking to the pupils at Grammar School No. 20 in Manhattan, asked "his audience of poor foreign boys" how many of them had read a life story of Lincoln. According to a *New York Times* reporter, four hundred boys raised their hands. This result came as no surprise to *Times* readers. The paper had started its Lincoln commemoration on the first of February, publishing the opening installment of a seven-part life of Lincoln, which appeared as part of a Lincoln essay contest for all schoolchildren in the Greater New York area.

The kids were invited to read this short biography—composed for the occasion by Frederick Trevor Hill, author of the recent book *Lincoln the Lawyer*—and write "original" essays of up to five hundred words drawing on Hill's account. To light a fire under the students and their families—"foreign" and "American" alike—the *Times* announced that one thousand pupils would win silver Tiffany medals imprinted with Lincoln's bust. The hundred best writers among them would also take home a five-dollar gold piece.[8]

Contending that Lincoln was a flesh-and-blood, ordinary individual, not a natural genius or the recipient of any special inspiration from on high, Hill encouraged everyone starting out in life to take him as a model. Lincoln proved that "character" could prevail in the race of life when a person lacked advantages of wealth, education, or personal attractiveness. Lincoln's "uncouth appearance," said Hill, had not worked "in his favor." As one young author wrote at the start of her essay, "Lincoln's is one of the homeliest faces in the American portrait gallery." All children could take him as just like them, and get busy, as he had done, developing their inner mettle.[9]

School officials and public figures endorsed the essay plan in glowing terms, and by the deadline of February 15, the twenty-second floor of the New York Times Building was piled high with almost ten thousand entries. Winners were announced two weeks later, and the medals, engraved with the winners' names, were handed out in late March. That gave the *Times* over a month to entertain readers with some of the children's essays, their ingratiating letters pleading for a medal, and their unsolicited drawings of Lincoln's face.

Some of the paper's daily updates developed story lines that took on lives of their own. Samuel Bussell, a fifteen-year-old boy from the Bronx, suffered from an enlarged heart and had been forced to withdraw from school. Being confined to home hadn't prevented him from reading the *Times*'s Lincoln installments in early February, or from submitting an essay without the required teacher's signature confirming that he'd produced it "without outside aid."

Learning of his illness, the paper dispatched an investigator to his home on Morris Avenue to verify that Samuel had indeed composed the essay himself. It quickly became clear that he was the author, and that his illness had taken a turn for the worse. Immediately a special panel of examiners read his essay, awarded him the prize, and had an engraved medal delivered to him. Samuel squirreled it away in his bed, and wrote the paper a thank-you note, closing with the hope that he "may be able to compete in other contests in the future." On February 27 Samuel died, with the medal showing Lincoln's face tucked into bed beside him.[10]

The moral tale featuring ten-year-old Gladys McKirnan caught readers' attention too. Before mailing her essay to the *Times*, Gladys had crossed out the words "without outside aid" on her teacher's certification form and scrawled in their place, "with a little help from mother." The judges were enchanted: "This frank confession is both unique and touching," the paper said. Not a single other author had owned up to the "little help" that some adult had surely supplied. "Gladys is beginning life well," said the *Times*. "She will make no false pretense. Young as she is, the example of Lincoln, which she has been studying with all her might, has had its influence upon her."

Several weeks later, the paper reported on Gladys's arrival at the *Times* office to pick up her prize. "For the benefit of *Times* readers who have read about Gladys and wondered what kind of girl she might be," the paper furnished a profile: "She is very small for her years, and has chestnut hair, and it falls down her back—not in a braid, but in a flood. And she has a quick, energetic manner, but it is modest for all that." When Gladys made it to the *Times*'s lobby "window" to claim her medal, the man on the other side could barely see her below the sill. "Who are you?" he asked. "I am the little girl who got some help from mother," she replied. That's all the information he needed. He retrieved the box marked "Gladys McKirnan" and handed it down to her, whereupon she retreated to a corner, opened the pasteboard box, and "let out some ecstatic screams."[11]

The *Times* received at least one essay from an African American pupil, eighteen-year-old Joseph Gomers. "As a negro," he wrote in his cover letter, "I cannot help feeling that your Lincoln competition would not be complete were the negroes not participants. I say so because I think of the connection he had had with our race and the great good results thereby." Apparently no longer in school, Joseph had his essay certified by a Sunday School teacher at the Bethel AME Church on West Twenty-Fifth Street in Manhattan, where the Reverend Reverdy C. Ransom had been preaching a militant egalitarian message since 1907. Ordinarily, when excerpting a student's letter, the *Times* offered some comment on it, but in this case the paper said nothing. Joseph didn't get a medal, but he did receive an honorable-mention certificate, mailed to him at his home on West Thirty-Sixth Street.[12]

THE *TIMES* essay contest had everything, and nothing, to do with "race." Apart from Joseph's cover letter, the relations between blacks and whites never came up at all. Frederick Trevor Hill had mentioned the Emancipation Proclamation in passing, but he avoided the legacy of emancipation altogether, and left out Lincoln's evolving views on race. Fourteen-year-old German immigrant Otto Haas, who had come to America eighteen months earlier, entitled his essay "Abraham Lincoln, Redeemer of the Black Race." But he didn't get that notion from Hill's *Times* installments.

The competition was nevertheless all about race, since the *Times* writers regarded immigration as the overriding race issue of the day. The tiny nine-year-old Russian Alexandra Kliatshco, who had arrived in America in 1906, became their poster child for all the "foreign races" destined to thrive in the free air of America. Her fervor for Lincoln, and the excellence of her English, drew euphoric praise. She proved that Lincoln's story could unite foreigners and native-born Americans.

Alexandra's father, a physician on Henry Street, proudly informed a reporter that his daughter had begun memorizing long passages of Russian poetry at the age of three. Her hunger for beautiful words transcended place, and now it had taken root in the land of Lincoln. "I'm a little foreign girl, and I have been here only a short time," her essay began, "but when I read about Lincoln, I thought that I might grow up a great woman as Lincoln was a great man." And it ended, "We cannot forget the love he bore us and he died leaving the world better than it was. I hope that I can be like Lincoln, unselfish, kind, thoughtful and modest."[13]

Lincoln loomed over the essay contest as the timeless prophet of individual advancement. His message underwrote a pacific intermingling of peoples, since all of the young, whatever their origins, could climb unimpeded to their desired goals. One after another, the writers repeated Frederick Hill's contention that Lincoln never took failure as defeat; he picked himself up, dusted himself off, and resumed the quest for success.[14]

Summing up the value of the essay contest, the *Times* said it had given perhaps a hundred thousand New Yorkers a centennial immersion into Lincoln's story. Reaching the children had mattered the most. The "conception of the great President" they had acquired "will not easily be effaced." Neither would the memory of having competed on what the *Times* kept insisting was the equal playing field of the contest—just like the American social order, which had never stopped rewarding men of ambition, no matter how homely their looks or unpolished their manner. As the children's own drawings of him suggested, Lincoln's body could help unite the nation through his unadorned appearance, the visible marker of a simple and trustworthy character.[15]

BY 1909, a number of northern states, including New York, had made Lincoln's birthday a holiday, enabling merchants to pitch him to citizen consumers free to shop on Friday, February 12. The Wanamaker's department store's enormous galleries in Lower Manhattan went all out for the centenary, putting on a "Lincoln Celebration" in its auditorium: an illustrated lecture on the president, followed by a screening of the ten-minute Edison film *The Blue and the Grey, or the Boys of '61*, accompanied by "favorite war songs." Capping the program, one "Mrs. Wilson" led the audience in belting out "The Star-Spangled Banner," joined by "fifes, drums, cornets, and trombones."

All of this historical excitement, Wanamaker's hoped, would incline customers to appreciate its "COLONIAL DAY" promotion, featuring a "Delightful Display of Reproductions of the Quaint FURNITURE of Our Forefathers . . . sedate, modest-priced, old-fashioned . . . Colonial mahogany Pieces, with their suggestions of the long ago . . . in whose simplicity is reflected the homely lives of our forefathers." Wanamaker's nostalgic ad copy used Lincoln and the Civil War to sell peaceful eighteenth-century charm.[16]

In 1909, most Lincoln advertisers, like the *Times* student essayists, took Lincoln as a man of the recent, accessible past. On February 12, the *Times* ran a boxed ad featuring nine companies (including Faber pencils and Bass Ale) founded before Lincoln's birth in 1809, and still going strong. The companies' excellence, like Lincoln's, was shown by the unbroken run of their good names down to the present.[17]

While the *New York Times* permitted only the most circumspect Lincoln ad copy, the *Chicago Tribune*—the Republican voice of a city with two million residents—featured straightforward commercial appeals in his name. The *Tribune* had been touting the city's development since Lincoln's day, watching contentedly as the population climbed from 30,000 in 1850 to 110,000 in 1860. On Sunday, February 7, 1909, the paper issued a colossal, 194-page issue (three times the usual size) that praised the still-exploding metropolis as much as it did the local and national hero.

The eighty-five-page Lincoln section began with a full-page engraving entitled "Lincoln's Vision—Chicago, Capital of the Great West," depicting him as a strapping, twenty-something man of the people. His sleeves rolled up to reveal two sturdy arms, young Mr. Lincoln is seated on a crate and has nodded off, leaning against a barrel, while reading law books by candlelight. The books have tumbled to the ground in front of him, and as he dreams, he conjures up the city's future: the skyscrapers of a booming urban center rise out of the mists of time—or is it industrial smoke?

Among the hundreds of advertisements sold for the centennial issue, at least fifteen made direct reference to Lincoln, and a few drew his body into their pitches. "Do You Keep Your Business in Your Hat Like

Lincoln?" asked the Derby Desk Company. The president had famously deposited important letters and notes in his tall silk hat, misplacing them, the ad suggested, with distressing regularity. Any "modern" businessman who hadn't upgraded from a dusty rolltop to a "sanitary flat top" rivaled Lincoln for inefficient, if endearing, work habits.[18]

"Nearly forty-four years since Lincoln's wonderful voice was last heard," declared an ad for "The Talking Machine Shop," located next to Orchestra Hall on Michigan Avenue. Regrettably, the store couldn't include Lincoln's voice in its "complete line of Victor Records," but it did come up with a consolation prize: "Do you know that you can hear President-Elect Taft on the Victor today, and will be able to hear him forty-four years from now?"[19]

A half-page advertisement for the J. I. Case Threshing Machine Company of Racine, Wisconsin, pushed the company's equipment "manufactured and sold under our world-famous trade-mark now known as 'Old Abe.'" The graphic display featured a drawing of the famous Civil War eagle "Old Abe," a battle-tested mascot of the Eighth Wisconsin Volunteer Infantry Regiment. A close look revealed that this aquiline "Old Abe" was wearing a small, circular halftone photo of Lincoln as a medallion around its neck.[20]

The Waterman pen company took out a full-page advertisement to commercialize nothing less than the signing of the 1863 Emancipation Proclamation. The bearded president is standing at a desk, his quill still moving as he finishes writing the words "shall be then thenceforward, and forever free—Abraham Lincoln." Behind his head, a disembodied hand is wielding an Ideal Fountain Pen to write on the ad copy, "Emancipation from Pen Troubles, L. E. Waterman Co." That flippant play on Lincoln the liberator got amplified in the text at the bottom of the ad, which identified the company—with offices in four American and nine foreign cities—as "the Emancipator of the Millions of Slaves to the Ink Bottle." A century later, this ad copy seems humorously irreverent, but also perhaps disrespectful to millions of actual slaves emancipated in 1865; many readers in 1909, too, must have winced as well as laughed.[21]

Tribune readers of the day were witnessing the birth of a new era for Lincoln's body and words. He had gone "public" in a brand-new way, transcending his republican frame of reference and emerging as a free-floating symbol. Yet advertisers could work the whimsical edges of his memory because so many people still imputed an aura of sanctity to his physical person along with his inspiring speeches and impeccable character.

The subtlest Lincoln advertising campaign in the *Tribune*'s centennial issue was the one the paper conducted on its own behalf. One drawing showed Lincoln, the "gawky" politician (as the *Tribune*'s text put it), planting "his feet on the edge of the editor's desk" and leaning back in his chair with perfect ease and confidence, indicating how completely at home he felt in editor Joseph Medill's office in the 1850s. Halftone photographic portraits of both men looked on from the sides of the article, as the etched version of Medill waited for the lounging Lincoln to finish reading a document.

This *Tribune* image connected Lincoln's elongated posture with his mental concentration. Many other Lincoln illustrations, during and after his life, relied on the same mind-body loop: his immense, stationary frame—lying prone or seated, legs bunched up or extended—signaling deep absorption in thought. In this case, Lincoln had stopped off at the *Tribune* to do his thinking, imbuing the paper too with his disciplined, probing spirit.[22]

THE *CHICAGO TRIBUNE* had good reason to be proud of the stunning eight-page "halftone section" of photographs in its Lincoln centennial edition of February 7, 1909. In the week leading up to it, daily display ads whetted the public's appetite for the stories and pictures to come. On February 2, a small oval halftone of the portrait taken by Samuel Altschuler in Chicago about three weeks after Lincoln's election in 1860 showed Lincoln studying the camera lens with a serious stare and a raised left eyebrow. He sported a neat haircut and shave, and his carefully manicured, U-shaped first growth of beard extended from the sides of his mouth down to his chin. The text quotes at length from the *Tribune*'s endorsement of Lincoln's candidacy on February 16, 1860, and concludes that Illinois readers will especially covet the souvenir paper "on account of The Tribune's intimacy with Lincoln in the early days."[23]

In its last promo for the centennial issue, the *Tribune* offered readers a classic Alexander Gardner shot from February 5, 1865, placing a wide margin of white space around it to

Samuel Altschuler's 1860 photograph of the president-elect.

magnify its visual impact. (The image appears as the frontispiece of this book.) Lincoln again looks straight at the lens, but without the raised eyebrow he seems positively beatific as he holds his hands serenely in his lap, exuding an aura of gentle contentment despite his drawn, wrinkled face. "Let us look at this picture," said the *Tribune* in the adjoining text. "Worn out by the willing sacrifice made of his life," this "Great Patriot . . . loved all his people as deeply as any mother ever loved her child."[24]

When they opened their five-cent Sunday papers to the halftone supplement, specially printed on calendered (smooth) stock, readers discovered that pages four and five presented a mind-boggling display of a hundred thumbnail-size portraits of Lincoln. Drawn from the collection of Osborn Oldroyd, caretaker of a Lincoln museum in the former Petersen house in Washington, DC, the photos had been shot between 1858 and 1865. (The paper mistakenly believed there was "no photograph extant showing the president as he was previous to 1858"—yet the dandified Lincoln shot by Nicholas Shepherd in the late 1840s had been displayed to great fanfare in *McClure's Magazine* in 1895.) These two pages alone—with the images arranged in ten neat rows of ten pictures each—turned the February 7 issue into a collectors' prize.[25]

Few people had ever seen a fraction of these images, and now, at a single glance, they could soak in the ever-evolving face of the people's hero. Halftone technology ensured that the details of his aging visage would become second nature to twentieth-century readers of newspapers and magazines. With the publishing of the Shepherd photo and three other pre-1858 images uncovered in the twentieth century, the public could contemplate Lincoln's physical transformation over his entire political career—from his arrival in Congress in 1847 to March 1865.

Of course, the slow shutter speeds of early photography had never captured, and so couldn't preserve, the range of Lincoln's bodily expressions, facial or otherwise. Deprived of his playful eyes and eruptive laugh, Americans were forced to take gravity or pensiveness as his default position. Of the 120 photographs of him available today, none shows a heartily smiling Lincoln. But the widely seen images of a solemn or severe presidential face, more deeply creviced and withered year by year, have helped generations of Americans comprehend how completely he gave himself to the Republic. In 1864, he wondered if he would survive the war. He and many others thought he might succumb to exhaustion.

AFTER SQUINTING at the thumbnails, readers could flip back to page one of the halftone section for a full-page photoengraving of sculptor Gutzon Borglum's 1908 bust of the president. Dramatic lighting turned this Lincoln into an ethereal presence rather than an earthly one and signaled Borglum's fulsome embrace of the Lincoln cult. Born in the Idaho Territory in 1867 of Danish immigrant parents, Borglum promoted his hero's virtues—and physical beauty—with aggressive exuberance.

"Dear Old Abe" had never deserved the labels "grotesque . . . gawky— or even awkward." No "man who could whip his way to the head of a band of ruffians [the Clary's Grove boys in New Salem], reason his way to the head of a town meeting, inspire and fire a nation, win and hold the hearts of millions"—could have deserved such description. Of course, Lincoln had never pleased "Old-World-trained eyes." For he moved "with free, easy stride, not Indian but Western—developed in the open road, where men, with bent head, study the unbroken trail."[26]

Since 1908, critics had disagreed about the merit of Borglum's forty-inch-high sculpture, which he had cut directly from a huge block of marble, rather than first making a clay model. Championing his own originality, Borglum assailed his detractors and bemoaned the academic takeover of what he considered an intuitive craft. Above all, he scorned imitation of the classical Greeks, which he thought shackled American art and kept citizens from properly celebrating their national exemplars.[27]

The *New York Times* assembled several artists who mocked Borglum's claim to originality (painter Everett Shinn called all of his work "utterly mediocre") and chastised him for imagining that a serious artist could escape the influence of the Greeks. But the *Chicago Tribune* found the Lincoln head "heroic in size and superb in conception . . . one of the most living portraitures yet done." Borglum's feel for popular tastes in art and patriotism propelled him down the path that led decades later to his monumental carvings at Mount Rushmore, where by 1939 the sixty-foot-high heads of Washington and Lincoln bookended those of Jefferson and Theodore Roosevelt.

The three-foot-high sculpted head from 1908 went on to become a beloved Lincoln likeness. The original marble bust adorned the US Capitol rotunda from 1911 until 1979, when it was relocated to the crypt, one floor below. Meanwhile, a bronze replica of the sculp-

The Springfield replica of Borglum's head of Lincoln took on a life of its own, outshining the original 1908 sculpture by taking root in the popular culture of post–World War II tourism.

ture, installed in 1931 at ground level just outside the president's tomb in Springfield, emerged as an intimate alternative to all the elevated, untouchable Lincolns in the land. Borglum's bust made the president's face accessible. After World War II, so many visitors and schoolchildren were rubbing Lincoln's metallic nose for good luck—a tradition that may have begun among soldiers headed off to war in the 1940s—that the replica turned into a lasting Illinois attraction.[28]

BY FEBRUARY 12, 1909, the *Tribune*'s centennial edition had become a sensation, and it helped trigger a big turnout for Chicago's hundreds of Lincoln events—orations, songfests, stereopticon lectures on the president (including one by Jane Addams at Hull House), dedications of over five hundred identical fifteen-pound bronze tablets of the Gettysburg Address (at schools and other institutions), and a twenty-one-gun naval artillery salute in Lincoln Park.

The marquee evening event put on by the mayor's Lincoln Memorial Committee took place at the enormous indoor pavilion at Dexter Park, adjoining the South Side stockyards. Ten to twenty thousand immigrant and native-born whites turned out, drawn by the promise of a five-hundred-voice chorus, a band concert by the First Regiment Band, and a "human flag" composed of five hundred children (girls in white dresses, boys in red or blue togas). The rollicking crowd—probably "the largest audience ever gathered in one building in Chicago," said the *Tribune*—stood squeezed together for three hours and joined in as the chorus boomed out some old favorites: "Tenting Tonight"; "Rally 'Round the Flag, Boys"; "America"; "Tramp, Tramp, Tramp"; and "The Star Spangled Banner."[29]

About two miles away, an African American centennial celebration at the massive brick Seventh Regiment armory was unfolding at the same time as the Dexter Park spectacular. The white leaders of the Lincoln Memorial Committee had worked with a Colored Citizens Committee to schedule an evening of competing, and de facto segregated, events. In its February 12 listing of the day's six mass meetings, the *Chicago Tribune* alerted readers that the 8:00 p.m. armory assembly was planned "especially for colored people." Between ten and fifteen thousand black citizens turned out, approximately one-quarter of the forty thousand African Americans residing in the city.[30]

In his keynote address, African American Methodist theologian John Bowen, president of Gammon Seminary in Atlanta, put emancipation forward as Lincoln's permanent legacy. The martyred president had never imagined "the removal of the shackles" as an end point. According to Lincoln, emancipation meant the liberated slave's "complete amalgamation into the body politic as a citizen of the mighty Republic." This conclusion followed from a simple application of Lincoln's 1858 "house divided" doctrine to postwar conditions: if the nation couldn't survive half-free and half-slave, neither could it survive after 1865 "with a great body of freedmen that have no right and title in the Republic as citizens."[31]

But Bowen believed 1909 was not the time to press for fulfillment of Lincoln's doctrine. He turned from Lincoln the prophet of equality and replaced him with Booker T. Washington's Lincoln, the model of character building. Of course African Americans faced unfair hurdles, he said, but down in Georgia—where conditions were much worse in the age of lynching than they were in Chicago—people had learned not to "weep over obstacles."

Instead, they courted white allies and focused on accumulating property. Blacks in Chicago, with their "greater privileges," should get busy "making character" instead of complaining about their burdens. "Every door is open to you," Bowen claimed. "You have yet to show . . . that you can wring out of your privileges the large good that we [in Georgia] have wrung out of our disadvantages."[32]

THE IDEA of emancipation didn't come up at all in the principal Chicago centennial address, which took place at 10:00 a.m. on February 12 in the elegant theater of the downtown Chicago Auditorium. Between four and five thousand listeners got to hear Woodrow Wilson, the president of Princeton University and a rising political star. An accomplished scholar of American politics, he delivered one of the best treatments of Lincoln's character ever written.

Born in Virginia and raised in Georgia and South Carolina, Wilson embodied in his personal life the North-South white reconciliation that propelled his political career. He had taught at Princeton since 1890 and had become its president in 1902. By February 12, 1909—two years before assuming the governorship of New Jersey, and four years before entering the White House—he had been studying and admiring Lincoln for decades. His oration in Chicago showed how much the future Democratic president shared with the current lame-duck Republican president as disciples of Lincoln.

Like Roosevelt, who spoke in Kentucky a few hours later, Wilson scoffed at the idea of honoring Lincoln by "merely remembering what he was"—that is, by consigning him to the Civil War era of great leaders, and dwelling on his heroic role in ending slavery and secession. "The tasks of this age," as Wilson put it, "are the only tasks to which we are asked to address ourselves." Too many people "elevate" Lincoln so they can "walk backward [into the future] and deplore the loss of such figures and of such ages." Properly celebrating him required "showing today that we have not lost the tradition of force which made former ages great." We shall live by "renewal," not by "recollection."

As "progressives," Wilson and Roosevelt plainly felt bedeviled by a pervasive traditionalism unwilling even to identify, much less solve, the quandaries of modern America. The civil religion of Lincoln, it seemed to them, had become an opiate. Living vicariously in a vanished era of war to the death over slavery and state rights let people ignore the true problems of 1909: how to position the United States among the other global powers and how to overcome what Wilson called "a division . . . not to say a warfare . . . among classes."[33]

Strong executive leadership would prove essential, said Wilson, and the leader Americans needed would qualify as a "man of the people"—a hackneyed phrase that Lincoln had reconceived. It didn't just mean that one had risen from a simple background, displayed an unpolished appearance, loved the company of one's fellow commoners, and grasped their concerns. All of that might be true, but the phrase had to be understood in republican as well as populist terms: Lincoln saw himself as a man of the *whole* people. He stood apart from any one class, interest, or region while remaining "cognizant" of all of them. In his detachment he represented the entire body politic.

"We should pray," said Wilson, "not only that we should be led by such men, but also that they should be men of the particular sweetness that Lincoln possessed." The sweetness, in Lincoln's case, was tied to aloofness as much as generosity. He kept his own counsel: "More remained unrevealed than was disclosed to our view."

> We feel that there was more promise in him when he died than when he was born; that the force was so far from being exhausted that it had only begun to display itself in its splendor and perfection. No man can think of the life of Lincoln without feeling that the man was cut off almost at his beginning.[34]

Lincoln made such a potent symbol of independent leadership—of standing for the entire diverse and divided public—because his particular body and character were constructed much like America itself. A variety of ordinary elements had come together in him, all of them commingling to create an entity never before seen. Sounding a lot like William Herndon, Wilson tied Lincoln's mind to his body. "Such was Mr. Lincoln," declared Wilson.

> Not a singular man; a very normal man, but normal in gigantic proportions,—the whole character of him is on as great a scale—and yet so delightfully informal in the way it was put together—as was the great frame in which he lived. That great, loose-jointed, angular frame that Mr. Lincoln inhabited was a very fine symbol of the big, loose-jointed, genial, angular nature that was inside.

Yet even when he was the most committed to a cause, such as defeating the rebellion, Lincoln had preserved his aloofness, his synoptic view.

In the midst of the crash of arms, he could sit quietly in his room and enjoy a book . . . could wander in fields of dreams, while every other man was hot with the immediate contest. Always set your faith in a man who can withdraw himself, because only the man who can withdraw himself can see the stage.

Seeing the whole, Lincoln could put himself in the shoes of his enemies, grasping the coherence of their worldview even as he strove to destroy their cause.[35]

WILSON'S STAGE METAPHOR was apt, since Lincoln had wandered in fields of dreams at the theater as much as he did in books—and his favorite books were the dramas of Shakespeare. The president would not have been surprised by the idea that someday his own character and political leadership would find the footlights. It ended up taking just a few decades, for on his hundredth birthday a matinee crowd of twelve hundred filed into New York City's Garden Theatre on Madison Avenue to watch thirty-five-year-old Benjamin Chapin perform the leading role in his four-act play *Abraham Lincoln at the White House*. Many were amazed at how skillfully Chapin made Lincoln come to life.

The strapping young Ohioan bore a certain natural resemblance to the president. A product of the state's Western Reserve—where "reverence for Lincoln is a heritage," he said, "and pretty nearly a religion"—he stood about six feet tall, with a thin frame, a high forehead, and dark, deep-set eyes. As a student at the University of Chicago, Chapin had read so much about "the martyred President" that he became an all-out disciple. He purposely mimicked his hero's stooped shoulders and shambling gait. That's when people started telling him he looked like Lincoln.[36]

By the early 1900s, Chapin was putting on full makeup, impersonating the president on lyceum and vaudeville stages around the North. Whether it was the twenty-minute vaudeville version or the two-hour lecture edition, he adapted the content to local audiences. Preparing for a 1905 performance at the Presbyterian National Union Convention in

New York City, he found out that some old-timers in the group remembered Lincoln's 1861 remarks at Manhattan's Astor House. Chapin promptly learned the short speech and opened his show with it.

In 1906, Chapin wrote and produced a scripted, three-hour play, *Abraham Lincoln in the White House*, with parts for Mary, Tad, Edwin Stanton, and a few others (all of them played by slightly built actors, the better to showcase the towering Lincoln). The drama was centered around Lincoln's experience of three pivotal moments: the fall of Fort Sumter in 1861, the Battle of Gettysburg in 1863, and the last day of his life, leading up to his departure for Ford's Theatre. Chapin mentioned the Emancipation Proclamation but kept it safely sequestered in the 1860s. Wary of "giving offense" to the South, he concentrated on Lincoln's now universally admired character: "I simply try to enter into the soul of the man," he told a reporter.

Chapin's Lincoln was saintly in his home life and in his politics—a man who met his wife's ill temper with forbearance, graciously pardoned a treacherous soldier, and disarmed the hard-nosed, intemperate Stanton with stories and jokes. This hero was a softly rendered man of charity: resolute, but never harsh; brooding, but never depressed. Unlike the iron-willed warrior summoned up by Roosevelt in Kentucky, Chapin's president did not atrophy physically as he approached his end. His body remained virile, and his spirit stayed self-effacing. Chapin created a figure that matched the Lincoln currently favored by whites in the North and South, the one whose image underwrote the ongoing North-South white rapprochement.[37]

Above all, Chapin's Lincoln *looked* like Lincoln, forcing many older spectators to do a double take. The face was a near exact copy as seen from the seats. Equally arresting were the iconic mannerisms. This president stretched out on the floor when he wished to mull over a problem, lying on his back with arms and legs stretching off in boyishly random directions. Commenting on his performance, Chapin said he saw "wonder and astonishment" on the faces of those over sixty, who remembered Lincoln from life. They "viewed me with that vacant, fascinated stare" of "hypnotic patients . . . as tho a ghost rather than the actor walked the boards." They swamped him after shows, addressing him as "Mr. Lincoln." "There was no joke nor flattery about this. Apparently I was Lincoln to them for a time."[38]

When he brought his act to the Liberty Theatre in Manhattan in April 1906, most critics found the play painfully amateurish. They urged parents to take their children to see it without expecting much illumination themselves. The *New York Times* generously noted that none of this was Chapin's fault. Experienced playwrights and actors could have done no better. You can't just take "the central figure in one of the greatest dramas that has ever stirred the hearts of men" and plop him down on a stage, expecting an engaging performance to ensue. A "master poet" combined with a "master psychologist" might *compose* such a play. But not even a "master player" could realize the character of Lincoln on the stage. Still, Chapin could be faulted for exaggerating Lincoln's personal sweetness and minimizing the "sterner" side of his leadership.[39]

In 1906, Chapin's show failed to catch on in Manhattan, and for three years he stuck to presenting his one-act "playlet" version on vaudeville stages as far west as Los Angeles. Were it not for the 1909 centenary, the four-act play would likely have died. The anniversary gave him his final six-day run at the Garden Theatre, but the critics were no more enthralled by his performance in 1909 than they had been in 1906.

In 1913, Chapin turned to film, and by 1915 he was in production with a biographical epic called *The Lincoln Cycle*. In 1917, four of Chapin's projected twelve episodes were playing in Manhattan at the Strand, a new "picture palace," and the star of the show was appearing in costume at World War I recruitment rallies. Hyping the upcoming series in 1915, the exhibitors' magazine, *Motion Picture World*, called attention to Chapin's command of Lincoln's appearance. "That sadly whimsical smile plays on Chapin's features as it did on Lincoln's face. The long gaunt body, the beautiful ugly features stand out in life from the pages of history. And young and old America can behold its hero once more."[40]

———

AS THEODORE ROOSEVELT'S presidency wound down in early 1909, he put the finishing touches on a plan to place Lincoln's face where Americans would see it and touch it every day—in their purses and pockets. The old Indian-head penny, in circulation since 1859, would be replaced by the Lincoln cent—a radical move, since no actual person had ever appeared on a circulating American coin. The penny was picked only because altering the face of the half-dollar—apparently Roosevelt's first choice—required congressional approval.

Remarkably enough, at this moment of near-universal enthusiasm for Lincoln, serious opposition to Roosevelt's idea emerged in the press. Traditionalists were alarmed: by keeping their coinage impersonal, republics distinguished themselves from autocracies. Republics honored not the reigning *person*, but the reigning *principle* (liberty) of the body politic. As the *New Orleans Picayune* put it, replacing the Indian head with Lincoln's image would "mark the visible and outward emblem of the transmogrification of the Republic into an empire."[41]

The *New York Times* agreed, reminding readers that when the US Senate had passed a bill in 1792 to put George Washington on the one-dollar coin, the House had rejected the idea as "a feature of monarchy." Since 1859, said the *Times*, the Indian figure had "typifie[d] the love of liberty and the possession of it." Roosevelt's tampering with that unvarying practice amounted to "a fresh whim of the most whimsical and self-satisfied Chief Magistrate we ever had." The "modest and humble" Lincoln "would never have consented to change a long-established custom by putting his own profile on the cent."[42]

True enough, Roosevelt might have replied, but Lincoln's own wishes were irrelevant to the case at hand. Roosevelt judged Lincoln's image a worthwhile substitute for the Indian head not because the move would have pleased Lincoln, but because Lincoln had, after his death, become a symbol of the whole people. The real question, as the *Picayune* pointed out, was not whether Lincoln would have approved, but whether Roosevelt was shifting the symbolic meaning of the penny from "liberty" to "great nation with imperial responsibilities."

The measured *Philadelphia Ledger* probably spoke for most people in 1909. Wary of the precedent Roosevelt was setting by unilaterally redoing the penny, the paper nonetheless conceded that Lincoln, like Washington, should certainly be put on a coin. Placing a person on a metallic "medium of exchange" was the highest honor a country could bestow. "Ephemeral" paper money and postage stamps, "soon canceled or destroyed," were suitable for the general run of public servants. Lincoln and Washington merited a consideration all their own. Like Roosevelt, the *Ledger* assumed Lincoln stood for both "liberty" and "nation." The only threat to liberty would come from a future president bent on immortalizing some undeserving public official. Congress should originate all future coin changes, not the president, and candidates should be limited to those who had been dead for fifty years or more.[43]

Up-and-coming thirty-one-year-old *Milwaukee Daily News* writer Carl Sandburg sided with the *Ledger*, finding it perfectly proper to put "the face of Abraham Lincoln on the copper cent." He speculated that the "great, good man" himself would be "perfectly willing" to adorn the new coin. As symbol in chief for "the people," Lincoln might object to being put on a fancier gold or silver coin, but not to gracing "the cheapest and most common coin in the country."[44]

In August, when the pennies finally made it to the subtreasuries in major cities for distribution, men and boys lined up by the thousands to buy a hundred new Lincoln pennies each. Many in the crowds intended to resell them for a profit, and for days the new coins were hard to get. Ultimately, over a hundred million pennies were issued in 1909, for a population of ninety-two million Americans. Critics loved medalist Victor D. Brenner's spacious layout, which showed the right-side profile of a bearded Lincoln, with the word "Liberty" prominently stretching across the empty space to his left. The phrase "In God We Trust" arched gracefully over his head at the top border of the coin, directly symmetrical to the phrase "E Pluribus Unum" on the reverse side. Even the *New York*

Times had to applaud the final result: "The entire design is noteworthy for its simplicity of line." Depicting Lincoln with his "face relaxed and a benign expression" had yielded a "handsome" coin.[45]

IN THE LONG RUN, the single most significant Lincoln event of 1909 may have been the decision by President Roosevelt's Council of Fine Arts to endorse one of three plans before Congress for a major new monument in the District of Columbia. Ever since 1902, plans had been afoot among Roosevelt, some congressmen, and a national cadre of architects and urban planners to complete a Lincoln memorial project in time for the centenary. But when the anniversary rolled around in February 1909, they remained deadlocked over which path to pursue. Rather than bringing different parties together, Lincoln's grandeur made each group dig in its heels.

One plan pushed a panoramic memorial highway linking Washington and Gettysburg. Many citizens, including Benjamin Chapin, considered this proposal the "modern" one, since it developed an original spatial vision made possible by the automobile. Meanwhile, aesthetically old-fashioned motorists wouldn't even have to give up their allegiance to stone edifices, for a wide "parking" area at the center of the roadway, as the *Washington Post* reported, would be "decorated with trees and monuments."[46]

Though the proposal got bogged down when Maryland and Pennsylvania representatives couldn't agree on the optimal route, support remained strong. Many congressmen in 1909 thought they could have their cake and eat it too: they could authorize the highway *and* build a stone edifice in the national capital. And for that installation, some powerful congressmen liked a plan to keep Lincoln close to the US Capitol building. Congress would purchase thirty-six acres between the Capitol and the nearby Union Station, where a grand Lincoln memorial would greet travelers arriving by rail in Washington.

This "Capitol extension" plan offered the decided advantage, according to Massachusetts congressman Samuel McCall, of keeping Lincoln's monument geographically separate from George Washington's obelisk on the Mall, ensuring that the sixteenth president would not be dwarfed by the first. Lincoln deserved as "noble and impressive" a memorial as Washington did, McCall told the House. To place his structure in the shadow of Washington's "would destroy the monumental balance of the city."[47]

But the thirty professional architects and artists appointed by the lame-duck Roosevelt to his Council of Fine Arts—including such luminaries as planner Daniel Burnham, architect Charles F. McKim, writer-artist John La Farge, and sculptor Daniel Chester French—rejected McCall's reasoning along with his site. It was the Capitol Hill plan, they thought, that would destroy the monumental balance of the city. In a letter to Roosevelt written on the eve of Lincoln's one hundredth birthday, the experts disparaged McCall's plan for having ignored both "the marked differences in scale of design" of the US Capitol and Union Station, and the "rapid descent of the ground from the Capitol to the station." These facts made the proposal "an architectural impossibility."

They also made the third project before Congress—a Lincoln memorial "on a line drawn from the Capitol through the Washington Monument"—"an absolutely necessary" one, "if the best result is to be obtained." Charles McKim had backed this "Potomac" location ever since he and Augustus Saint-Gaudens had toured the swampland west of the Washington Monument in 1901 and had driven a stake into the ground at the precise point where they thought a Lincoln monument should go.[48]

With the end of the Roosevelt administration on March 4, 1909, the Council of Fine Arts disbanded, but Congress authorized a new seven-person council, and President Taft appointed Daniel Burnham to chair it. In 1913, Congress approved the Potomac location and also endorsed the design of architect Henry Bacon for a Greek-temple monument. The stage was set for a historic collaboration between Bacon and the accomplished sculptor Daniel Chester French, the nephew of Benjamin French, who had overseen Lincoln's White House funeral in 1865. With his seated Lincoln on the National Mall, Daniel Chester French reimagined Lincoln's unassuming and quirky body as a commanding symbol of the nation.

PART THREE

The National Body
(1909–2015)

*Daniel Chester French's watchful and commanding Lincoln occupies
the main hall of the Lincoln Memorial, completed in 1922.*

CHAPTER TEN

Solidifying the Lincoln Cult: Two Memorials

*He was beginning to see what a little and willing piece of
sacrifice a man must be for the sake of a dark fame.*[1]
— CARL SANDBURG, 1926

I N THE LATE nineteenth century, northerners and black southerners enshrined Lincoln as their self-sacrificing hero. What the 1909
festivities accomplished was to hallow the Gettysburg Address as
the hero's holy text. These were words to recite in public, the core incan-
tation of the cult of Lincoln.

Along with images of his steady gaze and withered face—signs of
his physical and mental labor for the people—the verbal rituals of 1909
broadcast the Gettysburg Address as an emanation of his simple, unac-
countable genius. By this point, the exact historical reference of those
words mattered less than their rhythmic salute to America's high purpose
and Americans' readiness to die for it. They attached Lincoln to the nation
and attached twentieth-century Americans to the nation through him.

Two incomparably influential early-twentieth-century memorials to
Lincoln—Daniel Chester French's gargantuan marble statue in Washington and Carl Sandburg's massive six-volume biography—show how
profoundly Lincoln's body and words were intertwined in the mature
growth of the Lincoln cult. Both Sandburg and French turned to Lincoln

in the immediate wake of the 1909 events, and both men rode the wave
of the Lincoln cult to national distinction. Each followed in the footsteps
of a famous predecessor. Daniel French picked up where Augustus Saint-
Gaudens had left off at this death in 1907. Carl Sandburg, a well-known
poet before launching into his monumental biography, tried to duplicate
in prose the verbal veneration of Lincoln perfected by Walt Whitman in
blank verse.

French was picked by his neighbors in Concord, Massachusetts
(including family friend Ralph Waldo Emerson) to create the Minute-
man statue for the 1875 centenary of the "shot heard round the world." In
1893, Saint-Gaudens selected French to execute the (Chicago) Columbian
Exposition's centerpiece statue, the largest ever built in the United States:
a sixty-five-foot gold-leaf female figure titled *Statue of the Republic*. The
installation brought Daniel French a measure of national prestige to go
with the respect he'd already earned from his fellow sculptors. "A masterpiece," the *Chicago Tribune* called it, "the finishing touch in a scene of
splendor." French spent the summer of 1893 in Chicago soaking up the
plaudits, and during that time he surely visited Lincoln Park for an on-site
study of Saint-Gaudens's Lincoln masterpiece. The statue, as well as the
architectural setting designed by Stanford White—a semicircular, gradually ascending approach to the statue—had to be experienced in person.[2]

Two decades later, on Labor Day 1912, French unveiled his own
standing Lincoln at the Nebraska State Capitol (in the city of Lincoln),
and the homage to Saint-Gaudens's work is obvious. The Nebraska bronze
figure looks downward in deep concentration, left leg pitched forward,
just like the one in Illinois. But the settings diverge completely. Where
Saint-Gaudens silhouetted Lincoln against a canopy of trees and sky,
and backed him up with the chair from which he had just risen, French
placed him against a dominating 12×20-foot granite slab containing the
text of the Gettysburg Address.

Both sculptors portrayed Lincoln as an orator, but Saint-Gaudens
gave no indication of what he was about to say. The exact words were
of no consequence. What mattered was Lincoln's posture of contempla-

tion and readiness: his body at rest, yet in the act of thinking something through, maybe imagining the effect his words might exert on his audience. Saint-Gaudens captured the man's essential character, not a particular moment in history.

In Nebraska, French nailed down the occasion, realizing he could present a double "memorial": he could remember Lincoln *remembering* the Gettysburg dead of 1863. French gives Lincoln slumping shoulders—the better to show respect for the fallen. This leader knows the exact words he's going to speak. French's bronze, and the granite slab designed by his friend Henry Bacon—a veteran of the White City architectural team in 1893, and French's longtime collaborator—turned Lincoln into a Civil War prophet. His words, not his body, transmitted the call to republican virtue. The sculpted body signaled his strength as a leader and his sympathy for the dead. It basked in the reflected glory of his verbal inspiration.

HENCEFORTH, Lincoln's body no longer communicated its significance unless supported by his words. Henry Bacon made this plain in his successful proposal to build the Lincoln Memorial in Washington. In 1912, he told a *New York Tribune* interviewer (in all likelihood the paper's art critic Royal Cortissoz) that the Memorial's centerpiece—a "statue of heroic size expressing [Lincoln's] humane personality"—would be closely connected to "tablets" engraved with his "two great speeches": the Gettysburg Address and second inaugural address.[3]

Though French would not be officially approved as the sculptor until 1914, Bacon had given French the nod from the outset, and the two men had been sharing ideas all along. With French's Nebraska achievement in mind, Bacon called the planned statue and tablets "three memorials to the man himself." A fourth memorial—dedicated to the Union—lay in the ensemble of exterior elements, including the thirty-six Doric columns of the colonnade that surrounded the central building. They stood for the thirty-six states reunited under Lincoln's leadership.

*A twenty-first-century photo shows the full east–west layout of
the Mall, from the Lincoln Memorial to the US Capitol.*

Though Bacon drew up an alternative design featuring only two interior memorials to the man—the statue and the Gettysburg Address—he preferred the architecturally harmonious set of three, with the statue positioned between two flanking halls, each containing a textual tablet. The statue would magnify the tablets' authority, and they would reflect their power back onto Lincoln's body. In addition, the tripartite layout of the Memorial halls would echo the three visually interacting buildings stretching across the two-mile, east–west axis of the Mall: the Lincoln Memorial, the Washington obelisk, and the US Capitol. In Bacon's vision, the spatial unity of these three edifices, and of the two tablets and the statue, seamlessly mirrored the national unity achieved by Lincoln and symbolized by the exterior colonnade.

Upon entering the finished Lincoln Memorial, Bacon told the *Tribune,* visitors would first encounter the white marble statue, already visible from the outside through a wide entryway. Bacon would later briefly consider a standing position for Lincoln, but in 1912 he took for granted, given the horizontal thrust of the overall monument, that Lincoln would be seated. "The Washington Monument provides enough of the vertical," he said, "and in the Capitol you [also] have the [vertical] dome effect."

After encountering Lincoln, spectators would be drawn through four Ionic columns on each side of the statue into the smaller side halls containing the speech inscriptions, each topped with a mural presenting allegorical figures to display Lincoln's virtues. Bacon described an interacting force field created by the statue and tablets: Each of the three memorials would exert their "greatest influence" by being "secluded and isolated" from the other two, yet visitors would reconnect them as they went from hall to hall, sealing Lincoln's body and words in a single experience.

In his *Tribune* interview, Bacon didn't quite call the structure a "temple," though he might as well have. He likened it to the Greek Parthenon—the temple to Athena—and kept repeating that the essence of the entire monument lay in its "seclusion": the gradual "withdrawing" of the three memorials into its interior space (with the two speeches occupying the holiest recesses), and the isolation of the whole edifice from the "discordant irregularity" of nearby "secular buildings."

Lincoln and his words were well protected. The statue in the main hall guarded the entries to the side halls with their sacred verbal contents; the external colonnade shielded the main hall; and the colonnade was safeguarded by its location within a Mall purified of "the turmoil of ordinary affairs."[4]

Bacon's Greek design drew the fire of a few critics, including the dependably anticlassicist sculptor Gutzon Borglum, who took his case to Capitol Hill. He complained to Speaker of the House Joe Cannon, "We are about to spend two million dollars" on "a Greek temple . . . a cold, classical, meaningless temple of three thousand years ago. Into the middle of that we are going to drop a statue of Lincoln." Why not tell "our own [American] story?" Borglum pleaded. In his estimation, the proposed Memorial repeated the mistake of the Washington Monument, which had missed the chance to "record the work and life of a man who built this nation after eight years of one of the most trying wars that a little people ever had."[5]

A few "progressive" architects in Chicago, including George W. Maher, a renowned home designer, shared Borglum's frustration. Bacon's proposal "seems an effort to make of our Lincoln a 'Greek God,'" said Maher, and blissfully ignores "the western spirit—the dominant spirit which controlled" him. The Memorial should feature "sculptured monoliths" and "heroic bas-reliefs" depicting "minutely and accurately events in connection with his strenuous times and life."

Like Borglum, Maher thought he was protecting a Western folk hero against the Europeanizing East Coast elite, and shielding a simple man, shaped by American historical events, from deification as a transhistorical idol. What they both missed was that Bacon's Greek-inspired elevation of Lincoln fit the northern Protestant majority's sensibility to a tee: raising Lincoln to the heights of republican fame and evoking religious overtones that could be justified as secular. The Greek form permitted an elite of twentieth-century artists and architects to join hands with powerful congressmen in making Lincoln civically sacred *without* taking him as godlike.[6]

AFTER THE GROUNDBREAKING on Lincoln's birthday in 1914, it took over eight years to complete the Lincoln Memorial. The details of the statue emerged slowly, as Daniel French built larger and larger plaster models. He began with a three-foot-high version in 1916 and reached ten feet in early 1917. By that time, he and Bacon realized that the final statue needed to be twice the originally proposed ten to twelve feet in order to avoid looking minuscule beneath a sixty-foot ceiling.

French signed a new contract to raise the statue to nineteen feet, not counting its base, doubling the government's expenditure from $45,000 to $88,000. For some reason it took two years for the *Washington Post* to report the statue's increased size and price. Perhaps the *Post* was leery about publicizing the cost overrun in the middle of World War I. Even in 1919, with the war over, the paper found it necessary to defend the further expense by invoking "artistic purposes." "Naturally," said the *Post*, a statue of such gigantic size should cost more. "To give some idea of its enormousness it is said that the legs are six feet long."[7]

Of course, all of the measurements were now majestic. Lincoln's face measured three and a half feet high by two and a half feet wide. His thumbs were a foot long. The total height of the statue, including its eleven-foot seven-inch pedestal and plinth, came to thirty feet seven inches. The whole installation reached halfway to the ceiling. Lincoln would now dominate the space of the main hall, rather than being dwarfed by it.

As a steady stream of visitors has discovered since the Memorial opened in 1922, Lincoln sits calmly and intently in his massive chair of state, his strong hands poised atop the Roman-style fasces (bundled rods) that mark this place as the seat of power. The vertical rods carved into the front legs of the chair match the muscular fingers of his hands, and the four long fingers of each hand echo the four Ionic columns to either side of him, dividing the main hall from the side chambers.

Daniel French caught Lincoln in a living moment of physical exertion, just as Saint-Gaudens had done in Chicago. Here Lincoln's right foot extends over the edge of the chair's base, as if it's shuffling forward. His right hand clutches the armrest, his index finger lifting off the edge, while the left hand clenches into a fist. Lincoln's torso has seemingly settled back into his eternal seat, apparently at rest as his eyes gaze placidly toward the distant Capitol. But the busy hands and angular legs give away his mental vigilance. This throne-like chair is boxing him in, restraining him as much as supporting him.

"What I wanted to convey," French wrote privately three weeks before the Memorial's dedication, "was the mental and physical strength of the great President and his confidence in his ability to carry the thing through to a successful finish." If he, the sculptor, had succeeded, it was "probably as much due to the whole pose of the figure and particularly to the action of the hands as to the expression of the face."[8]

French issued no instructions to spectators on how to view, or understand, his Lincoln. People would see the looming figure according to the conceptions they brought into the hall. Some would think he looked godlike; others, human. Some would find him gentle; others, forbidding.

French made Lincoln's body active, but that only made his character and convictions more mysterious. Lincoln looks fidgety, but what's on his mind? People could summon the Lincoln of their choice. They could approach the statue as an aesthetic object, a historical symbol, or a kind of living civic spirit. Some would seek him out for mental guidance or patriotic inspiration.

This sculptural embodiment of Lincoln would not be rising from his chair, as the Saint-Gaudens Lincoln in Chicago did. Instead he would be instilling in future presidents—and citizens—the courage to rise confidently from theirs.

LIKE SAINT-GAUDENS IN 1887, French gave no visual hint that his Lincoln stood for either emancipation or union. Chicago's Lincoln represented republican character, and Washington, DC's Lincoln embodied resolute leadership, but neither one took a political position. French, like Saint-Gaudens, like Roosevelt and Wilson, believed it was time to leave mid-nineteenth-century issues behind.

Architect Henry Bacon, on the other hand, consecrated his entire structure to "union," as he never tired of repeating, and shunned the term "emancipation" altogether—a politically wise course for anyone seeking the support, or at least the acquiescence, of southern congressmen in the early twentieth century. Just to be sure everyone knew that union was the Memorial's controlling idea, and the main goal of Lincoln's presidency, Bacon placed a five-line pronouncement behind the statue's head, carved into the marble wall.

The words were not drawn from the Gettysburg Address, which French and Bacon had placed behind Lincoln's body in Nebraska. Written by *New York Tribune* art critic Royal Cortissoz, who had been promoting Bacon's design for a decade, they were added to the wall just before the dedication. For nearly a century, tourists have been snapping them in the background of photos of Lincoln.

IN THIS TEMPLE
AS IN THE HEARTS OF THE PEOPLE
FOR WHOM HE SAVED THE UNION
THE MEMORY OF ABRAHAM LINCOLN
IS ENSHRINED FOREVER

Bacon didn't eliminate every trace of emancipation from the Lincoln Memorial, for he approved a plan to mount canvas murals, sixty feet long and twelve feet high, in the south and north halls above the tablets containing the Gettysburg Address and the second inaugural. According to painter-illustrator Jules Guérin, these allegorical works were meant to represent "Emancipation and Reunion." "In general terms," he said, "the decoration on the south wall represents the emancipation of a race." Bacon, however, dropped the word "emancipation" in summing up the meaning of the mural in 1927 and said only that the "decoration" surmounting the Gettysburg Address expressed "in allegory the principles evident in the life of Abraham Lincoln."[9]

Spectators were hard-pressed to understand what was going on in the emancipation mural. It was positioned so high on the wall that it could barely be made out. And no explanatory text helped them decipher it. At the center of the south mural, the Angel of Truth lifts her arms and spreads her golden wings. A group of black slaves, most of them wearing brightly colored ceremonial skirts from the waist down, receive their freedom. These bondsmen and -women are slaves in general, patterned after classical models—not slaves living in the United States and being emancipated in the 1860s.

In the end, the Memorial's most powerful reminder of Lincoln the emancipator—and of the Lincoln willing to surrender his body for the freedom of all—lies in the speeches themselves. The "new birth of freedom" in the south hall's Gettysburg Address doesn't specifically mention the abolition of bondage, but the north hall's second inaugural brings slavery forth as the nation's original sin. In that address, six weeks before his death, Lincoln said the war's length seemed explicable to him only as a divinely ordained campaign to rid the nation of that sin—a sin of which North and South were equally guilty.

In the twentieth century, the Gettysburg Address rose to such heights of popularity for white Americans in part because it *didn't* mention slavery or emancipation. The "full measure of devotion" of the war dead could be detached from the "new birth of freedom" sparked by the Emancipation Proclamation. Lincoln's personal sacrifice could be deemed an act of dedication to the Republic in general, not to the liberation of those denied their equal part in it. Even the second inaugural could be updated: Lincoln's call for malice toward none and charity for all could be cemented in public memory while his dark reflections on the sin of slavery were set aside. For nearly a century now, the Memorial's north hall—with "the bondsman's two hundred and fifty years of unrequited toil" chiseled into the wall in the sentence right before "with malice to none"—has mounted a measure of resistance to such forgetting.

IN THEIR LINCOLN MEMORIAL dedication speeches on Memorial Day 1922, President Harding and Chief Justice William Howard Taft downplayed emancipation just as Bacon had done ever since 1912. Both speakers praised the Memorial as the living emblem of North-South reconciliation. "The Lincoln Memorial," said Taft, "is a shrine at which all can worship." Lincoln hadn't cared about emancipation, said Harding, nearly as much as he had about reunion. For a generation, that view had been shared by most whites, even though Lincoln, from 1863 on, had made plain that he cared equally about union and emancipation; the two were necessarily interlocked in his decision making.

In his speech, Taft contended—as many white southerners had been saying for decades—that Lincoln would surely have gone easy on the white South after the war. "Southerners know," he said, "that the greatest misfortune in all the trials of that section was the death of Lincoln. Had he lived . . . the trying days of reconstruction would have been softened. Rancor and resentment were no part of his nature." Taft got Lincoln's character right but drew the wrong conclusion from it. During the war, Lincoln had shown that, without rancor or resentment, he could go *hard* on the Confederate South. After the war, he might also, without rancor or resentment, have gone hard on antiblack intimidation and violence.[10]

Harding and Taft minimized the import of emancipation, but the Lincoln Memorial Commission, organizers of the dedication agenda on this Memorial Day, actively suppressed it. Headed by none other than Taft, the commission censored the speech of the program's invited black speaker, Robert Russa Moton, successor to Booker T. Washington as principal of the Tuskegee Institute.

Moton's advance text, submitted to the commission for approval, claimed that Lincoln's memorial would become "a hollow mockery, a symbol of hypocrisy," if the nation did nothing to further "the things for which he died," such as giving the "humblest citizen the full enjoyment of every constitutional privilege . . . Twelve million black men and women in this country are proud of their American citizenship" and ask only for "the full blessings of freedom." The speech actually delivered by Moton reversed ground and praised the nation for its steady advance toward Lincoln's goal of equality for all.[11]

Meanwhile, the African American *Chicago Defender*, impressed by the Memorial itself, took exception to Harding's and Taft's speeches and to the segregated seating for the small group of distinguished African Americans invited to the ceremony. Branding Harding and Taft, respectively, as "arch-founder" and "arch-expounder" of the Republicans' "Southern policy" of catering to white voters, the paper excoriated them for diminishing "the title that gives Lincoln deathless fame, that of Emancipator." The "enemies of Lincoln, of this Union, and [of] those to whom he gave life and liberty" had, with the unveiling of this Memorial, been handed the victory "they failed to gain on the field." The monument had been "opened" but not truly dedicated. The real dedication day would have to be put off until "juster and more grateful men come to power and history shall have rebuked offenders against the name of Abraham Lincoln."[12]

The segregated seating at the dedication raised few eyebrows among whites north or south—a sign of how completely their image of Lincoln the emancipator applied now only to the distant past. In response, as they had done for decades, many black Americans affirmed the liberator all the more uncompromisingly. They reiterated that Lincoln had given up his body for their freedom.

AFTER THE DEDICATION, W. E. B. Du Bois tossed off a seven-sentence editorial repeating Frederick Douglass's theme from 1876: the undeniable virtues of a very human leader. He applauded the president's unlikely growth from the conventional racism of his midwestern upbringing to his mature decisions to free the slaves, put black men in uniform, and recommend the vote for soldiers and other "intelligent" black men. Partial at first to "protecting slavery" where it had long existed, Lincoln had shown himself "big enough to be inconsistent," and ultimately proved himself a "brave man."[13]

Du Bois meant to be commending Lincoln, but taking note of Lincoln's early deficiencies struck some other black writers and readers as an unconscionable slandering of their hero. *Chicago Defender* columnist Roscoe Conkling Simmons, an experienced Republican Party hand and a nephew (by marriage) of the late Booker T. Washington, vilified Du Bois for mangling some facts about the early Lincoln (mistakenly claiming, for example, that he was "of illegitimate birth"—an error commonly made by earlier authors on Lincoln). Yet Simmons hammered Du Bois on much broader grounds, objecting to *any* negative information about Lincoln, even when grounded in fact.

No "colored man," said Simmons, "can afford to disgrace a name put above all names by his countrymen. What of expediency? If there was any proof of this charge against Lincoln[,] only a fool would repeat it." Simmons cleverly reminded the *Defender's* hundred thousand readers north and south that their supposedly illegitimate emancipator had restored *them* to legitimacy as free men and women with legally recognized families. "Once you were down; Lincoln picked you up. You were slaves; Lincoln made you free. Once your children were born out of wedlock; Lincoln gave them a name and a home. THIS MAKES LINCOLN SUBLIME."[14]

Simmons's appeal to expediency drove Du Bois to distraction. He was fed up with the impulse "to think of the Great as flawless," to prefer "not the real man, but the tradition of the man—remote, immense, perfect, cold and dead!" A social or political movement could flourish in the long run only by respecting and publicizing the facts, wherever they led. "The scars and foibles and contradictions of the Great do not diminish but enhance the worth and meaning of their upward struggle."

Lincoln would climb higher in people's estimation, thought Du Bois, the more truly he was known. "Lincoln was perhaps the greatest figure of the nineteenth century," he claimed. "Certainly of the five masters—Napoleon, Bismarck, Victoria, [Robert] Browning and Lincoln—Lincoln is to me the most human and lovable. And I love him not because he was perfect but because he was not and yet triumphed."[15]

For all their arch-backed acrimony, Simmons and Du Bois shared more than met the eye, as Booker T. Washington and Du Bois had a decade earlier: they both needed a Lincoln to revere and elevate, and so did the entire black community. Lincoln modeled a personal trajectory valuable for any young person to contemplate, not a story of self-making alone, but one of moral and political growth. Praising Lincoln gave blacks valuable leverage, permitting them to fault whites who failed to follow his example. Simmons and Du Bois disagreed only on whether to divulge the whole truth about the early Lincoln, especially his racial views. For Du Bois, those revelations made Lincoln accessible, protecting him against petrifying adulation.

The bitter standoff over airing Lincoln's flaws or suppressing them lost its urgency once African Americans found ways of acting regularly and publicly—not just on Emancipation Day—to build up his reputation as their ongoing emancipator. The Lincoln Memorial quickly proved its value for this purpose. As early as August 1926, the monument drew a crowd of African Americans for a noontime event. They were convention delegates in town for the annual meeting of the African Methodist Episcopal Zion Church. Some two thousand delegates had been meeting in Washington for several days, and convention organizers had scheduled "pilgrimages" to three sites: Frederick Douglass's home in Anacostia (he had died in 1895), the Tomb of the Unknown Soldier in Arlington Cemetery, and the Lincoln Memorial, already a surpassingly popular tourist destination.

The Zion group assembled at the Memorial to hear their bishop E. W. D. Jones deliver a eulogy entitled "Lincoln as an Emancipator, Immortal." Jones may have been the first African American speaker to answer the *Chicago Defender*'s 1922 plea for a true "dedication" of the monument at a later date. "The immortality of Lincoln," Jones declared, "will cluster around his emancipation of the slaves, rather than the preservation of the Union."[16]

IN THAT SAME summer of 1926, forty-eight-year-old Carl Sandburg, already a well-known poet and columnist for the *Chicago Daily News*, was adjusting to his new fame as a biographer of Lincoln. His *Abraham Lincoln: The Prairie Years*, a 960-page, two-volume boxed set, had been flying off the shelves since its release just before Lincoln's birthday, and startled reviewers were groping for words to sum up his achievement. "A new experience awaits the reader," began the *New York Times Book Review's* anonymous front-page rave. Sandburg had created a novel brand of biography, bringing Lincoln, and other characters, vividly to life, and placed them against the backdrop of "the surging, restless march of the westward movement," which "streams through this book like the recurrent theme of a symphony."[17]

The Prairie Years "seems destined to a classical place in our literature," gushed Van Wyck Brooks, renowned literary critic and celebrant of the heroic American spirit. He likened the book's steady flow to the mighty Mississippi River, "twisting and turning, exploring countless bays, fed by countless rivulets." Brooks noted what the *Times* reviewer did not: Sandburg's focus on "the growing menace of slavery." But he and other writers missed the author's recurrent attention to the sufferings of actual slaves, and to Lincoln's emerging awareness of their plight. *The Prairie Years*, already in its fourth printing by May, reminded white readers of the inhumanity of bondage and of its decisive impact on the young Lincoln.[18]

Born in 1878, the son of working-class Swedish immigrants, Sandburg had been raised in Galesburg, Illinois, site of the fifth Lincoln-Douglas debate exactly twenty years earlier. He left school at thirteen, worked odd jobs before enlisting in the Spanish-American War, returned to Galesburg at age twenty to attend classes at Lombard College (paying for them with a janitorial job), and there took a fancy to writing and speaking. He edited the college literary magazine and yearbook, fell in love with Walt Whitman's free-verse poetry, and tried his own hand at it. His early, turn-of-the-century poems went nowhere, but he took heart when knowledgeable friends gave their thumbs down not just to his own lines but also to several published poems of Stephen Crane and Emily Dickinson, which he'd slipped in, unidentified, among his own.

Gradually the rejection notices grew more positive and some of his work was published. He put together a talk on Whitman and found that his audiences (including "a Negro literary club on South State Street in Chicago" and "the guard house prisoners at Fort Sheridan") fell asleep at his canned lines but woke up when he read them Whitman's poetry. Just before World War I, Sandburg found his poems catching on with such literary lights as Edgar Lee Masters and Theodore Dreiser, leading to their publication in 1916. Many readers winced at the preachy sentiments in his collection *Chicago Poems*, but others took them as edgy affirmations of the city's supposedly youthful and masculine energy.[19]

The book's lead poem, "Chicago," first printed in Chicago's famous *Poetry* magazine in 1914, made a splash ("Hog butcher for the world . . . City of the Big Shoulders"), but apparently unnoticed by white critics in 1916 was the forty-third poem in the collection: "Nigger." "I AM the nigger," it starts, and "I" sums up the stereotypes pinned upon the dancing, singing, smiling black American. Amid the usual images, "I" invokes memories of slavery and leaves the reader with a long view of oppression. "Look at me," it ends. "I am the nigger."[20]

A moderate Socialist before the war, Sandburg described himself for *Who's Who* during the war as an "Independent." He still sided with "the people," but not the people conceived in Marxian terms as a prospective agent of egalitarian revolution. Leaving behind the idea of class struggle meant he'd be facing the future as an individual voice, not as the member of a movement. "I belong to everything and nothing," he declared. He would side with "all rebels everywhere all the time as against all people who are satisfied."[21]

In the summer of 1919, as he was researching a story for the *Chicago Daily News* on the miserable housing available to recent black migrants from the South, a race riot erupted at a Chicago "bathing beach." "A colored boy swam across an imaginary segregation line," Sandburg wrote. "White boys threw rocks at him and knocked him off a raft. He was drowned. Colored people rushed to a policeman and asked for the arrest of the boys throwing stones. The policeman refused." Rioting spread across the city, leading to the deaths of twenty blacks and fourteen whites, and in the fall, Sandburg's sixteen articles on the racial tumult were published in book form as *The Chicago Race Riots*, with an introduction by the Progressive luminary Walter Lippmann.[22]

Probing the ravages of race in post–World War I America, and letting go of his socialism, prepared Sandburg to appreciate Lincoln's sensibility. Militant about equalizing life chances for all, but averse to schemes for social reorganization, Lincoln supplied an attractively middle-of-the-road stance for a former leftist of Sandburg's sort. He could retain his zeal for the idea of equality while making provisional peace with the prevailing order of inequality.

SANDBURG began writing poems about Lincoln in 1914, and he published three of them between 1916 and 1918. "Abraham Lincoln's Father and Mother," written in 1914 but unpublished in Sandburg's lifetime, reads like the prospectus for a biography. Why write his life? To know more about who and what had formed him. The "I" of the poem was satisfied on this score already but imagined pursuing "the tragic or comic" ideas that others had built up about Lincoln.[23]

In the preface to *The Prairie Years*, Sandburg revealed the source of his satisfaction. For thirty years he'd planned on writing "a certain portrait" of Lincoln, one "placing him in the small-town Illinois where I grew up as a boy, and where I heard the talk of men and women who had eaten with Lincoln, given him a bed overnight, heard his jokes and lingo, remembered his silences and his mobile face." Sandburg believed that a new Lincoln would emerge from his pen, shaped by intimate knowledge of the midwesterners from whom his subject had sprung. Sharing Lincoln's roots, he would capture the "stalking and elusive Lincoln" that archival historians, poring over documented facts, could never reach. Lincoln's saga transcended the established facts, and the successful interpreter would soar above them too.[24]

Sandburg's Olympian assurance produced some evocative writing based on what his characters had "seen" and "heard"—by which he meant what a person in their time and place *might* have seen or heard. Thus, young Thomas Lincoln, who would become Abraham's father, had "heard" his eventual bride Nancy Hanks's "tremulous voice and seen her shaken with sacred desires in church camp-meetings; he had seen her at preachings in cabins when her face stood out as a sort of picture in black against the firelights of the burning logs." This fictional scene was based in part on a document, but one from 1918: Sandburg's own poem "Fire-Logs," which pictures Nancy sitting by a fire, logs crackling and flames lapping the fireplace to illumine her.[25]

Scholars have belittled Sandburg since the 1920s for providing no footnotes—an apt criticism for the cases in *The Prairie Years* where he quotes from historical sources. But there could be no footnotes for his grand pronouncements, personal recollections, fertile imagination, and lyrical riffs, which produced something vaster than a "life." Sandburg gathered all the facts and stories he could, apocryphal or not, and then swept majestically beyond them, whipping up an epic concoction that took Lincoln's mythic immensity as the most basic fact about him.

The more legendary folklore about Lincoln that was thrown into the mix, the better, since the lore had bubbled up from the purest source: the people. Let the niggling documentarians criticize him if they wished, scoffed Sandburg. They could only "rattle" Lincoln's "dry bones," while he gave Lincoln flesh. In Sandburg's eyes, the exuberant praise showered on *The Prairie Years* by newspapers, magazines, and book buyers confirmed his place as the hero's "authentic" interpreter.[26]

Vital to Sandburg's story were Lincoln's physical features, since they had helped carry the president, during his life, into popular mythology. Sandburg mingled Lincoln's body—"so bony and sad"—with his temperament and mood.

As he strode or shambled into a gathering of men, he stood out as a special figure to look at; some of the range of his feeling, the gamut of the solemn and comic, was registered in the angles of his body, in the sweeping lengths of extra long arms and legs, in the panther slouch of running and throwing muscles, in the wiry, rawbone frame that seemed to have been at home once handling an ax in tall timber, with the silent silhouette of an eagle watching.[27]

Lincoln's bizarre form could seem eerie as well as unusual. His body "looked like an original plan for an extra-long horse or a lean tawny buffalo, that a Changer had suddenly whisked into a man-shape." He resembled "a clumsy, mystical giant" of fable, and could almost be imagined as wholly nonhuman or inanimate: "a tall horse-chestnut tree or a rangy horse or a big wagon or a log barn full of new-mown hay," "something spreading, elusive, and mysterious."[28]

Earlier writers had split over whether Lincoln was in touch with the divine: Josiah Holland took him as a religiously attuned man of God, saintly in his moral perfection; William Herndon, as a secular man with natural gifts and human flaws. Millions of whites and blacks sensed God had tapped Lincoln for special service to the Republic, and had removed him when the task was finished. Sandburg blew up those dichotomous categories—natural and supernatural—seeing Lincoln instead as the historical emanation of a people's habits, longings, and fantasies. For all the hokey sentiment of some of the book's writing, Sandburg cleverly dispensed with an overworked split between Lincoln the ordinary man and Lincoln the more-than-human.

In his human essence, said Sandburg, Lincoln was already larger than life, a mythic creation of his community. Those who encountered him in the 1830s and early 1840s, before the rest of the country even knew he existed, had transformed him into an icon of self-making and folk wisdom. The only change in subsequent years was the height of his climb and the spread of his fame.

The Romantic Sandburg loved to linger on the bountiful nature and valorous public servants of the pre–Civil War era, but he kept nostalgia for the heroic days of yore in check by detailing Lincoln's struggles to maintain his emotional equilibrium. A culture wedded to the idea of self-creation spawned a lot of wandering, melancholic souls. Lincoln himself had spurned the notion of a succoring past. He adored certain historically rooted principles, but he didn't love the memory of his rustic upbringing and its many crushed spirits. In Sandburg's eyes, twentieth-century Americans needed Lincoln not because he had inhabited some wholesome village past, but because he could help them remember, amid impassioned social conflicts over race, immigration, religion, Prohibition, evolution, labor organizing, and urban-rural differences, that they comprised a common citizenry, not just a collection of class, ethnic, or interest groups.[29]

From the mid-1920s to the mid-1960s, Sandburg rode the Lincoln story to prominence of his own as Lincoln's kinsman and surrogate, nourished by the same rustling cornfields, imbued with the same democratic bearing. Without ever trying to impersonate him, Sandburg managed to evoke Lincoln's presence, and to let him speak for the people—a unified people that in the mid-1930s, a time of dissipating radical hopes, could stand up to the fascists. In one of his 107 prose poems in *The People, Yes*, published in 1936, Sandburg found an original formula for likening himself to Lincoln: labeling Lincoln a "poet" of the nation too. He asks if Lincoln counts as a composer of verse and offers all the proof he needs: "I have not willingly planted a thorn in any man's bosom." "I shall do nothing through malice; what I deal with is too vast for malice."[30]

IN THE 1920s few, if any, white reviewers noticed how emphatically *The Prairie Years* depicted the plight of African Americans. Sandburg had gone out of his way—and, as was his wont, beyond the available historical evidence—to claim that their plight had powerfully impinged on the young Lincoln's consciousness. In his twenty-seventh chapter, for example, he treated Lincoln's flatboat voyage down the Mississippi to

New Orleans in 1831. In the absence of any direct word from Lincoln about what he had done there, Sandburg embellished a tale based on a recollection (by William Herndon in 1882) of a recollection (by John Hanks, Lincoln's stepbrother, after the assassination) of what Hanks had supposedly witnessed thirty-five years earlier: Lincoln watching a New Orleans slave auction, where, as Sandburg wrote, "an octoroon girl was sold, after being pinched, trotted up and down, and handled so the buyer could be satisfied she was sound of wind and limb."[31]

Sandburg also supplied lengthy excerpts from a series of slave advertisements that he said Lincoln "saw" in the city (that is, could have seen). "One hundred dollars reward for return of a bright mulatto man slave, named Sam," Sandburg quoted. "Light sandy hair, blue eyes, ruddy complexion, is so white as very easily to pass for a free white man." In forty-two lines of slave advertisements, Sandburg cannily blended history (such advertisements really existed) and fiction (they were never mentioned by Lincoln). This method nicely suited his goal of building up the Lincoln lore that conveyed key features of his mature person, in this case his deep-seated antislavery feelings. Graphic stories, even if apocryphal, could communicate and preserve larger historical truths.[32]

School and public librarians had pushed *The Prairie Years* as a children's offering ever since publication. Anne Carroll Moore, a national figure in library work and children's literature, promoted Sandburg's book as "rich in the very facts children want to know." She pleaded for a one-volume edition for boys and girls, but she added, "We cannot afford to wait for it. The book as it stands is . . . for the whole family." She didn't have to wait long for the single volume. In 1928, Harcourt published an abridgment of the first twenty-seven chapters as *Abe Lincoln Grows Up*, a book, according to the publisher's note, for "boy and girl readers."

The slave advertisements and slave auction story were reprinted in full, and their impact was now heightened as they appeared at the end of the book, accompanied by a gripping full-page illustration of a slave market by renowned muralist James Daugherty. Young readers couldn't help imagining Lincoln's shock at the sight of a young black woman shielding

her chest from the attentive white buyers, while other slaves bowed their
heads in the foreground, awaiting their turn on the platform.[33]

THE TWO greatest Lincoln monuments of the 1920s—the Memorial
by Bacon and French, and Sandburg's *Prairie Years*—further swelled
the popular love of Lincoln that had swept the North and West in 1909.
In the long run, each of them magnified Lincoln as emancipator and
unifier, though in the 1920s, much more was said in mainstream white
media about his reuniting than about his liberating. It took the Great
Depression and the Democratic Party's courting of northern black
voters during Franklin Roosevelt's presidency (beginning in 1933)
to create the conditions for Lincoln's great leap forward as a racial
egalitarian.

By the late 1930s, a sizable cross-racial constituency had emerged
to work for a "new emancipation" linking job opportunities for African
Americans to expanded civil rights. The seventy-fifth anniversary of the
Emancipation Proclamation—on January 1, 1938—gave nationwide
publicity to Eleanor Roosevelt and other white liberals who had joined
the movement's ranks. At that point, as activists debated the proper path
forward, no one seems to have anticipated just how useful the Lincoln
Memorial would prove in fueling the cause. The first significant antiseg-
regation action at the Memorial, in 1939, took place there only as an
afterthought.[34]

The world-renowned African American contralto Marian Anderson
—blessed with a voice, said Arturo Toscanini, that comes along once
a century—had been invited to perform in Washington in the spring
of 1939 by Howard University. But the organizers had trouble booking
a venue large enough for her thousands of fans, black and white. The
Daughters of the American Revolution refused to let her appear in their
massive Constitution Hall on Eighteenth Street, a neoclassic edifice seating almost four thousand people. A few years earlier the DAR's refusal
might have passed unnoticed—black performers had been banned at the
hall, the largest auditorium in Washington, for almost a decade—and it

might have gone unnoticed again in 1939, had First Lady Eleanor Roosevelt, a DAR member, not resigned from the organization in protest.

The imbroglio deepened when Anderson was also blocked from singing at the district's white-only Central High School auditorium. A sharp public outcry forced the board of education into backing down: Anderson could perform at Central High, but only as a onetime exception to the continuing rule of segregation. Howard University turned down the board's offer, leaving the concert in limbo. Even at that point, after two turndowns and with no other hall on the horizon, the idea of using the Lincoln Memorial didn't come up in public discussion.

But privately, a handful of Interior Department and NAACP officials had begun mulling over the Memorial as a possible alternative. As soon as he heard the idea, Secretary of the Interior Harold Ickes understood the symbolic value of the seated, sainted Lincoln, and he quickly got President Roosevelt on board. "She can sing from the top of the Washington Monument if she wants to," FDR supposedly told him.[35]

On the cool Easter afternoon of April 9, 1939, the first ever civil-rights event at the Lincoln Memorial gathered a crowd of seventy-five thousand, about half black and half white. The concert lasted less than an hour, and apart from Harold Ickes's introduction of Anderson, it consisted of nothing but her seven musical selections. Putting the focus squarely on Anderson's art raised the issue of segregation much more powerfully than direct verbal condemnation of it could have done. In his opening remarks, Ickes simply told the bundled-up listeners stretching along both sides of the reflecting pool—and the vast radio audience tuned in to NBC's Blue Network—that "genius knows no color line."

> In this great auditorium under the sky, all of us are free. When God gave us this wonderful outdoors and the sun, the moon and the stars, He made no distinction of race, or creed, or color. [Applause] And 130 years ago He sent us one of his truly great in order that he might restore freedom to those from whom we had disregardfully taken it. In carrying out this task, Abraham Lincoln laid down his life, and so it is as appropriate as it is fortunate that today we stand reverently

and humbly at the base of this memorial to the great emancipator while glorious tribute is rendered to his memory by a daughter of the race from which he struck the chains of slavery.[36]

Draped in her flowing black velvet gown (with train) and warmed by her tan fur coat, Anderson was positioned with care on the temporary platform—newsreel cameras could catch the emancipator hovering approvingly behind her. Without any opening comment, she closed her eyes and launched into the national song featured for decades at African American Emancipation Day celebrations, and beloved by most Americans since its first performance in Boston in 1831. In 1925, a large chorus of African American children had belted it out inside the Lincoln Memorial's north hall, beneath the chiseled second inaugural address, as part of Washington's official Lincoln's birthday celebration.

> *My country, 'tis of thee,*
> *Sweet land of liberty,*
> *Of thee I sing;*
> *Land where my fathers died,*
> *Land of the pilgrims' pride,*
> *From every mountainside*
> *Let freedom ring!* [37]

News reports of the 1939 Marian Anderson event, in white and black papers alike, outdid one another in claiming no one had ever witnessed such an exalted moment. Thousands silently wept at the sound of Anderson's voice, at the injustice of her exclusion from the local halls, at the long history of African American suffering and deprivation, at the dawning of a new hope. Spectators fumbled for words to describe what had happened, telling journalists it had been the greatest day in Washington since Lindbergh's parade in 1927, or maybe since Armistice Day in 1918.

Many people pointed to the startling contrast between Anderson's tiny figure descending the monument's steps at the start of the concert and the colossal emancipator rising up behind her. By striding out from Lincoln's inner sanctum, and climbing back into that sacred space after the concert (to escape the surging crowd attempting to praise and touch her), Anderson intensified her closeness to Lincoln. And the size difference between them, far from reducing her importance, only accentuated her awesome power. She was singing for Lincoln as much as for the crowd, and at that moment it seemed that she alone possessed the vocal gifts to bring him a worthy offering on behalf of the whole nation. The beauty and purity of her art, unmixed with any overt political demand, honored him even as it consecrated the civil-rights cause as a mission above politics.

Black and white advocates of black equality took careful note of Anderson's luminous performance under Lincoln's beneficent gaze. Declaring their allegiance to him, and assembling again and again at the Memorial to recertify him as the emancipator, they could identify their movement with the nation's founding ideals of liberty and equality. The quest for civil rights would transcend politics by getting the country to fulfill its original promise. The ongoing work of emancipation would coincide with the task of reknitting a racially torn nation. Lincoln's two roles—liberator and unifier—split apart since the 1870s, could finally be reconnected.[38]

CHAPTER ELEVEN

The Hero on Screen, from Griffith to Gage

I'm a Lincoln nut. I've read three quarters of the books . . .
written about Lincoln.[1]

—HENRY FONDA, 1939

T HE SMASHING SUCCESS of Carl Sandburg's 1926 hymn to Lincoln, and to the village-pure midwestern culture that made him, aroused ardent interest among Hollywood moviemakers. Any biography of a historic figure that sold nearly fifty thousand copies in its first year would have seized their attention. But Sandburg's coming-of-age drama had scorched the best-seller lists at an unusually opportune time. Silent films were about to give way to talkies.

For years, beginning with *The Blue and the Grey; or, the Days of '61* (1908), the ten-minute Thomas Edison work shown at Wanamaker's in Manhattan for the centennial celebration, silent films had been putting Lincoln on screen. D. W. Griffith's racist Civil War saga *The Birth of a Nation* (1915) featured memorable scenes of the president—played by nonactor but Lincoln look-alike Joseph Henabery—dolefully pondering his plight as a reluctant warrior, and using his great height to intimidate the lesser (shorter) mortal Austin Stoneman, a conniving, self-aggrandizing version of Radical Republican Thaddeus Stevens. For that shot, Henabery stood on hidden wooden planks to make him look six foot four.[2]

In 1924, audiences were stirred by the twelve-reel silent *The Dra-*

matic Life of Abraham Lincoln. Nonactor and Lincoln look-alike George Billings made critics and spectators weep. "An epochal picture," said the *New York Telegraph*. Earlier performers had looked like Lincoln, added the *New York Tribune*, but Billings, for the first time ever, had "felt like him." The young critic Robert Sherwood (to become a famous Lincoln playwright and screenwriter in the 1930s) praised the production as "the first serious attempt" at a cinematic biography of *anyone*, with no catering to "fictional romance" as a come-on. Silent films—hardly "silent," with their sound effects and musical scoring—seemed fully equipped to inspire viewers with what the *Los Angeles Times*, commending George Billings, called Lincoln's "simple faith and rugged honesty."[3]

Silent cinema was reaching new heights as a dramatic art form, but the arrival of the sound track in the late 1920s promised an entirely novel Lincoln experience. Frame by frame, his familiar physical gestures and aura could be matched to the actor's voice. A talented interpreter might bring out Lincoln's whole persona, his full verbal repertoire interwoven with his bodily movements. At several major studios, the artistic and patriotic possibilities drove Lincoln film projects forward, even as Hollywood moneymen threw up caution signs. It was not self-evident, despite the success of *The Dramatic Life*, that a film biography of a saintly hero could entertain as well as instruct and glorify. The mass audience might not respond to high-minded edification.

Between 1930 and 1940, three studio films drawing on Sandburg's *Prairie Years* made it to the screen: Griffith's *Abraham Lincoln* (United Artists, 1930), John Ford's *Young Mr. Lincoln* (Twentieth Century Fox, 1939), and John Cromwell's *Abe Lincoln in Illinois* (RKO, 1940). A fourth, Frank Capra's *Mr. Smith Goes to Washington* (Columbia, 1939), didn't show Lincoln the man, but the characters couldn't stop talking about him, and Daniel Chester French's seated statue emerged as a virtual character in its own right. Griffith alone dared to take on Lincoln's presidential years, as he had already done in *The Birth of a Nation* fifteen years earlier. Ford and Cromwell stuck to the prairie years—not because Sandburg's 1926 work stopped there, but because New Salem and Springfield promised gripping personal drama. Lincoln's boyish innocence, bodily force, and social gawkiness could be played off his gathering wisdom about the world and himself.

All four films followed Sandburg in exuding heartfelt love for the hero. They embody the Lincoln cult so fully that even the one that appears initially to mock it (*Mr. Smith*) ends up reaffirming it. Into the 1950s, Lincoln piety found potent expression in numerous filmed depictions of him—from the CBS series of five episodes on the program *Omnibus* (scripted by James Agee) to the Academy Award–winning short film *The Face of Lincoln* (1955), a one-man performance by the Lincoln-loving sculptor Merrell Gage. After the 1960s, no Lincoln film as un-self-consciously worshipful as Gage's could possibly have been nominated for, much less win, an Academy Award.

D. W. GRIFFITH made the first move, tracking down Carl Sandburg in 1929 and inviting him to come to Hollywood. He wanted the high priest of the Lincoln faith to consult with him for a week at a fee of $10,000. Smelling a rat, Sandburg refused to endorse, with his brief presence, a project that he couldn't help oversee. He counterproposed a stay of several months for $30,000, far beyond Griffith's budget, and the collaboration died there.

Ironically, Griffith soon lost control of the film himself, as executives lined up to limit costs. They imposed a twenty-eight-day shooting schedule and resisted the director's appeal for more time on location. Despite the clampdown, Griffith and screenwriter Stephen Vincent Benét (author of the lengthy epic poem *John Brown's Body* in 1928) managed to eke out a film applauded by most reviewers of the day.[4]

A large number of them praised the film explicitly for having captured the Lincoln Americans loved. The forty-six-year-old Walter Huston, a veteran of the silent screen and of the song-and-comedy vaudeville stage for fifteen years before that, didn't look as much like Lincoln as George Billings did. But Huston, said the press, inhabited the very person revered by his disciples. "Huston is magnificent," raved the *Chicago*

Tribune, a major organ of the Lincoln cult. "His gaunt features, tall, bony figure and drawling voice, are those of the Lincoln with whom we became acquainted in grammar school."[5]

The makeup department at United Artists did what it could. Before filming began, they spent five weeks experimenting with "grease paint and pencil" to render the aging of Huston's character from his midtwenties to his midfifties. His "wrinkles, bushy brows, sallow, hollow cheeks, and melancholy eyes" composed "one of the most striking individual portraits of a man conceivable," said the *Washington Post*, and Huston, arriving on the set at 5:30 a.m. for an hour or two of makeup work every day, was turned into a workable approximation of the hero.[6]

A hefty six-footer, Huston gave Lincoln far too much bulk, but his easygoing camaraderie with the young he-men of New Salem—and even his nervous foot shifting while waiting for the chance to dance with Mary Lincoln—projected immense physical energy. Huston's tender byplay with Ann Rutledge made him a man's man too. This Lincoln never showed any nervousness around his supposed first love. Griffith puts the pair outdoors, with him splitting rails and her reading to him out of a law book. "You've taught me to love," he says, and Una Merkel, playing Ann giddily but with knowing assurance, comes back coyly with, "Have I taught you to like it?" Then they recline side by side under a capacious tree, giving her the chance to play with the cloth tie circling his neck. This pair is rapturously in love, and they agree to marry once Lincoln is out of debt.

Proving Lincoln's mainstream masculinity from the very start sets up Griffith's chief theme for the presidential years: this leader hates war and battles the Confederacy with a heavy heart. Given his already established manliness, we know he is not acting out of weakness. (In Griffith's 1915 *Birth of a Nation*, Lincoln dabs his eyes with a handkerchief after signing the first order for seventy-five thousand volunteers. In Griffith's 1930 *Abraham Lincoln*, the hero dabs his mouth.) Walter Huston makes a broken record out of the line "the Union must be preserved," while never speaking of emancipation. A brief tableau vivant of the signing of the Emancipation Proclamation plays out in complete silence.

Above all else, Griffith's Lincoln wished for peace between the sections. As the end of the war approached, Griffith shows him pardoning a young Union deserter. Soon we see an equally merciful Robert E. Lee, decked out in his elegant uniform, pardoning a Confederate soldier. Depicting Lincoln and Lee as mirror images of one another sets up the moral equivalence favored by Griffith: the greatest leaders of 1865, North and South, fought conscientiously for their favored goals, and with the fighting done, came together to restore the Union as it was in 1860, minus slavery but also without Radical Republican interference in race relations.

Several reviewers of the 1930 film bemoaned its fragmentary character—too many rushed scenes documenting the three decades of Lincoln's political life, hence little of the dramatic continuity that distinguished *The Birth of a Nation*. But even the most negative critics of Griffith's directing bowed down before Walter Huston's portrayal of Lincoln.

Mark Forrest of the British *Saturday Review* (the film ran in London for four weeks), called Huston "more than excellent . . . the best piece of acting which I have seen on the screen for a long time. He holds the picture together and con-

*Charles Edward Bull, pictured at the US Capitol in 1932, played Lincoln in two silent films—*The Iron Horse *(1924) and* The Heart of Maryland *(1927)—and toured the country as a striking Lincoln look-alike. Note Bull's left toe extending over the surface it's resting on, perhaps in homage to the masterpieces of Augustus Saint-Gaudens in Lincoln Park, Chicago, and Daniel Chester French at the Lincoln Memorial.*

veys the kindliness, the awkwardness and the strength of the man with sure touches."[7]

Griffith's entire project depended on Carl Sandburg's monumental creation *Abraham Lincoln: The Prairie Years*—the best, Griffith said, of the hundreds of Lincoln books he had read—and fittingly enough he ended his film with a salute to the other major Lincoln edifice of the 1920s. The final sequence begins with a shot of Lincoln's birthplace log cabin and ends with the Lincoln Memorial, as a swelling chorus sings the "Battle Hymn of the Republic." "Rare art," said the *Los Angeles Times* of the cabin-to-Memorial finale. "Fine symbolism this!" The closing benediction supplied by the Lincoln Memorial would become a standard devotional motif of the Lincoln cult.[8]

MARIAN ANDERSON'S sublime performance on the Washington Mall on Easter Sunday 1939 was not lost on the publicity department at Twentieth Century Fox in Hollywood. On Memorial Day 1939, seven weeks after her concert, she appeared in Springfield, Illinois, at the world premiere of director John Ford's *Young Mr. Lincoln*, starring Henry Fonda. Besides Anderson, the studio brought in three cast members from Los Angeles and a trainload of "more than 100 newspaper, magazine, and syndicate writers and photographers" from the East Coast, including radio personality Lowell Thomas, known to millions as the voice of the Movietone newsreels.[9]

The manufactured hubbub gave Springfield townspeople a solid day and night of "all the Hollywood trimmings," said the *Chicago Tribune*: lunch with the stars, autograph signing, a parade through the flag-draped downtown, and, beginning at 6:00 p.m., searchlights piercing the sky as guests arrived in sparkling evening attire. Introduced by Thomas, Anderson lit up the Fox-Lincoln Theatre (capacity 1,046) with the strains of "America," Schubert's "Ave Maria," and two spirituals—"Heaven, Heaven" and "My Soul's Been Anchored in the Lord." A live hookup flashed her voice—and Thomas's endorsement of the movie—to seventy-two stations over the Mutual radio network. For the packed house in Springfield, and listeners at home, Anderson's presence tied the film to the quest for racial equality.[10]

The film itself completely omitted the young Lincoln's concern about slavery, carefully emphasized by Sandburg's *Prairie Years*. Screenwriter Lamar Trotti, a prolific in-house writer at Fox, aimed to avoid Griffith's mistake of trying to cover the whole Lincoln story. But erasing politics from Lincoln's early adulthood, and centering on his rise to maturity as a lawyer, came at a huge cost in historical accuracy. First elected to the Illinois General Assembly in 1834 (at age twenty-five), Lincoln was already an officeholder at the time of Ann Rutledge's death in 1835—when the film portrays him as a callow youth just starting out. The film culminates in 1837, with attorney Lincoln's ingenious and successful defense argument in a fictional murder case. That's the very year when the historical Lincoln, a second-term member of the legislature, publicly affirmed, in opposition to a majority of his colleagues, "The institution of slavery is founded on both injustice and bad policy."[11]

Excluding the early political career, Trotti's story loses historicity but frees up space to probe the personal character that will later produce public greatness. Walter Huston's Abraham exhibited plenty of physicality, but not much inner life. Henry Fonda's Abraham is soulfully reflective and quietly charismatic. He broods over the three women he has lost in his life—his mother, Nancy (when he was nine); his older sister Sarah (when he was eighteen); and his friend Ann Rutledge (when he was twenty-six)—and uses fond memories of them to bolster his mission as an attorney. He longs to get close to the attractive Mary Todd but rebuffs her campaign to get close to him. First he needs to master the milieu of men. Fonda makes Lincoln humble and ambitious, unsure of himself yet determined. He gropes for maturity by endearing himself to others but tests his mettle by holding them to account.

Young Mr. Lincoln's boyish ways help him win over juries. This affable jokester can outduel his opponents in feats of logic, and outdo them in folksy simplicity. But the shambling-hick performance, sitting back with legs extended and boots resting on a table, can take him only so far. In Trotti's script, the transformation to mature adult and accomplished lawyer takes place when Lincoln decides to put his body in harm's way.

As he's preparing to defend two innocent, young-adult brothers against the charge of murder, Lincoln acts spontaneously to save them from a (fictional) lynch mob. Just before the drunken citizens of Springfield break through the jailhouse door with a battering ram, he sends them reeling backward with a single thrust of his leg against the timber. Bracing himself in the doorway, he dares anyone to try removing him. "I can lick any man here hands down," he yells. No one cares to take him on. By the time he's done, they've laughed at his self-deprecating wit and lowered their heads in shame as he cites the Sermon on the Mount. Now that Lincoln has made himself master of a mob, he's ready for major success in law and politics.

The film ends just as Griffith's *Abraham Lincoln* did, with a rousing "Battle Hymn of the Republic" playing over still shots of Daniel Chester French's seated Lincoln in Washington. With *Abraham Lincoln*, critics and reviewers gave the glory to Walter Huston. With *Young Mr. Lincoln*, it went equally to John Ford, Lionel Trotti, and Henry Fonda, with Fonda garnering accolades for actually embodying the young Lincoln.[12]

In the *New York Times*, Frank S. Nugent summed up the "once-in-a-blue-moon" performance of the star, calling it a rendezvous of nature and art in Fonda's person. Nature supplied the requisite "long legs and arms, a strong and honest face and a slow smile." All that was left for the makeup department was the "nose bridge, the "lank brown hair," and the "trace of a mole." The artist, meanwhile, "kindles the film, makes it a moving unity, at once gentle and quizzically comic."[13]

THE SECOND major Lincoln-based film of 1939 featured the monumental Lincoln rather than the living one—except that for Jefferson Smith, an incorruptible and newly appointed junior senator from an unnamed state in the mountain West, Lincoln is ever present as a spirit.

Unbeknownst to Smith, but instantly perceived by those around him, he also embodies many of Lincoln's presumed boyish features.

The recipient of eleven Academy Award nominations in 1940, Frank Capra's *Mr. Smith Goes to Washington* stars Jimmy Stewart as the child-like rube set down in a world of men. Arriving at Union Station in Washington, DC, the young innocent is so bedazzled by the sight of the US Capitol dome that he doesn't notice the three black porters left holding his bags as he disappears on a spontaneous sightseeing tour of the town. (The porters are played wholly for laughs; once they realize Smith is gone for good, they drop his bags and skedaddle.) When the bus reaches the Lincoln Memorial, Smith slowly climbs the steps and is transported by the sudden sight of his hero. "Gee whiz," he'll say later that day, "Mr. Lincoln, there he is, he's just lookin' straight at ya as ya come up those steps, just, just sitting there like he was waiting for somebody to come along."

No sooner does Smith enter the Lincoln temple than he hears the sound of a small white boy, standing next to his immigrant grandfather in the south wing, reading the chiseled Gettysburg Address as if he's saying his prayers. We learn that the grandfather is an immigrant only because the boy stumbles over the word "freedom," in "new birth of freedom." As the youngster fishes for the right pronunciation, his grandfather, beaming up at the address himself, says "freedom" out loud, in his heavy European accent.

Meanwhile, as the boy repeats the word "freedom," Capra cuts to a close-up of an older black man standing nearby, who removes his hat as he, too, gazes up lovingly at the address. It's a moment of sincere hero worship shared by a congregation of four—black man, white immigrant, small white boy, boyish white senator. Every other scene to this point in the film has been laced with comic exaggeration, many of them marked by "Boy Ranger" Jefferson Smith's wide-eyed entrancement at the nation's declared ideals. Now Capra invites his viewers to join the congregation of committed Lincoln faithful.

But during this "freedom" moment at the Lincoln Memorial, Jefferson Smith sees only the grandfather and the young boy, not the grateful

African American elder. Only the theater audience sees the black man. (The close-up of him may have been added after the main shooting at the Memorial wrapped up; there is no visual evidence in the shot that he is actually there with the other actors.) Smith didn't notice the black porters at the station, and at the Memorial he doesn't see the African American Lincoln admirer, doesn't see Jules Guérin's horizontal *Emancipation* mural right above the Gettysburg Address, and doesn't see any connection between Lincoln's "new birth of freedom" and the racial segregation of the 1930s.

Written by Sidney Buchman, who received an Oscar nomination for Best Adapted Screenplay, the film draws on the long-standing stereotype that Lincoln was "simple as a child." The script tacks back and forth between Jeff's surface immaturity and underlying wisdom. Stewart plays an original hybrid. On the one hand, he's a Lincoln-loving naïf, infatuated with old heroes but clueless about how the world works. On the other hand, he's a prospective martyr, willing to live, or die, in obedience to Lincoln's simple preference for right over wrong—a moral conviction for which he is prepared to go, literally, to the mat.

Step by step, Smith's old-school patriotic idealism is revealed as a higher realism. The corrupt Senator Joseph Paine (Claude Rains) and his alluring daughter Susan mock Smith by calling him "Honest Abe," but savvy Senate staffer Clarissa Saunders (Jean Arthur) sees deeper.

When Smith's longtime idol Senator Paine betrays him in false testimony to a Senate committee, he takes refuge at the Lincoln Memorial, where Saunders finds him alone, in tears, sitting on his packed suitcase. "I had a hunch I'd find you here," she says. She reminds him of what he said when he first saw the Lincoln statue. "You said he was sitting up there waiting for someone to come along. You were right . . . I think he was waiting for you, Jeff. He knows you can do it. So do I." With that, he perks up, calls her "Clarissa" rather than "Saunders," gives Lincoln a brisk salute, and marches off with her to learn the intricacies of the filibuster.

In the long history of Lincoln commemoration, admiring disciples from William Herndon to Theodore Roosevelt and Woodrow Wilson had rebelled against its complacency. Ritualized veneration sucked the life out of Lincoln the man, said Herndon, or, as Roosevelt and Wilson believed, stole energy from the urgent tasks confronting the present. Sidney Buchman gave this criticism a comic update, satirizing Lincoln piety but all in the interest of rekindling it. Jefferson Smith earns his childlike faith in Lincoln and the Declaration of Independence by suffering for them, throwing his body into the fight for the "people" and against their corrupt overlords.[14]

IN AUGUST 1939, with *Young Mr. Lincoln* still playing in theaters and *Mr. Smith Goes to Washington* in final production for its October release, shooting began on yet another Lincoln feature, *Abe Lincoln in Illinois*, released to critics' raves in January 1940. That made three major studio releases touching on Lincoln in seven months. Yet while the Lincolns of *Young Mr. Lincoln* and *Mr. Smith Goes to Washington* stood for right over wrong without broaching the wrong of racial subordination, *Abe Lincoln in Illinois* propelled Lincoln into the battle against European fascism, invoking his name in the fight against racial discrimination in Europe.

Playwright Robert Sherwood crafted the screenplay from his own twelve-scene, Pulitzer Prize–winning drama, which had been thrilling theater crowds since October 1938. It ran on Broadway for a solid year, and it was still on tour in Chicago when the movie opened in Washington. Play and film were hailed from the outset as galvanizing defenses of democracy, and the show's star—Canadian-born actor Raymond Massey—joined Sherwood in promoting the story as a call to action against fascism. "There really isn't such a great difference between Lincoln's fight and ours," Massey told an interviewer in October 1938. Lincoln had attacked "the policy of indifference to evil" when it came to slavery; democrats of the late 1930s combated the same policy in the case of "dictatorship."[15]

The film's premiere on January 23, 1940, at the RKO Keith's Theatre in Washington, DC, brought the issue of racial discrimination to the fore even before the curtain went up. Eleanor Roosevelt and dozens of other dignitaries, including the film's cast, had to cross an informational picket line to get in. Protestors were targeting the theater's whites-only admission policy. In a letter to the *Washington Post*, John Lovell Jr., secretary of the local NAACP, wrote, "The Washington community can lay no claim to a belief in this picture or in Abe Lincoln himself so long as it will tolerate the denial of the stand he took, evidenced by the exclusion of Negroes." For her part, Eleanor Roosevelt apologized for crossing the line but went ahead and took her seat in the "box of honor" adjoining Sherwood's and Massey's entourages.[16]

Mrs. Roosevelt told the *Post* she was most impressed by the snippets of Lincoln's oratory, and *Post* columnist Nelson Bell concurred: Massey spoke Lincoln's words with a "fervor" that "transcends realism and approaches reality." In the play's stirring ninth scene, Lincoln gives his longest speech. He is squaring off against Stephen Douglas in the summer of 1858, delivering an oration pieced together by Sherwood from several speeches and letters. It features some of Lincoln's greatest phrases, mobilized to expose the basic idea behind antidemocratic movements in any era.[17]

That idea, as Sherwood's Lincoln puts it, is "the tyrannical principle" that places one person or group on top of another, "the same spirit that says, 'you toil and work and earn bread, and I'll eat it.'"

As a nation, we began by declaring, "All men are created equal." There was no mention of any exceptions to the rule in the Declaration of Independence. But we now practically read it, "All men are created equal except Negroes." If we accept this doctrine of race or class discrimination, what is to stop us from decreeing in the future that "All men are created equal except Negroes, foreigners, Catholics, Jews, or—just poor people?" That is the conclusion toward which the advocates of slavery are driving us.[18]

Massey could so persuasively tether the concerns of the 1940s to those of the 1850s in part because, like Benjamin Chapin thirty years earlier, he looked so much like Lincoln. His frame, height, and facial structure came strikingly close to Lincoln's. At forty-two years of age and six foot two, he presented the rangy, craggy outline that people expected of their rail-splitter. His deep-set eyes and hollowed-out cheeks gave his face a tragic veneer, as if, like Lincoln, he'd weathered a long storm. Massey far surpassed Henry Fonda or Walter Huston in the Lincoln look-alike contest, and in using his tired body to evoke the whole country's weary pilgrimage through adversity. For the years of war that lay just ahead, Massey helped reaffirm Lincoln as the body and face of the nation—one dedicated, as Sherwood's president-elect tells his Springfield neighbors from the rear of the train departing for Washington, to "the fulfillment of an ancient dream, which men have held through all time, that they might one day shake off their chains and find freedom in the brotherhood of life."[19]

THE SCRIPTS of *Abraham Lincoln*, *Young Mr. Lincoln*, and *Abe Lincoln in Illinois* had all depended for their very existence on Sandburg's *Abraham Lincoln: The Prairie Years*. In 1939 and 1940, the last two films inadvertently returned the favor, heightening public awareness of the president at the exact moment when Sandburg's four-volume sequel, *Abraham Lincoln: The War Years*, was hitting the stores. Released in time for Christmas shoppers in December 1939, this colossal new work renewed Sandburg's unofficial tenure as the nation's Lincoln laureate.

The two-volume *Prairie Years* had reached 360,000 words; the four-volume *War Years* topped a million and weighed in at eight pounds. Certifying Sandburg's position as chief Lincoln sage, Robert Sherwood redefined the rave review (on page one of the *New York Times Book Review*) by claiming it was "so great a work" that it could not be properly assessed at this time: "It will require great reading and great reflection before any true appreciation of its permanent value can be formed."

Three months after the outbreak of war in Europe, Sandburg's *War Years* could only be heralded, not scrutinized. For Sherwood, Lincoln was needed in 1939 as the time-transcending hero of democratic freedom, and Sandburg was needed as his interpreter.[20]

The mid-twentieth-century American war years began in 1941, and before they ended, television programmers were already joining movie theaters in putting Lincoln on screen. In the spring of 1945, NBC produced Sherwood's play *Abe Lincoln in Illinois*, presenting its three acts live on three evenings in April and May. At that point there were fewer than ten thousand home sets in the entire country. By 1952, a third of American households (fifteen million) had acquired televisions, and CBS's high-minded arts program *Omnibus* rewarded them with an innovative five-episode series on Lincoln's early life written by novelist and film critic James Agee—a fan of Sandburg's freewheeling fictionalizing, but one who pushed well beyond the master's devotional mind-set. Agee discomfited many among the mass of Americans who loved Sandburg's storytelling because it made Lincoln sacrosanct.

The brainchild of the Ford Foundation's TV-Radio Workshop, *Omnibus* aired for ninety minutes on Sunday afternoons, and the half-hour Lincoln segments appeared every few weeks between November 1952 and March 1953. Placing Lincoln in the midst of ballet, opera, drama, instrumental music, and profiles of other great men asserted his place as an American cultural treasure. (He shared the lineup on November 16 with Leonardo da Vinci, and on March 29 with Lord Byron.) At times the shows expressed Sandburg-style sentiment. Filmed on location, Agee's scripts were meant to show how the land and common people of Kentucky, Indiana, and Illinois "were like the father and mother of Lincoln's greatness."[21]

The screenwriter followed Sandburg's method, using documented facts as starting points but refusing to be fenced in by them. He, too, was after bigger game than a sequence of certified events and speeches. Promising to be "true to history," he would nevertheless build on "legend whenever it seemed truer than fact." Naturally, one legend that seemed indispensable to Agee—as it had to Sandburg, Griffith and Benét, Ford and Trotti, and Cromwell and Sherwood—concerned Ann Rutledge.

But Agee used the intimacy of Abraham and Ann to set off the psychic crisis of Lincoln's twenties. This Abraham is played (by Royal Dano) as a fifties-style existentialist, alienated from the culture around him. He keeps gazing into the distance, his entire body stiff and constricted, despite the warm entreaties of Ann (played by the twenty-two-year-old Joanne Woodward). After Ann's demise, a stricken Lincoln spreads his full frame over her grave, his face planted in the dirt, suspecting that he was the cause of her death. He had put political ambition over love, leaving her forsaken and vulnerable to disease.

So many viewers and newspapers complained about Agee's speculative foray into Lincoln's heart and mind that the show staged a mock judicial proceeding. At the conclusion of the March 19, 1953, broadcast, series host Alistair Cooke moderated a good-natured examination of the evidence: was *Omnibus* at fault for misleading the public about Ann and Abraham? With Cooke on the bench as "judge," Agee squared off against Columbia University historian Allan Nevins about Lincoln's relationship with Ann Rutledge.

Nevins declared that there was "no historical truth in the story that Lincoln was in love with Ann Rutledge, much less that he was ever engaged to her." Agee countered by defending "reasonable conjecture" as a pathway to truths that historical documents could not touch. Nevins didn't bend: Agee's story was "90 percent legend," and he had "tampered with the truth." After garnering Agee's genial concurrence that his script neither attained nor aspired to "historical truth," Cooke wryly judged *Omnibus* guilty of "non-willful misrepresentation, and maybe unconscious fraud," all "mitigated by the imagination and talent of Mr. Agee."[22]

It's impossible to tell how many people tuned in to the *Omnibus* Lincoln episodes, but the series as a whole started strong, procuring premium payouts from advertisers and initially attracting a substantial share of the audience. Syndicated TV columnist John Crosby reported in January 1953 that viewership had "slipped quite a bit since then."

Crosby suggested that the first Lincoln episode, "The Beginning and the End" (broadcast during the program's second week on the air), helped spur the drop-off. The film began with the assassination, deathbed, and funeral train, and then flashed back to Lincoln's childhood. Crosby considered the death scene in the Petersen house "gruesome"—"they all but embalmed him in front of our eyes"—and a brief view of the open coffin revolted him.[23]

Still working on his novel *A Death in the Family* in 1953 (it won the Pulitzer Prize in 1958), Agee was captivated by Lincoln's postmortem body and by the national mourning for him. *Omnibus* went to the trouble of assigning a second unit (headed by the young and unknown director Stanley Kubrick) to film a funeral-train sequence. The train is shown draped in mourning cloth as it rolls through the countryside, its bells, whistles, and hissing steam engine joined on the sound track by Walt Whitman's "When Lilacs Last in the Dooryard Bloom'd," read by director Norman Lloyd. Shots from inside the train captured Whitman's and Sandburg's people: a farmer standing with his horse, head uncovered; men and women standing at a crossroad, holding flowers; a young boy chasing after the train through tall grass; a family at night gathered by a bonfire beside the tracks.

Agee and Kubrick inserted a public viewing of the corpse during a station stop. A few spectators board and pass slowly by Lincoln's open coffin (Royal Dano gamely lies inside). The last mourner in the line is an old black woman. With no soldiers present to whisk her along, she takes her time bending over the body and admiring it. Slowly and meticulously, she deposits a sprig of lilac on his bier.[24]

FOR THE REST of the decade, and into the 1960s, local stations around the country and the national television networks produced regular Lincoln programming, unself-consciously promoting his civic cult. Jack Lemmon appeared as John Wilkes Booth, Lillian Gish as Mary Lincoln, and Raymond Massey as Lincoln in the teleplay of Jim Bishop's best-selling

1955 novel *The Day Lincoln Was Shot*, an hour-by-hour account of Lincoln's and Booth's activities on April 14, 1865. For Lincoln's birthday in 1960—with 87 percent of American households now owning sets—Los Angeles viewers could make an evening of it: at 7:00 p.m., a local travel show profiling "Lincoln Country" in Illinois; at 7:30 p.m., the popular Academy Award–winning short subject *The Face of Lincoln*; and at 8:30 p.m., a network variety show with Julie Andrews among the performers "handling the musical chores and Carl Sandburg, without whom no Lincoln's birthday would be complete, speaking in his measured magnificent language of the man Lincoln."[25]

The only Lincoln film of any length to have won an Academy Award (in 1956) as the best picture in its category, *The Face of Lincoln* develops a touchingly simple concept. The unassuming, sixty-three-year-old sculptor Merrell Gage of the University of Southern California takes a smooth, egg-shaped mound of clay ("because most human heads are egg-shaped," he says with a sly glance at the camera) and in twenty minutes turns it into the head of Lincoln. First he holds up Leonard Volk's 1860 "life mask" of the aspiring presidential candidate, running his fingers over it to show the difference between the left and right sides of his face. On the left side, Lincoln's skin is stretched tight, conveying, in Gage's homespun judgment, the president's "power" and "decisiveness." It gives him his "firm, true look," the gaze of a shrewd lawyer. On the right side, a relaxed muscle makes the corner of his lip protrude slightly, suggesting gentleness to Gage—the look of the "humanitarian and philosopher."[26]

These innocent speculations about Lincoln's physical features obscure what's really happening: Gage is establishing his intimacy with Lincoln's image, speaking of him like an old friend. He sets down the mask, turns to the clay, and digs in with fingers, thumbs, and small sculpting instruments. Meanwhile, keeping his eyes locked on Lincoln, he converses amiably about some of "the events that changed his face." The very first event he mentions depicts the twenty-two-year-old Lincoln as the future emancipator: drawing on Sandburg's story of the 1931 flatboat trip to New Orleans, Gage reports that Lincoln stayed at a boardinghouse right across the street from a slave market, with "men and women being sold like cattle."

When Gage relates Lincoln's "nervous breakdown" after the death of Ann Rutledge, the camera pans slowly around the back of Lincoln's head, keeping the focus on Gage. He appears to be bucking up his sorrowing friend by smoothing out his lapels. When the Civil War arrives, Gage makes Lincoln age rapidly, deepening the hollows of his cheeks and the wrinkles in his forehead. Gage's fingers are working hurriedly by the time he starts telling the tale of Appomattox and the final week of Lincoln's life. His voice slows down for the trip to Ford's Theatre, even as his hands speed up to complete the crow's-feet beside Lincoln's eyes and the creases around his mouth.

"You know the rest of the story," says Gage. He swivels Lincoln's head away from the camera, adding, "You know how the assassin's bullet forever turned his face from us." The "Battle Hymn of the Republic" swells up as Gage concludes, "The spirit of Lincoln lives on. Wherever there's a struggle for human freedom his deeds are remembered."[27]

In the winter of 1956, nominated for an Academy Award in two categories—documentary short and two-reel short—*The Face of Lincoln* was booked briefly into a few commercial theaters. (It went on to prevail against the two-reel competition, including *The Battle of Gettysburg*, but lost to Disney's short documentary *Men against the Arctic*.) In Manhattan it opened at the Little Carnegie on Monday, March 5, on a bill with a filmed version of Mozart's *Don Giovanni*, and the *New York Times* reviewer called Gage's work "an interesting and oddly eloquent short."[28]

Perhaps one or two of the Little Carnegie's patrons, hearing Merrell Gage speak his final words about Lincoln living on in later struggles for freedom, called to mind a feature story they'd seen the day before in the Sunday *New York Times*. It gave detailed attention to a three-month-old "phenomenon unprecedented in American race relations, a Gandhi-like passive resistance campaign waged by Negroes with religious fervor against the city bus lines" in Montgomery, Alabama.[29]

CHAPTER TWELVE

Standing in Lincoln's Shadow

*We are getting more from a dead Republican than we are
getting from live Democrats and live Republicans.* [1]

—ADAM CLAYTON POWELL JR., 1957

I N DECEMBER 1955, a young black minister in Montgomery took
the reins of a fledgling drive to integrate the city's buses. In less
than a year and a half he would be standing in front of the Lincoln
Memorial appealing for racial justice. That event drew a disappointing
crowd, half the size he'd hoped for. Six years later, in 1963, he would
return to the Memorial, his reputation preceding him. And the Lincoln
statue would rise again to the symbolic place where Marian Anderson
had left it in 1939.

On March 22, 1956, only hours after Merrell Gage accepted his Academy Award at the Pantages Theatre in Hollywood, a circuit court judge
in Montgomery handed down his verdict in the case of *Alabama v. Martin Luther King*. The twenty-seven-year-old Baptist minister had been
leading the local bus boycott for seventeen weeks, following the refusal
of forty-two-year-old Rosa Parks to give up her seat to a white passenger.
Judge Eugene Carter—a World War I veteran and a Bible class teacher
at the Methodist church across the street from King's Dexter Avenue
Baptist Church—found King guilty of breaking a 1921 state law banning
all organized boycotts except those with "just cause or legal excuse."

With the Montgomery campaign, a decade of civil-rights agitation began, and so did a new era for Lincoln. But King didn't publicly embrace him at the start. He was too busy building a religiously based movement for equality. Lincoln, and the Lincoln Memorial, would prove indispensable later, once the movement had staked out the moral high ground through devotion to Jesus and his doctrine of loving one's enemies.

After rendering his guilty verdict in March 1956, Judge Carter went easy on King in the sentencing phase, telling the courtroom audience (in *New York Times* paraphrase) that King had always "urged his followers to observe a policy of non-violence." Released on bond, the young preacher told a revved-up crowd of two thousand packed into the Holt Street Baptist Church that God had chosen Montgomery for a test. In this city, at the heart of the former Confederacy, the spirit of freedom might take new root and radiate across the South.[2]

Just three days later, King got "a hero's welcome" from an interracial crowd of twenty-five hundred squeezed into the Concord Baptist Church in Brooklyn, New York. Introduced by a Jewish rabbi and a Catholic priest, he appealed for contributions to support "a fight for justice and democracy." He made no mention of Lincoln or any other American advocate of equality, harping instead on the method of nonviolence. To this northern audience King spoke of Gandhi as well as Jesus; together they summed up the philosophy and practice of nonviolent resistance to evil. Hateful opponents would run up against the discipline of love—a love of enemies, he quipped, that differed from "the way you love your wife." It was a powerful, God-given love for "our brother men, white and dark." Jesus had modeled it first, and in twentieth-century India, Gandhi had shown "it could work."[3]

A columnist for the African American *New York Amsterdam News* called the boycott leader "transcendentally brilliant" for inaugurating a new phase of emancipation. As Lincoln had attacked the legal structure of slavery, King had taken on the legal structure of segregation. But King leapt beyond Lincoln in mobilizing the slaves' descendants for a moral struggle, persuading "his own people that really they are superior to the hateful whites"—"humble and superior." When the yearlong Montgomery boycott ended in victory for the protesters—integration of the city's buses—the *New York Times* predicted that readers would hear again from "the Rev. Martin Luther King Jr.," whose "name should be remembered." The paper praised him for "learning and maturity far beyond his twenty-seven years."[4]

AMERICANS didn't have to wait long for more news of King. On May 17, 1957, six months after the Montgomery triumph, he mounted the steps of the Lincoln Memorial in Washington as the final speaker at an event called the Prayer Pilgrimage for Freedom. Already, the crowd of twenty thousand (half the hoped-for number) had heard Congressman Adam Clayton Powell Jr. of Manhattan challenge Congress to implement the Supreme Court's 1954 *Brown v. Board of Education* decision banning segregated schooling. His clenched right fist raised above his head, Powell berated Democratic and Republican officials for doing less about inequality than the dead Republican enthroned behind him.[5]

The event brought King's oratory to thousands of listeners—including a live radio audience—for the first time. And for much of the black and white press, it made him the undisputed leader of the civil-rights movement. King called his speech "Give Us the Ballot," and once again he insisted on strict spiritual discipline on the part of those provoking social change. "With the statue of Abraham Lincoln directly behind him," noted the *Washington Post*, King announced the key strategic aim of a civil-rights campaign built on the love of enemies: never attempt to "defeat or humiliate the white man." The mostly black audience answered him with call-and-response approval: to his hearty injunction to love evildoers while detesting their deeds—"We've got to love," he shouted—the crowd yelled back, "go ahead," "oh yes," and other cries of support.[6]

Still King didn't mention Lincoln. He seemed to realize that a program of nonviolent civil disobedience was ill suited to the symbolic sponsorship of the hero rising up behind him. King was twenty-eight years old in 1957, when he stood beneath Lincoln's statue and called for the breaking of unjust laws (and accepting one's punishment). Lincoln was twenty-nine in 1838, when he told the Springfield Lyceum that "reverence for the laws" must become "the political religion" of the nation. Even "bad laws," until they were repealed, "should be religiously observed."[7]

Combining love and justice enabled King to position his forces as more religious *and* more militant than the lawyers of the NAACP, whose legal work he praised in his speech but also judged insufficient. It would take coercive force to break down the edifice of segregation and yield "an integration based on mutual respect." You didn't have to like your enemies; you just had to love them impersonally while you went about patiently dismantling their vile social system. The civil-rights contingent had to do two jobs at once: exposing the violence that always lay just below the surface of a segregated society, and signaling the collaborative spirit of the integrated society that would replace it.

Within six months of his trip to the Lincoln Memorial, King had found a way to bring Lincoln into the movement. Disregarding the president's unusable perspective on the law, he praised his personal character. If Lincoln couldn't lend support to civil disobedience, he could certainly endorse the forgiving of one's detractors. In his November 17, 1957, Dexter Avenue Church sermon titled "Loving Your Enemies," King held Lincoln up as an ethical master. Few politicians, he said, would have forgiven Edwin Stanton for the treatment he had meted out to Lincoln in Cincinnati in 1855—scoffing at his legal stature and, for good measure, ridiculing his appearance. Yet less than a decade later, Lincoln turned around and chose Stanton as his secretary of war. The president showed that "the power of love" could overwhelm the rigid barriers between people. King declared Lincoln his ally in preaching emancipation from hate.[8]

ON AUGUST 28, 1963, six years after the prayer pilgrimage had brought twenty thousand people to the Lincoln Memorial, an interracial crowd of two hundred thousand descended on the Memorial to mark the centenary of the Emancipation Proclamation. On a brilliant eighty-two-degree day, a vast television audience ("virtually every household in the nation," said *New York Times* TV critic Jack Gould) got a glimpse of King's stature as a real-life emancipator, amid thousands of signs and banners demanding jobs and equality for all.

All three networks carried his midafternoon speech, following substantial coverage of the noontime march down Constitution Avenue from the Washington Monument to the Memorial, captured by cameras perched atop government buildings. "The unforgettable stroll" of hundreds of thousands down the eight-lane, tree-lined avenue struck Gould as "an editorial in movement . . . The gentle entrance and exit of so much petitioning humanity" could be delivered only by television, not by a newspaper's "frozen word or stilled picture." Thirty-five cameras carried live images of the day's drama, including one placed "high in the Washington monument," revealing a distant Lincoln presiding over a mass of spectators stretched out to the east of the Memorial and packed against the sides of the reflecting pool.[9]

Five minutes shorter than his twenty-minute "Give Us the Ballot" remarks in 1957, the finely wrought "I Have a Dream" conveyed an assurance of ultimate victory in the campaign for equal rights. Yes, unmerited suffering could still be expected, but it would prove fruitful spiritually and temporally. King saluted Lincoln with ho-hum blandness at the start— calling the author of the Emancipation Proclamation "a great American"—but he paid him fervent, indirect homage at the end of the speech, as he performed the rhythmic and operatic "I have a dream" sequence.

The start of it summed up a recurrent theme in Lincoln's speeches from the 1850s. Like Lincoln at Gettysburg, King appealed to the Declaration of Independence: "We hold these truths to be self-evident, that all men are created equal." Like Lincoln in his Dred Scott speech, King implored citizens to embrace their founding creed. Each generation should draw closer to the original goal. King, like Lincoln, had discerned the signs of the times, recognizing a moment of opportunity. Neither of them created the moment; both glimpsed the opening door and held it open with oratorical and political talent.

As King spoke, a television camera zoomed in on Lincoln seated in his temple. The benevolent father calmly received from King's lips the familiar words of Jefferson on self-evident truths, apparently anointing King as a fellow prophet of equality. In 1957, the minister had stood on the same steps and spoken as a Christian: the sorrows of Good Friday, he said, will eventually give way to the joys of Easter. In 1963 he spoke as a national leader, twice quoting the Hebrew scriptures—sacred texts to Jews and Christians alike—and inviting God's children of all faiths to join hands and pursue the age-old American dream.

Appropriately, the sixty-four-year-old Marian Anderson had come out on the platform earlier that afternoon to sing "He's Got the Whole World in His Hands." She was supposed to have sung "The Star Spangled Banner" at the start of the program, but she'd been held up in traffic. The obvious selection for Anderson would have been "My Country 'Tis of Thee," her signature anthem from 1939, but it was King who threaded those lyrics into the pitch-perfect conclusion of his speech. The ringing tones of "I Have a Dream" thus recalled Anderson's 1939 performance, just as it echoed the generations of African Americans who had intoned "My Country 'Tis of Thee" to close their Emancipation Day festivities.

The next day, James Reston, chief columnist for the *New York Times*, caught the significance of King's "melodious and melancholy voice . . . crying out his dreams to the multitude," joining "the symbolism of Lincoln and Gandhi" to "the cadences of the Bible." A massive social movement was building, and Reston found just the right Lincoln quotation to mark the moment. "I think," he'd written to Gov. Andrew G. Curtin of Pennsylvania in 1861, "the necessity of being ready increases. Look to it."[10]

MARTIN LUTHER KING began his "I Have a Dream" speech by invoking the president whose marble features rose up behind him, the author of the Emancipation Proclamation. King knew very well that Lincoln's 1863 decree did not free many slaves right away, but he also knew that it came as a streaming ray of hope to the rest of them. Some made their way to Union lines, and freedom; others waited for the defeat of the Confederate armies in the spring of 1865, or for the Thirteenth Amendment, ratified that fall to make slavery or involuntary servitude illegal except as punishment for a crime of which a person "was duly convicted."

Lincoln died knowing the amendment *would* be ratified, and aware that he would be hailed as the president who had overseen the destruction of slavery in the United States. No other "great death" in world history, said Whitman, in his late-nineteenth-century lecture "The Death of Lincoln"—

> not Caesar in the Roman senate-house, or Napoleon passing away in the wild night-storm at St. Helena—not Paleologus, falling, desperately fighting, piled over dozens deep with Grecian corpses—not calm old Socrates, drinking the hemlock—outvies that terminus of the secession war, in one man's life, here in our midst, in our own time—that seal of the emancipation of three million slaves—that parturition and delivery of our at last really free Republic, born again, henceforth to commence its career of genuine homogeneous Union, compact, consistent with itself.[11]

A century later, as King spoke at the Lincoln Memorial, all but a handful of Americans had lost contact with Whitman's "stage of universal Time." They couldn't sense that they stood in the symbolic shadow of Napoleon, much less the Greeks or Romans. For Americans in 1963, Lincoln occupied an eternal sphere of his own, mirroring the exceptional stature of the twentieth-century American nation. Nearly all could agree that the United States was special among world powers—either uniquely virtuous, or uniquely aware of the gap between its moral promise and performance.

In 1963, thanks to the civil-rights movement and to King in particular, millions could feel the tug of Lincoln's vision, and of Jefferson's before him. They could mobilize around the ideal of equality, focusing on the overt second-class citizenship of Jim Crow in the South, while mostly averting their eyes from the subtler patterns of segregation and discrimination deeply grooved into life in the North too. King shrewdly summoned the memory of Lincoln to give the movement some vestigial historic resonance, while stretching the campaign to include a social equality never contemplated by Lincoln.

ON SATURDAY, November 23, 1963, less than three months after the "I Have a Dream" speech, the banner headline of the *Chicago Defender* read KENNEDY, LIKE LINCOLN, KILLED . Immediately, the paper's publisher, John Sengstacke, called the loss of Kennedy "the greatest blow that the Negro people have sustained since the demise of the great Emancipator." In spontaneous November 22 interviews on the city's South Side, black Chicagoans also called Lincoln to mind. "President Kennedy was good to the Negro," said Yvonne Stigler at Weeks' Barber Shop on Forty-Seventh Street. He was "the second man that ever stood up for the Negro . . . The other president stood up for us was shot also."[12]

The Lincoln parallel prevailed in other Saturday papers too. The banner headline in the *Baltimore Sun* read KENNEDY MURDERED BY DALLAS SNIPER, and the capital letters beside his photograph at the top of page one said, "PRESIDENT DESCRIBED AS 'MARTYR,' HIS FATE COMPARED TO LINCOLN'S." Instantly, black and white Americans knew that this event demanded comparison to Lincoln's sudden removal a century earlier.[13]

Flying east with her husband's body on Friday afternoon, Jackie Kennedy turned to Lincoln like everyone else. Surely she called to mind the comments JFK had made about Lincoln's death, in her presence, in early 1962. At a White House seminar on Lincoln led by historian David Donald, the president asked the first question: If Lincoln had served out his second term and been forced to deal with Reconstruction, would later generations have ended up judging him such a great president? As Jackie

recollected the scene in a 1964 interview, Donald came around to agree-
ing with JFK that "it was better for Lincoln that he died when he did." In
the fall of 1962, after the Cuban Missile Crisis ended well for Kennedy
(the Soviet Union withdrew its missiles from Cuba), he told Jackie, as she
recalled, "Well, if anyone's ever going to shoot me, this would be the day
they should do it."[14]

Before arriving in Washington on November 22, 1963, Jackie Kennedy knew that the funeral ceremonies had been scheduled for Monday the twenty-fifth. When the plane taxied to a halt at Andrews Air
Force Base around 6:00 p.m., Angier Biddle Duke, the State Department's chief of protocol, was waiting for her on the tarmac. He offered
to help her however he could. "Find out how Lincoln was buried,"
she told him. Immediately he dispatched a team of researchers to the
Library of Congress, and before dawn the next day, Mrs. Kennedy had
their report.[15]

During her wakeful Friday night at Bethesda Naval Hospital, she had
already leafed through a book featuring pictures of Lincoln's funeral.
She'd called the White House and asked a messenger to retrieve it from
a second-floor bookshelf. (It could easily have been the final volume of
Carl Sandburg's ubiquitous best seller of 1939, *Abraham Lincoln: The
War Years*, with its fifty-page, illustrated account of the 1865 mourning
rituals.) The book may have given her the idea of putting a riderless horse
in the funeral procession, and of using Lincoln's wooden catafalque to
support JFK's coffin during the lying-in-state at the US Capitol.

The White House volume and the Angier Duke report would have
confirmed what the historically informed Mrs. Kennedy already knew:
some of the trappings of Lincoln's funeral could be imitated, but its
inner dynamic lay beyond reach. The people's expectations in 1865
were entirely different from those of 1963. Lincoln's mourners clamored to see his corpse. To them, a lying-in-state meant an open coffin,
enabling a stream of men, women, and children to bid farewell to the
body of their departed hero.

In Lincoln's case, the bereaved were especially insistent: they needed

Old Bob, bedecked with a mourning blanket, stands in front of Lincoln's former Springfield home on May 4, 1865.

to ponder their martyr's bruised face. And they wished to say goodbye in person; if they couldn't be present, they wanted to read detailed newspaper descriptions of exactly how his body looked. They would soon buy engravings and lithographs depicting his dying body surrounded by family and friends. Had Lincoln's mourners encountered only a flag-draped coffin, as Kennedy's did, they'd have been inconsolable.[16]

Even when Mrs. Kennedy copied such a simple detail as the riderless horse, she was fashioning a new symbol as much as retrieving an old one. Yes, she could place a horse in the mourning procession, empty boots reversed in the stirrups, right behind the coffin, just as in Lincoln's Springfield funeral. The sight of him would once more suggest the lost warrior, never to mount his steed again.

But in 1963, the sleek sixteen-year old gelding Black Jack, a regular performer on the funeral circuit, couldn't call to mourners' minds the personal bond between man and animal that sixteen-year-old Old Bob, Lincoln's own horse, had evoked in 1865. Black Jack had lost his commander in chief. Old Bob had lost his actual owner and rider (until 1861), the man who had fed him apples and patted his mane as they trudged through the mud on the central Illinois legal circuit. Old Bob brought the physical Lincoln to mind, the workaday Lincoln rooted in a small state capital of fifteen thousand people. Less than a month before the Springfield funeral, the town's residents had paraded Old Bob through the downtown streets to celebrate Robert E. Lee's surrender at Appomattox. With Lincoln eight hundred miles away in Washington, they invoked his presence by pulling his horse around the city at the head of their procession. Spectators in 1865 could readily impute to Old Bob, as he plodded from downtown Springfield to Oak Ridge Cemetery, some of their aching bereavement.[17]

IN NOVEMBER 1963, the national cult of Lincoln was still flourishing. Jackie Kennedy lent majesty to her husband's funeral by summoning up Lincoln, and ordinary Americans could use their feelings about him to make sense of JFK's death. On the weekend before the funeral, they began creating a list of resemblances between the losses of Kennedy and Lincoln. Kennedy's murder might be profoundly shocking and wholly inexplicable, but at least it was mysteriously tied to Lincoln's. The *New York Times* came up with alluring historical patterns the morning after Kennedy's shooting: JFK had been elected exactly a century after Lincoln, and every president elected at twenty-year intervals since 1840 had died before leaving office.[18]

By 1964 the list of parallels had grown longer. Both Lincoln and Kennedy were succeeded by vice presidents named Johnson, each one a southern Democrat with a six-letter first name. Both victims were shot on a Friday, by John Wilkes Booth and Lee Harvey Oswald, respectively (fifteen letters each)—Lincoln in a theater named after Ford, and Kennedy in a Lincoln convertible made by Ford. These and other weird coincidences pointed, in the eyes of many, to a strange order underlying the gut-wrenching reversals of the public domain.

Yet absent from the list was the single biggest resemblance between the deaths of Lincoln and Kennedy, one that helps account for the appearance of the list in the first place. Kennedy's death seemed so devastating in part because like Lincoln—and unlike the two other assassinated presidents, James Garfield in 1881 and William McKinley in 1901—he lost consciousness at the instant he was shot. Suddenly, like Lincoln, he was no more. Citizens had trouble taking the news in. CBS news anchor Walter Cronkite modeled the disorientation, his eyes dodging the camera as he dealt with the catch in his throat. People wandered aimlessly, tears rolling down their cheeks, stomachs clenched, weak in the knees. To make some sense of senseless facts, many clutched after the hidden forces of history.

With a half century's distance on the loss of JFK, one can see that the similarities between his and Lincoln's deaths are dwarfed by two big differences. In 1865, when their "chief magistrate" was stolen from them, northerners had to confront a new reality. They could call on no precedent for comfort. No previous president had ever been assaulted, much less killed. (On a visit to the Capitol, Andrew Jackson had disarmed a would-be attacker.) The shock at Lincoln's loss was mixed with bewilderment about its meaning for the Republic.

In addition, while many people in 1963 called John F. Kennedy a "martyr," they had a tough time identifying what he had been martyred *to*. What cause had he espoused, and then willingly fallen for? Like James Garfield and William McKinley, he was in the strictest sense a victim, not a martyr. A special grief gripped Kennedy's mourners not because of his sacrifice for some ideal, but because of his youth. He'd been snuffed out at age forty-six, deprived of the chance to reach for the greatness Lincoln had achieved before his death at age fifty-six. Kennedy stood for potential denied; Lincoln, for promise fulfilled.[19]

No one in 1963 said that Kennedy had died a good death, and that people should be happy for him. In 1865, the mourning for Lincoln was premised on the belief that for him this *was* a good death. "It was a euthanasy [dying well]," as the *Troy (NY) Daily Times* put it, "a death in the very climax of physical and moral victory." Lincoln's work of saving the nation and liberating the slaves was more or less complete. To be given the gift of martyrdom at that very moment was to be given the perfect republican exit.[20]

In *Patriotic Gore*, his much-discussed 1962 study of two dozen Civil War–era writers, including Lincoln, critic Edmund Wilson came the closest of anyone in the Kennedy era to comprehending what northerners had taken for granted in 1865: that however devastating, Lincoln's death seemed fitting, something to feel grateful for in the midst of one's grief, something indeed that Lincoln may have anticipated. "It was as if he had not only foreseen the drama but had even seen all around it with a kind of poetic objectivity, aware of the various points of view that the world must take toward its protagonist. In the poem that Lincoln lived, Booth had been prepared for, too, and the tragic conclusion was necessary to justify all the rest . . . it was morally and dramatically inevitable that this prophet who had crushed opposition and sent thousands of men to their deaths should finally attest his good faith by laying down his own life with theirs."[21]

KENNEDY'S MURDER, and President Johnson's decision to honor him by putting civil-rights legislation on a fast track, enabled the black-white alliance led by Martin Luther King to reach its peak of achievement. "After 100 years of talking" about Lincoln's cause, LBJ said to a joint session of Congress on November 27, 1963, the time had come to enact the "dream of equal rights for all Americans, whatever their race or color." King called Johnson's speech an audacious and historic assertion of the nation's ideals.[22]

Passage of the bills barring discrimination in public accommodations (1964) and in voting (1965) guaranteed King his place as the prime hero of the civil-rights era. But as he stood triumphantly behind President Johnson at the signing ceremony for the Voting Rights Act on August 6, 1965, he was on the verge of stepping out from Lincoln's symbolic shadow. Five days after the ceremony, the Watts district in Los Angeles exploded in a six-day riot that killed thirty-four people, and King soon announced, according to the *Los Angeles Times*, that the riot was less "racial" than people assumed. It was actually "a class revolt" pitting the disadvantaged against the advantaged.[23]

He had always differed from Lincoln on the propriety of civil disobedience, and he would always uphold Lincoln's admonition to hate the sin but not the sinner. But now King departed from Lincoln's rights-based outlook, for antidiscrimination statutes couldn't put most of the poor anywhere near even the bottom rung of Lincoln's beloved ladder of opportunity.

This move carried huge repercussions for black and white attitudes toward Lincoln, and for Lincoln's continued stature as face of the nation. Spreading urban riots and an expanding war in Southeast Asia made countless younger blacks and whites choose King's path, not Lincoln's. Class justice trumped racial justice. The century-long African American reliance on the martyred president—and his physical sacrifice—to foster hope for the future was now hanging by a thread.

By the spring of 1967, King had broken with Lyndon Johnson over Vietnam—the colossal spending on the war, he felt, should be invested in the campaign against poverty—and by the fall he was calling for a poor people's encampment in Washington, a base for nonviolent actions to create "massive dislocation" in the nation's capital. The goal, he wrote in the issue of *Look* magazine dated April 16, 1968, was an "Economic Bill of Rights for the Disadvantaged": guaranteed employment for the able-bodied, guaranteed income for everyone else. Militant nonviolent action would start on April 22 and last for two or three months.

King presented this course as a middle path: yes, it would inconvenience a great many people, but it would also stave off urban rioting, including possible "guerrilla warfare." Now King made no reference to Lincoln or his Memorial. The demonstrators in Washington would build a "Resurrection City" near the Memorial, but south of the reflecting pool and beyond the sight line of the Daniel French statue. The seated Lincoln would offer no symbolic endorsement of this assembly. The *Look* article showed how far King had traveled since August 1963. In his "I Have a Dream" speech, he had announced the "poverty" theme at the start, but then suppressed it to accentuate the goal of equal rights. Now he was pushing guaranteed employment or guaranteed income for everyone—a program light-years away from Lincoln's ladder-of-opportunity mind-set.[24]

More than any other major newspaper, the *New York Times* had resolutely promoted Martin Luther King since the Montgomery bus boycott of 1955, but after getting wind of his plan for the poor people's campaign in the fall of 1967, the *Times* backed off. King's "massive dislocation . . . would certainly violate the rights of thousands of Washingtonians and the interests of millions of Americans." King's legacy, in the eyes of many liberals, was now jeopardized. But so, in the estimation of many blacks and whites, was Abraham Lincoln's. His bedrock belief in equal opportunity now appeared antiquated—unobjectionable as an ideal, but irrelevant at a time when unequal results seemed structured into the American "system."[25]

Even as he distanced himself from Lincoln politically, Martin Luther King was preparing himself for an eventual martyrdom that would necessarily—if it happened—resemble Lincoln's. Since Montgomery in 1955, King had contemplated the prospect of assassination. In early 1968 it appeared he was expecting it. Within days of his death on April 4, the *Chicago Defender, Washington Post*, and other papers reprinted his February 4 "Drum Major" sermon at Ebenezer Baptist Church in Atlanta, outlining the eulogy he wished to receive one day. He hoped someone would say he had dedicated his life to the service of others and to the love of humanity. He wanted someone to mention that he had tried to accomplish what Jesus commanded: he had done his best to feed the hungry, clothe the naked, and visit the imprisoned.[26]

The night before he died, speaking to the sanitation workers of Memphis, King seemed to be saying his time had arrived. He spoke of a trip he'd taken to Palestine, where he drove along the Jericho road and understood why Jesus had chosen it as the setting for the Good Samaritan story. In the time of Jesus, it was a dangerous path. Calling himself a Good

Samaritan for stopping in Memphis to help the workers, King implied he resembled the wounded victim too. He'd been stabbed in a Harlem bookstore a decade earlier and barely survived. That very morning his flight from Atlanta had been delayed by a bomb threat directed at him.

By the end of the speech, King was saying goodbye. He'd already been to the mountaintop. People in the crowd shrieked and moaned even before he added that he might not get to the Promised Land with them. If his time had come, he wanted to be remembered as a martyr, not as a victim. He wanted to die with a profession of faith on his lips. Like Jesus in the Garden of Gethsemane, he was saying to his Father, "Not as I will, but as thou wilt."[27]

In the vortex of 1968 America, this martyrdom, unlike Lincoln's in 1865, carried a strong scent of defeat. It demonstrated the strength of King's faith but also disclosed the weakness of his current cause. His imagined middle path toward economic justice had borne little fruit. To his left, many black and white radicals endorsed King's goal but belittled his bedrock belief in nonviolence, which reeked to them of unmanly surrender or feckless idealism. To his right, many liberal blacks and whites mourned their pre-1965 champion of equal rights, and expunged from memory as quickly as they could his final three years of antiwar radicalism and guaranteed-income advocacy.

Major liberal newspapers returned King to his heroic civil-rights activity of 1955–65. The *Washington Post*'s April 5 obituary appeared to have actually been *written* in 1965: it made no mention of his final radical years. Likewise, the *Post*'s April 6 editorial encomium skipped over King's calls for economic justice and made no mention of his Poor People's campaign, due to begin in the city in a month. For the *Post*, King's public career had culminated and ended in his "dream" of equality, "so stirringly recited at the Lincoln Memorial" in 1963.[28]

In his retrospective piece on King on April 7, *New York Times* editorial board member Herbert Mitgang, a well-published authority on both Abraham Lincoln and Carl Sandburg, did take full account of King's recent "battle for economic rights" and his "skirmish against the war in Vietnam." He then placed the martyr back where he belonged, "in the shadow of the Lincoln Memorial," where King had become "the symbol of hope for reconciliation" between whites and blacks.

Mitgang laid down the liberal template that would gather massive strength a generation later: King's martyrdom resembled Lincoln's in advancing "the war for equal rights." Like Lincoln, King had left behind a text that Americans could treasure, intertwining his "dream" with the Bible, the Constitution, and "America" (for many years an alternative title for "My Country 'Tis of Thee"). Drawing so prominently on those holy texts, religious and secular, he'd set up his "I Have a Dream" for the same enshrinement earlier accorded the Gettysburg Address. And his prophetic stature, like Lincoln's, was magnified by a sacrificial death, a physical offering for American ideals.[29]

ON JUNE 6, 1968, a mere two months after King's killing, the *New York Times* ran an absurdly familiar-sounding banner headline: KENNEDY IS DEAD, VICTIM OF ASSASSIN. Within minutes of winning the California Democratic presidential primary, Robert Kennedy had been shot at close range at the Ambassador Hotel in Los Angeles. Less than five years had passed since his older brother's assassination. "With the death of Robert Kennedy, following the murder of his brother and the murder of Martin Luther King," said Arthur Schlesinger Jr. (a former JFK adviser, historian, and public voice of liberalism), "we have killed the three great embodiments of our national idealism in this generation. Each murder has brought us one stage further in the downward spiral of moral degradation and social disintegration."[30]

The loss of three such leaders in five years sucked the remaining wind out of reformist liberalism. The piling up of assassinations made it seem futile to pursue electoral politics as a pathway to change. History had conspired against bringing ideals to fruition in American life. Lincoln the symbol—and Lincoln the man's old hope for incrementally realizing the dream of the Declaration of Independence—was submerged under a tidal wave of disillusionment.

—————

ON APRIL 29, 1968, between the King and Robert Kennedy assassinations, the rock musical *Hair* opened to acclaim from most critics and befuddlement or bedazzlement from most of the public. The show's four-year Broadway run—with eight concurrent regional spinoffs and its megahit LP recording—made millions familiar with the raw and irreverent "Happy Birthday, Abie Baby," sung by four black cast members in act two. Sporting a silk top hat, the one female performer in the group recites the first part of the Gettysburg Address after the three men sing gleefully—and perhaps mockingly—of their emancipation by Lincoln.

The men hail "Massa" Lincoln for having freed them, calling him (with either derisive irony or brash endorsement) "emanci-mother-fuckin-pator of the slaves." Then the woman begins chanting the Gettysburg Address in classic fashion, with a more or less respectful delivery of "Four score and seven years ago, our fathers brought forth on this continent a new nation." But gradually her tone grows satirical, tongue-in-cheek, and possibly dismissive. She faults the Address for not including *all* the forefathers. And before she reaches "conceived in liberty, and dedicated to the proposition that all men are created equal," she pauses to ponder whether her entire recitation is a corny and conventional exercise (whether, as she puts it, "it's too [hokely?] Stokely," an apparent invocation of black-power activist Stokely Carmichael.[31]

The background singers then intone two choruses of "Happy birthday, Abie Baby, happy birthday to you," concluding the last verse with a staccato shout: "Bang!" A pistol-toting, white assassin has interrupted the play by shooting "Lincoln." But his African American victim refuses to die. She mocks the very word "Bang" and tells the assassin she will never die for a white man.[32]

The "Abie Baby" scene in *Hair* plays havoc with viewer and listener expectations. There's no way to tell whether it affirms or denies Lincoln's symbolic importance in the struggle for equality. It's impossible to say whether it cherishes or derides his memory, or whether the lines are to be taken seriously at all. Lyricists Gerome Ragni and James Rado left these questions unanswered. They wanted to provoke rather than assert. They let audience members decide what it all meant and decide how shocked they should feel by profanity directed Lincoln's way.

Ragni and Rado surely knew some spectators would feel assaulted by, and alarmed at, anyone toying with the Gettysburg Address. They knew others would find "Abie Baby" refreshingly iconoclastic, liberating Lincoln's great deeds and words from the prison house of piety. Regardless, it was obvious to all that public utterance on the subject of Lincoln had taken a new turn. The old cult of him was by no means dead, but it had received a hearty and jubilant slap in the face.

Ragni and Rado also realized that "Abie Baby" had seized on some of the emotions that were driving a sizzling public debate over Lincoln's credibility as an emancipator. A couple of months earlier, in February 1968, Lerone Bennett Jr., a senior editor at *Ebony* magazine, had written a blistering essay assailing Lincoln's reputation as the "great emancipator," under the title "Was Abe Lincoln a White Supremacist?"

Like Martin Luther King, Bennett attended Atlanta's Morehouse College in the late 1940s, and in 1962 he had published *Before the Mayflower: A History of Black America*. King had never doubted the sincerity of Lincoln's antislavery convictions or his gradual acceptance of greater political equality for black men. But Bennett went after Lincoln root and branch, adopting, in effect, Malcolm X's doctrine of self-defense: the black community needed protection against the myth of a benevolent Father Abraham who had delivered them from slavery.

Was Lincoln a white supremacist? Bennett gave a resounding "yes." The "real" Lincoln had been a lifelong racist who wished to engineer "a black exodus" from the United States. Bennett didn't say so, but it turned out, according to him, that William Howard Taft and Warren G. Harding had been right all along in their dedication speeches at the Lincoln Memorial in 1922. "Abraham Lincoln," Bennett declared, "was *not* the Great Emancipator."

It didn't matter to Bennett that Frederick Douglass and W. E. B. Du Bois had already assessed the white-supremacy charge and decided that it contained at most a partial truth, or that the only black exodus Lincoln had ever envisioned was the emigration of African Americans to places they wished to go. In analyzing the past, Bennett kept both eyes firmly fixed on the present, when "a real emancipation proclamation has become a matter of national survival." Judged by the needs of 1968, Lincoln's so-called emancipation looked to Bennett like clever deception. Black Americans had been conned by the "Massa Linkun myth" into believing that the Civil War president cared about them.[33]

Bennett's picture of Lincoln as a white supremacist may not have changed many minds on that score, but it added force to the general current of disfavor directed at old political icons. Since 1865, most African Americans had held on to Lincoln—and his sacrificial death—as a succoring memory. The gift of his very life had helped them endure when hope for the future was seeping away. Now, like King, many blacks sensed that Lincoln had done all he could do for them. Only eight weeks after Bennett's essay was published, Martin Luther King himself supplied a new martyr for the late twentieth century, one who had surrendered his life for social equality and political equality alike.

WHILE "ABIE BABY" was confounding expectations about Lincoln at the Biltmore Theatre on Broadway—in the 1,750 performances of *Hair* put on between 1968 and 1972—a stunning Lincoln look-alike was taking the stage dozens of times a day at Disneyland in California, as he had since the summer of 1965. Unlike the *Hair* characters, this Lincoln impersonator never mentioned equality or slavery. Instead he spoke of "liberty," in a script based heavily on the twenty-nine-year-old Lincoln's Lyceum address of 1838. "Reverence" for the law should be taught so assiduously "in colleges" and all other schools that it would become the "political religion" of the nation.

The Illinois-born Walt Disney, a lifelong Lincoln buff and an uncanny judge of popular taste, had conjured up this robotic president before it was possible to build him. Disney "imagineers" developed the first "audio-animatronic" prototype in time for the 1964 World's Fair in New

York City, where *Great Moments with Mr. Lincoln* anchored the Illinois pavilion. In a promotional film for the fair that aired on *The Wonderful World of Disney*, Walt held up the same "life mask" of Lincoln that Merrell Gage had scrutinized in *The Face of Lincoln*. The Disney Lincoln, said Walt, was "so lifelike that you might find it hard to believe."

A reedited version of the World's Fair film shows a well-dressed audience of adults and children sitting in rapt attention as Lincoln delivers his lines. He moves his lips, blinks, shifts his weight, and swivels his head up and down and side to side, but his limbs are nearly motionless. With none other than Royal Dano—the star of James Agee's *Omnibus* films— supplying the baritone voice, Lincoln's tone is grave and preachy. The threat to America comes from no foreign adversary, he says, but from internal disorder. Lincoln's voice swells to an emphatic peak when he begs all Americans to make a religion out of obedience to law. The audience performs the part of silent worshippers in the civic cult of Lincoln.[34]

This Lincoln doesn't identify the lawbreakers, but in 1964 the implication couldn't be missed: civil disobedience, like that sponsored by the civil-rights movement since 1955, was un-American. The actual Lincoln of 1838 had been worried about mob violence, not civil disobedience. But that doesn't mean he would have countenanced civil disobedience, which, as King said repeatedly, was designed to provoke violence without practicing it. That distinction would have been lost on Lincoln.

Despite debuting the year after King's "I Have a Dream" speech, Disney's Lincoln remained oddly detached from the very topics—race and slavery—that had driven the real man's political career beginning in 1854. The decision in *Great Moments* to highlight Lincoln's 1838 speech—supplemented with general passages on "liberty" taken from three later speeches—implied that the emancipator had plenty to say in 1964 about how domestic disorder threatened freedom, but nothing to say about how racial injustice threatened freedom. Omitting Lincoln's mature views on citizen equality didn't place him beyond twentieth-century debates on race, however. It simply turned him into a "law-and-order" man.

The World's Fair audience, according to the *New York Times*, initially found the Lincoln facsimile unconvincing. The "32 channel magnetic tape" sending electronic impulses to "activate pneumatic and hydraulic valves" produced movements that the spectators judged stiff and cumbersome. During the fair's winter recess in early 1965, Disney engineers reworked the mechanism, and attendance more than doubled in the spring and summer. Some spectators now exclaimed to pavilion personnel that this Lincoln must be "a man impersonating a machine."[35]

The tenth-anniversary celebration of Disneyland in Anaheim, California, took place in July 1965, less than a month before the Watts rioting erupted only twenty miles to the west. To mark the milestone, Walt Disney himself unveiled a duplicate Lincoln at the park's revamped five-hundred-seat Opera House on "Main Street, USA." A reporter from the *Los Angeles Times* wondered why the five-minute Lincoln oration didn't include the Gettysburg Address. According to the *Times*, Disney said he "felt that the speech was famous enough without requiring repetition at Disneyland."[36]

Before Disneyland's Lincoln stood up to make his appeal for liberty and obedience to law, spectators were treated to a nine-minute narration featuring slides of American history up to Lincoln's time. At the start, colorful paintings show two groups of Europeans arriving by ship— Pilgrims reaching Plymouth Rock in the seventeenth century, and poor, hopeful immigrants passing by the Statue of Liberty in the nineteenth. The arrival by ship of African slaves goes unacknowledged, and Lincoln's rise to prominence unfolds with no mention of African Americans at all. In voice-over, he does mention in passing that God "hates injustice and slavery." But viewers don't learn that Lincoln's preoccupation with slavery fueled his return to politics in the 1850s and propelled him to victory in the election of 1860.

THE CULT of Lincoln didn't disappear after 1968, but even when its forms persisted, its spirit lagged. Gradually its rituals departed from local parades, public assemblies, and school pageants. The Gettysburg Address persisted by floating free of Lincoln festivities as such. It evolved into an unofficial national speech of wide application—joining "Amazing Grace," originally an abolitionist hymn, as an all-purpose text for occasions of civic renewal or national stocktaking. (The Gettysburg Address was recited by Governor George Pataki of New York at Ground Zero on the first anniversary of the 9/11 attacks on the World Trade Center in Manhattan.)

Lincoln's birthday on February 12 remained an official holiday in a handful of northern states, but pious public commemoration of Lincoln went out of style. A few civic sites and observances (mostly in Illinois, Kentucky and Washington, DC) and pay-for-admission locales like Disneyland maintained a flicker of the former northern adulation for a leader regarded by masses of Americans, for a century after his death, as an altogether unique joining of wise man, holy man, and lovingly remembered friend.

CHAPTER THIRTEEN

Reviving the Emancipator

Lincoln had revolutionized the Revolution, giving people
a new past to live with that would change their future
indefinitely.[1]

—GARRY WILLS, 1992

I N THE FINAL YEARS of the Vietnam quagmire and the first years
of the Watergate disclosures, it seemed beside the point to dwell on
American ideals in general—or Lincoln's ideals in particular. The
connection between ideals and realities appeared to be broken. In an
atmosphere of disillusionment with government—when, in the eyes of
many, government itself seemed oblivious to American ideals—Lincoln
was bound to languish as symbol of the nation.

On February 12, 1973, only two hundred people turned out for the
fiftieth annual wreath-laying ceremony at the Lincoln Memorial. "Very
disappointing," said Commander Frederick Hunt, the head of the Washington, DC, branch of the Military Order of the Loyal Legion of the
United States, an organization founded by Union officers soon after the
assassination in 1865. Hunt blamed the low turnout on President Nixon.
President Johnson had come to the ritual remembrance every year from
1964 to 1968, Hunt said, but Johnson's successor had stayed away.

To make matters worse, Hunt added, the news media were ignoring
patriotic events. "If this were a flag burning, all three networks would be

here in force." In 1973, Walter E. Washington, the black mayor of Washington, DC, followed Nixon's example, citing a "scheduling conflict." Six members of the "National Socialist White Power Party" did show up, brandishing swastikas on their armbands. Beneath the Lincoln statue they left a wreath with the words "champion of racial separation."[2]

Newspapers commonly noted the loss of public fervor for Lincoln. "Very Little of Lincoln in Lincoln's Birthday," said the *New York Times* in 1976. "Almost all" New York City stores held "Presidents' Birthday Sales," not Lincoln's Birthday sales, and "almost none" of the stores displayed pictures of Lincoln (or Washington). "There was hardly a commemoration in sight." The Civil War president's image was sighted only "on the money that changed hands at cash registers."[3]

In 1973, Hollywood producer David Wolper, a longtime Lincoln admirer, decided to give the president his due in a television miniseries called *Sandburg's Lincoln*, dedicated to the poet's memory (he died in 1967) as well as Lincoln's. The program's six fifty-minute episodes appeared irregularly between September 1974 and April 1976, each of them scripted by a different screenwriter and treating a different theme in Lincoln's life. That fragmented design put pressure on the iconic American actor Hal Holbrook, Wolper's choice for the lead role, to provide some measure of continuity.

Famous since the 1950s for his one-man stage show as the acerbic but endearing Mark Twain, Holbrook had also performed briefly as Lincoln. In January 1963, to mark the centenary of the Emancipation Proclamation, the off-Broadway Anderson Theatre in New York City put on a revival of Robert Sherwood's *Abe Lincoln in Illinois*. Holbrook leapt at the chance to add another iconic sage to his repertoire, and Ed Sullivan, the high priest of variety television, leapt at the chance to bring Holbrook back to his live Sunday evening show, where he'd performed as Twain in 1956.

On Sullivan's broadcast of February 10, 1963, which also featured the Three Stooges and Patti Page, Holbrook recited Robert Sherwood's familiar medley of Lincoln passages on equality and tolerance—

including "We now practically read it, 'All men are created equal except Negroes'"—this time for a live audience of ten or eleven million viewers. Holbrook gave the *Ed Sullivan Show* a pointed civil-rights moment less than a month after George Wallace's installation as governor of Alabama. "Segregation now, segregation tomorrow, segregation forever," Wallace had declared in his inaugural speech, standing on the very spot where Jefferson Davis had been inaugurated as president of the Confederacy in 1861.[4]

David Wolper's Lincoln of the 1970s diverged dramatically from Robert Sherwood's of the late 1930s and the early 1960s revival. "You tend to become cynical about myths these days," Holbrook told the press in 1974. He thought Robert Sherwood and Raymond Massey had made Lincoln too "noble." "My job," he added, "is to create an illusion. To make people feel they are seeing Lincoln."[5]

He meant that literally. Holbrook sat for a three-hour metamorphosis every morning during three months of shooting: rubber eye bags, cheekbones, forehead and nose, ears and lips, followed by the fake hair, eyebrows, and beard. Only the actor's eyeballs were left visible. Once the physical components of the "illusion" were in place, Holbrook faced the challenge of tying external appearance to inner character. The scripts didn't make this an easy task, since they presumed that the hero's character could be detached from his beliefs.

Holbrook portrayed a folksy midwesterner with the gift of gab, a sweet-tempered family man patient to a fault with his emotionally erratic wife, and an "unwilling warrior" (the title of one episode) quick to mourn the loss of any soldier. This Lincoln proved adept at courtroom law and backroom politics, but his heart lay in the hearth, and in the down-home stories that endeared him to the common folk. Holbrook delivered not so much "Sandburg's Lincoln" as the spitting image of Carl Sandburg himself. He played Lincoln as an avuncular, beaming man of the heartland, full of generous goodwill for all.

Sandburg's Lincoln gave a reverential portrait of the president, but that didn't stop it from contributing to the erosion of the Lincoln cult.

The scripts were written in 1973 and 1974, just as the Vietnam War and Watergate were making millions dubious about their government's role in the world and about the legitimacy of the "imperial presidency." *Sandburg's Lincoln* surrendered the grand public hero—the symbolic head of a democratic world power, the author of majestic words on freedom, the republican martyr to liberty. Instead, Holbrook would "humanize" him. "I want to take him out of the stone and marble and give him some flesh and blood."[6]

But Holbrook's portrayal didn't just remove Lincoln from his pedestal. The scripts of *Sandburg's Lincoln* removed the president from his writing desk and made him such a chatterbox that he never found the time to mull over his country's destiny. Excising from the series the uniquely gifted wordsmith, the brooding ethical thinker, the lifelong antagonist of the idea of slavery, and the religious seeker pondering the workings of Providence didn't "humanize" Lincoln. It denied him his particular way of being human. It unwittingly sacrificed him to the anti-ideals atmosphere of the early 1970s.

The real Sandburg would have loved Holbrook's depiction of the simple man from the provinces who had vanquished the polished politicians of the East. But he'd have cringed at the neglect of Lincoln's greatest words, the ones that voiced his dedication to the ideal of equality. The Dred Scott speech of 1857, the Gettysburg Address of 1863, and the second inaugural of 1865 all went missing. The final minute of the first inaugural, appealing for national unity and cross-sectional friendship, made the cut, as did a few lines of the April 11, 1865, Reconstruction speech (but not the ones recommending that southern states grant voting rights to some black men).

Avoiding the president's commitment to emancipation would have struck Sandburg as unconscionable. The episode "Unwilling Warrior," which aired in September 1975, ended with Lincoln disembarking at the dock in Richmond, Virginia, on April 4, 1865, and proceeding on foot with his entourage toward the just retaken Confederate White House. Erasing emancipation from this scene required real dedication.

Thirty-five years earlier, Sandburg had portrayed that scene in *Abraham Lincoln: The War Years*, evoking the dense crowds of "black folk, some silent and awe-struck, others turning somersaults and yelling with joy as though their voices and bodies could never tell what they wanted to tell." On this day—their first moment of actual freedom—thousands of jubilant African Americans—men, women, and children—"reached hands toward him in greeting and salute." Of course, David Wolper didn't benefit from a budget permitting a Cecil B. DeMille–style epic. But a close-up of Lincoln accosted by a small group of ecstatic black men and women, calling out and straining to touch him, could have done the job.[7]

Instead, Holbrook's Lincoln picks his way through deserted streets, stepping gingerly around slain Confederate soldiers who litter the ground. Dead white people have replaced rejoicing black people. There were no dead Confederate soldiers lying on Richmond streets in 1865 because no battle took place there; southern troops had evacuated the city before Union forces arrived. Holbrook's Lincoln catches a glimpse of a single living person: a vaguely menacing and disheveled white woman peering at him from a second-story window. No one in his party notices two cowering black men hiding in a doorway, depicted, in complete ignorance of the actual historic moment, as being terrified at the sight of the Union visitors. When he gets to Union headquarters and sinks contentedly into Jefferson Davis's chair, the president can only think about the approaching end of the fighting. He drinks a glass of water and sighs, "It's over."

Many viewers watching that scene in September 1975, when it aired on NBC, connected Lincoln's sense of deliverance to their own relief at the recent end of hostilities in Vietnam. In retrospect, one can see what else was "over" by 1975. *Sandburg's Lincoln* had preserved a nostalgic interest in the humble man from the provinces, but it had surrendered the century-old northern and African American understanding of Lincoln's body as a voluntarily surrendered gift. The series ended on the afternoon of April 14, 1865, hours before his assassination. It alluded to his approaching victimization, but it gave up the old conviction that he'd offered the last full measure of his devotion.

———

SANDBURG'S LINCOLN revealed the sagging fortunes of the public
Lincoln icon even as it covered its tracks by extolling the affability and
charisma of the man. A half decade later, the novelist-playwright-essayist
Gore Vidal set out to finish the job, destroying any vestiges of the larger-
than-life Lincoln, including his reputation as the unblemished exemplar
of midwestern virtue. Vidal gave Sandburg his comeuppance, and cut
Lincoln down several pegs too.

Born in 1925, the year before Sandburg published *The Prairie Years*,
Vidal spent his early years in Washington, DC, where he grew close to his
grandfather Thomas Gore, a longtime Democratic senator from Okla-
homa. Through him, the precocious boy was exposed to the real world
of politics during Franklin Roosevelt's first term (1933–37). At the same
time, he was constructing an ideal world of politics. Like a cosmopolitan
version of Jimmy Stewart's young Jefferson Smith, Vidal roamed around
the Lincoln Memorial and other monuments, imagining himself "in
ancient Rome" but sharing Smith's infatuation with Lincoln. A notebook
from Vidal's early years contains his own drawing of the president's face.
"Beneath it," he recalled in 1991, "I wrote, in a reverent if slovenly hand,
'Now he belongs to the ages.' "[8]

Having been seduced as a youngster by the reigning Lincoln piety,
Vidal made up for it in adulthood by assailing the "national god" pur-
veyed by Sandburg's "six-volume scrapbook" of praise. In 1981, he publicly declared war on whatever remained of Sandburg's influence. Calling
him a "poet of the second rank" and "biographer of awesome badness,"
Vidal accused Sandburg of creating a hero in his own image, a "warm,
gentle, shy, modest" Lincoln. Vidal preferred the aloof, tough-minded
Lincoln of Edmund Wilson's 1962 *Patriotic Gore*, the already classic
account of northern and southern writers involved in, or shaped by, the
Civil War. "The actual Lincoln," Vidal wrote, closely paraphrasing parts
of Wilson's thirty-page essay on the president, "was cold and deliberate,
reflective and brilliant . . . a man of intellectual arrogance and unconscious assumption of superiority."[9]

Wilson, writing at the start of the Kennedy presidency, faulted Lincoln for being all too keen to vanquish the South and to restrict state rights, but he also lent his weight to the cult of Lincoln—as long as it stuck to honoring the president's well-earned authority as a visionary and a poet whose "style was cunning in its cadences, exact in its choice of words, and yet also instinctive and natural."

In his own day, said Wilson, Lincoln used gripping language to teach millions to read the signs of the times. By "laying down his own life," he had tied his personal story to that of the nation. He himself planted the seeds of his later symbolic stature. "If you are tempted to suspect that the Lincoln myth is a backward-reading invention of others, a closer acquaintance with the subject will convince you that something like the reverse is true . . . Lincoln has conveyed his own legend to posterity in an even more effective way than he did to the America of the [eighteen] sixties."[10]

Writing two decades later, during the Reagan era, Gore Vidal couldn't muster Wilson's modulated enthusiasm for the Lincoln legend. For Vidal, Sandburg's cloying sentimentalism had vitiated the entire enterprise of locating heroism in Lincoln's career. The "American nation-state," meanwhile, had been tarnishing the Lincoln symbol for generations, throwing its weight around the international community while claiming disingenuously to act "with malice toward none" and "with charity for all" other countries. Now, in the wake of Vietnam and Watergate, Vidal thought Lincoln would have to be reconfigured from the ground up, reimagined as the mere mortal whose political wizardry had laid the groundwork for the imperial American nation of the twentieth century.[11]

To drive home exactly how ordinary, and unsaintly, Lincoln had been, Vidal latched on to a tale first told by William Herndon in 1891, two months before his death at age seventy-two. Sometime in the mid-1830s, when Lincoln was in his twenties, he'd supposedly picked up a case of syphilis. It was "about the year 1835–36," Herndon claimed in a private letter, when "Mr. Lincoln went to Beardstown [on the Illinois River] and during a devilish passion had connection with a girl and caught the disease." Herndon believed that having contracted the disease, Lincoln might well have passed it on to Mary, whom he married in 1842, and through her to some of their sons, leading possibly to their early deaths.[12]

Having chipped away, beginning in 1981, at the image of a sacrosanct Lincoln, Vidal took his anti-Sandburg slant to an immense readership in the 1984 *Lincoln: A Novel*—the fourth-biggest-selling work of hardcover fiction that year (a first printing of two hundred thousand copies, thirty weeks on the *New York Times* Best Seller list, and by 1988 over a million copies sold). He introduced a much younger (forty-three-year-old) Herndon as a character in his story, brought him to Washington in 1862 to visit his law partner at the White House—a trip the real Herndon did take—and followed him on an entirely invented evening adventure to a DC brothel in the company of Lincoln secretary John Hay.[13]

When the fictionalized Hay urges Herndon not to tell the president of their seedy escapade, Herndon offers, "Oh, I don't think our friend [Lincoln] would be too shocked by this." He proceeds to disabuse Hay of his innocent notion that the young Lincoln had never been "concerned with fleshly as opposed to political unions." He'd visited prostitutes more than once, Herndon tells him, speaking some of the exact words the elderly Herndon had written privately to Jesse Weik in 1891: "Mr. Lincoln had gone over to Beardstown, where, during a devilish passion, he had connection with a girl and caught the disease [syphilis]." Before Vidal's by now drunken Herndon can finish telling Hay that Lincoln may have transmitted the affliction to Mary and his children, he's interrupted by the arrival at his side of the comely "red-haired waiter-girl" he'd been eyeing ever since entering the establishment.[14]

In his thirty-three-hundred-word review of *Lincoln: A Novel*, and of Vidal's career, *Newsweek*'s book critic Walter Clemons heartily seconded the author's assertions, tossing out Sandburg's "sentimental icon" in favor of the "political genius" formed, like any hardy nineteenth-century youth, by the down-to-earth habits of the frontier. Clemons took Herndon's syphilis tale as historical fact, underscoring its truth by contrasting it to Herndon's mere speculation about Lincoln's transmitting the disease to his family. Journalistic balance prompted Clemons to quote historian

Stephen B. Oates—"there is not a shred of truth" even to the syphilis contention, said Oates—but Clemons gave the game to Vidal. He had proved a "more careful historian" than Oates, Clemons thought, since he had quoted Herndon's late-nineteenth-century claim, and done so without "embellishment."[15]

Despite the word "novel" in his title, Vidal wished to be taken seriously as a historian. In his afterword he claimed that his main characters "said and did pretty much what I have them saying and doing." He obtained the imprimatur of Harvard scholar David Donald, a major authority on Herndon as well as Lincoln, thanking him at the end of the afterword "for his patient reading—and correction—of the manuscript."

A decade later, in an interview, Donald asserted that Vidal had "accepted a good many of my suggested revisions. But on occasion he would refuse." Donald didn't specify which of his proposed changes were rejected, and he didn't object retroactively to any of Vidal's interpretations. By letting Vidal claim his endorsement in 1984, and by silently signing off on the book's syphilis episode, Donald lent vital support to the author's campaign to scuttle Lincoln the saint.[16]

TARGETING Lincoln's body for a symbolic takedown through the syphilis account was only one of Vidal's devices for showing that Lincoln's virtues had been overblown by generations of fawning idolaters. Though impressed by the president's ambition, and his facility for imposing his will on his contemporaries, Vidal also denigrated him as a dictatorial strongman, faulting him for suspending habeas corpus during the war and even for taking on the Confederacy in the first place. "The Civil War didn't need to take place," he told an audience at the New York Public Library. "If Lincoln had followed Secretary of State Seward's line[,] he could have let the Southern states go, and then in time taken them back, as they had no place to go."[17]

In *Lincoln: A Novel*, Vidal has John Hay implausibly observe that "the Southern states had every Constitutional right to go out of the Union," and that Lincoln simply asserted his own personal power, knowing all along "he would be obliged to fight the greatest war in human history." Lincoln accomplished much more, in Vidal's view, than saving the Union from being split in two. He instilled a mystical *idea* of union in public consciousness, and used force to deepen its hold. He set the nation on course to replace the states as the sovereign power for all Americans.[18]

Convinced of Lincoln's single-minded quest for national power, Vidal took the easy next step: the president had fought the war wholly for union, not for emancipation. His eloquent support at Gettysburg for the notion that "all men are created equal" had only covered up his actual—and unchanging—belief. "He wanted the Negroes freed," Vidal writes, "and he wanted them out of North America," colonized in a foreign land for their own good. For even if, in Lincoln's eyes, "the colored race" was not by nature "inferior to the white," he felt sure northern and southern whites would never tolerate giving them an equal chance at true freedom.[19]

For years after his book's publication, Vidal bickered with a string of professional historians over his three-pronged campaign to diminish Lincoln's heroic standing. The syphilitic (hence unsaintly) Lincoln was a Union-aggrandizing warmonger, not a peacemaker, and a lifelong colonizer, not a liberator. He underscored all three claims when NBC aired the four-hour miniseries *Gore Vidal's Lincoln* on two successive evenings in March 1988. Starring Sam Waterston as Abraham and Mary Tyler Moore as Mary—and scripted by Hollywood veteran Ernest Kinoy with no input from Vidal—the program conceded substantial ground to Vidal's opponents. It dropped the syphilis saga altogether, and turned the commander in chief into a reluctant warrior rather than a craftily aggressive nationalizer.

Of Vidal's three preoccupations, the show preserved only his image of Lincoln as a committed colonizer, but in press interviews he pitched his other talking points. In a cover story for its weekly TV section, the *Washington Post* took his syphilis story as a fact and featured his ideas that Lincoln resembled Caesar in his imperial ambition, and fought the war "not to end slavery" but "to preserve the union, at any cost."[20]

For all his interest in Lincoln's alleged sexual and medical history, *Lincoln: A Novel* dwelt only minimally on its subject's physical appearance. *Gore Vidal's Lincoln* followed suit by rejecting a Holbrook-style visual impersonation. Sam Waterston plays Lincoln largely without makeup. Viewers are looking at the actor, not at "Lincoln"—a deft maneuver for drawing them away from what Vidal called the Sandburg–Mount Rushmore icon.

The un-made-up Waterston looked appropriately slim, and tall enough, at six foot one, to suggest the president's general body type. But as TV critic John O'Connor noted in his *New York Times* review, Waterston "never quite conveys the 'bulk' of the man, the sheer presence that never failed to impress those who met him." Though he tries to voice Lincoln's high-pitched regional twang, Waterston's boyish, forty-seven-year-old face doesn't come close to evoking the drawn visage of the president in his early to midfifties. Lacking Holbrook's transformative mask, Waterston couldn't help looking "like a high-school thespian determined to play Lincoln."[21]

Lincoln: A Novel did appear to latch on to the idea that Lincoln had died a martyr. Vidal's John Hay, looking back at the assassination, "was now more than ever convinced that Lincoln, in some mysterious fashion, had willed his own murder as a form of atonement" for the horrible and awe-inspiring exploit of "giving so bloody and absolute a rebirth to his nation." Though there is plenty of evidence that he saw his public life as a service rendered to the people, a service that necessarily put his life at risk, there is no evidence that the actual Lincoln ever willed his own murder.[22]

IN RETROSPECT, it's evident that even as NBC was airing *Gore Vidal's Lincoln*, the novelist's vision of Lincoln as the "would-be colonizer of the ex-slaves" was losing ground to the resurgent idea that Lincoln qualified as one of their resolute liberators. Two magisterial books of 1988—James McPherson's *Battle Cry of Freedom: The Civil War Era* and Eric Foner's

Reconstruction: America's Unfinished Revolution, 1863–1877—placed Lincoln's embrace of emancipation at the center of the history of the war and its aftermath.[23]

Princeton professor McPherson's nine-hundred-page tome was climbing the best-seller lists a month before *Gore Vidal's Lincoln* appeared on NBC. Ten months after the book's release in February, it had sold over a hundred thousand copies. The Vietnam War had ended thirteen years earlier, and the publication of military history—stalled as long as readers were getting all the military news they could handle from their daily newspapers—was now booming again. Yet *Battle Cry of Freedom* went far beyond the armed struggle of the Civil War. As a volume in the prestigious *Oxford History of the United States* series, it covered political, social, and economic topics too. And it gave full attention to Abraham Lincoln as commander in chief, politician, and lifelong antagonist of slavery. McPherson had been arguing for Lincoln's commitment to emancipation for many years, but now *Battle Cry of Freedom* brought his views to a vast public.[24]

Yes, McPherson granted, President Lincoln took his time before committing publicly to emancipation. He was preparing the foundation for it, wary of losing border slave states to secession. To Lincoln, emancipation and union always went together in principle. He never subordinated the goal of emancipation to the goal of union. He simply conceded that enacting legal freedom for slaves had to wait until the Union was firmly protected. And as it turned out, protecting the Union depended on bringing thousands of African Americans into the US Army. Emancipation, enlistment, and union all went together.[25]

In essays published after *Battle Cry of Freedom* came out, McPherson gladly surrendered the old saw that "Lincoln freed the slaves." He acknowledged that thousands of slaves had risked everything for liberty well before the Emancipation Proclamation or the Thirteenth Amendment. Yet McPherson argued that *without* Lincoln in the presidency, the vast majority of slaves might *not* have found liberation for decades to come. It was his insistence in 1861 that war was preferable to compromise that enabled a steady flow of slaves to begin freeing themselves, and enabled other slaves to imagine an approaching end to their captivity.[26]

Eric Foner's *Reconstruction* added to the rehabilitation of the emancipator by shielding Lincoln from the drubbing dished out by Gore Vidal and many other liberals and radicals since the late 1960s. In their eyes, Lincoln had done little more than cast the slaves loose, depositing them in a free-labor market and proclaiming, in effect, "Now that you're free, go fend for yourselves." The limited freedom of 1865, in the eyes of Lincoln's critics, resembled the limited freedom of 1965, when black poverty remained untouched by federal civil-rights legislation.

By the late 1980s, with LBJ's war on poverty now a distant memory, Lincoln's incremental approach to extending freedom seemed commendably realistic to many of the liberals who twenty years earlier had snickered at his legalism and gradualism. They found in Foner's *Reconstruction* a Lincoln who "genuinely abhorred slavery," and who drew praise from Frederick Douglass: "He did not let me feel for a moment that there was any difference in the color of our skins."

Foner cautioned against romanticizing Lincoln as a liberator—the president probably "did not approach any policy, even emancipation, primarily in terms of its impact on blacks"—but he dropped the idea, dear to Vidal, that Lincoln had remained a colonizer for life. By issuing the Emancipation Proclamation, Lincoln had "ignored entirely both compensation [to slave owners] and colonization."[27]

From his dual position as a leading professional historian and a major voice on the left, Foner played a substantial if indirect part in quashing Gore Vidal's cachet as a Lincoln interpreter. Acting independently of one another, McPherson and Foner created a new line of defense for the emancipator. Without directly seeking to discredit Vidal, they both helped render his views passé.

SPEAKING IN 1991 at Harvard University, Gore Vidal contended that the key threat to his nonheroic Lincoln—the lusty frontiersman turned nation-building visionary with a default preference for getting African Americans to relocate out of the country—came from filmmaker Ken Burns, whose documentary *The Civil War* had attracted a mass audience to the Public Broadcasting Service for five successive evenings in September 1990. About fourteen million viewers tuned in each night (an average of 13 percent of all those watching TV), surpassing the PBS ratings record set by Carl Sagan's *Cosmos* in 1980.[28]

True, Burns and his scriptwriter, Geoffrey Ward, had left Lincoln's colonization schemes out of the script. Their superbly produced ten-hour photographic, musical, and literary extravaganza made repeated mention of emancipation and of Lincoln's support for it. Never had television viewers been offered such graphic access to the devastation of American slavery, and to the hopes for freedom that led thousands of slaves to bolt for Union camps—thus proclaiming their emancipation before Lincoln did. The program also took note of the dire conditions faced by African Americans once they were free.

But Burns didn't leave Vidal completely behind. As Eric Foner and other historians soon pointed out, Ken Burns's *Civil War* ended up subordinating the black experience of emancipation and Lincoln's role in it to the "poignant family drama" (Burns's phrase) that divided white Americans north and south. Excellent early episodes kept both black and white perspectives on the war in play, along with military battles and political debates. As the series moved toward its conclusion, however, the romance of reunion among warring whites forced emancipation into the background.[29]

At that point, *The Civil War* pitched toward one of Gore Vidal's favorite themes: this war really didn't need to happen. Burns didn't join Vidal in blaming Lincoln personally for fighting an unnecessary war. He just left his audience to ponder the suggestion that if they'd only tried harder, Americans could have found a way to compromise rather than kill off 2 percent of their population.

Well before the final episode, it became clear that the emotional core of the show concerned the courage of individuals and the horrific loss of life, all followed by a decades-long healing process within the national white family. With fratricide among white Americans, and their quest for postwar reunion, emerging as *The Civil War*'s through line, emancipation could only figure, at best, as an essential sidebar.

This structural split in the script—white national unity and disunity on one track, black emancipation on another—was inadvertently announced at the stirring end of the first episode. There, Ken Burns created the most memorable scene of the entire series. Almost a quarter century later, many viewers remember it as a spellbinding moment. The haunting melody of "Ashokan Farewell," composed by Jay Ungar in 1982, sets a pensive tone as voice-actor Paul Roebling reads the heartrending 1861 letter that Rhode Island major Sullivan Ballou wrote to his wife Sarah just before the Battle of Bull Run.

In view of what may well befall him, Ballou declares his love for her and his love for the nation. He takes for granted that love of country must sometimes collide with love of family and spouse. This is one of those times. He must pay his citizen's debt to the revolutionary ancestors who created the original union. Committing his body to a fight for republican government, Ballou inadvertently sums up Lincoln's chosen path, publicly expressed at Independence Hall in Philadelphia only months earlier. Rather than surrender that principle of self-rule—for all men everywhere—Lincoln had said he "would rather be assassinated on this spot." When Ballou did fall at Bull Run, he became the kind of hero identified in his just-written letter: a citizen surrendering "all my joys in this life" to defend the people's cause.[30]

To the richly resonant voice of Paul Roebling reading the letter, and to the violin, bass, and acoustic guitar accompaniment, Ken Burns added a succession of six unforgettable photographs, each showing a married couple from North or South—husbands in uniform with stalwart wives sitting or standing beside them. Six bonded pairs, twelve lovers depicted with tragic intimacy, all alike in fidelity to family and to their chosen cause—and they are all white.

The addition of even a single black couple would have deepened the scene dramatically, and cautioned white viewers against inferring that

*An unidentified Union soldier, probably from
Maryland, poses with his wife and daughters.*

the individual losses suffered by whites on both sides, and the calamitous breakup of the white national family, express the central meaning of the war. It would have conveyed visually the fact that many of the 180,000 black soldiers in the Union army suffered the same family separations that whites did, and that the gains of emancipation compensated in part for the human losses on all sides.[31]

The Civil War does feature well-known black actor Morgan Freeman reading the 1862 letter of fugitive slave John Boston written to his "dear wife" Elizabeth (but placed in the middle, not at the end, of episode three, and with no inspired background music to imbue it with transcendent significance). It echoed the personal sentiments contained in Ballou's letter. "I trust the time will come when we shall meet again," Boston wrote, "and if we don't meet on earth we will meet in heaven where Jesus reigns."[32]

By the final episode of *The Civil War*, as Eric Foner noted, the program had strongly implied that the Confederacy and Union could be seen as moral equivalents. The series presented the two warring parties as equally "composed of brave men fighting for noble principles." Each side produced a symbolic leader—Lincoln and Lee—to embody its "noblest features," and in time the white citizens of each section would come to honor both men.[33]

Meanwhile, popular historian Shelby Foote, the principal talking head of *The Civil War* and a master storyteller, added to the atmosphere of moral equivalence. Enjoying the extended final word at the end of the last episode, he concluded, "We [Americans] think that we are a wholly superior people. If we'd been anything like as superior as we think we are, we would not have fought that war." He was repeating what he'd said at the very start of the series: the Civil War erupted "because we failed to do the thing we really have a genius for, which is compromise."[34]

But as Barbara Fields—professor of history at Columbia University and the show's second-most-often-featured talking head—had earlier pointed out, the Civil War was ultimately *caused* by the original compromise of the revolutionary generation: permitting slavery to persist in the land of freedom. By 1861, the only "compromise" available was to put off an inevitable reckoning. Either the secessionists would give up on slavery extension, or the Republicans would accede to it. Shelby Foote's retrospective endorsement of compromise, given his prime editorial position in the series, pushed *The Civil War* to the brink of proclaiming that achieving emancipation and blocking the expansion of slavery mattered less than preventing the war.[35]

Ken Burns placed the subject of death at the heart of his story, and that decision removed emancipation—and Lincoln's own career as a liberator—from the script's central track. Lincoln's death, by contrast, was well covered in a thirteen-minute stretch of the final episode: the basic facts of the assassination and funeral train were laid out, and the atmosphere of numbed disbelief around the deathbed—and among the African Americans clustered in the rain outside the White House— was beautifully evoked.

LOOKING BACK, it's obvious that the late-twentieth-century fading of interest in Lincoln's identity as an emancipator was only temporary. During his period of declining fortunes—from the late 1960s to the late 1980s—his image as a liberator was both scoured and restored. African Americans by and large gave up their special historic tie to him. Their devotion to his bodily sacrifice as a sign and promise of eventual equal citizenship passed into the realm of cherished memory, or was forgotten altogether. It had lost its visceral power as a lifeline, as a sure source of hope.

But many of the radicals and liberals, black and white, who gravitated back toward the political center after Vietnam found Lincoln's political sagacity—on emancipation and other issues—not only defensible, but laudable. His eloquent speeches on American ideals between 1854 and 1861 demonstrated his *realism*. He knew his words could help steel northerners for their historic responsibility: to preserve their Republic by *not* compromising on slavery extension. Like Sullivan Ballou before Bull Run, black and white men would choose to offer their lives for the vision Lincoln had voiced.

As late-twentieth-century blacks and whites reembraced the emancipator, however, they did not revive the old awareness of Lincoln's physical commitment to republican rule. They rhapsodized about the president's miraculous words and his capacity for self-correction, while for the most part falling silent about his putting his body at risk. Their republican hero spoke eloquent truths and maintained a firm moral compass. He outclassed everyone else at encapsulating basic principles, knew when to compromise, and understood when compromise could prove fatal.

His body remained intriguing to some, but not because he had jeopardized it for the people, or because his physical withering stood as a sign of his ardor for public service. His physicality took on a life of its own, apart from what it had meant to him and his contemporaries. Speculation about his possible medical conditions now enjoyed free play, the evidence generally falling short of probability but in the nature of the case never succumbing to complete refutation. At one time or another, as one recent historian sums up his alleged physical ills, Lincoln was said to have exhibited signs of aortic regurgitation, ataxia, cancer, cardiac insufficiency, congestive heart failure, crossed eyes, epilepsy, hypogonadism, Marfan syndrome, MEN_2B, mercury poisoning, syphilis, thyroid problems, and tuberculosis.[36]

But it's the eloquent Lincoln who took center stage in the 1990s. In the spring of 1992, a year and a half after *The Civil War* aired on PBS, a bold rendering of the wordsmith appeared in Garry Wills's Pulitzer Prize–winning *Lincoln at Gettysburg: The Words That Remade America*. Wills's Lincoln saved the nation for equality by spinning a verbal masterpiece. His task on November 19, 1863, was to transform a bloody battlefield—where in early July fifty thousand men had been killed, wounded, or lost—into a resting place for eight thousand souls. He ended up accomplishing a lot more than his appointed task of dedicating the cemetery.

Lincoln, Wills wrote, reiterated his theme from the 1857 Dred Scott speech—"the Declaration as the expression of a transcendent ideal to be approximated" over time—but he went further by asserting that the Declaration of Independence qualified as a "founding document" of the nation. In 1776, Jefferson's cohort had announced the pursuit of equality for all as a *national* goal. For in that year, thirteen years before the Constitution of the United States went into effect, they had, as Lincoln contended, "brought forth upon this continent a new nation."

Lincoln built on earlier thinkers and activists in retrofitting equality into the nation's founding, said Wills—especially Daniel Webster and Theodore Parker. He followed Webster in particular, seeing the Declaration not as the expression of an ideal or spirit alone, but as "the sovereign act of a single people." Americans had reconfigured themselves, in that proclamation, as a body politic. Their decision could not be undone by any disgruntled member of that body. This viewpoint was not original to Lincoln, Wills conceded, but the sanctity of the Gettysburg moment, and his own literary skill, gave his formulation unparalleled cultural power. Words had consequences.[37]

Wills rightly believed Lincoln meant the address to speak to the future, and if one follows it through subsequent generations, the ironies pile up. White northerners learned to cherish it as a holy text in the late nineteenth and early twentieth centuries when it *didn't* stand, in their eyes, for a continuing pursuit of black equality. Yet by the 1950s, deeply grooved cultural fondness for the address had prepared many whites— thousands of whom had memorized it in school—to comprehend what Martin Luther King meant, at the Lincoln Memorial in 1963, when he repeated that "all men are created equal" and tied that sanctified phrase to "the fierce urgency of now."[38]

Lincoln at Gettysburg swept onto the best-seller lists in the summer of 1992, greeted with wonder-struck enthusiasm and vehement criticism from the same reviewers. The trained classicist Wills had struck the increasingly popular emancipation chord with "intoxicating originality," as the *Chicago Tribune* remarked, elevating Lincoln's brief remarks to the lofty company of Pericles's funeral oration. Many historians faulted Wills for giving the president's words too much power to create a new American faith in equality all by themselves. Grassroots social move- ments had created the mass fixation on equality that Lincoln could sum up in his virtuoso performance on the Gettysburg battlefield.[39]

But this line of commentary often missed Wills's main point. Of course Lincoln didn't single-handedly create a consciousness of equal- ity among Americans. But carefully and poetically chosen words could, and in this case did, take on a life all their own. Himself the product of the mass republican consciousness, Lincoln expressed its essence with uncanny brevity, economy, and beauty, just as Jefferson had done in the opening sentences of the Declaration. Like Jefferson, Lincoln was carry- ing out an *intellectual* mission, and in that respect he surpassed everyone else in his day, including his own earlier self, the author of repeated, passionate endorsements of the Declaration.

The paperback edition of *Lincoln at Gettysburg* spent the summer of

1993 on the *New York Times* Best Seller list, a testament to Wills's literary talent and to a rebirth of liberals' hopes in the early days of William Jefferson Clinton's presidency. Surging interest in Lincoln as emancipator—an emancipator with his eye set on the future—helped prepare the way for a twenty-first-century Democratic presidential candidate who chose to make Lincoln his personal calling card.

CHAPTER FOURTEEN

Lincoln Sightings at the Bicentenary: Obama, Disney, Spielberg

Behind me, watching over the union he saved, sits the man who . . . made this day possible.[1]

—BARACK OBAMA, 2009

O N APRIL 19, 2005, President George W. Bush and fledgling US senator Barack Obama sat on the same sun-drenched outdoor stage in Springfield, Illinois, for the dedication of the Abraham Lincoln Presidential Library and Museum. The sparkling edifice offered state-of-the-art technology to rival that of the Walt Disney Company—hardly a surprise, since former Disney "imagineer" Bob Rogers had overseen the high-tech elements. The ALPLM exhibits featured an eerie holographic Lincoln, as well as several true-to-life Lincoln figures, including one seated beside Mary in a mock-up of the Ford's Theatre box.

Lincoln's "living" person was thus portrayed both as a disembodied, timeless spirit and as a finite physical man. His dead body was invoked too: an entire room of the vast complex—"40,000 square feet of space dedicated to Abraham Lincoln," as PBS anchor Ray Suarez told his viewers—was made over as a replica of the Old State Capitol rotunda as it looked in May 1865, with Lincoln lying in state. The black-and-silver coffin shimmered under the black-cloth canopy of the catafalque, and the words

"I would rather be assassinated on this spot than surrender it"—that is, the principle of equality in the Declaration of Independence—were inscribed overhead. To accommodate twenty-first-century sensibilities, this coffin remained closed.[2]

As the headliner on April 19, President Bush spoke for twenty minutes, praising Lincoln's defense of liberty and claiming his endorsement for the work of building democracy in other parts of the world, such as Iraq and Afghanistan. Just beginning his second term, Bush was relaxed and confident. He laughed that he had something in common with the sixteenth president: they had both been derided as hicks by the eastern press.

Barack Obama, in only his seventh week as the junior senator from Illinois, crammed a polished historical analysis of Lincoln's character and temperament into a five-minute talk. He came across as earnestly professorial, probing Lincoln's identity for what it might reveal about America's exceptional openness to talent. Bush was seeking Lincoln's mantle as leader of a world power. Obama was seeking Lincoln's idiosyncratic story as a way of publicizing his own. The travails of this "homely and awkward" man, said Obama, were "etched in every crease of his face, reflected in those haunted eyes." The sixteenth president's "painful self-awareness"—consciousness of his failings and limitations—had yielded an attitude of humility, a habit of welcoming new ideas. For all his early misgivings about black equality, and his slow lurch toward emancipation, he had ultimately stood firm in the face of "slavery's dark storm."[3]

Between the lines, Obama had disclosed something vital about his own trajectory, and about the way he would help to reconfigure Lincoln over the next half decade. He cared a lot more about the president's character than he did about exactly what kind of emancipator he was. Others might cavil about Lincoln's colonization plans, or his views on African Americans' rights, but Obama cared much more about Lincoln's experience of *self*-emancipation. He took Lincoln personally, as a model for finding one's distinctive American identity.

Asked by *Time* magazine to submit an essay amplifying his Springfield remarks, Obama claimed that his own humble beginnings and unlikely rise to national office resembled those of his famous forebear. "When I moved to Illinois 20 years ago to work as a community organizer, I had no money in my pockets and didn't know a single soul." The subsequent success of a black man "with a funny name," with "a father from Kenya and a mother from Kansas," was trumped only by that of "a child born in the backwoods of Kentucky with less than a year of formal education."

In the *Time* article, Obama also came up with a direct historical tie to Lincoln, binding them across the ages. Obama had just spoken in Galesburg, Illinois, site of Lincoln's fifth debate with Stephen Douglas in the 1858 US Senate race. Lincoln had lost that contest and probably never imagined that one day a black man would win it. Yet Lincoln's career had laid essential groundwork for Obama's later victory. His "arguments that day would result," nearly 150 years later, "in my occupying the same seat that he coveted. He may not have dreamed of that exact outcome. But I like to believe he would have appreciated the irony."[4]

ON SATURDAY, February 10, 2007, less than two years after the dedication of the Abraham Lincoln Presidential Library and Museum, the Springfield temperature dipped far below freezing on a cloudless blue day. Outside of Lincoln's Old State Capitol, a hatless Barack Obama, warmed by the heater hidden inside his podium, told thousands of excited supporters he was running for president. He had served seven years as a state senator in Springfield (1997–2004), and he had begun his one term as a senator in Washington in 2005. Lincoln had spent eight years as an Illinois state representative (1835–43) and one term in Washington as a congressman (1847–49).

The new candidate tethered his speech to Lincoln's great "house divided" address, delivered only a few hundred feet away in the Capitol's Hall of Representatives on June 16, 1858. The country was split between slavery and freedom, Lincoln had said, and the standoff could not last forever. Slavery would eventually either be permitted everywhere in the

United States or banned everywhere. If northerners just went about their business, allowing slavery's defenders to mold the "public heart" into not minding if the institution expanded, they would wake up one day to find they were living in slave states themselves.[5]

Taking Lincoln's theme of division and applying it to twenty-first-century America, Obama claimed it was politics in general, not any single issue, that had "divided us for too long," preventing us from being "one people, reaching for what's possible, building that more perfect union." If citizens did nothing, they'd end up with negativism: a "small" politics of petty point scoring and the "chronic avoidance of tough decisions."

The senator thrust Lincoln's name into the very sentence that announced his campaign: "In the shadow of the old State Capitol, where Lincoln once called on a house divided to stand together, where common hopes and common dreams still live, I stand before you today to announce my candidacy for president of the United States of America." Putting himself "in the shadow" of Lincoln's statehouse let Obama pay homage to Martin Luther King too: forty-four years earlier King had begun the "I Have a Dream" speech by placing himself in the figurative shadow of the great emancipator. Lincoln had "moved a nation" to expunge the line separating "slave and free"; King's civil-rights cohort had overcome the legal split between the races, giving twenty-first-century Americans the chance to take on their problems "as one people."

The young presidential hopeful reminded the chilled crowd why voters could support a first-term US senator who had served in Washington for barely two years: he offered the same simple, self-reliant beginnings as Lincoln. He'd come to Illinois as a young man "without money or family connections." His initial salary of $13,000 a year as a community organizer had kept him modestly lodged in genteel poverty. After a few years, like Lincoln, he had undertaken a legal career, having already demonstrated, like his predecessor, a grasp of "the power of words." A gift for language had eased each man's move from legal practice to political office.

Similarly, Obama let his Springfield audience ponder how much his

body resembled Lincoln's. "The life of a tall, gangly, self-made Springfield lawyer tells us that a different future is possible . . . beneath all the
differences of race and region, faith and station, we are one people." The
tall, self-made man on the platform believed that the racial difference
between him and Lincoln was dwarfed by the similarity of their lanky
frames and their upward trajectories. The bond between two Illinois politicians, across the centuries and across racial lines, stood for the links
that twenty-first-century Americans could forge among themselves.

SINCE 2005, critics had been pounding Obama for presuming to compare his life to Lincoln's. "There is nothing wrong with Barack Obama's
résumé," wrote *Wall Street Journal* columnist Peggy Noonan, a former
Reagan speechwriter, "but it is a log-cabin-free zone. So far it also is a
greatness-free zone." Save the highfalutin Lincoln talk until you have
achieved something, Noonan chided. She was on target about the men's
educations: Obama's private schooling had lifted him far above the son
of a subsistence farmer raised in the almost schooling-free zone of rural
Kentucky and Indiana. But the young candidate had never come close to
claiming any of Lincoln's "greatness." Moreover, Obama had *under*stated
the biographical and historical resemblances between him and Lincoln.[6]

Each man stood for something startlingly new in American politics.
Lincoln was the first president to spring from the ranks of the people
without brandishing educational credentials or military honors to grease
his path. This "naturally" groomed man—and unnatural-looking one—
had somehow climbed to the top without the usual markers of achievement. He seduced northeastern Republican gatekeepers in 1860 by
outthinking and outspeaking the stylish.

Obama presented another kind of novel identity: the first candidate
to declare with pride that he had sprung from an interracial and international couple. Globalization was embedded in his earliest experience. In
their persons, Lincoln the western man of nature, spawned by the most
ordinary of the people, and Obama the multicultural product of Kenya

and Kansas, embodied cutting-edge facts about a rapidly evolving world. Obama qualified as "postracial" not because race didn't matter any more, but because the ways it mattered couldn't be so easily pinned down. As the 2008 election would show, race alone could no longer block a black person's path to the presidency. Obama would take down the "whites only" sign at 1600 Pennsylvania Avenue.

In addition, Obama resembled Lincoln in political sensibility and historical placement. As young men entering public life, each had coped with the sense that his generation had missed the main event—in Lincoln's case, the Revolution and the founding of the nation (he was born three weeks before the fourth president, James Madison, took office); and in Obama's, the civil-rights movement's decade of victories over Jim Crow, from Montgomery in 1955 to Selma in 1965 (Obama was born in 1961).

Where the senator diverged dramatically from Lincoln was in freely publicizing his unusual biographical journey, placing it at the heart of his campaign. "In no other country on earth is my story even possible," he had said at the 2004 Democratic National Convention in Boston. To vote for Obama was to endorse America's, and Lincoln's, principle of the fair chance. It was to choose hope over cynicism, he said in Boston, "the hope of slaves sitting around a fire singing freedom songs," or of "a skinny kid with a funny name who believes that America has a place for him too." Obama implied in Boston that Illinois voters could make history by electing him to the US Senate in the fall, and many of those in the hall chanting "O-ba-ma" at the end of his speech expected to be supporting him someday for an office higher than senator.

A Lincoln transported to 2004 (and briefed on a century and a half of social change) would have been horrified not by Obama's blackness, but by a candidate's personal story pushing political principles to the margin. In 1860, Lincoln let William Dean Howells and other campaign writers take care of his biography. He would have agreed with Peggy Noonan about the virtue of keeping one's quirky self in the background.

In fact, Obama comfortably interwove identity and policy. He had written a book on each: *Dreams from My Father* (1995), on his creation of a stable cross-racial and multicultural self, and his quest to embed that self in a career of public service; *The Audacity of Hope* (2006), on how he approached the overriding issues of the day, and how Lincoln served him as the ultimate political practitioner and sage. Both books sketched out a campaign like the young Lincoln's (in the 1838 Lyceum speech) to build up social and political solidarity in a post-heroic age—laying a groundwork of trust across racial, regional, and party lines, preparing the way for a later run at reform.

As he began imagining a political career, Obama recognized his developing ties to Lincoln's political sensibility: navigate between moralizing certitudes of the Left and Right, bridge differences by listening to opponents but demand they engage in reasoned argument. "Emancipation" would now mean improving education, housing, and health care for all disadvantaged groups—an approach more likely, in the twenty-first-century political climate, to aid the black poor than race-specific proposals could. "Union" would mean locating common values shared by all Americans, whatever their disagreements. Lincoln was needed as the model for everyone's unobstructed quest for self-improvement. The old African American sense of a special bond with Lincoln, already mostly sloughed off in the late twentieth century, could be safely retired.

Giving up the group tie to Lincoln created an opening for individual blacks like Obama to rediscover his significance. In the emotional flourish that concludes *The Audacity of Hope*, Obama describes a visit to the Lincoln Memorial at night, calling to mind Jimmy Stewart's vigil at Lincoln's marble feet in *Mr. Smith Goes to Washington* (1939). But a child of the 1960s, Obama can't think of the Memorial without thinking about Martin Luther King. And it's King's martyrdom that seems to have kept Lincoln's sacrifice fresh in Obama's mind.

> At night, the great shrine is lit but often empty. Standing between marble columns, I read the Gettysburg Address and the Second Inaugural Address. I look out over the Reflecting Pool, imagining the crowd stilled by Dr. King's mighty cadence, and then beyond

that, to the floodlit obelisk and shining Capitol dome. And in that place, I think about America and those who built it. This nation's founders, who somehow rose above petty ambitions and narrow calculations to imagine a nation unfurling across a continent. And those like Lincoln and King, who ultimately laid down their lives in the service of perfecting an imperfect union.[7]

BARACK OBAMA'S inauguration in January 2009 took place three weeks before Lincoln's two hundredth birthday, and the forty-fourth president strode into office signaling his devotion to the sixteenth at every turn. On January 17, the Obamas rode into Washington in an inaugural train from Philadelphia to Washington, repeating the last part of Lincoln's trip in 1861 (without the secret, off-schedule passage through Baltimore). Obama took the oath of office on January 20 with his hand resting on the same Bible Lincoln had used. After his inaugural address, assorted members of Congress convened for a banquet of delicacies from the 1860s.

Perhaps the most striking Lincoln moment occurred on January 19, when television cameras covering the inaugural concert caught Obama loping diagonally up and across the steps of the Lincoln Memorial. Reaching the microphone, he thanked Lincoln for making his election possible. The sight of Daniel Chester French's statue rising up behind him summoned for many viewers the history of African American appearances at the Memorial, with the black president completing a trajectory launched seventy years earlier at the Easter Sunday concert of Marian Anderson.

Yet Obama's love for Lincoln provoked opposition from some blacks, who had voiced displeasure as soon as he declared himself a candidate in 2007. Four decades after his famous *Ebony* magazine article "Was Lincoln a White Supremacist?," Lerone Bennett Jr. appeared at a Covenant with Black America conference and informed an audience of thousands that Lincoln "would have been horrified" at the prospect of a black president, for he'd always wished to rid America of black people.

In 2000, Bennett had published a book-length version of his case in *Forced into Glory: Abraham Lincoln's White Dream*: Lincoln had sought to "deport" all African Americans—a plan Bennett thought worthy of the label "ethnic cleansing." True enough, Lincoln had used the word "deportation," but in the mid-nineteenth century that term didn't signify forced expatriation. Lincoln's colonization idea might merit scorn, but not because it was coercive. He had always made clear that he saw resettlement as voluntary, and no one at the time was confused on that score.[8]

In his probing PBS documentary *Looking for Lincoln* (2009), and in a concurrent essay titled "Abraham Lincoln on Race and Slavery," Henry Louis Gates Jr. gave Bennett a serious hearing. Gates noted the pain he'd felt himself at finding out that Lincoln, as late as 1862, had publicly urged black Americans to find another place to live. Yet Gates pivoted back to Lincoln, as Douglass and Du Bois had done before him. The fundamental fact about Lincoln was his capacity for growth, and over the course of his presidency he had grown steadily in his grasp of racial justice.[9]

Meanwhile, Obama's fondness for Lincoln sent many disgruntled conservatives to the anti-Lincoln works of Charles Adams and Thomas DiLorenzo. Since the early 2000s, these two writers had been vilifying Lincoln for trampling on state rights and personal liberties. Their Lincoln combined a love of big government and federal taxes with a tyrannical penchant for defying the Constitution and for waging war on innocent civilians.[10]

Adams relates that, as a child and college student, he was "force-fed Lincoln adoration," complete with worship of "the martyr and the dying God." Collective veneration of the nation's suffering servant had pulled the wool over Americans' eyes, blinding them to Lincoln's wily assault on the Republic. Adams saw no further use for Lincoln's body, but the assassination served his argument well. John Wilkes Booth could be compared to Brutus, for whom, as Adams put it, "the killing of a tyrant was a patriotic act."[11]

Adams shares with Lerone Bennett Jr. a lingering indignation at having been bamboozled as a child by the myth of the kindly emancipator.

DiLorenzo makes his kinship with Bennett explicit, calling Bennett's *Forced into Glory* "an especially powerful critique" of Lincoln the liberator. That book confirms DiLorenzo's belief that Lincoln wished to deport the slaves, not emancipate them, and cynically used his apparent concern for their welfare to camouflage his real goal of imposing the iron boot of an "omnipotent Lincolnian state."[12]

DiLorenzo's Lincoln also fought an utterly needless war in order to extend the power of his centralizing regime. Slavery had nothing to do with the Civil War, since Lincoln could have used his "dictatorial powers" to "spend tax dollars on compensated emancipation." DiLorenzo *needs* the president to have been a dictator so that he could have persuaded or commanded slave owners to give up their way of life without a fight. Having posited Lincoln's unanswerable authority, DiLorenzo can then conclude, "He never gave peaceful emancipation a chance."[13]

In the ideological climate following Obama's 2008 election, it's not surprising that his Lincoln-based appeal for a new politics of dialogue sounded to so many conservatives like diversionary cover for another expansion of big government. Liberals, meanwhile, eyeing the prospective prize of independent voters, could rejoice that so many conservatives seemed now to spurn even a center-right Lincoln—the business-friendly leader effusively celebrated by the Republican Party into the mid-twentieth century. In 1957, President Eisenhower's official inaugural program gave Lincoln a full page of small-print praise, noting that as he delivered his second inaugural address, his "gaunt frame was stooped, and his kindly face was stamped with sadness" at the war's casualties. Six weeks later, "the whole Nation mourned the loss of this great and noble man."[14]

In 2008, many liberals also rejoiced that Lincoln and Obama had become entwined as beacons of hope for a more progressive America. This idea was strikingly visualized by Bob Staake in "Reflection," the cover image for the *New Yorker's* postelection issue of November 17. It's a double sighting—of Lincoln and Obama. The tiny Lincoln statue is visible inside a glowing white Lincoln Memorial seen at night from the middle of the reflecting pool. Obama is depicted in the form of the illu-

minated "O" in the word "Yorker," the first letter of his name rising like
the moon in a star-studded sky and bestowing its light on the Memorial.
Change is in the air.

"Why is the cover great?" asked Arthur Hochstein in *Time* magazine.
"It doesn't do a victory dance. Rather, it whispers to the [liberal] reader . . .
'Everything's okay now—we have our country back.' It's set at night, a
time when creepy things happen, but also a time when people sleep, safe
and sound."[15]

IN THE 1990s, with rising public awareness of Lincoln's deeply held
antislavery convictions, Disneyland's *Great Moments with Mr. Lincoln*
looked more and more out of date. In 1992, historian Eric Foner took
his young daughter to the park, and was shocked at the anachronism
of *Great Moments.* The opening historical overview ignored the central
duality of the American past—slavery and freedom—and the Lincoln
figure's script made matters worse. The words were all his, but they'd
been cherry-picked to make him preoccupied with the threat to liberty
posed by internal divisions—not the threat to liberty posed by inequality
and discrimination. Dozens of times a day Lincoln spun a one-sided story
about himself. He needed liberating from his erroneous self-conception.

Thanks to a friend employed by Disney, Foner got through to company officials who took his complaint seriously. They promised to think
about the *Great Moments* problem, but first they asked for his help in
rewriting the historical introduction at Disney World's Hall of Presidents
in Orlando, Florida. Foner duly produced a new script that highlighted
the original promise of the Declaration of Independence—equality for
all men—and the centuries-long struggle to implement it, and his recast-
ing was accepted.

Disneyland came next. In Foner's retrospective view, the Rodney
King riots in nearby Los Angeles in April 1992 (following the beating by
police of a black motorist) led some at Disney to look kindly on modify-
ing *Great Moments.* In 1994, outlining a new opening narrative to bring

out "Lincoln's greatness," Foner explained to the company that Lincoln had risen to the occasion during the Civil War "by adopting the policies, including emancipation, necessary to preserve the Union, and by rallying the Northern people in speeches that linked the nation to the original ideals of liberty, equality, and opportunity."[16]

Disney had little to lose in bringing change to *Great Moments*. Attendance at the attraction had tanked since the 1970s—one more sign of the end of the Lincoln cult. (The exhibit had even been shut down from 1973 to 1975, as officials debated whether to get rid of it.) Sandy Spurgeon, who worked as a hostess at the exhibit through the 1980s and '90s, and saw the show "thousands of times," remembers only an occasional Opera House crowd running into the hundreds. The usual turnout for the fifty daily shows in summer—and half that number in winter—was twenty or thirty people. By the 1990s, Disneyland's president was freely admitting to the *Los Angeles Times* that *Great Moments* was "the least-trafficked attraction we have." Yet it was impossible to drop it. "We talked about removing [it in 1990]," the *Times* quoted him as saying, "and we got killed. People said it was not yours to make the decision."[17]

WITH A VOLUBLE PUBLIC committed to keeping *Great Moments*, but not interested in actually going to see it, Disney's imagineers were handed an unusual opportunity to try something different. They took their time—perhaps because in the late 1990s they were busy building California Adventure, a new park adjacent to Disneyland. In the year 2000, they got back in touch with Foner about a radical redesign of the Lincoln show. They would scrap the old one entirely and present a short drama featuring a fictional late-1863 encounter at the White House between Lincoln and several guests. His conversation with them would help him decide what to say in mid-November at the dedication of the Gettysburg Cemetery.

With Foner's urging, the group of guests in the new program came to include Frederick Douglass, along with photographer Mathew Brady and a fictional veteran of the Gettysburg battle named Jonathan Cunningham. Spectators would wear stereo headphones and experience the entire show from Private Cunningham's standpoint—as he sits for a Brady picture, as he meets Lincoln and Douglass, as he loses a leg in a battle. The dual themes of emancipation and of Lincoln's unassuming warmth with his guests would drive the program. The scripted dialogue, accompanied by photos of the principals, would culminate in a performance of the Gettysburg Address by the animatronic Lincoln—speaking in the historically correct tenor voice rather than the familiar baritone of Royal Dano.

Disney show writer Steven Spiegel crafted the script and ran it by Foner. They both wanted Frederick Douglass's visit to help Lincoln focus his thoughts on the Gettysburg speech. That placed the action in early November 1863, *after* the actual Lincoln received his invitation to speak at the cemetery dedication. But the actual Douglass had come to see Lincoln in August 1863. Foner assured Spiegel that it was fine to put Douglass in the White House after Lincoln received the Gettysburg offer. Resequencing known facts in a dramatic presentation was acceptable as long as it served a larger truth—in this case the truth that as he thought about his speech, Lincoln was already formulating the war's legacy: a new birth of freedom for all Americans (as he tells Douglass in the script).[18]

The revamped *More Great Moments with Mr. Lincoln* finally opened in July 2001. Spiegel's script brought home the central place of emancipation in Lincoln's quest for union, as well as the historic role of Brady's camera in Lincoln's rise to political power. Near the start of the show, Brady's photo of 1860 (see p. 7 of this book) is projected, and he speaks of the struggle to make his subject look good. His legs dominated his frame, and his ears and nose dominated his face. A straight-on shot, cut off at the thighs, would draw the viewer to his eyes and his mental force.

Brady's trouble picturing Lincoln points back to Woodrow Wilson's insight into the Lincoln paradox. He managed to represent the people visually by looking like none of them, and he managed to represent most northerners politically by seeing the nation as few could see it. Lincoln came the closest to taking it whole, synoptically, not through the eyes of an "interested" party.

In addition to supplying *More Great Moments* with the character of Frederick Douglass, Eric Foner provided the gist of the show's dialogue about emancipation: The president tells Douglass that in 1861 his purpose in pursuing the war was to protect the union, not to liberate the slaves. But with the Emancipation Proclamation in 1863, ending slavery emerged as an integral war aim. Douglass promises to help recruit black soldiers; Lincoln commends him, calls him "Frederick," and asserts that without them the war would likely end in Union defeat.[19]

The Spiegel-Foner edition of *More Great Moments* ran from 2001 to 2005, when it was shut down to make room for a fiftieth-anniversary program on Disneyland hosted by Donald Duck and actor Steve Martin. As Lincoln's 2009 bicentenary approached, Disney decided to build a next-generation "Autonomatronic" Lincoln figure—and to revert to the old history lesson and speech. Pilgrims and European immigrants, liberty and the threat to it from domestic weakness, were back in; slavery, emancipation, and African Americans were out.

A Disney official explained that *More Great Moments* had run afoul of the public. He didn't mention any opposition to the emancipation theme, or to the new dramatic structure of the show. He claimed that people just missed the deep ringing tones of Royal Dano. "We changed the voice in the previous show," said Tony Baxter, senior vice president for creative development at Disney Imagineering, "and we got tremendous negativity, so we brought back this voice, which has kind of been the voice of Abraham Lincoln for 45 years."[20]

In 2014, Disneyland's *Great Moments* was still unveiling its trusty Royal-Dano Lincoln three times every hour. This Lincoln had "reforgotten" slavery and emancipation, reverting to what he didn't know in 1965. Physically, the 2009 version of Lincoln's body sported a fleshier face and bigger shoulders than the previous model had, making him even less like the wrinkled, hollow-cheeked man of the 1860s. He could now swing his arms for emphasis, but he still couldn't reach up to grasp his lapels.

When I saw this reconstructed Lincoln in 2012, I was struck by how he draws attention to himself by slowly swiveling his head, apparently gazing at one audience member after another. He looks realer than ever, with sixteen miniature motors subtly manipulating his silicone skin as he speaks. His chest swells, his fingers twitch delicately, and if you sit in the front row you can occasionally hear him breathing in and out. When he finally sits down and the lights fade out, it's easy to remember—at least if you grew up under the thriving Lincoln cult of the 1950s and early 1960s—that this president made it his mission to seek out his fellow citizens.

A MOMENTOUS transatlantic telephone call in 2010 may have been responsible for convincing Daniel Day-Lewis to play Abraham Lincoln in Steven Spielberg's film of 2012. Hard at work in New York City on the *Lincoln* screenplay, Tony Kushner was staring at a photo he'd just received from Spielberg. It was a shot of Day-Lewis, whom Spielberg and Kushner had recently met in Ireland. They'd flown there at Day-Lewis's invitation—he'd read Kushner's script in 2009 and liked it—and they hoped to persuade the two-time Academy Award Best Actor to accept the role of the president. After meeting with them for two or three days—including a stop at a pub, where Spielberg had taken the photo with his cell phone—the inveterately cautious Day-Lewis would only promise to keep mulling over the offer.

Back in New York, Kushner was pondering the picture of Day-Lewis. It showed him in profile, and Kushner was flabbergasted when he realized that it captured Lincoln's silhouette as much as Day-Lewis's. And the actor wasn't wearing any makeup. Walking through Greenwich Village, he got the actor on the phone in Ireland and related his Lincoln sighting. "Look in the mirror," he said. "God is telling you something."[21]

After consulting his mirror and getting pleas from other luminaries, Day-Lewis succumbed to the swelling tide and took the lead role in *Lincoln*. The film gave the president's physical persona the most careful

on-screen attention it had received since Henry Fonda's performance
in *Young Mr. Lincoln* in 1939. And the combined talents of Spielberg,
Day-Lewis, and Kushner (the latter in frequent touch with Doris Kearns
Goodwin, who amicably "badgered" him about getting his Lincoln to tell
stories), created a fictive president who embodies not the "real" Lincoln—
an impossible goal—but an eerily "true" Lincoln. Viewing the film, you
periodically have to remind yourself that this is *not* the man who mas-
tered mid-nineteenth-century northern politics, voiced enduring American ideals, and put the commonweal ahead of his own well-being.[22]

Born in 1946, Spielberg grew up, like most American children of his
vintage, pledging allegiance to Abraham Lincoln. He was a small boy
when an uncle took him to the Lincoln Memorial. The statue scared him.
"I was only five or six," he recalled in 2012, "and it was so much bigger
than me . . . I remember being afraid of that space, but just before we
left, I dared to look up at the face of Abraham Lincoln. The second I saw
that visage, I relaxed completely. That's the first impression of Lincoln
I ever had." Later, as a student and Eagle Scout, he took Lincoln as a
leader and "brilliant thinker," and held him up as a "role model."[23]

At first, Day-Lewis had found the idea of playing Lincoln "preposterous," "outlandish." The distance between him and Lincoln seemed
impassable. Born in London in 1957, as a child he knew Lincoln only
from the Civil War trading cards contained in bright-pink packs of
Bazooka bubble gum. But Kushner's multidimensional take on Lincoln
as politician, thinker, wit, and family man made the offer tantalizing, as
did Day-Lewis's exposure to Lincoln's own prose.

Still he hesitated. Making the project work meant locating a plausible
approximation of Lincoln's "voice"—not the mere timbre or pitch of it,
but the full resonance of it as an instrument and sign of character. Acts
of speech, for Day-Lewis, emerged from the physical and moral being
of the whole person. Body language interacted with the sound of words.

Finally Lincoln's "voice" came to him. Day-Lewis didn't experience
a *sighting* of Lincoln, as Spielberg had, but a *hearing* of him. As he
explained it, he actually caught a version of Lincoln speaking into his

"mind's ear." Then he worked on embedding that particular Lincoln in his own body. This wasn't the only true Lincoln to be found, said Day-Lewis, but it was the authentic Lincoln that he had been given. Unlike Benjamin Chapin a century earlier, Day-Lewis didn't aim for verisimilitude. Day-Lewis preferred the goal of original impersonation, not imitation of the original. Creative interpretation was more likely than imitation to represent—make present—the dead hero.[24]

At the start of the film we hear Lincoln's voice before we see him. It's nighttime in early February 1865, and the camera has zoomed in on Private Harold Green, a uniformed black soldier, busily describing the most recent action he's seen in the war. A member of the 116th US Colored Regiment, he's about to ship out from Washington to North Carolina for the Battle of Wilmington, along with the rest of his unit, which we see milling around in the background. The off-camera Lincoln (we presume that's who it is) asks him his name, in the soft, high-register voice that Day-Lewis discovered for him.

Gradually the camera retreats to reveal another black soldier who has joined the conversation, and as it pulls further away we get a glimpse of the back of the man whom they're addressing. He's casually sitting on a raised platform only a few feet in front of them. They're looking up at him, but not in awe. They're freely interacting with a welcoming, unpretentious man. Already, before getting our first glimpse of Lincoln's face, we've learned the most essential truth about his body: its accessibility to his public. The first Republican chief magistrate—head citizen—took his republican station seriously.

Almost two minutes of this scene go by before Spielberg cuts to a front view of the president. Day-Lewis sits on a nondescript bench near the edge of a reviewing stand. His stovepipe hat rests on the bench beside him, and in the dim light of evening it resembles in its shape and lines the simple wooden barrels arrayed beside the bench. This chief executive occupies not a throne, but a common man's perch.

Day-Lewis instantly evokes Lincoln, but not because he matches up with him completely in physical appearance. The *Lincoln* makeup crew did spend seventy-five minutes each morning dressing him and preparing his hair and the furrows on his face. They used the "stretch and stipple" technique, painting on a substance that can be molded with the fingers into wrinkles on the brow or crow's-feet beside the eyes. These slight alterations did give Day-Lewis some of Lincoln's drawn and weary mien, but as chief makeup artist Lois Burwell put it, this was "not a look-alike" effort, but an attempt to capture "the *feel* of Mr. Lincoln." The actor sitting on the bench *looks* like Lincoln mostly because he *seems* like Lincoln—approachable and attentive, fully at the soldiers' disposal.[25]

The second black soldier, Corporal Ira Clark, feels comfortable enough with the president to press him about racial inequality: true, equal pay in the army has finally been enacted, but what about equal entry into the officers' corps, and what about the vote? Lincoln changes the subject, asking Clark what he'll do after the war. The corporal is sure only that he won't settle for the job of bootblack or barber. The mention of hair cutting gives Lincoln his chance to lighten the exchange. With a little grin, he says, "I've yet to find a man could cut mine so it'd make any difference." Private Green appreciates the levity and comes right back at the president, in a jocular tone: "You got springy hair for a white man." Lincoln loves the reference to his body and ups the comical ante: "Yes, I do. My last barber hanged himself. And the one before that. Left me his scissors in his will."[26]

Soon the camera pulls back to show that Lincoln's bench rests beneath a canopy, and suddenly the reviewing stand looks a lot like a gallows. The vertical and diagonal timbers behind Lincoln frame his body perfectly and foreshadow the fate, only two months away, to which viewers in the theater know he is condemned. They now suspect that this film, no matter what its chronological coverage, will take up the iconic American story of Lincoln's death.

Up walk two young white soldiers, hemming and hawing as they grope for words. They broach the topic of Lincoln's remarks at Gettysburg, which they both witnessed fifteen months earlier. "Could you hear what I said [there]?" Lincoln asks them. The first soldier launches into a mechanical recitation of the Gettysburg Address, but the president, disconcerted by the display of rote memory, tries twice to stop the speech—as if to say (to the film audience as much as the soldiers), "Stop worshipping my oratory and start thinking about what it means. I didn't ask if you could *remember* my words, I asked if you could *hear* them." The two white soldiers don't make it as far as "the new birth of freedom," because all the troops are summoned to their units.

Having heard Lincoln interrupt the white soldier's recitation, Corporal Clark, the African American cavalryman, picks up the thread and finishes the speech. He turns it into a lesson for the president, asking him, in effect, if *he* can hear it: "That we here highly resolve that these dead shall not have died in vain." This time Lincoln doesn't try to stop the speech. "That this nation, under God, shall have a new birth of freedom." Lincoln is seized by his own words, feeling the force in them. As Clark disappears into a drifting fog, the camera slowly zooms in on Day-Lewis's right shoulder from the back. He turns his head slightly to his right to reveal the strategic movement of his eyelid. First a blink, then a widely opened eye: accompanied by a meditative piano piece, Lincoln is contemplating the course of black freedom.

THE NIGHTTIME scene at the gallows-reviewing stand announces Lincoln's proximity to the people and signals the intertwining of his Gettysburg speech, his body's fate, and the future of African American freedom. In the next scene, Secretary of State Seward (played by David Strathairn) rides with Lincoln in an open carriage, wondering why the president is so determined to rush the Thirteenth Amendment (abolishing slavery) through the House of Representatives. It makes more sense to Seward to put off the vote until the new, more heavily Republican House convenes later in the year. Yet Lincoln remains committed to acting on the amendment before the end of February, keeping his reasons to himself. "I like our chances now," he tells Seward.

Two more nighttime scenes follow directly, both of them intimate and ominous like the first. At the reviewing stand, it was the film's viewer, not Lincoln, who sensed that his time was limited. Now death squeezes its way into Lincoln's consciousness. We see Abraham chatting with his wife Mary (played by Sally Field) as they sit comfortably in her small, shadowy boudoir, warmly lit on a chilly evening. Her husband is stretching out in a signature Lincoln pose, one of his legs extended full length to the top of another chair, the other bent and resting on an ottoman. After 1865, Americans were never allowed to forget that the martyred president had been beloved in his own day for his contemplative calm and his boyish simplicity, traits signaled in prints, plays, and films by letting him lie on his back, or lean back in a chair, propping his feet up on a tree, a wall, or a piece of furniture.

The topic for Mary and Abraham's conversation is a recurrent dream well known to American newspaper readers in April 1865. It's the fast-moving-ship dream that the real Lincoln discussed with his cabinet on the morning of April 14. Kushner's script makes Lincoln worried about the excessive speed of the ship as it hurtles toward the distant shore—a concern that he eagerly unloads on Mary so that she can fret about it with him. These spouses are often depicted as opposites: irrational, tempestuous Mary; and rational, long-suffering Abraham. But they shared, among other things, a passion for the interpretation of dreams, especially *his* dreams. Analyzing them helped sustain their bond. Her readiness to absorb his worries let them feel close. We can tell these two people are deeply connected by the play of their minds as they dissect, and disagree about, the ship dream. Mary can't help dwelling on the threat of assassination. Once she has gripped that idea, Abraham can wave away his anxiety about the speeding ship and get back to affairs of state.

The next nighttime scene continues developing the death theme. Having left Mary's boudoir, where the couple commiserated but never touched, Abraham seeks out his eleven-year-old son, Tad, sleeping on the floor of his office. Lincoln ambles up to Tad with awkward, shuffled steps and slowly, creakily bends down to sit beside him by the fire. He picks up the two photographic glass plates that Tad was viewing before nodding

Lincoln *the film grounds the president's wartime well-being in his mostly wordless physical intimacy with Tad, as suggested by this retouched 1864 Anthony Berger shot of them examining a photo album.*

off, and lets the flames illuminate them. They show images of slave children. He clears away the toy soldiers strewn about the child, making room for himself to lie down.

Then he revives the boy with a kiss on his forehead, the signal for Tad to roll onto his father's back. The camera zooms in on the arm of a chair that Lincoln grabs for leverage as he rises up slowly, limb by limb, with his son clinging to his neck. Tad is awake enough to say, "Papa I wanna see Willie" (his dead older brother, lost at age eleven in 1862). "Me too, Taddie," Lincoln whispers, "but we can't." "Why not?" "Willie's gone. Three years now. He's gone." Neither of them has recovered from Willie's death. They cling to each other in his absence. Abraham's grief over Willie ghosts all his steps.[27]

KUSHNER'S SCREENPLAY keeps Lincoln's public work tethered to his private life. The president gathers strength for the battle in the House of Representatives by hugging his young son, by dumping his anxieties on his wife, by telling his stories and jokes, by pondering one of Euclid's common notions with two soldiers in the telegraph office: "Things that are equal to the same thing are equal to each other," he tells them. (Read: since blacks are human and whites are human, they're equal to each other.) All the while, the president oversees the dishing out of patronage appointments to ensure enough votes for the Thirteenth Amendment. He's a master at finding the right kind of appeal for each man—moral or material (never cash, just jobs). Always the smartest thinker and tactician in the room, he outreasons and outwits hesitant cabinet members and legislators.

The film could have left Lincoln at his victory in the House, savoring the approaching constitutional end to slavery. Instead, the script depicts the liberator's final move, months later, on the subject of black freedom: publicly endorsing suffrage for some African American men. It's early evening on April 14, 1865, and Lincoln is bantering with friends in a White House sitting room about his April 11 speech on Reconstruction. They note that Thaddeus Stevens had criticized it for not granting the vote to all black men, but House Speaker Schuyler Colfax commends the president for being the first chief executive in American history to endorse even limited black suffrage.

Viewers are left with a Lincoln moving into the next stage of emancipation, advancing from the negative liberty of the Thirteenth Amendment—no more slavery—to the positive liberty of the right to vote. With that, a cheerful Lincoln scurries off for Ford's Theatre, telling his friends he has to depart, though he'd rather stay. He shuffles down the long hallway, landing his flat feet on the carpet, not his heels. It's the last time Colfax or the film's viewers will see him alive.

The mistake of some writers on Lincoln, from Herndon to Vidal, has been to suppose that humanizing the iconic hero—turning the monument back into a man—means cataloguing his flaws. There's no reason *not* to show his flaws, as Kushner does with graphic precision in a battle scene between Abraham and Mary. They're arguing about whether to permit their grown son Robert to enlist in the army. Abraham assures Mary that Robert will get a safe spot on General Grant's staff, but she is convinced that some lethal shred of shrapnel, or the same infection that killed Willie, will seek him out and find him. The dispute degenerates quickly. If Robert dies in the army, she says, she won't be able to forgive her husband, whose egregious sins multiply the longer she speaks. He counters by telling her to think about others for once, not just herself.

Finally, Abraham screams her into submission, tossing his arms about like a crazed dervish. Once he has silenced her, he coldly adds that his grief over their young son matched hers heartache for heartache, but he was forced to suppress it so that he could keep living. "I wanted to crawl . . . into the vault with his coffin," he taunts, measuring his sorrow against hers. The fight ends without reconciliation. Over the weeks to come they realize that their joint sorrow has taken too large a toll on their marriage. Riding in an open carriage in early April 1865, they agree to try, at long last, to give up being servants to their grief.

The Abraham versus Mary quarrel reveals flaws in both spouses, and thus humanizes them both, but it is not typical of the way Kushner's script makes Lincoln a real human being. His writing and Day-Lewis's acting bring the transcendent American symbol down to earth by rooting him in his body—including his dead body as it lies on William Clark's bed at the Petersen house on April 15, 1865.

The deathbed scene lasts less than a minute, but that's long enough to portray a simple man reduced to the final simplicity. His body has expired on the sheets of a borrowed bed, his head resting on a blood-stained pillow. The tableau-vivant gathering of friends and family is wholly secular. The Reverend Phineas Gurley, who at Edwin Stanton's request uttered a prayer for Lincoln at the actual death-bed, is omitted.

Yet Spielberg leaves hints of the religious sentiment that per-meated the room in 1865. A bright white light shines down on Lin-coln from above. Although he is lying on his back—with his beige nightshirt pulled up to reveal his calves—his knees are bent and his legs are pushed unnaturally over to his right, where they lie side-

Alexander Gardner photo of Lincoln, November 8, 1863.

ways on the bed. This was not the position he would have died in. He has been placed in this pose.

The careful placement of the corpse will invoke for some viewers familiar with traditional Christian art the knees-bent pose of Jesus as he expires on the cross. For others it will signify the fragility of an utterly human Lincoln, the imposing physical specimen reduced, at the end of his "pilgrimage road" (in the phrase of his favorite poem "Mortality," by William Knox), to the common end. The Clark bedroom scene confirms the film's through line, beginning at the gallows-reviewing stand. The president's death asserts the meaning of his life as martyrdom to liberty.

The tone of veneration built into the film's portrayal of the warm father, the witty storyteller, the peerless politician, and the sacrificial servant didn't prevent it from capturing the real man. Kushner built his script on the conviction that "full, open-hearted affection" for Lincoln is fully deserved. Day-Lewis agreed: "I never thought it possible to love a man I've never met . . . I've had reverence for historical figures, and I've had heroes . . . but Lincoln was a man I grew to love. That was a unique experience in my life." In the film's official featurette, released in January 2013, Day-Lewis added, "It's the man himself that invites you, because he was so open . . . [he was] insanely accessible" at a time when it was "physically very dangerous to be accessible."[28]

The 2013 Academy Awards telecast took place on February 24, 2013, and forty mil-

Daniel Day-Lewis's pensive Lincoln.

lion Americans watched Daniel Day-Lewis win his third Oscar for Best Actor, the most for any male performer in the eighty-five-year history of the awards. His fellow actors leapt to their feet in a standing ovation, as if to say they had rarely seen anyone command a role so masterfully, with every turn of phrase and every gesture. Day-Lewis created a Lincoln that future generations may take as a treasured cultural inheritance.

A CERTIFIED MASTERWORK, almost universally praised by critics, *Lincoln* showed its cultural reach by provoking some well-made YouTube spoofs and a memorable *Saturday Night Live* parody. Lincoln himself would have enjoyed the humor of "Impatient Lincoln," a two-minute video satirizing Spielberg's trailer, which had featured Day-Lewis's president bellowing the words "now, now, now" and pointing his finger angrily at those who doubted the urgency of passing the Thirteenth Amendment. Produced by Flashback Films, "Impatient Lincoln" depicted other moments when Lincoln couldn't help barking "now, now, now"—when a chess opponent was taking too long for a move, when a kitchen maid told him breakfast wouldn't come for half an hour, and so on.

In the five-minute *Saturday Night Live* sketch, writer Seth Meyers and comic Louis C. K. showed, perhaps for the first time ever, that it's possible to honor Lincoln's sacrifice while making fun both of him *and* of his assassination. Louis C. K. put on Lincoln's beard, mole, and familiar duds—black hat, black coat, black tie—just enough to signify "Lincoln" without seriously trying to look like him. But his key move was to engage Lincoln's worries from the president's point of view.

Speaking into a handheld mike, he played his Lincoln as a comedian dredging up his thoughts about death, uttering them in the unmistakable idiom of 2012: "One thing I'm really sure of is that someone's going to murder me. I just know I'm totally getting murdered. This is not even a question. Like, when they murder, whoever murders me, when I get murdered, it's just going to say, 'it happened,' and you're just going to know what 'it' is."

This bit played on the preoccupation that had gnawed at countless northerners on April 15, 1865, the day of Lincoln's death: knowing that he had thought about assassination in the abstract, they wondered if he'd sensed it was really coming in that blossoming spring of Union victory. It comforted them to think he'd had an inkling of his fate. They wanted him to have known about it ahead of time. The ideal death took place only after a person had prepared for it.

Louis C. K.'s Lincoln knows he's going to be murdered, and he knows why: for years he's taken the risky path of preaching equality in a nation split between slavery and freedom. Reconciled to dying for the founding American principle that everyone was born equal, Louis C. K.'s Lincoln feels sorry for the detectives who will go out looking for his murderer. They'll face an endless search, since the killer could be anyone among the millions who applaud the inequality and injustice of slavery. Louis C. K.'s Lincoln imagines a bedraggled investigator assigned to the hunt, sizing up the futile task ahead: "Let's see, who might have done it, oh, I don't know, everybody from the middle of the country down, maybe they, maybe one of them did it, maybe they had a motive like, I [Lincoln] ruined the whole way they do everything."[29]

IN 2012, Lincoln the emancipator found his interpreter in Day-Lewis and his screenwriter in Kushner, just as, in the late 1930s, Lincoln the defender of freedom found his actor in Raymond Massey and his writer in Robert Sherwood. *Abe Lincoln in Illinois* supplied a heroic face of the nation for the fight against fascism, while Spielberg's *Lincoln* enshrined the liberal symbol from the heady days of civil-rights struggles—a symbol shunned by many in the 1970s and '80s and rediscovered in the 1990s. After *Abe Lincoln in Illinois* appeared in 1940, it took seven decades for Hollywood to produce another feature film on the mature Lincoln. One wonders whether Day-Lewis's acknowledged mastery of the role—a judgment that midcentury critics had also conferred on Massey—may block another serious Lincoln film for decades to come.

In the meantime, Lincoln's image will circulate freely through American and global popular culture, turning up across the spectrum from theatrical releases to video games, all of them packaged for home entertainment systems, personal computers, and mobile devices. Much of Timur Bekmambetov's *Abraham Lincoln: Vampire Hunter* (2012), a film released six months before Spielberg's, actually looked like a video game. This adaptation of Seth Grahame-Smith's 2010 novel played cleverly on the president's actual prowess with an ax, setting him in motion as a fearsome antislavery superhero ("president by day, hunter by night" said the movie poster). The vampires had chosen sides in the North-South conflict, cottoning to the slaveholders, whose enchained chattels supplied a steady source of blood. The vampires had also killed Lincoln's mother, giving him a second reason to hunt them down—vengeance as well as hatred of slavery.

Vampire Hunter did not rival Spielberg's *Lincoln* for critical or commercial success in the United States, but it alerted many viewers to the creative world of video games that has lately reached new sophistication in graphic design and historical reference. Dozens of video games have mentioned Lincoln, but Ken Levine's award-winning "first-person-shooter" game *BioShock Infinite* (2013) plays on Lincoln's body with humor and invention. This is the third BioShock game in a best-selling franchise that began in 2007, with Lincoln as a symbol of resistance for the "Vox Populi," a group of dissenters battling a white-only elite of "Founders" who have in effect seceded from the United States and are running their own cloud city of "Columbia." The Founders cherish John Wilkes Booth as a hero and saint, and revile Lincoln as a devil (public depictions of him in Columbia give him menacing horns).[30]

Like *Vampire Hunter*, *BioShock Infinite* appeals to the image of Lincoln the emancipator as a way of draping some gruesomely violent entertainment in the mantle of a good cause. The two portrayals also play freely on the historical fact that President Lincoln, rightly remembered as a man of peace, also distinguished himself as a warrior. American slavery was destroyed because he used his armies to defeat its supporters on the ground, not because it somehow expired of its own anachronistic weight. With his Emancipation Proclamation in 1863, Lincoln declared, in effect, that the war for reunion had become a war against slavery too, and in November 1864 his own vox populi, given the chance to turn him out of office, reelected him by a comfortable margin.

FIVE MONTHS LATER, at Lincoln's death, most of those who had voted for him thought it was now a good time for him to depart. Already, as Ralph Waldo Emerson said four days after Lincoln expired, "the terror and ruin" of his passing were "burning into glory" around him. But as the years passed, many came to see that Lincoln still had vital work to do. He might have succeeded where Andrew Johnson failed: reknitting the country while somehow shielding African Americans from violence and extending their freedom to include a measure of political, if not social, equality.

Yet even if Lincoln hadn't completed his work in April 1865, he exemplified, more fully than anyone before him, the ideal republican life course: self-improvement in youth, public service in adulthood, and sacrifice for the people at the peak of his powers. For one who had worried in his early thirties about having "done nothing to make any human being remember that he had lived," he'd come through rather better than he could have hoped for—easily surpassing his goal, as his friend Joshua Speed remembered it, of connecting "his name with something that would redound to the interest of his fellow man."[31]

A Note on Sources

WHILE THERE is no extensive literature on Lincoln's body as such, countless books by scholars and popular writers have touched on the theme, and many of these are referenced in the endnotes. A massive output of work has described the assassination, the deathbed, the mourning rituals, and the memorials to Lincoln written and built, but surprisingly little of it has assessed the range of meanings that black and white Americans gave to his "sacred remains."

A small sample of the secondary sources on the funeral period that proved helpful to me (in addition to those mentioned in the endnotes) are David B. Chesebrough, *No Sorrow like Our Sorrow: Northern Protestant Ministers and the Assassination of Lincoln* (Kent, OH: Kent State University Press, 1994); Carolyn L. Harrell, *When the Bells Tolled for Lincoln: Southern Reaction to the Assassination* (Macon, GA: Mercer University Press, 1997); Shirley Samuels, *Facing America: Iconography and the Civil War* (New York: Oxford University Press, 2004), especially chapter 5, "Lincoln's Body"; James L. Swanson, *Bloody Crimes: The Chase for Jefferson Davis and the Death Pageant for Lincoln's Corpse* (New York: Morrow/HarperCollins, 2010); and Thomas Reed Turner, *Beware the People Weeping: Public Opinion and the Assassination of Abraham*

Lincoln (Baton Rouge: Louisiana State University Press, 1982). Martha Hodes, *Mourning Lincoln* (New Haven, CT: Yale University Press, forthcoming 2015), is sure to contribute to our grasp of the funeral era.

The avid study of historical "memory" since the 1980s sparked important work on Americans' and non-Americans' remembering of Lincoln, including Richard Carwardine and Jay Sexton, eds., *The Global Lincoln* (New York: Oxford University Press, 2011); Betsy Erkkila, "Lincoln in International Memory," in *The Cambridge Companion to Abraham Lincoln*, ed. Shirley Samuels (New York: Cornell University, 2012), 155–82; Barry Schwartz, *Abraham Lincoln and the Forge of National Memory* (Chicago: University of Chicago Press, 2000), and *Abraham Lincoln in the Post-heroic Era: History and Memory in Late Twentieth-Century America* (Chicago: University of Chicago Press, 2008; and Merrill D. Peterson, *Lincoln in American Memory* (New York: Oxford University Press, 1994).

Peterson's comprehensive account—which built deftly on such earlier works as Roy P. Basler, *The Lincoln Legend: A Study in Changing Conceptions* (Boston: Houghton Mifflin, 1935)—proved essential for my book, as he makes at least brief mention of nearly everything to do with his subject from 1865 to the 1980s. His broad coverage permitted me to focus more pointedly than he could on a theme such as Lincoln's body, while benefiting from many of his insights and formulations.

Historian David Blight's trenchant review of Peterson's book in the *Journal of American History* (December 1994, pp.1265–67) made me realize that the best way to build on Peterson was to show how Americans' conceptions of Lincoln were actually put to use after 1865. Among the most significant uses, Lincoln was drafted into campaigns to support, or oppose, extending civic equality to black people. Blight's works on Frederick Douglass and on Americans' memories of the Civil War—especially *Race and Reunion: The Civil War in American Memory* (Cambridge, MA: Belknap Press of Harvard University Press, 2001)—convinced me that the story of Lincoln's body had to follow two tracks that had become distinguishable as early as 1860. From the time of Lincoln's nomination for the presidency, African Americans and white Americans developed intersecting but independent approaches to Lincoln and to what made his body so memorable.

On black-white variations in perceptions and memories of Lincoln, I've learned from many books and articles, including the following works not mentioned in the endnotes: Ira Berlin and Leslie Harris, eds., *Slavery in New York* (New York: New Press, 2005), especially chapter 10, "Securing Freedom: The Challenges of Black Life in Civil War New York," by Iver Bernstein, 289–324; Allen C. Guelzo, "How Abe Lincoln Lost the Black Vote," *Journal of the Abraham Lincoln Association* 25 (Winter 2004): 1–22; Steven Hahn, "But What Did the Slaves Think of Lincoln?" in *Lincoln's Proclamation: Emancipation Reconsidered*, ed. William A. Blair and Karen Fisher Younger (Chapel Hill: University of North Carolina Press, 2009), 102–19; Edna Greene Medford, "'Some Satisfactory Way': Lincoln and Black Freedom in the District of Columbia," *Washington History* 21 (2009): 4–21; and Barry Schwartz, "Collective Memory and History: How Abraham Lincoln Became a Symbol of Racial Equality," *Sociological Quarterly* 38 (Summer 1997): 469–96.

All writers on Lincoln depend on the documentary collections assembled by the most tireless of their scholarly peers. I drew on four of them for information and also for inspiration: perusing books like these, one witnesses the actual historical record being assembled. Michael Burlingame's two-thousand-page biography *Abraham Lincoln: A Life* (Baltimore: Johns Hopkins University Press, 2008), two volumes, available online from the Lincoln Studies Center of Knox College, cites an extraordinary range of primary sources and stands as both a breakthrough biography of Lincoln and a virtual archive of commentary on him.

Herndon's Informants: Letters, Interviews, and Statements about Abraham Lincoln, edited by Douglas L. Wilson and Rodney O. Davis (Urbana: University of Illinois Press, 1998) contains a treasure trove of memories of those who knew or crossed paths with Lincoln in his young adulthood. The volume celebrates William Herndon's devotion to his friend and mentor, and in transcribing and contextualizing 634 documents it exemplifies the highest achievement in scholarly editing.

So does the indispensable *Recollected Words of Abraham Lincoln*, edited by Don E. Fehrenbacher and Virginia Fehrenbacher (Stanford, CA: Stanford University Press, 1996), a brave effort to rate the reliability of words attributed to Lincoln by friends and acquaintances. A compelling treatise on the question of how we know what we think we know about the past, *Recollected Words* argues implicitly for protecting Lincoln's well-documented words from adulteration by the supposed statements put into his mouth after his death by others—some of whom quite naturally wished to demonstrate for posterity how close they had been to the Great Man and his inmost thoughts.

The ten volumes published by the Freedmen and Southern Society Project at the University of Maryland—under the general title *Freedom: A Documentary History of Emancipation, 1861–1867*—gather thousands of documents, some of which throw into poignant relief the hopes that many slaves placed in the Lincoln of their dreams. Expertly contextualized by the editors, the records often reveal the startling ways in which emancipation actually took place under the ultimate aegis of Lincoln's policy making. For example, the volume titled *The Black Military Experience*, edited by Ira Berlin, Joseph P. Reidy, and Leslie S. Rowland (Cambridge: Cambridge University Press, 1982), shows that the successful recruitment policy in the border states had undermined slavery so effectively by 1864 that some black men just walked away from slavery without bothering to enlist in the army. In Missouri, white legislators tried unsuccessfully to compel all black men who'd left their masters to enlist (p. 190).

Along with the documentary works, I benefited immensely from the many published collections of Lincoln images. Among those not mentioned in the endnotes, I recognize with pleasure the astonishing quality of the volumes published by photo collector Frederick Hill Meserve and his descendants for the last century. Meserve's privately issued *The Photographs of Abraham Lincoln* appeared in 1911 "on heavy rag paper," as

Carl Sandburg wrote in the 1944 popular edition, "with durable boards, cased, the type large bold-face, the pages wide-margined, $35 a copy, and the edition limited to one hundred copies" (p.23).

Dorothy Meserve Kunhardt and Philip B. Kunhardt Jr. published a striking photographic record of the assassination and funeral period titled *Twenty Days* (New York: Harper & Row, 1965, reissued in 1993); and Philip B. Kunhardt III, Peter W. Kunhardt, and Peter W. Kunhardt Jr. issued, among other books and films, the historically informed *Looking for Lincoln: The Making of an American Icon* (New York: Knopf, 2008) and the visually innovative *Lincoln, Life-Size* (New York: Knopf, 2009), which includes Harold Holzer's excellent brief history of published Lincoln photo collections.

Among the many other useful books of Lincoln images, one stands out for its scintillating reproductions and skillful contextualizing: Harold Holzer, ed., *Lincoln and New York* (New York: New-York Historical Society, 2009), which includes both the editor's masterly "The Lincoln Image: Made in New York" (pp.126–67) and Michael Kammen's probing treatment of the funeral events: "Mourning for a Lost Captain: New York City Comes to Terms with a National Tragedy" (pp.226–61).

The cultural distance traversed over the century between the centenary of 1909 and the bicentenary of 2009 can be neatly measured by contrasting the respectful historical analysis of Lincoln in the twenty-first-century Holzer and Kunhardt volumes to the reverential celebration contained in Francis Trevelyan Miller's *Portrait Life of Lincoln* (Springfield, MA: Patriot, 1910). "Sit down with me and turn these pages in reverie," Miller tells the reader in the "Introductory," for the pictures will reveal "the strongest character that American civilization has produced . . . he may justly be entitled The Greatest American."

THE BASIC SOURCES for this book are the newspapers, magazines, books, illustrations, photographs, films, and sculptures that brought images of Lincoln's body, as well as extensive commentary about it, to masses of Americans from the mid-nineteenth century to the present. Diaries, personal journals, and private letters also come into play when they shed light on public perceptions. There can be no sharp distinction, in any case, between public and private texts, since even the "private" ones often circulated among small numbers of citizens, and hence helped shape ideas and feelings about Lincoln's body and about the body politic. Blacks and whites—along with some Asian Americans, Latino Americans, and Native Americans for whom documentary evidence is unavailable, not yet assembled, or simply overlooked—created incipiently public meanings about Lincoln every time they placed a picture of him on a wall of their private dwellings.

Fortunately for me, online databases expanded dramatically during the years I worked on this book, making it possible to canvass a large number of African American and white periodicals and newspapers. Accessible Archives, African American Newspapers (1827–1998), Chronicling America, The Making of America, 19th Century US Newspapers, and ProQuest—each of them containing many papers or journals—are supplemented by the online archives of such important publications as the (Democratic) *Brooklyn Daily Eagle*, *Harper's Weekly* (HarpWeek), and the *Springfield (MA) Republican*.

Thousands of other documents relevant to Lincoln's body were not digitized at the time of my research, and I consulted a fair portion of them the old-fashioned way, by trekking to the archives. My principal destinations were the Abraham Lincoln Presidential Library and Museum, American Antiquarian Society, Gilder Lehrman Institute of American History, Henry E. Huntington Library, Indiana State Museum, Library of Congress, (the former) Lincoln Museum in Fort Wayne, Indiana (its holdings have been relocated to the Indiana State Museum and the Allen County Public Library), National Museum of Health and Medicine, New-York Historical Society, and New York Public Library. The manuscript and print collections, as well as clipping files, that provided material ultimately used in the book are listed in the endnotes.

My website for this book (richardwfox.com) features a listing of the library holdings that I examined (and that other researchers may find helpful), a sampling of the original documents that I found most interesting, a gallery of Lincoln-related images not reproduced in this book, and an original video essay prepared by two filmmakers, revealing how some twenty-first-century visitors to Henry Kirke Brown's Lincoln monuments in Manhattan and Brooklyn think and feel about Lincoln.

In 1869, as he dedicated the Brooklyn statue before a crowd of 15,000 onlookers, local pastor Richard Storrs predicted that, generations hence, the people of Brooklyn would still be inspired by it. In the spring of 2014, only a few passersby in Brooklyn or Manhattan stopped to study either statue or to pose for a photo beneath them. (Children eagerly climbed on them, and skateboarders rested on their plinths.)

But when directly asked about the monuments, some black and white strollers voiced their attachment to the bronzes and the man they depict. As the trees burst with color around them (and as the Brooklyn Lincoln seemed to revel in its beautifully restored setting), the sculptures appeared to settle into the valued historical landscape of New York City and the nation. The brief interviews in this little film thus contribute their share to the ongoing cultural history of Lincoln's body.

Acknowledgments

THE UNSUNG HEROES of historical studies are the librarians, archivists, curators, and conservators who tend to the documents and artifacts. Every researcher depends on the interest as well as the expertise of these specialists, who frequently make one's day by holding up a folder or an object and saying, "You may also want to see this."

Among those who contributed directly to this project, I want to single out, by institution: Abraham Lincoln Presidential Library and Museum (James Cornelius and Thomas Schwartz); American Antiquarian Society (Georgia Barnhill, Joanne Chaison, Vincent Golden, Lauren Hewes, Philip Lampi, Jaclyn Penny, Elizabeth Pope, and Laura Wasowicz); Henry E. Huntington Library (Cathy Cherbosque, Robert Ritchie, and Jenny Watts); and Lincoln Financial Foundation in Fort Wayne and Indianapolis, Indiana (Jane Gastineau, Cindy Van Horn, and Kara Vetter). For financial assistance in support of my Lincoln research, I am grateful to the Mellon Foundation, the Gilder-Lehrman Institute, and the University of Southern California (Dornsife College Dean's Office).

Soon after I began working on this project, I had the good fortune to encounter three leading Lincoln authorities—Michael Burlingame, Harold Holzer, and Thomas Schwartz—and they all took pleasure in welcoming a new laborer to the vineyard. I first met Michael Burlingame in the Madison Reading Room at the Library of Congress, and subsequently I ran into him accidentally at libraries in Indiana and Massachusetts. Each time, we enjoyed comparing notes on the day's discoveries. Harold Holzer's contagious enthusiasm for Lincoln, and for writing books about him, has impressed me since the afternoon when I first sat in his office at the Metropolitan Museum of Art, admiring all the Lincoln-related items adorning his shelves and walls. Thomas Schwartz introduced me to the Lincoln sights in Springfield, took me through the Abraham Lincoln Presidential Library and Museum, and shared his detailed knowledge of Lincoln's life and death. All three of them conveyed the truth that the more one knows about Lincoln, the more one knows that vital questions about him remain unanswered.

Many people helped me edge this book toward its final form. I am especially grateful to my fellow historians who read manuscript drafts and sent me ideas for improving them: Casey Blake, Michael Burlingame, Cathy Cherbosque, Cathy Corman, Karen Halttunen, Daniel Walker Howe, Michael P. Johnson, Stephen Kantrowitz, Louis Masur, Steven J. Ross, Michael Vorenberg, Robert B. Westbrook, and Ronald C. White Jr. Many others, over many years, shared insights about Lincoln and his era in conversations or correspondence, spurring me on in my thinking about him; that group includes David Blight, Richard Carwardine, Catherine Clinton, David Brion Davis, Ann Fabian, James Kloppenberg, Jackson Lears, Stephanie McCurry, John McGreevy, Martha Sandweiss, John Stauffer, Joan Waugh, Jennifer Weber, and Sean Wilentz.

To David D. Hall: thanks for one day reaching up onto a shelf of your bookcase, pulling down the nine gray volumes of Lincoln's *Collected Works*, and handing them to me with the words, "You need these more than I do." To my USC colleagues Philip Ethington and Vanessa Schwartz: thanks for your continuous instruction in how to make sense of pictures as historical texts. To Ron White: thanks for all of the Lincoln illumination you have dispensed in dinners shared at McCormick and Schmick's, booth 401, in downtown LA.

And to my far-flung family members: thanks for all your interest and all your gifts of Lincoln's body—from the Metropolitan Museum of Art reproduction of Lincoln's right hand to the bobblehead president sitting on his Lincoln Memorial throne and the T-shirt that recreates an Alexander Gardner photo of his face and shoulders with nothing but the black and gray letters that are spelling out the words of the Gettysburg Address.

My expert copy editor Stephanie Hiebert went beyond catching mistakes of grammar or spelling. She flagged ambiguous passages and proposed words better suited to my meaning. Norton editorial assistant Anna Mageras guided the manuscript through the initial stages of production, giving me quick and nuanced counsel about what needed doing. I thank them both for very intensive work and very patient explanations.

James Cornelius, Lincoln Curator at the Abraham Lincoln Presidential Library and Museum, squeezed many hours of meticulous labor on behalf of this book into his already hectic schedule, saving me from errors of fact and tone. It's been a joy knowing him, and learning from him about Lincoln, over the last five years. The streaming insights of Elizabeth Beverly into Lincoln's world and ours inform these pages at every turn. Over three decades I've learned that no one reads visual and verbal texts more deeply and generously than she does.

Wielding a lively editorial pencil, Alane Salierno Mason paid my chapter drafts the compliment of taking issue with them, pressing for more clarity, more economy, more energy. As a critical reader she somehow manages to keep sentences, sections, and the sweep of a manuscript in her mind's eye all at once. That shaping vision has made her the coproducer of this book, and for her years of commitment to it I express my profound gratitude. To Jill Kneerim go my thanks, once again, for her warm support, and in this case, for landing the project at Norton and in the sure hands of Alane Salierno Mason.

Abbreviations Used in Notes

AL	Abraham Lincoln
ALPLM	Abraham Lincoln Presidential Library and Museum, Springfield, IL
CH Trib	*Chicago Tribune*
CW	*Collected Works. The Abraham Lincoln Association, Springfield, Illinois*, ed. Roy P. Basler (New Brunswick, NJ: Rutgers University Press, 1953–1955), 9 vols.
FLIN	*Frank Leslie's Illustrated Newspaper*
JALA	*Journal of the Abraham Lincoln Association*
JISHS	*Journal of the Illinois State Historical Society*
LA Times	*Los Angeles Times*
LFFC	Lincoln Financial Foundation Collection, Fort Wayne, IN (Allen County Public Library) and Indianapolis, IN (Indiana State Museum)
NY Herald	*New York Herald*
NY Times	*New York Times*
NY Trib	*New York Tribune*
NY World	*New York World*
WA Post	*Washington Post*

Notes

Preface

1. Steven Spielberg, speaking at the Richmond Forum, Richmond, VA, Jan. 5, 2013, http://www.youtube.com/watch?v=Ag9PGQez_Pg (at 7:50 min.).

2. John Heilemann and Mark Halperin, *Game Change: Obama and the Clintons, McCain and Palin, and the Race of a Lifetime* (New York: Harper, 2010), 83 ("totemic"). Sales figures for Goodwin and Donald (not counting e-books) are cited in Stefanie Cohen, "Four Score and 16,000 Books," *Wall Street Journal,* Oct. 12, 2012. Goodwin described her phone call from Obama at a Harvard University conference on Lincoln in April 2009. In "What's So Special about a Team of Rivals?" *NY Times,* Nov. 20, 2008, historian James Oakes notes that Lincoln followed standard presidential practice in appointing his competitors to cabinet posts.

3. Doris Kearns Goodwin, *Team of Rivals: The Political Genius of Abraham Lincoln* (New York: Simon & Schuster, 2005), xix.

4. Spielberg, Goodwin, and Kushner discussed their collaboration in great detail at the Richmond Forum, Richmond, VA, Jan. 5, 2013, http://www.youtube.com/watch?v=Ag9PGQez_Pg.

5. David Donald, "The Folklore Lincoln," *JISHS* 40 (Dec. 1947): 377.

6. AL, "Message to Congress in Special Session," Jul. 4, 1861, in *CW,* 4:440. The *reason* to protect republican institutions against secessionist attack, Lincoln concluded in this message, was to ensure for all Americans "an unfettered start, and a fair chance, in the race of life" (ibid., 438).

7. Albert D. Richardson, *The Secret Service, the Field, the Dungeon, and the Escape* (Hartford, CT: American Publishing, 1865), 319–20.

8. Charles Davis diary entry, May 7, 1864, in Charles H. Davis [Jr.], *Life of Charles Henry Davis [Sr.], Rear Admiral, 1807–1877* (Boston: Houghton, Mifflin, 1899), 303.

9. [Henry Villard], "Our Springfield Correspondence," *NY Herald*, Nov. 22, 1860.

Chapter One: Lincoln's Body Politic

1. On the origins of "Honest Old Abe" and "rail-splitter," see Michael Burlingame, *Abraham Lincoln: A Life* (Baltimore: Johns Hopkins University Press, 2008), 1:249–50, 598–99.

2. Donn Piatt, *Memories of the Men Who Saved the Union* (New York: Belford, Clarke, 1887), 29–30.

3. Walt Whitman to Nathaniel Bloom and John F. S. Gray, Mar. 19, 1863, in Whitman, *The Correspondence*, ed. Edwin Haviland Miller (New York: New York University Press, 1961), 1:82.

4. Allan Nevins, ed., *A Diary of Battle: The Personal Journals of Colonel Charles S. Wainwright, 1861–1865* (New York: Harcourt, Brace & World, 1962), 10. Wainwright didn't think much of Stanton's looks either, describing him as "a long-haired, fat, oily, politician-looking man."

5. Rutherford B. Hayes to Laura Platt, Feb. 13, 1861, Rutherford B. Hayes Presidential Center, Fremont, OH. Thanks to Curator of Manuscripts Nan Card for sending me a copy of Hayes's letter.

6. "Two Faces of Lincoln," *Newark (OH) Advocate*, Aug. 24, 1860; "Old Abe's Personal Pulchritude," *Petersburg Express* (probably Virginia), reprinted in the *Fayetteville (NC) Observer*, May 31, 1860.

7. Richardson, *Secret Service*, 325 (see preface, n. 7).

8. Harold Holzer, Gabor S. Boritt, and Mark E. Neely Jr., eds., *The Lincoln Image: Abraham Lincoln and the Popular Print* (1984; Urbana: University of Illinois Press, 2001), 1–78, details the building up of Lincoln's visual identity across multiple interacting media—photography, lithography, engravings, woodcuts—in the presidential campaign of 1860.

9. "ABE THE GIANT KILLER!" classified advertisement for an engraving from "a Photograph of Hesler of Chicago," *NY Trib*, May 31, 1860. In her book *Mathew Brady and the Image of History* (Washington, DC: Smithsonian Institution Press, 1997), 17, Mary Panzer discusses the 1860 Lincoln carte de visite, which appeared via woodcut on the cover of *Harper's Weekly*, Nov. 10, 1860.

10. Aiming to establish a de facto party line on the presidential candidate's appearance, Republican Rufus F. Andrews told a crowd of thousands at the Young Men's Republican Union ratification meeting in Brooklyn on May 22, 1860, that Lincoln was "a homely man—not an ugly man, but a homely man." "The Presidential Campaign," *NY Herald*, May 23, 1860.

11. Benjamin F. Shaw, "Owen Lovejoy, Constitutional Abolitionists, and the Repub-

lican Party," in *Meeting of May 29, 1900 Commemorative of the Convention of May 29, 1856 That Organized the Republican Party in the State of Illinois,* ed. Ezra M. Prince, Transactions of the McLean County Historical Society 3 (Bloomington, IL: Pantagraph, 1900), 68.

12. "Mr. Lincoln in New York," *NY World,* Feb. 20, 1861. The *World* didn't specify that the "standard" complexion of the "western fever and ague districts" was a dark one, but that seems to be what the paper meant. Lincoln had mentioned his "dark complexion" in the personal sketch that he'd sent to newspaperman Jesse W. Fell in 1859 for distribution to the Republican press in 1860 (with the proviso that no one should learn he had written it). *CW* 3:512.

13. Villard, "The Republican Mecca," *NY Herald,* Oct. 20, 1860.

14. AL, "Speech at Springfield, Illinois," Jul. 17, 1858, in *CW* 2:506.

15. Ibid., 513.

16. AL, "Speech at Peoria, Illinois," Oct. 16, 1854, in *CW* 2:274. Iver Bernstein supplies helpful background on the "body politic" in this era in "Abraham Lincoln's Body and Body Politic," in *The Lincoln Forum: Rediscovering Abraham Lincoln,* ed. John Y. Simon and Harold Holzer (New York: Fordham University Press, 2002), 135–59; and in "Political Evil and the Body Politic in Mid-Nineteenth-Century America," in *The Problem of Evil: Slavery, Freedom, and the Ambiguities of American Reform,* ed. Steven Mintz and John Stauffer (Amherst, MA: University of Massachusetts Press, 2007), 231–59.

17. AL, "Address to the New Jersey Senate at Trenton, New Jersey," Feb. 21, 1861, in *CW* 4:236.

18. "The Speech of Abraham Lincoln," *NY Trib,* Feb. 28, 1860.

19. "The Presidential Campaign," *NY Herald,* Feb. 28, 1860.

20. Lincoln's phrase "a house divided against itself cannot stand" was a well-known formulation taken from the synoptic gospels (Matthew, Mark, and Luke—e.g., Matthew 12:25). The house in question was not a physical dwelling, but a household or clan. Jesus was explaining that no "kingdom," "city," or "house" could survive internal division. Lincoln expanded the house image to fit the nation, thus equating the house with the body politic.

21. AL, "Speech at Peoria," in *CW* 2:248.

22. Ibid., 274.

23. AL, "Remarks at Little Falls, New York," Feb. 18, 1861, in *CW* 4:223.

24. AL, "Remarks at Westfield, NY," Feb. 16, 1861, in *CW* 4:219.

25. AL, "Speech at Cincinnati, Ohio," Feb. 12, 1861, in *CW* 4: 198.

26. AL, "The Incoming Administration: Progress of the President Elect . . . ," *NY Times,* Feb. 23, 1861.

27. Harold Holzer, ed., *Dear Mr. Lincoln: Letters to the President* (Reading, MA: Addison-Wesley, 1993), 341–42. Holzer's *Lincoln President-Elect* (New York: Simon & Schuster, 2008) gives detailed treatment of Lincoln's security dilemmas during the four-month preinaugural period.

28. William Seward to John Bigelow, Jul. 15, 1862, in *The Assassination of Abraham Lincoln . . . and the Attempted Assassination of William H. Seward, Secretary of State, and Frederick W. Seward, Assistant Secretary, on the Evening of the 14th of April, 1865: Expressions of Condolence and Sympathy Inspired by These Events* (Washington, DC: Government Printing Office, 1867), 134.

29. Editorial, *NY World*, Feb. 25, 1861.

30. "The Conspiracy against the President," *NY Times*, Feb. 27, 1861.

31. "Mr. Lincoln in Washington," *NY Times*, Feb. 25, 1861 (editorial, p. 4).

32. "Extraordinary Flight," *New York Evening Post Semi-weekly*, Feb. 27, 1861.

33. "Mr. Lincoln's Progress [Cleveland to Buffalo]," *NY Herald*, Feb. 17, 1861.

34. "President Lincoln's Opinions Touching Assassination," *New Haven Palladium*, May 29, 1865, evening edition—gives an extensive excerpt from Charles Halpine's report (published sometime in the previous five or six weeks, probably in the *New York Citizen*) of his 1862 conversation with Lincoln about his personal security. A journalist and humorist, Halpine had served on General Halleck's staff during the Civil War. Reprinting Lincoln's comments in his book *Baked Meats of the Funeral* (New York: Carleton, 1866), 108–9, Halpine conceded that he was reconstructing Lincoln's words—a rare instance of humility among the hundreds of people who claimed, after the assassination, exact recall for words Lincoln had supposedly uttered to them years or decades earlier. On the public's access to Lincoln's office, perhaps even more liberal at times than Halpine recalled, see Ronald D. Rietveld, "The Lincoln White House Community," *JALA* 20 (Summer 1999): 29–30.

35. Edwin Stanton telegram to AL, Apr. 3, 1865, in *CW* 8:384–85.

36. AL telegram to Edwin Stanton, Apr. 3, 1865, in *CW* 8:385.

37. I discuss Lincoln's Richmond experience in "Lincoln's Practice of Republicanism: Striding through Richmond on April 4, 1865," in *The Living Lincoln*, ed. Thomas A. Horrocks, Harold Holzer, and Frank J. Williams (Carbondale: Southern Illinois University Press, 2011), 131–51; and in "'A Death-Shock to Chivalry, and a Mortal Wound to Caste': The Story of Tad and Abraham Lincoln in Richmond," *JALA* 33, no. 2 (2012): 1–19.

38. "The Celebration Last Night," *Washington Evening Star*, Apr. 12, 1865; Elizabeth Keckley, *Behind the Scenes; or, Thirty Years a Slave and Four Years in the White House* (1868; New York: Oxford University Press, 1988), 176.

39. "The Celebration Last Night," *Washington Evening Star* (including full text of Lincoln's prepared policy speech). The *Star* added that Lincoln gave the audience something to enjoy when he asked Senator James Harlan of Iowa to speak after him. The crowd greeted his digs at the fallen Confederacy—for example, "I hope no one will annoy the American people with the suggestion that you 'can't conquer the South'"—with jeers and cheers.

40. In *The True Story of Mary, Wife of Lincoln* (New York: Harper, 1928), 243, Katherine Helm (Mrs. Lincoln's niece) claimed that Booth, playing the vil-

lain in the *Marble Heart* performance, had pointedly targeted the president by glaring at him while uttering threatening lines from the play. A member of Lincoln's party supposedly remarked to him, "He looks as if he meant that for you," to which Lincoln allegedly replied, "Well, he does look pretty sharp at me, doesn't he?"

41. John Wilkes Booth, "To Whom It May Concern," [Nov.] 1864, in *"Right or Wrong, God Judge Me": The Writings of John Wilkes Booth*, ed. John Rhode-hamel and Louise Taper (Urbana: University of Illinois Press, 1997), 124–27.

42. Ibid., 154. (written in his diary while on the run, Apr. 21, 1865).

43. AL, "Last Public Address," Apr. 11, 1865, in *CW* 8:403.

44. AL, "Protest in Illinois Legislature on Slavery," Mar. 3, 1837, in *CW* 1:75.

45. AL, "To Albert G. Hodges," Apr. 4, 1864, in *CW* 7:281–82.

Chapter Two: Last Words, Last Breath

1. Henry James, *Notes of a Son and Brother, and the Middle Years* (Charlottesville: University of Virginia Press, 2011), 336.

2. Schuyler Colfax to Isaac N. Arnold, May 1, 1867, in Don E. Fehrenbacher and Virginia Fehrenbacher, eds., *Recollected Words of Abraham Lincoln* (Stanford, CA: Stanford University Press, 1996), 113.

3. Schuyler Colfax, "Memorial Address," Apr. 30, *CH Trib*, May 1, 1865.

4. "The Grand Display Last Night," *Washington Evening Star*, Apr. 14, 1865; Roeliff Brinkerhoff, *Recollections of a Lifetime* (Cincinnati, OH: Robert Clarke, 1900), excerpt reprinted in Arthur M. Markowitz, ed., "Tragedy of an Age: An Eyewitness Account of Lincoln's Assassination," *JISHS* 66 (Summer 1973): 207 (Grover's Theatre transparency).

5. Charles Leale's 1865 notes on his evening at Ford's Theatre became available for the first time in 2012. I discuss them in "A 'New Find' in 2012" at http://richardwfox.com. Michael W. Kauffman, *American Brutus: John Wilkes Booth and the Lincoln Conspiracies* (New York: Random House, 2004), supplies excellent detail on Ford's Theatre, including the houselights and the types of people in the audience on April 14.

6. John Deering Jr. to Miss E. M. Griggs, Apr. 26, 1865, reprinted in *Lincoln Lore*, no. 1478 (Apr. 1961): 4. According to Cindy Van Horn of the Lincoln Financial Foundation in Fort Wayne, Indiana, who examined the original letter, Deering is misidentified as "Downing" in some standard secondary sources—for example, Timothy S. Good, *We Saw Lincoln Shot: One Hundred Eyewitness Accounts* (Jackson: University Press of Mississippi, 1995), 65–69.

7. Lincoln's last full evening of entertainment took place on March 21, when he and Mary took a box at Grover's Theatre to see the opera *La Dame Blanche*. "German Opera," *Washington Evening Star*, Mar. 22, 1865.

8. Edwin Bates to his parents, Apr. 15, 1865, in Good, *We Saw Lincoln Shot*, 34. Some members of the audience heard Booth say "the South is avenged," and

others (including Booth himself) claimed he'd shouted "sic semper tyrannis" before leaping to the stage. But most newspapers reported that he'd uttered the three-word Latin phrase in full view of the audience from the empty stage. In its Saturday, April 15, 1865, editions, the *New York Herald* had Booth crying "sic semper tyrannis" from the Lincoln box; but the following day it claimed "he planted himself upon the stage and assumed a tragical posture, flourishing a dagger," and then shouted the phrase as he "faced the audience." "Our Loss," Apr. 16, 1865.

9. "Revulsion," *Cincinnati Daily Commercial*, Apr. 18, 1865.

10. In "The Insanity of Assassination," the *New York Evening Post* (Apr. 18, 1865) took the republican William of Orange, like Lincoln, as "the soul of the body politic."

11. *St. Louis Democrat* article excerpted in "President Lincoln's Death," *Louisville Journal*, Apr. 19, 1865; Henry Ward Beecher sermon, Apr. 23, *Independent* (New York), May 4, 1865, reprinted in *Our Martyr President, Abraham Lincoln: Voices from the Pulpit of New York and Brooklyn* (New York: Tibbals and Whiting, 1865), 37.

12. H. Montgomery, *The Life of Major-General William H. Harrison, Ninth President of the United States* (Philadelphia: Porter & Coates, 1852), 372; Freeman Cleaves, *Old Tippecanoe: William Henry Harrison and His Time* (New York: Scribner, 1939), 342; H. Montgomery, *The Life of Major-General Zachary Taylor* (New York: Miller, Orton, 1857), 431; "Telegraphic Intelligence," *Charleston Mercury*, Jul. 10, 1850 (dispatch of Jul. 9, 8:10 p.m.). In his Chicago eulogy for Taylor in 1850, Lincoln summed up Taylor's last words as "I have done my duty, I am ready to go." AL, "Eulogy on Zachary Taylor," in *CW* 2:89.

13. *FLIN*: "Last Words," May 31, 1862; "Last Hours of Judge Douglas," Jun. 15, 1861.

14. AL to Andrew Johnston, Apr. 18, 1846, in *CW* 1: 378. After the assassination, the *Chicago Tribune* ("Poem by Abraham Lincoln," Apr. 17, 1865) claimed he'd authored the poem himself, and many other papers, including Lincoln's hometown *Illinois State Journal* ("Poetry," Apr. 21), gladly agreed. The mistaken attribution made some sense. He'd patterned his own 1846 poem "My Childhood Home I See Again," based on a trip back to Indiana in 1844, on Knox's. But Lincoln gave an even grimmer portrait of life's decay and death's reign than Knox did. Among his childhood friends, he wrote, one had succumbed to mental degeneracy and half were dead. Published in an Illinois newspaper in 1847, Lincoln's poem is included in John Hollander, ed., *American Poetry: The Nineteenth Century* (New York: Library of America, 1993), 1:552–55.

15. "Our Loss," *NY Herald*; Shepard to her father, Apr. 16, 1865, in Rufus Rockwell Wilson, ed., *Lincoln among His Friends: A Sheaf of Intimate Memories* (Caldwell, ID: Caxton, 1942), 391.

16. "The Nation's Loss," *NY Trib*, Apr. 17, 1865.

17. Colfax, "Memorial Address."

18. Drs. King and Leale, both twenty-three years old, were relative novices com-

pared to the twenty-nine- or thirty-year-old Dr. Taft, but Taft later praised the medical skills of Dr. Leale. Taft was close to the Lincolns, and as head surgeon at the Church Hospital on H Street in the early war years (the Episcopal Church of the Ascension had been "improvised as a hospital"), he'd seen a lot of Mary and Abraham. She would distribute "wine and flowers," and he would make a game of "measuring height" with any tall soldier he could find. "Back to back they would stand and knock heads together, the President of the United States and the private in the regular army." "Lincoln's Last Hours," *NY Trib*, Oct. 14, 1900.

19. "The blood of the First Magistrate . . . dabbled the robe of an actress!" exclaimed the *Washington Chronicle* on Apr. 16 (quoted in the *Illinois State Journal*, Apr. 22, p.1).

20. Charles A. Leale, "Lincoln's Last Hours," Address Delivered before the . . . Loyal Legion, Feb. 1909, 7–8; Charles Sabin Taft, "Medical Notes on . . . Lincoln," *Medical Record*, Apr. 1, 1893, 388.

21. William H. DeMotte, "The Assassination of Abraham Lincoln," *JISHS* 20 (Oct. 1927): 426.

22. Terry Theodore, "Laura Keene and Mr. Lincoln," *Lincoln Herald* 73 (Winter 1971): 203.

23. David Rankin Barbee, "President Lincoln and Doctor Gurley," *Abraham Lincoln Quarterly* 5 (Mar. 1948): 23. The Lincolns attended New York Avenue Presbyterian, where the president enjoyed Gurley's sermons, but Lincoln never embraced the tenets of orthodox Christianity (the doctrine of sin made sense to him, but not the doctrine of redemption via divine grace and the atonement of Jesus). In his speech, Gurley indicted Booth for having been "addicted to tragedy," and for having "made the stage his home" (ibid., 24). I comment further on Lincoln's religion in "Lincoln's Religious Quest," *Slate*, Jan. 18, 2006, http://www.slate.com/id/2134450. See also the supple analysis of Mark A. Noll in "The Struggle for Lincoln's Soul," *Christianity Today*, Feb. 9, 1998.

24. *Boyd's Washington and Georgetown Directory* 3 (1865): 199; George Francis to [his niece] Josephine, May 5, Chicago History Museum.

25. DeMotte, "Assassination," 426; Fred Petersen (William Petersen's son), quoted on the attempted hanging in J. C. Hemphill, "Deathbed Relics Here Tell of Lincoln Tragedy," *NY Times*, Feb. 9, 1913.

26. Brinkerhoff, *Recollections*, excerpt reprinted in Markowitz, "Tragedy of an Age," 210.

27. In 1865 the term "assassination" was a word in transition. Sometimes it connoted a killing, sometimes only an attack with intent to kill. The *New York Herald* gave it the latter meaning in its first telegraphic dispatch from Washington, late in the evening on April 14: "Washington was thrown into an intense excitement a few minutes before eleven this evening, by the announcement that the President and Secretary Seward had been assassinated and were dead." "Details of the Assassination," Apr. 15, 1865.

28. Maunsell B. Field, "Particulars of the Death of Mr. Lincoln," *Philadelphia Inquirer*, Apr. 17, 1865. Another page-one interview with Field was published in the *New York Times* (in "Our Great Loss") on the same day; both interviews were conducted on the afternoon of April 15, and both were reprinted in many papers.

29. Maunsell B. Field, *Memories of Many Men and of Some Women* (New York: Harper, 1874), 322.

30. From the April 22, 1865, issue of *Philadelphia Medical and Surgical Reporter*, the *Chicago Medical Examiner* reprinted part of Charles Taft's "paper on the last hours" of Lincoln, detailing the urgent effort to warm up the president with "sinapisms over the entire anterior surface of the body" and "artificial heat to the extremities." "Assassination of President Lincoln," May 1865, 310.

31. Orville Hickman Browning, *The Diary of Orville Hickman Browning*, ed. Theodore Calvin Pease and James G. Randall (Springfield, IL: Trustees of the Illinois State Historical Library, 1925–1933), 2:20 (young man informing Stanton); Gideon Welles, *The Diary of Gideon Welles*, ed. Howard K. Beale (New York: Norton, 1960), 2:286 (Major Eckert); this 1960 Norton edition reprints the original nineteenth-century diary, not the 1911 revision of it that is available online.

32. "Personal," *Cleveland Plain Dealer*, quoted in *FLIN*, Feb. 8, 1862. Stanton's efficient telegraphic work on April 14–15, 1865, is documented in *The War of the Rebellion: A Compilation of the Official Records of the Union and Confederate Armies* (Washington, DC: Government Printing Office, 1880–1901), available on the "Making of America" website, http://digital.library.cornell.edu/m/moawar/waro.html, series 1, vol. 46, pt. 3: Correspondence, 756–85.

33. About the same time that official news began flowing from the Petersen house to the nation's newspapers—in the early morning of April 15—the Tenth Street crowd was dispersed and barriers were erected at the corners of E and F Streets.

34. James Tanner to Henry Walch, Apr. 17, 1865, reprinted in *American Historical Review* 29 (Apr. 1924): 516; "Tanner Also Present: Was in the Group Around the Deathbed of Lincoln," *WA Post*, Apr. 16, 1905. In the 1920s, Tanner's memories (slightly revised) appeared widely as "The Passing of Lincoln," e.g., *Indianapolis Star*, Sept. 19, 1920.

35. Charles Sabin Taft, "Abraham Lincoln's Last Hours," *Century*, Feb. 1893, 635; Tanner to Walch, Apr. 17, 1865, 515–16.

36. Leale, "Lincoln's Last Hours," 12. Edward Steers Jr., in his thoroughly researched *Blood on the Moon: The Assassination of Abraham Lincoln* (Lexington: University Press of Kentucky, 2001), estimates that fifty-seven people entered the bedroom during the night to pay their respects to the president, and concludes that no more than twelve people can be confirmed as standing by the deathbed when Lincoln expired. He counts a total of fourteen physicians at the president's deathbed at one time or another (pp. 268, 313, n. 25).

37. Leale, "Lincoln's Last Hours," 12.

38. Ibid., 6, 11.

39. Field, *Memories*, 324–25; Welles, *Diary*, 2:286–87; "Lincoln's Last Hours," *NY Trib.*

40. Fred Petersen, quoted in Hemphill, "Deathbed Relics."

41. "Our Loss," *NY Herald.*

42. Interview with Field in "Our Great Loss," *NY Times.* Historian Karen Halttunen notes that in Lincoln's day, the ideal passage from life to death involved no physical pain or mental suffering. The *Herald* reporter's depiction of Lincoln's body carried that hoped-for dénouement to its Romantic extreme: in death he looked positively, ebulliently alive. A painless deliverance permitted those left behind to focus on, and control, their pain and suffering as mourners. Halttunen, *Confidence Men and Painted Women: A Study of Middle-Class Culture in America, 1830–1870* (New Haven, CT: Yale University Press, 1982), chap. 5.

43. "Our Loss," *NY Herald.* The authoritative Edward Steers, in *Blood on the Moon*, 331, n. 2, lists these six men among the twelve people definitely present in the room when Lincoln died. Had they heard Stanton's alleged words, one or more of the six would likely have mentioned them in their diaries or letters soon after the assassination, but none did.

44. John G. Nicolay and John Hay, *Abraham Lincoln: A History* (1890; New York: Century, 1917), 10:302. John Hay was present in the Petersen house during the night of April 14–15, but according to Steers, he did not remain in William Clark's bedroom until 7:22 a.m.

45. A few writers have asserted that Stanton really said, "Now he belongs to the angels." "Ages" does rest on shaky ground, but at least Hay and Tanner, who both vouched for it decades after the assassination, had been present at the Petersen house. (Tanner, less attuned to literary rhythm than Hay, put Stanton's "now" at the end of the sentence: "He belongs to the ages now.") For more details on the unfounded "angels" case, see my essay "A Phrase for the Ages" at http://richardwfox.com.

Chapter Three: The Martyr and His Relics

1. *New York Journal of Commerce*, Apr. 15, quoted in "Press Eulogies of President Lincoln," *Washington National Intelligencer*, Apr. 17, 1865. The full quotation reads, "The whole people will mourn. The blow is struck at the heart of the nation, and it is felt in every fibre of the body, social and politic."

2. I discuss the outpouring of feeling among French republicans on hearing of Lincoln's death in "When the Grieving Went Global," http://richardwfox.com.

3. AL, "Address before the Wisconsin State Agricultural Society, Milwaukee, Wisconsin," Sept. 30, 1859, in *CW* 3:480.

4. "President Lincoln Shot by an Assassin," *NY Times*, Apr. 15, 1865; George Templeton Strong, *The Diary of George Templeton Strong*, ed. Allan Nevins and Milton Halsey Thomas (New York: Macmillan, 1952), 3:582–83. Also in the

one-volume abridgment: George Templeton Strong, *The Diary of George Templeton Strong*, abridged by Thomas J. Pressly (Seattle: University of Washington Press, 1988), 294–95.

5. Reminiscence of Louise Coffin Smith, undated typescript, LFFC, Allen County Public Library.

6. Untitled advertisement, *NY Trib*, Apr. 21, 1865 (mourning paraphernalia, p. 5); "Mourning in the Metropolis," in "Our Loss," *NY Herald*, Apr. 16, 1865.

7. Editorial comment, *Springfield Republican*, Apr. 19, 1865.

8. DeMotte, "Assassination," 428 (see chap. 2, n. 21); "Our National Loss," *NY Trib*, Apr. 18, 1865.

9. *New York Freeman's Journal and Catholic Register*, Apr. 29, 1865 (Apr. 17 letter from Nashville correspondent "Charlie").

10. *NY Herald* (all 1865): "Mourning in the Metropolis," Apr. 16; "The Metropolis," Apr. 19; "The Metropolis," Apr. 21. The article on Apr. 21 reminded readers of Lincoln's well-publicized fondness for *Macbeth*. As he passed through Philadelphia on April 23, journalist Charles A. Page counted at least twenty mottoes featuring Macbeth's famous lines on King Duncan. "Reception of the Remains of Abraham Lincoln," *NY Trib*, Apr. 25, 1865.

11. "The President's Death," *Baltimore American and Commercial Advertiser*, Apr. 17, 1865.

12. AL, "Address at Cooper Institute," Feb. 27, 1860, in *CW* 3:541; Burlingame, *Abraham Lincoln*, 1:281 (see chap. 1, n. 1).

13. "George W. Julian's Journal—The Assassination of Lincoln," *Indiana Magazine of History* 11 (Dec. 1915): 330.

14. Strong, *Diary*, 3:583–84 (see chap. 3, n. 4).

15. "The National Calamity," *NY Times*, Apr. 16, 1865. Quotations from the Wall Street event are from the *Times*; virtually identical accounts are found in the *New York Tribune* ("The Wall-St. Meeting," Apr. 17) and the *New York Herald* ("Mourning in the Metropolis," Apr. 16). Papers across the North picked up these reports beginning on April 17.

16. Garfield blended Matthew 12:44 and Joshua 7:1 in his "let this my house . . . this accursed thing."

17. Edwin Stanton to Charles Francis Adams (telegram), Apr. 15, 1865, in *War of the Rebellion*, series 1, vol. 46, pt. 3, 785 (see chap. 2, n. 32).

18. Welles, *Diary*, 2:282–83 (see chap. 2, n. 31).

19. Frederick W. Seward, "Recollections of Lincoln's Last Hours," *Leslie's Weekly*, Feb. 4, 1909, 107. Seward's 1909 account of the dream interpretation session during the cabinet meeting is identical to the one he first published in his study of his father, *Seward at Washington, as Senator and Secretary of State* (New York: Derby and Miller, 1891), 275. See Fehrenbacher and Fehrenbacher, *Recollected Words*, 398 (see chap. 2, n. 2).

20. Strong, *Diary*, 3:591 (see chap. 3, n. 4); "Interesting Incidents of Mr. Lincoln's Last Days," in "Mourning," *NY Herald*, Apr. 18, 1865. The *Boston Herald* (Apr.

20) and many other papers printed the story, transmitted by the Associated Press.

21. Gideon Welles, "Lincoln and Johnson," *Galaxy*, Apr. 1872 (reprinted in the *Oneida Circular*, Apr. 29, 1872, under the title "Lincoln's Dream") gives the "dark and indefinite shore." For the original text of the diary entry, which mentions no shore at all, see Fehrenbacher and Fehrenbacher, *Recollected Words*, 486 (see chap. 2, n. 2). The Fehrenbachers assert that Welles "later" added "towards an indefinite shore," and then, in 1872, made it "towards a dark and indefinite shore" (ibid., 547, n. 492).

22. The Catholic press was decidedly "Copperhead" (anti-Lincoln and antiwar) from the start of the conflict. The country's leading Catholic intellectual, Orestes Brownson, wrote in late 1861 that only two of the North's twelve Catholic newspapers—the *New York Tablet* and the *Pittsburgh Catholic*—could be counted on to support the Lincoln administration. Five others, according to historian Kenneth J. Zanca, could be relied on to oppose the war effort. Brownson, "Slavery and the War," *Brownson's Quarterly Review*, Oct. 1861, discussed in Zanca, "The Lion Who Did Not Roar . . . Yet: The Editorials of James A. McMaster—May 1860 to May 1861," *American Catholic Studies* 122 (Fall 2011): 26. Many priests and bishops tried to get their flocks to mourn the martyred president. Father Thomas Mooney at St. Bridget's in Manhattan gave a moving tribute to Lincoln during a special service on the day after his funeral ("The National Mourning," *NY Times*, Apr. 21, 1865). On the American Catholic response to the Civil War, consult John T. McGreevy, *Catholicism and American Freedom* (New York: Norton, 2003), chaps. 2 and 3.

23. Albert Daggett to his mother, Apr. 16, 1865, reprinted in *Lincoln Lore*, Apr. 1961, 2–3; William Clark to his sister Ida, Apr. 19, 1865, quoted in Louis A. Warren, "The Petersen House," *Lincoln Lore*, Apr. 17, 1939, 1.

24. Official autopsy report, *The Medical and Surgical History of the War of Rebellion* (Washington, DC: Government Printing Office, 1875), vol. 2, pt. 1 (first surgical volume), 306.

25. "Our Great Loss," *NY Times* (see chap. 2, n. 28).

26. Taft, "Lincoln's Last Hours," 636 (see chap. 2, n. 35). Another army doctor at the autopsy, thirty-two-year-old Robert Reyburn (later an attending physician at the bedside of the dying President Garfield) "very urgently pleaded" to no avail for some of Lincoln's hair. But a clump of it had fallen to the floor in the general ardor for acquisition, and a military officer allegedly told him, "Doctor, I can't give you any of the President's hair, but . . . if you capture it I shall make no objection." The young doctor "seized upon the precious relic at once." Reyburn, *Fifty Years in the Practice of Medicine and Surgery, 1856–1906* (Washington, DC: Beresford, 1907), 20.

27. Augusta L. Curtis affidavit, May 11, 1926, 1–2, National Museum of Health and Medicine.

28. "The Features of the Dead," in "The Rites," *NY Herald*, Apr. 20, 1865.

29. Drew Gilpin Faust, *This Republic of Suffering: Death and the American Civil War* (New York: Knopf, 2008).

30. *Boyd's Washington and Georgetown Directory* (Washington, DC: Hudson Taylor, 1864), 330.

31. "Viewing the Remains," *CH Trib*, May 2, 1865.

32. George Alfred Townsend, "The Great Tragedy," *NY World*, Apr. 19, 1865. This report was widely reprinted—for example, in *CH Trib*, Apr. 20, 1865.

33. Henry Bellows sermon, Apr. 16, published in the *New York Evening Post*, Apr. 18, 1865, and reprinted in *Our Martyr President*, 49–63 (see chap. 2, n. 11).

34. George Dana Boardman and A. D. Mayo sermons, Apr. 16, 1865, in "The Martyred President: Sermons Given on the Occasion of the Assassination of Abraham Lincoln," Emory University website, http://beck.library.emory.edu/lincoln (Boardman, 34, 44–45; Mayo, 13).

35. Rabbi Isaac Leeser, "Lincoln's Death," Apr. 15, 1865, in Emanuel Hertz, ed., *Abraham Lincoln: The Tribute of the Synagogue* (New York: Bloch, 1927), 133, 135.

36. Samuel Myer Isaacs, "The President's Death," Apr. 19, 1865, in Hertz, *Abraham Lincoln*, 76–77.

37. Isaac Wise, "Funeral Sermon," Apr. 19, 1865, in Hertz, *Abraham Lincoln*, 98; Bertram Wallace Korn, *American Jewry and the Civil War* (Philadelphia: Jewish Publication Society of America, 1951), 189. Rabbi Wise soon emerged as a nationally renowned leader of Reform Judaism. His assertion about Lincoln was reported on page one of the *Cincinnati Commercial*, Apr. 20, 1865 (in a sampling of sermons from the day before), and roundly mocked in the *Philadelphia Press* ("Anxious for Reflected Honor," May 4, 1865) and other papers.

38. "Improving the Late Dispensation: The Rev. M. L. P. Thompson," *Cincinnati Daily Enquirer*, Apr. 28, 1865; "A Clerical Harangue," *Brooklyn Daily Eagle*, May 18, 1865, reprinting the Reverend Motly's remarks from an unnamed paper. The Democratic *Enquirer* was responding to the April 23 sermon given by Republican Presbyterian minister M. L. P. Thompson, published in the *Cincinnati Gazette*, Apr. 25, 1865. The Democratic *Daily Eagle* was one of many like-minded papers to target Motly's words: on May 23 the *Bloomville (NY) Mirror* reprinted them from the *Allen County (OH) Democrat*.

39. "The Safety of the President," *NY Times*, Apr. 24, 1865.

40. Henry J. Raymond, *The Life of Abraham Lincoln* (New York: National Union Executive Committee, 1864), 83.

41. "Safety of the President," *NY Times*. Ted Widmer, "'A Very Mad-Man,'" *Opinionator* (blog), NYTimes.com, Mar. 19, 2011, http://opinionator.blogs.nytimes.com, gives background on the Lincoln-Raymond connection.

42. To Raymond, Lincoln's march through Richmond on April 4 exemplified his

irresponsible courting of danger, and with his return to Washington, "his personal demeanor in all respects remained unchanged." Henry J. Raymond, *The Life and Public Services of Abraham Lincoln* (New York: Derby and Miller, 1865), 681, 693.

43. Ibid., 724. An appendix compiled by Francis Carpenter included six pages on Lincoln's "religious experience" (pp. 730–35).

Chapter Four: African Americans and Their Emancipator

1. "Reflections," *Colored Citizen* (Cincinnati, OH), Nov. 7, 1863.

2. "The Great Event," [Frederick] *Douglass' Monthly*, Feb. 1863, 795.

3. Mrs. Lou Griffin, quoted in "Missouri Ex-slave Story," in *Born in Slavery: Slave Narratives from the Federal Writers' Project, 1936–1938*, vol. 10, *Missouri Narratives*, 143–44, WPA Slave Narrative Project, American Memory, Library of Congress, http://memory.loc.gov/ammem/snhtml/snhome.html.

4. "Charlie Davenport, Ex-slave, Adams County," in *Born in Slavery*, vol. 9, *Mississippi Narratives*, 38.

5. "Mary Wallace Bow, Ex-slave 81 Years," in *Born in Slavery*, vol. 11, *North Carolina Narratives*, 150.

6. "Susan Snow, Ex-slave, Lauderdale County," in *Born in Slavery*, vol. 9, *Mississippi Narratives*, 138. William H. Wiggins, *O Freedom!: Afro-American Emancipation Celebrations* (Knoxville: University of Tennessee Press, 1987), 71, relates more slave stories about Lincoln.

7. L. S. Thompson, *The Story of Mattie J. Jackson* (Lawrence, KS: Printed at Sentinel Office, 1866), 11, available at Documenting the American South, University of North Carolina, http://docsouth.unc.edu. Thanks to Matthew Amato for this reference.

8. I give a short account of Lincoln's encounter with Richmond's African Americans in "Don't Drown, Massa Abe, for God's Sake!" at http://richardwfox.com.

9. Frederick Douglass, *The Life and Times of Frederick Douglass* (1881), in his *Autobiographies* (New York: Library of America, 1994), 785–86, 809. The most probing words Douglass ever wrote about Lincoln—in his speech at the dedication of the Emancipation Memorial in Washington in 1876—will be examined in Chapter 8.

10. John P. Jones to his wife, Mary, Oct. 3, 1862, in *"I Take Up My Pen"—Complete Transcripts from the Exhibition*, Gilder Lehrman Institute of American History, http://gilderlehrman.org.

11. Carl Schurz to Theodore Petrasch, Oct. 12, 1864, in Carl Schurz, *Intimate Letters of Carl Schurz, 1841–1869*, trans. and ed. Joseph Schafer (Madison: State Historical Society of Wisconsin, 1928), 309.

12. "Frederick Douglass at the Cooper Institute," *NY Trib*, Feb. 7, 1863, reprinted in [Frederick] *Douglass' Monthly*, Mar. 1863, 804–5.

13. AL, "Eulogy on Henry Clay," Jul. 6, 1852, in *CW* 2:132.

14. Frederick Douglass, "The Negro Exodus from the Gulf States," a paper read in Saratoga, New York, Sept. 12, 1879, *Journal of Social Science* 11 (May 1880), reprinted in *The Frederick Douglass Papers, Series One: Speeches, Debates, and Interviews*, vol. 4, *1864–80*, ed. John W. Blassingame and John R. McKivigan (New Haven, CT: Yale University Press, 1991), 526. For the utilitarian response of one black leader, Richard T. Greener, to Douglass's republican universalism, see Nell Irvin Painter, *Exodusters: Black Migration to Kansas after Reconstruction* (New York: Knopf, 1977), 247–48; the exodus was justified, said Greener, by "the greater good which will accrue to the greatest number."

15. Welles, *Diary*, 2:288, 290 (see chap. 2, n. 31).

16. "Andy Johnson and the Black Race," *NY Trib*, May 8, 1865.

17. Andrew Johnson speech to "the Colored Men of Nashville," Oct. 24, 1864, in *The Papers of Andrew Johnson*, vol. 7, *1864–1865*, ed. LeRoy P. Graf (Knoxville: University of Tennessee Press, 1986), 253.

18. Frederick Douglass, "Our Martyred President," Apr. 15, 1865, in *Frederick Douglass Papers: Series One*, 4:76–77.

19. Taft, "Lincoln's Last Hours," 636 (see chap. 2, n. 35); "The City Yesterday," *NY Herald*, Apr. 18 ("damned nigger"). Figures on the decline of black residency in New York City are given in Iver Bernstein, *The New York City Draft Riots* (New York: Oxford University Press, 1990), 267. Other reports of attacks on those expressing anti-Lincoln sentiments can be found in (all dates are 1865): "The Feeling in Washington," *CH Trib*, Apr. 17; "Thrown Overboard," *Brooklyn Daily Eagle*, Apr. 17; "Mourning," *NY Herald* (see chap. 3, n. 15); and "The General Gloom" (including a dispatch from San Francisco), *Cincinnati Enquirer*, Apr. 17. For plaintive letters to the editor from accused citizens seeking to exonerate themselves, see *NY Herald*, Apr. 19, and *NY Trib*, Apr. 19. Many other cases of arrest for anti-Lincoln speech (including the arrest of a policeman) are itemized in "Dissenters from the Popular Idea," *NY Trib*, Apr. 18, and "The City," *Philadelphia Press*, Apr. 17.

20. Editorial, *New York Freeman's Journal and Catholic Register*, Apr. 22, 1865. When he first heard about Lincoln's death on April 15, McMaster said to himself, "'Some Puritan exterminationist must have done it!' Indeed, it was the only *rational* explanation of the crazy act! It inures [i.e. redounds] to the exclusive benefit of these" (ibid.).

21. "Andrew Johnson's Record," *Crisis* (Columbus, OH), May 3, 1865, referring to an Andrew Johnson speech of Dec. 12, 1859.

22. "The Funeral Train in York," *Cartridge Box* (a weekly published by the York US Army Hospital), Apr. 29, 1865.

23. "Abraham Lincoln," *Elevator* (San Francisco), Apr. 21, 1865, Black Abolitionist Archive, University of Detroit-Mercy.

24. Henry Ward Beecher, "The National Bereavement," *NY Times*, Apr. 24, 1865.

25. "The National Loss," *NY Trib*, Apr. 19, 1865. This story said "perhaps" a majority of those lining up for the White House lying-in-state were African Americans.

26. Charles A. Page, "A Second Account," *NY Trib*, Apr. 20, 1865.

27. "The Love of the Freedmen for the Late President," *Independent* (New York), May 11, 1865; "Frederick Douglass on President Lincoln," *National Anti-Slavery Standard*, Jun. 10, 1865.

28. "The Colored Baltimore Delegation," *Philadelphia Inquirer*, Apr. 20, 1865.

29. *NY Trib*: C. A. Page, "The Funeral Pageant," Apr. 22, and "Baltimore and Harrisburg," Apr. 25, 1865. The official military dispatch from Baltimore also noticed the racial mingling of the "laboring classes, white and black." E. D. Townsend to Edwin Stanton, Apr. 22, 1865, in *War of the Rebellion*, series 1, vol. 46, pt. 3, 886 (see chap. 2, n. 32).

30. "The Funeral," *NY Herald*, Apr. 24, 1865; "The Funeral Pageant," *NY Weekly Trib*, Apr. 29, 1865. In 1865, the word "thrilled" meant "chilled," implying weird or ominous surprise, not delight or exhilaration. In that era, a "thrill" went up your spine.

31. Reminiscence of Louise Coffin Smith, undated typescript, LFFC, Allen County Public Library.

32. C[harles] A. Dana [assistant secretary of war] to Maj.-Gen. John A. Dix, Apr. 24, *NY Times*, Apr. 25, 1865. For details on the New York imbroglio, see the unpublished letter of black preacher J. Sella Martin, Apr. 24, 1865, in C. Peter Ripley, ed., *The Black Abolitionist Papers* (Chapel Hill: University of North Carolina Press, 1992), 5:317–19.

33. *NY Trib*, Apr. 25, 1865: "The Colored People" [J. W. B. Pennington letter, Apr. 21], p. 7; [Pennington et al.,] "Appeal to Colored Citizens," p. 4. The paper asked citizens living along the route to welcome the freedmen's wives and children into their homes to view the procession (p. 6). "Our Tribute," *NY Herald*, Apr. 26, 1865, gives the figure of two thousand blacks marching in the procession, but the same article (obviously rushed to press) also gives the number as "several hundred," thus making the lower figure of two hundred, as reported in both "The Procession," *NY Times*, Apr. 26, and "Obsequies of Abraham Lincoln," *NY Trib*, Apr. 26, much more likely. In a striking anticipation of affirmative-action debates in our own time, Rochester's *Semi-weekly Union and Advertiser*, defending the Common Council for a principled, race-blind standard of inclusion—and thus exclusion of late applications from blacks and whites alike—judged that "so far as there is legitimately any reason to complain of distinction of color, it proceeds from the effort to discriminate in favor of the negro, instead of against him!" ("The Negro Mourners in New York—Justice to the Common Council," Apr. 28, 1865).

34. "Obsequies of Abraham Lincoln," *NY Trib* (the banner); George Templeton Strong, *Journal, 1862–1875*, 121, New York Historical Society (original man-

uscript diary). Editors Allan Nevins and Milton Thomas omitted this entry about the marchers in the published Strong, *Diary* (see chap. 3, n. 4). Strong assumed that all of the Manhattan mourners had stuck to waving, but the *Tribune* reported repeated applause—for the African Americans alone—throughout the procession. "It was evidently deemed inappropriate, on such a day, to notice particularly any but those who needed public recognition to retrieve the honor of the city."

35. *New York Weekly Day-Book*: "Mr. Lincoln's Inaugural Address," Mar. 11, 1865; "'The Constitution as It Is and the Union as It Was' the Sole Salvation of the Country," Apr. 8, 1865; "The Death of the President," Apr. 22, 1865; "A Stultified City," May 6, 1865.

36. *Pottsville (PA) Democratic Standard*, Apr. 22, 1865: "Matchless Impudence" and "A Misogen Dance."

37. AL, "Speech at Springfield, Illinois," Jun. 26, 1857, in *CW*: 2:409.

38. "The President's Funeral," *NY World*, Apr. 26, 1865.

39. M, "From Our Indiana Corresponding Editor" [Apr. 17], *Christian Recorder*, Apr. 29, 1865.

40. "The Jubilee of Friday," *Columbus Gazette*, Apr. 21, 1865.

41. Ruth, "Chicago Correspondence" [May 3], *Christian Recorder*, May 20, 1865.

42. "Tribute to the Memory of Mr. Lincoln from Colored Citizens," *Albany Evening Journal*, Apr. 26, 1865. The night before they walked in the Chicago procession, the four hundred black marchers met to pass a set of resolutions, and one of them, like the Albany AME statement, showed how consciously African American mourners tried to avoid implying that anything good could possibly have come out of—or ever come out of in the future—Lincoln's assassination: "We do not wish to be understood as mitigating the crime of assassination," they declared. Yet "we do believe . . . that the fact and circumstances of his death, like that of all martyrs for a cause, will tend ultimately to promote that cause and to defeat its enemies." "President's Funeral," *CH Trib*, May 2, 1865.

43. "Assassination of President Lincoln," *Black Republican* (New Orleans, LA), Apr. 22, 1865, Black Abolitionist Online Archive, University of Detroit-Mercy, http://research.udmercy.edu/find/special_collections/digital/baa.

44. J. T. Mills, "Interesting Interview with the President," *NY Trib*, Sept. 9, 1864. (An earlier, unpublished version, "Interview with Alexander W. Randall and Joseph T. Mills," is in *CW* 7: 506–8.)

Chapter Five: Rolling Funeral, Living Corpse

1. I have elided two sentences from the start of George Alfred Townsend's lengthy description of Lincoln's body as he lay in state in the White House on April 18 and 19: "Death has fastened into his frozen face all the character and idiosyncrasy of life. He has not changed one line of his grave, grotesque countenance,

nor smoothed out a single feature." His color turned out to be lifelike as well: "The hue is rather bloodless and leaden; but he was always sallow." "Appearance of the Corpse," *NY World*, Apr. 20, 1865. Townsend's report was reprinted everywhere in the North, and in some parts of the South. The brand-new *Colored Tennesseean* reprinted it on May 6, 1865.

2.   In "Folklore Lincoln," 377 (see preface, n. 5), Donald described the Lincoln cult as almost a "religion."

3.   B. F. Morris, comp., *Memorial Record of the Nation's Tribute to Abraham Lincoln* (Washington, DC: Morrison, 1865), 103–4.

4.   Carl Sandburg, *Abraham Lincoln: The War Years* (New York: Harcourt, Brace, 1939), 4:387–413, plus six pages of photographs; David Herbert Donald, *Lincoln* (New York: Simon & Schuster, 1995), 599. Some recent biographies do mention the funeral period—for example, Allen C. Guelzo, *Abraham Lincoln: Redeemer President* (Grand Rapids, MI: Eerdmans, 1999), 450–53, and Burlingame, *Abraham Lincoln*, 2:819–33 (see chap. 1, n. 1).

5.   J. G. Holland, *Life of Abraham Lincoln* (1866; Lincoln: University of Nebraska Press, 1998), 526. (This edition features an excellent introduction by Allen Guelzo on the history of Lincoln biography.)

6.   Ibid., 529, 532.

7.   Henry Ward Beecher sermon, Apr. 23, 1865, in *Our Martyr President*, 47 (see chap. 2, n. 11); "The Great Heart of the Nation," *Philadelphia Press*, Apr. 18, 1865.

8.   Anson Henry to his wife, May 8, 1865, Anson G. Henry Papers, ALPLM.

9.   Mary Lincoln to Charles Sumner, Jul. 4, 1865, in *Mary Todd Lincoln: Her Life and Letters*, ed. Justin G. Turner and Linda Levitt Turner (1972; New York: Fromm International, 1987), 256.

10.   Dr. Adonis, "Letter from Washington," *CH Trib*, Apr. 26, 1865.

11.   Benjamin Brown French, *Witness to the Young Republic: A Yankee's Journal, 1828–1870*, ed. Donald B. Cole and John J. McDonough (Hanover, NH: University Press of New England, 1989), 471, 507. French's nephew, the sculptor Daniel Chester French, created the seated Lincoln for the Lincoln Memorial (dedicated in 1922).

12.   "Our Grief," *NY Herald*, Apr. 17, 1865. In his best-selling *Myths after Lincoln* (1929; New York: Press of the Readers Club, 1941), 106, journalist Lloyd Lewis reduced Stanton's position to politics. If mourners saw the bruises on Lincoln's face, they would support the Radical Republicans' stringent Reconstruction policies. "With the undertakers under their thumbs," said Lewis, "the corpse of Lincoln itself could be turned into a weapon against the Lincolnian policy of mercy toward [white] Southerners." But even if Stanton's goal was primarily political, as Lewis alleges with no documentary evidence, Stanton would also have wanted mourners to recognize Lincoln's republican devotion to them: he had died a *martyr's* death, not just any death.

13. Leigh Huntley diary, Apr. 18 and 20, 1865, Huntley Papers, ALPLM.

14. George Alfred Townsend, "Thousands Coming to Get a Last Look at the Features of the President," *NY World*, Apr. 19, 1865.

15. "The Funeral of President Lincoln," *Zion's Herald and Wesleyan Journal*, Apr. 26, 1865, listed "the only ladies present."

16. "The Day of the Obsequies," *Elevator* (San Francisco), Apr. 21, 1865, Black Abolitionist Online Archive, University of Detroit-Mercy, http://research. udmercy.edu/find/special_collections/digital/baa.

17. "Emerson Address at Concord" [Apr. 19], reprinted in *Philadelphia Press*, May 4, 1865, and many other papers, including *Littell's Living Age*, May 13, 1865.

18. "Dr. Holland's Address," *Springfield Republican*, Apr. 20, 1865.

19. Five seats of state government—Harrisburg, Albany, Columbus, Indianapolis, and Springfield—were selected to host a lying-in-state. Trenton, the capital of New Jersey, got no lying-in-state, since Philadelphia was so close by.

20. "George W. Julian's Journal," 336 (see chap. 3, n. 13); Wachusett [G. B. Woods], "The Funeral Journey," *Boston Daily Advertiser*, Apr. 22, 1865 (details on train passengers).

21. Ozias Hatch to Julia Hatch, Apr. 23, 1865, Hatch Papers, ALPLM; "Appearance of the Deceased," *Philadelphia Inquirer*, Apr. 24, 1865; C. A. P. [Page], "In Philadelphia," *NY Trib*, Apr. 25, 1865; Louisa Clark Olmsted to Parmelee Calkins Olmsted, Apr. 24, 1865, in R. Gerald McMurtry, "Lincoln's Funeral at Philadelphia," *Lincoln Herald* 46 (Jun. 1944): 43.

22. "The City Hall," *NY Times*, Apr. 25, 1865; "The Features of the Deceased President," *New York Evening Post*, reprinted in *Boston Journal*, Apr. 25, 1865. "The Remains in New York," *CH Trib*, Apr. 25, 1865 (apparently from the Associated Press) said "the remains will not again be exposed to view until their arrival at Springfield." Springfield officials were aghast at the news, since a cancellation of Chicago's lying-in-state would likely provoke a stampede from the Windy City to the state capital.

23. "Our Dead President," *NY Trib*, Apr. 28, 1865; "The Funeral Train," *NY Herald*, Apr. 28, 1865.

24. "The Remains on View Yesterday," *NY World*, Apr. 26, 1865; "The President's Remains at Albany," *Rochester Semi-weekly Union and Advertiser*, Apr. 28, 1865 ("growing yet darker"); "Funeral Obsequies at Albany," *Troy Daily Times*, Apr. 27, 1865 ("kindly face"). "President Lincoln's Remains in Albany," *Zion's Herald and Wesleyan Journal*, May 17, 1865, found Lincoln's flesh "much discolored, forcibly reminding us that the bodies of great men, too, must wither and decay."

25. C. A. P. [Page], "From Buffalo Westward," *NY Trib*, May 1, 1865 (dispatch written in Cleveland on April 28).

26. "The Funeral Cortege," *CH Trib*, Apr. 28, 1865. "The President's Obsequies," *Illinois State Journal*, Apr. 28, 1865, reprinted the cables exchanged between

the members of the Illinois delegation and their Springfield colleagues on April 26 and 27.

27. C. A. P. [Page], "The Funeral Progress," *NY Trib*, May 1, 1865.

28. Advertisement, *Rochester Semi-weekly Union and Advertiser*, Apr. 28, 1865.

29. "J. Wilkes Booth," *NY World*, reprinted in the *Cincinnati Enquirer*, May 3, 1865.

30. A "star," explained the *New York World*, "belongs to no one theater, but travels from each to all, playing a few weeks at a time . . . sustained . . . by the regular or stock actors." George Alfred Townsend, "John Wilkes Booth," *NY World*, Apr. 28, 1865. Townsend claimed (in "Thousands Coming to Get a Last Look") that "the President had never spoken with Booth but wished to make his acquaintance, and said so. Booth evaded the interview."

31. "How Booth's Body Was Disposed Of," *Boston Advertiser*, reprinted in *NY Trib*, May 5, 1865. Cf. "Booth's Body," *Albany Evening Journal*, May 2, 1865; and Junius Henri Browne, "The Disposal of Booth's Body," *NY Trib*, May 11, 1865.

32. "The Obsequies of President Lincoln," *Crisis* (Columbus, OH), May 3, 1865. All a Republican paper could offer in modest criticism of Stanton was the wish for a "somewhat different" itinerary: a direct train from Washington to Springfield via Pittsburgh, with public viewings at the final stop for those authentic pilgrims intent on viewing the president's body. "The Martyr in Our City," *Buffalo Morning Express*, Apr. 27, 1865.

33. P. D. Day, "A Memorial Discourse on the Character of Abraham Lincoln," Jun. 1, 1865, in "Martyred President," 6 (see chap. 3, n. 34).

34. "The Obsequies of Mr. Lincoln," *Chicago Times*, May 2, 1865; "President's Funeral," *CH Trib* (see chap. 4, n. 42).

35. Abraham Lincoln, "Farewell Address at Springfield, Illinois," in *CW* 4:190. In the version published in the *Illinois State Journal* the day after Lincoln spoke in 1861, Lincoln says, "With these few words I must leave you—for how long I know not." The *Journal* reprinted that first version in its May 3, 1865, edition, as Lincoln's body arrived for the lying-in-state.

36. C. A. P. [Page], "A Retrospect," *NY Trib*, May 8, 1865; "The Arrival of the Remains of President Lincoln," *Illinois State Journal*, May 4, 1865.

37. "The President's Obsequies," *NY Times*, May 4, 1865; L. A. Gobright, *Recollection of Men and Things at Washington, during the Third of a Century* (Philadelphia: Claxton, Remsen & Haffelfinger, 1869), 362–63; Ida M. Tarbell, *The Life of Abraham Lincoln* (1900; New York: Lincoln History Society, 1908), 4:56.

38. "A Girl in the Sixties: Excerpts from the Journal of Anna Ridgely (Mrs. James L. Hudson)," *JISHS* 22 (Oct. 1929): 444–45 (May 7, 1865, entry).

39. Edward Cox Davis had composed this funeral march in 1861 for General Nathaniel Lyon, recently killed at Wilson's Creek, Missouri. Balmer and Weber,

the St. Louis music publishers, turned it down, but they came running back to Davis in 1865 to see if they could release it as "Lincoln's Funeral March." Thanks to James Cornelius for these and other details on the May 4 events in Springfield.

40. "The Funeral," *Bloomington Pantagraph*, May 8, 1865.

41. Walter B. Stevens, *A Reporter's Lincoln*, ed. Michael Burlingame (Lincoln: University of Nebraska Press, 1998), 190. (This volume updates a 1916 work.)

42. Simpson's address was widely reprinted in the North (e.g., *Illinois State Journal*, May 5, 1865; *NY Trib*, May 5, 1865), with a corrected version printed the next day.

43. "Guard at the President's Tomb," *Illinois State Journal*, May 6, 1865.

44. "Procession," *NY Times* (see chap. 4, n. 33).

Chapter Six: The First Lincoln Memorials

1. Bryant's poem appeared in many newspapers in late April (e.g., *CH Trib*, Apr. 29, 1865), and in *Littell's Living Age*, May 6, 1865. A volume of 165 poems dedicated to Lincoln was published in July (*Poetical Tributes to the Memory of Abraham Lincoln* [Philadelphia: Lippincott, 1865]), and Bryant's opened the book. At least fifty of the poets were women. Occasionally, a female poet performed at a public memorial service—for example, Mrs. H. C. Gardner, "Abraham Lincoln Is Dead!," East Weymouth MA, Apr. 19, *Zion's Herald and Wesleyan Journal*, May 3, 1865.

2. Emma D., "Died: Abraham Lincoln," *Schenectady Evening Star*, Apr. 25, 1865. So many Lincoln poems had arrived at the *Chicago Tribune* by late April that the paper pleaded tongue in cheek for readers to stop mailing them in. Poetry had swarmed up "like the frogs of Egypt . . . We beg our authors not to take it to heart if we find ourselves compelled to part with poems we think exceedingly smart, when we've more than enough to fill a cart . . . It is not *every* man can be a poet / No more than every sheep can be a go-at." "Our Poets and Poetry," Apr. 30, 1865.

3. Libertus Van Bokkelen sermon, St. Stephen's Church, Baltimore, Apr. 16, *American and Commercial Advertiser* (Baltimore), Apr. 20, 1865.

4. George Bancroft to Elizabeth Bancroft, Sept. 1861, in M. A. De Wolfe Howe, *The Life and Letters of George Bancroft* (New York: Scribner, 1908), 132.

5. "Our Tribute: Services at Union Square," *NY Herald*, Apr. 26, 1865.

6. "Reflections," *Colored Citizen* (see chap. 4, n. 1).

7. "Mr. Bancroft's Oration," *NY Times*, Apr. 26, 1865. Ever the Jacksonian Democrat, Bancroft implied that the "people" were the ultimate emancipators: "As he [Lincoln] walked with them side by side, [he] inspired them with their own wisdom and energy" (ibid.).

8. "Abraham Lincoln," *NY Times*, Feb. 13, 1866. By this point, Bancroft had

become a speechwriter for President Johnson, already locked in battle with the congressional Republicans who would impeach Johnson two years later (the Senate would fail by one vote to convict the president).

9. "Eulogy of Hon. Charles Sumner," in *A Memorial of Abraham Lincoln* (Boston: Ticknor and Fields, 1865), 134.

10. Charles Sumner to John Bright, Jun. 5, 1865, in *The Selected Letters of Charles Sumner*, ed. Beverly Wilson Palmer (Boston: Northeastern University Press, 1990), 2:304.

11. "Abraham Lincoln," *NY Times*, Jun. 2, 1865; "Eulogy of Hon. Charles Sumner," 147, 151.

12. "Eulogy of Hon. Charles Sumner," 127. On June 5, Sumner told Bright he felt "very sanguine that we shall succeed," since "there is prodigious unanimity of sentiment for the colored suffrage." Sumner to Bright, Jun. 5, 1865, in *Selected Letters*, 304. But an editorial attacking his memorial address in Henry Raymond's *New York Times* on June 3 must have given him pause. The *Times* called for an indefinite period of "probation" before southern states should be expected to let African Americans vote, since most former slaves were "field-hands—illiterate, ignorant of even the existence of government, and just as incompetent to form opinions on political subjects as the cattle by their side." "Negro Suffrage in the South," *NY Times*, Jun. 3, 1865.

13. Colfax, "Memorial Address" (see chap. 2, n. 3). Like Bancroft's and Sumner's, Colfax's address was widely reprinted in northern newspapers.

14. "Colfax on Lincoln," *NY Times*, Apr. 20, 1883.

15. Walt Whitman, "In Mem of A. L.," in *Notebooks and Unpublished Prose Manuscripts*, ed. Edward F. Grier (New York: New York University Press, 1984), 2:768. Whitman had tossed off his first brief effort, the twelve-line "Hush'd Be the Camps Today," right after the assassination. Like much popular poetry at that juncture, Whitman's poem dwelt on the people's affection for their lost hero. "Sing poet in our name," his mourning soldiers plead, "Sing of the love we bore him."

16. Whitman, "When Lilacs Last in the Dooryard Bloom'd," canto 1, in *Complete Poetry and Collected Prose* (New York: Literary Classics of the United States, 1982), 459. The phrase "martyred chief" was in common usage in April 1865; Whitman used "martyr chief" as the closing words of his lecture "The Death of Lincoln," delivered to eastern audiences in the late 1870s and early 1880s. "A Poet on the Platform," *NY Trib*, Apr. 15, 1879.

17. Whitman, "When Lilacs Last," cantos 6, 10, 16; "Walt Whitman," *NY Times*, Dec. 2, 1866. The *Times* adored "When Lilacs Last in the Dooryard Bloom'd" but said that Whitman's *Leaves of Grass* "wallows exultingly in unredeemed and irredeemable indecency and filth . . . Until the social circle, the dinner table and the fireside are deemed fitting theatres for every topic and for every act for which the sanction of Nature can be invoked, this volume cannot be accepted

as fit for the audience which it seeks and claims." Whitman had managed, with "Lilacs" and his other Lincoln and Civil War poems, to please the literary gate-keepers as well as a large reading public.

18. Walt Whitman to Nathaniel Bloom and John F. S. Gray, Mar. 19, 1863, and Whitman to James P, Kirkwood, Apr. 27[?], 1864, in Whitman, *Correspondence*, 1:82–83, 215 (see chap. 1, n. 3).

19. Whitman notebook entry, Oct. 31 and Nov. 1, 1863, in Whitman, *Notebooks and Unpublished*, 2:539.

20. Whitman, "When Lilacs Last," cantos 6, 18, 20.

21. Ibid., cantos 6, 15, 16.

22. Whitman, "O Captain! My Captain!," in *Complete Poetry*, 467.

23. "The Presidential Progress," *NY Herald*, Feb. 20, 1861.

24. Whitman, "Death of Abraham Lincoln," in *Complete Poetry*, 1037–39, 1042, 1046.

25. Herndon to Holland, May 26, 1865, in Allen C. Guelzo, "Holland's Informants: The Construction of Josiah Holland's 'Life of Abraham Lincoln,'" *JALA* 23 (Winter 2002): 18.

26. Herndon to Holland, May 26, 1865, in Guelzo, "Holland's Informants," 18 ("inner life"). The excerpt in the *New York Times*, Dec. 31, 1865, captured the striking appeal of Herndon's December 12 lecture; the excerpt in the *Illinois State Journal*, Dec. 13, 1865, reprinted in *CH Trib*, Dec. 15, 1865, did not. The full text of Herndon's original "character" manuscript (he delivered the second half of it in a Springfield lecture on December 26) was printed for the first time as "Analysis of the Character of Abraham Lincoln: A Lecture by William H. Herndon," *Abraham Lincoln Quarterly* 1 (Sept. and Dec. 1941), 343–83, 403–441.

27. A lengthy, eloquent statement written by his brother Elliott may have suggested to Herndon the basic structure, and some of the content, of his lecture. Lincoln's "mind," Elliott wrote, "partook [of] the incongruities of his body." *Herndon's Informants: Letters, Interviews, and Statements about Abraham Lincoln*, ed. Douglas L. Wilson and Rodney O. Davis (Urbana: University of Illinois Press, 1998), 459.

28. "Abraham Lincoln; the Characteristics of His Life as Seen by his Law Partner," *NY Times*, Dec. 31, 1865. Here and in the following paragraphs, I quote only from sentences of the address that appeared in the *Times*, since those were the passages read by a national audience. I restore Herndon's idiosyncratic punctuation and original phrasing whenever the *Times* altered it, but I don't restore his original misspellings. (Herndon's sentences are available in the *Abraham Lincoln Quarterly* 1 [Sept. 1941], 356–59, 364, 366, 381–82.)

29. Francis Bicknell Carpenter's popular book *Six Months at the White House with Abraham Lincoln* (New York: Hurd and Houghton, 1866) brought a twenty-eight-page excerpt of Herndon's lecture to national attention. Perhaps out of

deference to Mary Lincoln's feelings, Carpenter dropped the number "23" and had Herndon say, "I do not think he knew what real joy was for many years" (326). Released in August 1866, *Six Months* had sold fifteen thousand copies by December. "The publishers have not been able to supply the demand," Carpenter wrote to Herndon on Dec. 24, 1866, in *Herndon's Informants*, 522.

30. "Abraham Lincoln," *CH Trib*, Nov. 28, 1866.

31. William Henry Herndon, *Abraham Lincoln, Miss Ann Rutledge, New Salem, Pioneering, and the Poem: A Lecture* (Springfield, IL: Kessinger, 1910), 9. This sixty-seven-page pamphlet reprints the entire lecture (which was delivered in the Old Sangamon County Courthouse in November 1866), as issued by Herndon in a broadside printing of 1866. Identical excerpts were published in the *New York Times* (Nov. 24, 1866), the *Chicago Tribune* (Nov. 28, 1866), and other papers. Here and in what follows, I quote (with one identified exception) from the *Times* excerpt—"A Curious and Interesting Romance," *NY Times*, Nov. 24, 1866—which faithfully reproduces Herndon's printed text. I give a longer account of the 1866 lecture, and of Abraham's love for Ann, in "Lincoln's First and Final Love? William Herndon's Ann Rutledge" at http://richardwfox.com.

Chapter Seven: Monuments for the Ages

1. "The Monument," *NY Trib*, May 17, 1865; "Lincoln Memorials—Monumental Art," *NY Times*, Jul. 8, 1865.

2. "Monuments," *Independent* (New York), May 11, 1865; Charles Sumner, "Speech in the Senate on . . . a [proposed] Statue of Abraham Lincoln [by Vinnie Ream]," Jul. 27, 1866, in *Charles Sumner: His Complete Works* (Norwood, MA: Norwood Press, 1874), 14:171.

3. Jesse K. Dubois, "History . . . of the National Lincoln Monument Association," speech delivered Oct. 15, *CH Trib*, Oct. 16, 1874.

4. "Abraham Lincoln," in *Harriet Hosmer: Letters and Memories*, ed. Cornelia Carr (London: John Lane, 1913), 368. In his book *Standing Soldiers, Kneeling Slaves* (Princeton, NJ: Princeton University Press, 1999), chap. 4, Kirk Savage recounts the story of Hosmer's star-crossed creation.

5. The highlight of the 1876 dedication ceremony was Frederick Douglass's subtle and impassioned testimonial to Lincoln, discussed in Chapter 8.

6. AL, "Address before the Young Men's Lyceum of Springfield, Illinois," Jan. 27, 1838, in *CW* 1:115.

7. F. Lauriston Bullard, *Lincoln in Marble and Bronze* (New Brunswick, NJ: Rutgers University Press, 1952), 8–9. In *Summers with Lincoln: Looking for the Man in the Monuments* (New York: Fordham University Press, 2008), 217, James A. Percoco estimated that there were 191 public Lincoln "statues" (including busts) in the United States, 42 of them in Illinois. See also "Lincoln

Statues across the Country" on the Looking for Lincoln website, http://pbs.org/wnet/lookingforlincoln.

8. "Abraham Lincoln," *NY Times*, Oct. 22, 1869.

9. John C. Hamilton to Henry Kirke Brown, Oct. 1865, quoted in Bullard, *Lincoln in Marble*, 33–34.

10. "The Lincoln Statue on Union Square," *NY Trib*, Oct. 1, 1870.

11. "Home and Foreign Gossip," *Harper's Weekly*, Aug. 3, 1872. Kirk Savage discusses the National Lincoln Monument Association's open competition in *Standing Soldiers, Kneeling Slaves*, 100–103.

12. *CH Trib*: "Abraham Lincoln," Oct. 15, 1874; "The Lincoln Monument," Oct. 16, 1874.

13. H. M. Turner, "Wayside Dots and Jots," *Christian Recorder*, Oct. 25, 1877.

14. The wooden coffin that John Power helped move in 1876 was not the famous black-and-silver coffin from the funeral processions of 1865. That iconic container had been retired on account of wear and tear in 1871. By 1874, Lincoln's remains were lying in a lead-lined cedar coffin that could fit inside the new marble sarcophagus.

15. Thomas J. Craughwell, *Stealing Lincoln's Body* (Cambridge, MA: Harvard University Press, 2007), gives a fine summary of how the absurd plot developed.

16. National Lincoln Monument Association statement, Apr. 14, 1887, in John Carroll Power, *History of an Attempt to Steal the Body of Abraham Lincoln* (Springfield, IL: Rokker, 1890), 96.

17. "Lincoln's Body," *CH Trib*, Apr. 15, 1887.

18. "A Guarded Grave," *LA Times*, Apr. 15, 1887; "Lincoln Buried at Last," *NY Trib*, Apr. 15, 1887. On the same date (the twenty-second anniversary of Lincoln's death), front-page stories on the reburial also appeared in the *Atlanta Constitution, Baltimore Sun, Boston Globe*, and other papers.

19. "To End a Disgrace," *CH Trib*, Dec. 18, 1894.

20. "Lincoln's Body Rests at Last," *CH Trib*, Apr. 25, 1901.

21. "Lincoln's Face Shown to Few," *CH Trib*, Sept. 27, 1901; "Opened Casket Despite Protest," *Daily Pantagraph* (Bloomington, IL), Sept. 27, 1901; "Martyr Is Now at Rest," *Illinois State Journal*, Sept. 27, 1901. Thomas Lynch, a St. Louis undertaker who claimed to have actually chalked Lincoln's face for the May 3, 1865, public viewing in Springfield, told the *State Journal* he couldn't explain how the president's face had turned black by 1887 and reverted to white by 1901. Maybe the copious amounts of rouge chalk and amber he had brushed on in 1865 "to completely hide the discoloration of the skin" had "through some unexplainable action asserted itself and [given] the skin the white appearance seen" in 1901. "Says Face Was Chalked," *Illinois State Journal*, Sept. 29, 1901.

22. "Fresh Literature," *LA Times*, Nov. 6, 1887.

23. The *Sunday Inter-Ocean* (Chicago)—"In Memory of Lincoln" (Oct. 23, 1887)—gave full-page, seven-column coverage to the unveiling ceremony, and

noted the importance of the "heavy chair" in relieving "the long form [Lincoln's frame] of its ungainly proportions."

24. "The Martyr President," *CH Trib*, Oct. 23, 1887. This story was picked up by papers around the country, including the *Madison [Parish] Times* in Tallulah, LA ("Lincoln Statue," Nov. 12, 1887), which printed a very respectable line drawing of the sculpture.

25. Mariana Griswold van Rensselaer, "Saint Gaudens's Lincoln," *Century*, Nov. 1887, 37. In the same issue, painter and critic Kenyon Cox saluted Saint-Gaudens for reviving American sculpture, starting with his 1880 statue of Admiral David Farragut in Manhattan's Madison Square. Free copies of the magazine were sent to newspapers all over the country, spawning local stories about Saint-Gaudens. The *Century*'s reproduction (p. 38) of *Standing Lincoln* is available at "Making of America," ebooks.library.cornell.edu/m/moa/browse. html.

26. Over time, the *Standing Lincoln* took on a life of its own as a symbol of American ideals and goodwill. Replicas were sold and installed at home and abroad: by 1920, Lincoln was standing outside the Palace of Westminster in London's Parliament Square; and in 1966 the statue was dedicated in Mexico City's Parque Lincoln.

Chapter Eight: Black Emancipation, White Reunion

1. "Monument to Lincoln," *NY Trib*, Apr. 15, 1876. See the close-up of the statue at http://presidentsusa.net/lincolnpark2.jpg.

2. In Douglass, *Frederick Douglass Papers: Series One*, 4:428 (see chap. 4, n. 18), editors John Blassingame and Robert McKivigan accept Freeman Murray's 1916 claim that Douglass disliked the pose of Thomas Ball's kneeling slave. They quote "observers" at the ceremony in 1876 who allegedly heard Douglass say that the statue "showed the Negro on his knees when a more manly attitude would have been indicative of freedom." Murray himself mentioned not "observers," but a single witness, John W. Cromwell, who wrote those words to Murray four decades after the event (Cromwell did not claim Douglass spoke those exact words—just words to that effect). Supposedly, Douglass had declared to the entire crowd his disapproval of the slave's depiction. If so, one of the reporters present would likely have heard the same thing Cromwell heard, and reported it. Freeman Henry Morris Murray, *Emancipation and the Freed in American Sculpture* (Washington, DC: Author, 1916), 199. As Kirk Savage points out in *Standing Soldiers, Kneeling Slaves*, chap. 4 (see chap. 7, n. 4), the posture of the slave was hotly debated before the dedication, leading to changes in its design.

3. "Negro Suffering and Suffrage in the South," *Christian Recorder*, Jul. 1, 1865.

4. "Douglass on Lincoln," *NY Times*, Apr. 22, 1876. The 360-word sentence is

structured as anaphora: the phrase "under his rule" comes at the start of nine straight clauses, building a crescendo for Lincoln the emancipator.

5. Unnamed former slave, quoted in "Missouri Ex-slave Story," in *Born in Slavery*, vol. 10, *Missouri Narratives*, 225–26 (see chap. 4, n. 3).

6. Booker T. Washington, *Up from Slavery* (New York: Doubleday Page, 1901), 8.

7. Solon Robinson speech, Mar. 26, 1867, reported in letter from Lucy Chase, a northern white teacher, to Fred May, in "Northern Visions of Race, Region and Reform," American Antiquarian Society Online Resource, http://faculty. assumption.edu/aas/Manuscripts/Chase/03-00-1866.html. The AAS site dates the letter "March, 1866," but internal evidence (including the date of Robinson's speech, "Tuesday March 26th") shows that the year was 1867. Robinson's words appear to have been reconstructed after he delivered them. At first glance, Chase's letter appears to describe Robinson as a black minister, but she actually notes that he was a (white) writer for the *New York Tribune*. For more on Robinson's interest in the African Americans of Charleston, see http:// library.syr.edu/digital/guides/r/robinson_s.htm.

8. "Emancipation Day at Frederick, Md.," *Baltimore Sun*, Aug. 25, 1881.

9. Joshua A. Brockett, "The Emancipation Proclamation," *African Methodist Episcopal Review* 8 (Apr. 1892): 418.

10. *Richmond Whig*, May 12, 1863, quoted in "Late Southern News," *NY Trib*, May 16, 1863. Michael Davis, *The Image of Lincoln in the South* (Knoxville: University of Tennessee Press, 1971), 98–104, lays out the southern reactions to the assassination.

11. *Augusta Chronicle*, cited in "The Voice of the Press," *NY Times*, Sept. 20, 1881.

12. "The South Sincerely Mourning," *NY Times*, Sept. 21, 1881.

13. "James A. Garfield," *NY Times*, Sept. 20, 1881.

14. *NY Times*: "South Sincerely Mourning," Sept. 21, 1881; "Ex-soldiers Grasping Hands," Sept. 23, 1881.

15. "New England's Great Day," *NY Trib*, Dec. 23, 1886. Soon Grady's speech became famous in the North, the South, and abroad as a classic of American eloquence. Raymond B. Nixon, *Henry W. Grady* (New York: Knopf, 1943), 245–53, samples the northern testimonials to its grandeur. The *New York Tribune*, while praising Grady's oratory, reminded readers that southern "prejudice and fraud" had deprived African American men of the vote, a right they had widely exercised in the late 1860s and '70s (ibid., 247).

16. *NY Trib*: "The News of Brooklyn," Feb. 13, 1896; "Lincoln and the Negro," Feb. 13, 1899.

17. "Colored Men Protest," *NY Trib*, Oct. 4, 1900.

18. AL, "Address before the Wisconsin State Agricultural Society" (see chap. 3, n. 3); AL, "Annual Message to Congress," Dec. 3, 1861, in *CW* 5:52.

19. Jane Addams, *Twenty Years at Hull-House* (1910; Urbana: University of Illinois Press, 1990), 15, 19–20, 25.

20.　"Lincoln His Theme," *CH Trib*, Feb. 13, 1896.

21.　"Secretary Hay on McKinley," *New York Observer and Chronicle*, Nov. 28, 1901.

22.　"President Roosevelt's First Message," *NY Times*, Dec. 4, 1901.

23.　"McKinley, Martyr to Envy and Hate," *NY Trib*, Sept. 19, 1901.

24.　"Last Speeches on President's List," *NY Times*, Jun. 5, 1903.

25.　"Call Roosevelt Second Lincoln," *NY Times*, Feb. 14, 1905.

26.　Ibid.

27.　Roosevelt's article "Character and Success," *Outlook*, Mar. 31, 1900, 725–27 ("bodily vigor"), spells out the physical, intellectual, and ethical components of "the strenuous life" more fully than does "The Strenuous Life," his well-known 1899 speech. Both are reprinted in *The Strenuous Life: Essays and Addresses* (New York: Century, 1900).

28.　"Roosevelt Praises Lincoln as Fighter," *NY Times*, Feb. 13, 1909. This report quoted Roosevelt's extemporaneous ending ("whose blood was shed . . ."); the *WA Post* ("Roosevelt's Tribute to Lincoln," Feb. 13, 1909) did not.

29.　Luke E. Wright, "Lincoln and the Lost Cause," in Nathan William MacChesney, ed., *Abraham Lincoln: The Tribute of a Century, 1809–1909* (Chicago: McClurg, 1910), 261.

30.　Calvin Dill Wilson, "The Little Farm That Grew a Man," *Midland*, Mar. 1, 1909.

Chapter Nine: Celebrating the Centenary of 1909

1.　Brief wire service reports announcing Villard's "Call" appeared in many northern papers without editorial comment. The *Chicago Tribune* ("Rights of Negro to Be Defended," Feb. 13, 1909), came close to adding an endorsement, running as a subheadline the sentence, "Appeal Says Blacks Are Robbed of Right to Vote in the Southern States." David Levering Lewis shows how the NAACP emerged out of Villard's "Call" in his *W. E. B. Du Bois*, vol. 1, *Biography of a Race, 1868–1919* (New York: Holt, 1993), 386–407.

2.　William English Walling, "The Race War in the North," *Independent* (New York), Sept. 3, 1908.

3.　"Indicts Six More on Riot Charges," *CH Trib*, Aug. 22, 1908. Donnegan may well have encountered Lincoln in Springfield in the 1850s. Richard E. Hart, "Springfield's African Americans as a Part of the Lincoln Community," *JALA*, Winter 1999, 40, n. 15, mentions two other African American Donnegans living in the town during Lincoln's residence there.

4.　"Honor at Springfield," *NY Trib*, Feb. 13, 1909.

5.　Ibid.

6.　"Will Celebrate Lincoln's Birth," *San Francisco Chronicle*, Feb. 7, 1909. Many white southerners had come to admire Lincoln—he would have saved them from Radical Reconstruction, they felt sure—but that sentiment didn't translate into a groundswell of enthusiasm for him on February 12, 1909. In the former Confederate states, Lincoln was dutifully mentioned in some public schools, and feted with enthusiasm in black churches and at reunions of blue and gray war veterans. See, for example, "Blue and the Gray Join in a Tribute to Lincoln," *Atlanta Constitution* Feb. 15, 1909.

7. "Whole City to Join in Honoring Lincoln," *NY Times*, Feb. 11, 1909.

8. "The Day in the Schools," *NY Times*, Feb. 13, 1909. Famous Hearst newspaper editor Arthur Brisbane joined the Lower East Side pupils of PS 177 on Market Street in "chanting" the Gettysburg Address. Probably "chanting" means "reciting," not "singing," but even recitation suggests the air of civic piety that marked the day. Other urban papers, including the *Philadelphia Ledger* and the *Cleveland Press*, also conducted Lincoln essay contests for schoolchildren. The *Ledger* received almost five thousand essays and dispensed six hundred awards at a civic assembly on March 19, 1909. An audience of five thousand kids watched the governor and mayor present the prizes. "Lincoln Prizes Awarded," *NY Times*, Mar. 20, 1909.

9. Frederick Trevor Hill, "Lincoln's Legacy of Inspiration," *NY Times*, Feb. 7, 1909; Senta Jonas, "Sketch by a Little Girl" ("one of the homeliest faces"), *NY Times*, Feb. 28, 1909.

10. *NY Times*: "Plucky Boy Invalid Wins Lincoln Medal," Feb. 18, 1909; "Sam'l Bussell Dies, Medal Beside Him," Feb. 27, 1909. On February 28, the *Times* published a family photo of young Bussell, along with pictures of its top ten essayists.

11. *NY Times*: "With a Little Help from Mother," Feb. 16, 1909; "Winners of the Lincoln Competition," Feb. 28, 1909; "Winners Rush to Get Lincoln Medals," Mar. 20, 1909.

12. *NY Times*: "Prefaces His Essay by Lincoln's Will," Feb. 19, 1909 (gives Joseph's last name as Gomes); "Children to Whom Certificates Have Been Awarded," Feb. 28, 1909 (gives his last name as Gomers). Radical preacher Reverdy C. Ransom and his very large church were well known to *Times* readers (e.g., "Vote against Taft, Negro Preacher Cries," *NY Times*, Sept. 28, 1908).

13. Alexandra Kliatshco, "Little Alien's Wisdom," *NY Times*, Feb. 28, 1909. For more on Alexandra, see "New York Times Essay Contest" at http://richardwfox. com.

14. "Impressions of an Examiner," *NY Times*, Feb. 21, 1909, lays out the cultural differences revealed in the essays.

15. "The Lincoln Essays," *NY Times*, Feb. 28, 1909.

16. Wanamaker Galleries advertisement, *NY Times*, Feb. 12, 1909.

17. "A Century in Business: Firms in Existence since the Birth of Lincoln," *NY Times*, Feb. 12, 1909.

18. Derby Desk Company advertisement, *CH Trib*, Feb. 7, 1909.

19. Talking Machine Shop advertisement, *CH Trib*, Feb. 7, 1909.

20. J. I. Case Threshing Machine Company advertisement, *CH Trib*, Feb. 7, 1909.

21. Waterman Company advertisement, *CH Trib*, Feb. 7, 1909.

22. "Lincoln and the Tribune," *CH Trib*, Feb. 7, 1909.

23. "Lincoln and the Tribune" (advertisement), *CH Trib*, Feb. 2, 1909.

24. "Lincoln's Last Photograph," *CH Trib*, Feb. 6, 1909. In 1909, the February 5 Gardner photos were thought to have been taken in April, and to have been the last ever taken of him. In fact, Henry Warren took the last photograph of the living Lincoln at the White House on March 5.

25. "The Centenary of Abraham Lincoln's Birth," *CH Trib*, Feb. 7, 1909. The centennial edition cost a nickel, but only those who reserved an advance copy got it for that price. On February 7, newsstands and newsboys commanded a quarter or more for it.

26. Gutzon Borglum, "The Beauty of Lincoln," *Everybody's Magazine*, Feb. 1910, 218. Borglum's marble Lincoln bust can be viewed at http://www.aoc.gov/capitol-hill/busts/abraham-lincoln-bust. Many newspapers ran stories in 1909 about Lincoln's physical appearance—for example, "Lincoln's Personal Appearance," *CH Trib*, Feb. 7, 1909; "Not a Homely Man," *Boston Globe*, Feb. 12, 1909; "Lincoln Not Ugly, She Says," *Baltimore Sun*, Feb. 14, 1909.

27. Borglum defended his outlook in "Individuality, Sincerity and Reverence in American Art," *Craftsman*, Oct. 1, 1908. Gustav Stickley's "Arts and Crafts" magazine *The Craftsman* summed up Borglum's approach to sculpting Lincoln: spontaneity tethered to precise measurements of Lincoln's head; to immersion in all known Lincoln images; and to the theory that the president's "intellectual" activity was centered on the right side, and "spiritual" activity on the left. "All the Varying Phases of Abraham Lincoln's Character Shown in Gutzon Borglum's Great Portrait Bust," Apr. 1, 1908, 27.

28. "American Art—from Different Points of View," *NY Times*, Oct. 11, 1908; "How This Edition Was Made," *CH Trib*, Feb. 7, 1909. A 1987 tourist guide (Alfred Borcover, "Springfield: Capital Sights in the Land of Lincoln," *CH Trib*, Jun. 7, 1987) singled out the Borglum bronze, lending it an air of mystery as well as intimacy. "A woman pauses at the bust," wrote Borcover, "touches the shiny nose rubbed by many before her and says: 'We'll see you, old boy,' and slowly walks on. The sense you get here, and it's rather spooky, is that Lincoln died recently."

29. "Deeds of Lincoln Sway All Chicago," *CH Trib*, Feb. 13, 1909.

30. "This Is Lincoln Centennial Day," *CH Trib*, Feb. 12, 1909.

31. J. W. E. Bowen, "The Liberation of the Negro," in MacChesney, *Abraham Lincoln*, 91–92 (see chap. 8, note 28).

32. Ibid., 96–97.

33. Woodrow Wilson, "Abraham Lincoln: A Man of the People," in MacChesney, *Abraham Lincoln*, 27–28 (see chap. 8, note 28).

34. Ibid., 17, 29.

35. Ibid., 22, 29–30. Wilson the Democrat pointed toward, but stopped short of articulating, the kind of new "nationalism" soon advocated by Herbert David Croly, an avid student of Lincoln, in his *The Promise of American Life* (1909; New York: Dutton, 1963). Individual rights and local privileges, said Croly, had gotten out of hand. A new "nationality"—not chauvinist sentiment, but a new consciousness of collective purpose (akin to Lincoln's republican body politic)—could underwrite a democratic "individuality" premised on social responsibility. All the dust kicked up in the nineteenth-century stampede to get ahead had obscured the truth that "the nation is so much more than a group of individuals . . . the nation has an individuality of its own" (407).

36. "To Portray Lincoln on the Stage," *NY Times*, Feb. 4, 1906.

37. Ibid.

38. Benjamin Chapin, "Lincoln in the Hearts of the People," *Independent* (New York), Feb. 11, 1909. Photos of Chapin are available at the New York Public Library's Digital Gallery, http://digitalgallery.nypl.org/nypldigital/index.cfm.

39. "Abraham Lincoln as a Stage Figure," *NY Times*, Apr. 1, 1906.

40. "Chapin, the Star of the Lincoln Cycle," *Motion Picture World*, Aug. 7, 1915, 1022.

41. "The New Orleans Picayune," *NY Trib*, Aug. 7, 1909.

42. "The Indian on the Cent," *NY Times*, Feb. 20, 1909.

43. "Shall Heads of Great Men Be Placed on U.S. Coins?" *Philadelphia Ledger*, reprinted in *Wall Street Journal*, Feb. 15, 1909.

44. Carl Sandburg, "Lincoln on Pennies," *Milwaukee Daily News*, n.d. [1909], http://in.gov/lincoln/teachers.html ("Lincoln on Pennies by Carl Sandburg," lesson-plan menu).

45. "New Lincoln Pennies Here," *NY Times*, Aug. 4, 1909.

46. "Vary on Memorial," *WA Post*, Feb. 12, 1909.

47. Ibid.

48. "Lincoln Memorial Site," *NY Times*, Feb. 18, 1909.

Chapter Ten: Solidifying the Lincoln Cult: Two Memorials

1. Carl Sandburg, *Abraham Lincoln: The Prairie Years* (New York: Harcourt, Brace, 1926), 1:480.

2. "Is a Model of Art," *CH Trib*, Jan. 29, 1893.

3. "A Memorial to Lincoln Worthy Alike of the Nation and the Man," *NY Trib*, Jan. 7, 1912. On the selection of Bacon and French as the Lincoln Memorial's architect and sculptor, respectively, and on the political and cultural conflicts that marked the building of it, two works are essential: Kirk Savage, *Monument Wars* (Berkeley: University of California Press, 2009, and Christopher A. Thomas, *The Lincoln Memorial & American Life* (Princeton, NJ: Princeton University Press, 2002).

4. "Memorial to Lincoln," *NY Trib.*

5. Gutzon Borglum, "The Betrayal of the People by a False Democracy," *Craftsman*, Apr. 1, 1912, 7.

6. George W. Maher, "The Lincoln Memorial and American Ideals," *Construction News*, Jan. 11, 1913, 11.

7. "Great Lincoln Statue Is Doubled in Size," *WA Post*, Oct. 5, 1919.

8. Daniel Chester French to Charles Moore, May 13, 1922, quoted in Michael Richman, *Daniel Chester French* (New York: Metropolitan Museum of Art for the National Trust for Historic Preservation, 1976), 184.

9. Jules Guerin, "The Mural Decorations," *Art and Archaeology* 13 (Jun. 1922): 259; Henry Bacon, "The Architecture of the Lincoln Memorial," in *The Lincoln Memorial, Washington* (Washington, DC: US Government Printing Office, 1927), 45.

10. "Harding Dedicates Lincoln Memorial; Blue and Gray Join," *NY Times*, May 31, 1922.

11. Adam Fairclough, "Civil Rights and the Lincoln Memorial: The Censored Speeches of Robert R. Morton (1922) and John Lewis (1963)," *Journal of Negro History* 82 (Autumn 1997): 408–16.

12. *Chicago Defender*, Jun. 10, 1922: "Harding Truckles to South at Dedication"; M. LeCount Chestnut, "Mock Ideal of Lincoln at Memorial." Chestnut described the segregated seating for invited blacks and identified ten of the African American dignitaries who laudably "withdrew" from the event rather than accept seats in the "bloc d'Afrique"—"that sector of squalid conscience."

13. W. E. B. Du Bois, "The World and Us," *Crisis* (New York), Jul. 1922, 103.

14. Roscoe Simmons, "The Week," *Chicago Defender*, Jul. 8, 1922. Du Bois's *Crisis* had just praised Robert S. Abbott's weekly *Chicago Defender* for its modern plant; its staff composed of "college men from Harvard and elsewhere, business men and experts"; and its national circulation of "over 100,000 copies monthly." (Black porters helped make it national by carrying the paper south on interstate trains.) "Horizon," *Crisis* (New York), Jun. 1922, 74–75. Andrew M. Kaye details Simmons's political dealings in "Colonel Roscoe Conkling Simmons and the Mechanics of Black Leadership," *Journal of American Studies* 37 (Apr. 2003): 79–98.

15. W. E. B. Du Bois, "Again, Lincoln," *Crisis* (New York), Sept. 1922, 199–201.

16. "A. M. E. Zion Convention Praised by Governors," *WA Post*, Aug. 5, 1926; "A. M. E. Zion Quadrennial Convention Closes in D. C.," *Chicago Defender*, Aug. 14, 1926. Scott A. Sandage, "A Marble House Divided: The Lincoln Memorial, the Civil Rights Movement, and the Politics of Memory, 1939–1963," *Journal of American History* 80 (Jun. 1993): 143, calls the AME Zion Church delegates' visit to the Memorial "a mass religious service."

17. "When Lincoln Rode the Circuit," *NY Times Book Review*, Feb. 14, 1926.

18. Van Wyck Brooks, "Carl Sandburg's Lincoln," *Forum*, Apr. 1926, 632, 634.

19. Carl Sandburg, *Ever the Winds of Chance* (Urbana: University of Illinois Press, 1983), 156–57. Sandburg drafted this second volume of his autobiography in 1955–56.

20. Carl Sandburg, "Chicago," in *Selected Poems*, ed. George Hendrick and Willene Hendrick (San Diego, CA: Harcourt Brace, 1996), 3–4; and "Nigger," in *The Complete Poems of Carl Sandburg*, rev. ed. (New York: Harcourt Brace Jovanovich, 1970), 23.

21. Sandburg to L. W. Payne Jr., Dec.3, 1926 ("for ten years I have been designated in Who's Who as an 'Independent'"), and Sandburg to Romain Rolland, ca. Oct.1919, in *The Letters of Carl Sandburg*, ed. Herbert Mitgang (New York: Harcourt, Brace & World, 1968), 243, 169–70.

22. Sandburg, *The Chicago Race Riots, July, 1919* (1919; New York: Harcourt, Brace & World, 1969), 3.

23. Sandburg, "Abraham Lincoln's Father and Mother," in *Selected Poems*, 89–90. In addition to three Lincoln poems he published between 1916 and 1918 ("In a Back Alley," "Fire-Logs," and "Knucks"), the book contains four other previously unpublished Lincoln poems by Sandburg ("Lincoln," "Mr. Lincoln and His Gloves," "Journey and Oath," and an untitled verse), at least three of them written in 1914 and 1915.

24. Sandburg, *Lincoln: The Prairie Years*, 1:vii.

25. Ibid., 1:13; Sandburg, "Fire-Logs," in *Selected Poems*, 79.

26. Sandburg to William Allen White, Oct. 20, 1928, in Sandburg, *Letters*, 262.

27. Sandburg, *Lincoln: The Prairie Years*, 2:284, 1:304.

28. Ibid., 2:285.

29. I address Lincoln's aversion to nostalgia in "Abraham Lincoln's Nostalgia" at http://richardwfox.com.

30. Sandburg, *The People, Yes* (1936; San Diego, CA: Harcourt Brace Jovanovich, 1990), 134 (poem no. 57). Sandburg quoted Lincoln accurately on not planting a thorn in any man's bosom (*CW* 8:101), but not on avoiding malice; the final line should have been the less poetic "what I deal with is too vast for malicious dealing" (*CW* 5:346).

31. Sandburg, *Lincoln: The Prairie Years*, 1:110–11. To believe that Lincoln witnessed the slave auction in New Orleans not only requires accepting the truth of an 1882 recollection of a late-1860s recollection of an 1831 event; it also requires *rejecting* Lincoln's own written assertion in 1860 that John Hanks had not accompanied him to New Orleans in 1831, but had gone with him only as far as St. Louis. For the full particulars, consult Burlingame, *Abraham Lincoln*, 1:56–57 (see chap. 1, n. 1).

32. Sandburg, *Lincoln: The Prairie Years*, 1:109–10.

33. Anne Carroll Moore, "Recent Books for Children," *Bookman*, Apr. 1926, 209; Carl Sandburg, *Abe Lincoln Grows Up* (1928; San Diego, CA: Harcourt Brace Jovanovich, 1975), 218–21.

34. George Edmund Hayes, "The New Emancipation," *Chicago Defender*, Nov. 19, 1938; "Negro Gains Hailed by Mrs. Roosevelt," *NY Times*, Feb. 11, 1938.

35. Sandage, "Marble House Divided," 144. Raymond Arsenault details the NAACP and Department of the Interior deliberations about the Memorial in *The Sound of Freedom: Marian Anderson, the Lincoln Memorial, and the Concert That Awakened America* (New York: Bloomsbury Press, 2009), 145–50.

36. Edward T. Folliard, "Ickes Introduces Contralto at Lincoln Memorial," *WA Post*, Apr. 10, 1939. Susan Stamberg, "Denied a Stage, She Sang for a Nation," NPR Morning Edition, Apr. 9, 2014, is archived with excellent photos at http://www.npr.org/2014/04/09/298760473/denied-a-stage-she-sang-for-a-nation. Anderson's performance of "My Country 'Tis of Thee" on Apr. 9, 1939, is at https://www.youtube.com/watch?v=mAONYTMf2pk.

37. "Capital Tribute to Lincoln One of Simplicity," *CH Trib*, Feb. 13, 1925 ("ranks upon ranks of little colored children" singing at the Memorial). In 1927 the *Chicago Defender* published "a model program" for Emancipation Day celebrations, advising that they begin with James Weldon Johnson's hymn "Lift Every Voice and Sing" and end with "My Country 'Tis of Thee," to be "sung by entire audience" ("Emancipation Celebration Set for Jan. 1," Dec. 31, 1927).

38. Sandage, "Marble House Divided," 135–67, notes the Lincoln Memorial's development as a sacred space. Charles I. Griswold offers thoughtful reflections on the Memorial in relation to its surrounding monuments in "The Vietnam Veterans Memorial and the Washington Mall: Philosophical Thoughts on Political Iconography," *Critical Inquiry* 12 (Summer 1986): 688–719.

Chapter Eleven: The Hero on Screen, from Griffith to Gage

1. Henry Fonda, *Fonda: My Life*, as told to Howard Teichmann (New York: New American Library, 1981), 125.

2. A Lincoln photograph first appeared in a motion picture in Edwin S. Porter's *The Martyred Presidents* (1901), and Edison's *Uncle Tom's Cabin* (1903) made the first use of Lincoln's stationary image in a film drama (he was shown as the liberator standing over the kneeling slave). Mark S. Reinhart's indispensable catalogue counts twenty-eight film depictions of Lincoln before Griffith's silent *Birth of a Nation* (1915), and another twenty-nine before Griffith's talkie *Abraham Lincoln* (1930). Reinhart, *Abraham Lincoln on Screen*, 2nd ed. (Jefferson, NC: McFarland, 2009), 225.

3. Robert E. Sherwood, "The Silent Drama," *Life*, Feb. 14, 1924, 24; Helen Klumph, "Terms 'Lincoln' Greatest Film," *LA Times*, Jan. 27, 1924.

4. Arthur Lennig, "'There Is a Tragedy Going On Here Which I Will Tell You Later': D. W. Griffith and Abraham Lincoln," *Film History* 22 (Mar. 2010): 41–72, gives copious details on Griffith's dealings with United Artists and includes production photos from scenes cut after the film's initial release in

New York City. The early prints included a prologue depicting a slave ship whose human cargo is writhing below deck while the crew throws a dead slave overboard. (Stephen Vincent Benét's *John Brown's Body* also begins with a slave ship.) When the studio abridged the film months later to make it eligible for double-feature bookings, the slave ship scene was cut. The original opening has been restored in the most recent Kino DVD (2002).

5. Roberta Nangle, "Film Reveals Lincoln with Jokes, Sorrows," *CH Trib*, Sept. 19, 1930.

6. "Make-up Vital in Making an Accurate Abe," *WA Post*, Dec. 21, 1930.

7. Mark Forrest, "The Martyred President," *Saturday Review* (London), Feb. 28, 1931, 303.

8. Edwin Schallert, "'Lincoln' Life Revisualized," *LA Times*, Dec. 15, 1930. Cf. Mordaunt Hall, "Mr. Griffith's First Talker," *NY Times*, Aug. 26, 1930: "There is a finely conceived flash at the end, with a log cabin dissolving into the majestic Lincoln memorial."

9. Nelson B. Bell, "Zanuck 'Pulls Fast One' with 'Young Mister Lincoln,'" *WA Post*, May 29, 1939; "'Young Mr. Lincoln' Has Its Premiere," *NY Times*, May 31, 1939 (trainload).

10. "Lincoln's Town Turns Out for Film Premiere," *CH Trib*, May 31, 1939 ("all the Hollywood trimmings"). Anderson reprised her performance at the Los Angeles premiere on June 2, adding a third spiritual to the recital ("Trampin"). Edwin Schallert, "'Young Mr. Lincoln' Gains Gala Preview Approval," *LA Times*, Jun. 3, 1939.

11. "Protest in Illinois Legislature on Slavery," Mar. 3, 1837, in *CW* 1:74–76; Sandburg, *Lincoln: The Prairie Years*, 1:211–12 (see chap. 10, n. 1).

12. In early 2014, a Google search for "images" of "Young Mr. Lincoln" yielded an extensive gallery of stills showing how Ford and Fonda tied Abraham's strapping body to his confident, gracious, and searching temperament.

13. Frank S. Nugent, "The Screen," *NY Times*, Jun. 3, 1939.

14. On Buchman's personal politics, see Michael Kazin, *American Dreamers: How the Left Changed a Nation* (New York: Knopf, 2011), 186–88. When he wrote *Mr. Smith Goes to Washington*, Buchman was a Communist—a fact that Capra concealed from Columbia officials.

15. Raymond Massey, quoted in Theodore Strauss, "Abe Lincoln of 45th St.," *NY Times*, Oct. 30, 1938. "The policy of indifference to evil" is a line spoken by Massey's Lincoln in the play and movie. Sherwood based it on Lincoln's words from his Peoria speech of October 16, 1854: "This *declared* indifference, but as I must think, covert *real* zeal for the spread of slavery, I can not but hate" (in *CW* 2:255). Cf. Raymond Massey, "Lincoln and Democracy," *Abraham Lincoln Quarterly* 1 (Jun. 1940): 99, where he quotes his own lines from Sherwood's script—"indifference to evil"—and mistakenly attributes them to the historical Lincoln.

16.   *WA Post*: "A Lincoln Memorial," Jan. 24, 1940; "For Every American," Feb. 5, 1940; Nelson B. Bell, "'Abe Lincoln in Illinois' Given De Luxe Premiere," Jan. 23, 1940.

17.   Bell, "'Abe Lincoln in Illinois' Given"; Robert Emmet Sherwood, *Abe Lincoln in Illinois* (New York: Scribner, 1939), 131.

18.   Sherwood, *Abe Lincoln in Illinois*, 138. Sherwood added "Jews" and "poor people" to Lincoln's original words: "When the Know-Nothings get control, [the Declaration] will read 'all men are created equal, except negroes, and foreigners and catholics [*sic*].'" AL to Joshua Speed, Aug. 24, 1855, in *CW* 2:323.

19.   Sherwood, *Abe Lincoln in Illinois*, 183 (this line is omitted in the film).

20.   "Lincoln of Carl Sandburg," *NY Times Book Review*, Dec. 3, 1939, 1, 14.

21.   James Agee's on-air comments, February 6, 1955, introducing the one-hour *Omnibus* film *Mr. Lincoln*, which condensed the five original half-hour episodes of 1952–53 ("The Beginning and the End," "Nancy Hanks," "Growing Up," "New Salem," and "Ann Rutledge") and was rebroadcast as a Lincoln's birthday special in 1959. It is available on DVD under the title *Omnibus: James Agee's Mr. Lincoln and the Civil War*.

22.   The debate between Agee and Nevins is offered as a "bonus" on the *Mr. Lincoln* DVD.

23.   John Crosby, "Attracting an Audience," *Boston Globe*, Jan. 11, 1953. According to Crosby, *Omnibus* reached 30 percent of the viewers in its time slot. Looking back in 1954 at the show's first two years, *Variety* gave it good marks. "Such productions as the film series on 'Young Lincoln' will continue to go before the cameras, since the package was one of the best pullers for 'Omnibus.'" "Comes 'Omnibus' Revolution," *Variety*, May 12, 1954, 26, 34.

24.   *Omnibus* aired its Royal-Dano-in-the-coffin sequence in January 1953, a few months after *Life* magazine, the *Boston Globe*, the *Chicago Defender*, and other papers published a never-before-seen photograph of the actual Lincoln lying in his coffin in Manhattan's City Hall on April 24, 1865. That photo, shot by Jeremiah Gurney Jr. and immediately confiscated (and, it was thought, destroyed) by Secretary of War Stanton, was accidentally discovered in 1952. Gurney's camera had been positioned so far away from Lincoln's body—40 feet across the City Hall rotunda—that the photo left the face barely recognizable. *Life* magazine's colossal enlargement (fourteen inches high and thirteen inches wide; "Speaking of Pictures," Sept. 15, 1952, 16–17) was touched up to make him easily identifiable.

25.   Cecil Smith, "Face of Lincoln Will Light Tube," *LA Times*, Feb. 12, 1960.

26.   As of May 2014, *The Face of Lincoln* (1955) was available at https://archive.org/details/face_of_lincoln. For more on Gage, see my essay "And the Oscar Goes to . . . *The Face of Lincoln*" at http://richardwfox.com.

27.   Terence Mal, "Film, Sculpture Tell the World About the Face of Abe Lincoln," *LA Times*, May 10, 1964.

28. Bosley Crowther, "Screen: Colorful Mozart," *NY Times*, Mar. 6, 1956.

29. Wayne Phillips, "Montgomery Is Stage for a Tense Drama," *NY Times*, Mar. 4, 1956.

Chapter Twelve: Standing in Lincoln's Shadow

1. Ordained a Baptist minister in Harlem in the 1930s, Powell was elected to Congress in 1945 and served for a quarter century. From the start he assailed both major parties for giving up Lincoln's ideals, e.g., "Both Major Parties Ignore Negroes, Powell Asserts," *Atlanta World*, Mar. 30, 1947.

2. Wayne Phillips, "Negro Minister Convicted of Directing Bus Boycott," *NY Times*, Mar. 23, 1956.

3. Stanley Rowland Jr., "2,500 Here Hail Boycott Leader," *NY Times*, Mar. 26, 1956.

4. Councilman Earl Brown, "50,000 People," *New York Amsterdam News*, Apr. 7, 1956; "Battle against Tradition: Martin Luther King Jr.," *NY Times*, Mar. 21, 1956; "Integration in Montgomery," *NY Times*, Dec. 22, 1956. These two papers provided especially fine civil-rights coverage in the late 1950s and early 1960s.

5. Jay Walz, "Negroes Hold Rally on Rights in Capital," *NY Times*, May 18, 1957.

6. "Crowd Chants for the Ballot at Pilgrimage," *WA Post*, May 18, 1857; King, "Give Us the Ballot," May 17, 1957, Martin Luther King, Jr. Research and Education Institute, http://mlk-kpp01.stanford.edu.

7. AL, "Address before the Young Men's Lyceum," in *CW* 1:112 (see chap. 7, n. 6).

8. King, "Loving Your Enemies," sermon preached Nov. 17, 1957, Martin Luther King Jr. Online, http://mlkonline.net.

9. *NY Times*: Val Adams, "T.V.: Coverage of March," Aug. 29, 1963; Jack Gould, "Television and Civil Rights," Sept. 8, 1963.

10. James Reston, "'I Have a Dream . . . ,'" *NY Times*, Aug. 29, 1963; AL to Andrew Curtin, Apr. 8, 1861, in *CW* 4:324. The *New York Amsterdam News* used fifteen reporters at the march, and put King's entire speech on pages one and two of its September 7 issue, along with several dozen photographs of the day's events.

11. Whitman, "The Death of Lincoln" (1879), in *Complete Poetry*, 1045 (see chap. 6, n. 16).

12. *Chicago Defender*, Nov. 23, 1963: Ernestine Cofield, "Kennedy's Assassination Worst Tragedy since Lincoln's Death Says Sengstacke," Ted Coleman, "Kennedy, like Lincoln, Killed / A Dear, Dear Friend Is Dead."

13. Peter J. Kumpa, "Kennedy Murdered by Dallas Sniper," *Baltimore Sun*, Nov. 23, 1963.

14. Jacqueline Kennedy Onassis, *Jacqueline Kennedy: Historic Conversations on Life with John F. Kennedy: Interviews with Arthur M. Schlesinger, Jr., 1964* (New York: Hyperion, 2011), 251.

15. "Footnotes to the Assassination: The Kennedy Sense of History," *NY Times*, Dec. 2, 1963.

16. The open-coffin custom continued for the assassinated James Garfield in 1881 and William McKinley in 1901, and for the other two deceased presidents who lay in state at the Capitol before Kennedy: Warren Harding in 1923 and William Howard Taft in 1930. No president since Taft has been given an open-coffin viewing in the Capitol. Hoover, Eisenhower, Johnson, and Reagan did lie in state there after Kennedy, but they lay in closed coffins. *Memorial or Funeral Services in the Capitol Rotunda* (Washington, DC: Senate Historical Office, 2005).

17. Jack Raymond, "Riderless Horse an Ancient Tradition," *NY Times*, Nov. 26, 1963. The rambunctious Black Jack, chosen for his good looks and unencumbered by mourning cloth, is pictured prancing in the Kennedy funeral procession at http://flickr.com/photos/34882515@N08/5513641940. In Lincoln's Washington funeral procession on April 19, his horse Tommy, "led by two grooms, caparisoned," followed the hearse. Morris, *Memorial Record*, 96 (see chap. 5, n. 3).

18. "Deaths in Office Show a 20-Year Coincidence," *NY Times*, Nov. 23, 1963.

19. *Life* magazine's editorial "The 72 Hours and What They Can Teach Us" (Dec. 6, 1963, 4), labored to articulate the cause it believed JFK had been martyred to. "The Kennedy martyrdom is a . . . tragedy of freedom," said *Life*, "a political tragedy of [a] classical kind." JFK had unwittingly died defending the Bill of Rights, which "guaranteed all of us, including not quite certifiable madmen, the right to move freely and to bear arms."

20. "The Assassination of the President," *Troy (NY) Daily Times*, Apr. 29, 1865, reprinting an editorial from the *Springfield Republican*.

21. Edmund Wilson, *Patriotic Gore: Studies in the Literature of the American Civil War* (1962; New York: Oxford University Press, 1966), 130.

22. *NY Times*, Nov. 28, 1963: Tom Wicker, "Johnson Bids Congress Enact Civil Rights Bill with Speed"; "Negroes Praise Johnson Speech."

23. "Dr. King Defends His Stand on Vietnam Issue," *LA Times*, Aug. 22, 1965.

24. King, "Showdown for Nonviolence," *Look*, Apr. 16, 1968, 24–25.

25. *NY Times*: Walter Rugaber, "Dr. King Planning to Disrupt Capital in Drive for Jobs," Dec. 5, 1967; "The Responsibility of Dissent," Dec. 6, 1967.

26. "King Spells Out Eulogy," *Chicago Defender*, Apr. 8, 1968; "King Gave Outline for Eulogy," *WA Post*, Apr. 7, 1968.

27. King, "I've Been to the Mountaintop," Apr. 3, 1968, Martin Luther King, Jr. Research and Education Institute, http://mlk-kpp01.stanford.edu; Matthew 26:39 (King James Version). Instantly, civil-rights leaders hailed King as a martyr to the cause. *Chicago Defender*: "Jesse Jackson, King Aides Vow to Carry On," Apr. 6, 1968; "Did He Give Life in Vain?," Apr. 8, 1968.

28. *WA Post*: "Dr. King, Apostle of Non-violence, Drew World Acclaim," Apr. 5, 1968; "Martin Luther King, Jr.," Apr. 6, 1968.

29. *NY Times*: Murray Schumach, "Martin Luther King Jr.: Leader of Millions in Nonviolent Drive for Racial Justice," Apr. 5, 1968; Herbert Mitgang, "The Race Crisis: A Non-violent Man Is Martyred," Apr. 7, 1968.

30. "Community Reacts to Another Killing," *New York Amsterdam News*, Jun. 15, 1968.

31. The "Abie Baby" lyrics are transcribed from the original-cast recording of May 1968. The official 1969 Pocket Books edition of the musical's script included many songs, and presented the "emancipator" opening to "Abie Baby," but it left out the Gettysburg Address and Stokely Carmichael segments that followed. Gerome Ragni and James Rado, *Hair: The American Tribal Love-Rock Musical* (New York: Pocket Books, 1969), 154. The current official *Hair* website provides a link to all of the show's original lyrics at http://stlyrics.com, but the line "Oh, come on, it's too [hokely?] Stokely" has been omitted.

32. Plot is subordinated to mood, sensibility, and cast-audience interaction in *Hair*, but technically speaking, the four black characters and the white assassin in the "Abie Baby" scene are being conjured up by one of the white male leads during a drug-induced reverie.

33. Lerone Bennett Jr., "Was Abe Lincoln a White Supremacist?," *Ebony*, Feb. 1968, 35–42. The article caused an immediate stir, provoking a quick rejoinder from Herbert Mitgang, the resident Lincoln expert at the *New York Times*. "Was Lincoln Just a Honkie?," *NY Times Magazine*, Feb. 11, 1968, 35, 100–106.

34. The performance is available at http://youtube.com/watch?v=mvfjvBO2l2Y. This video splices together Walt Disney's promotional pitch for the 1964–65 World's Fair (which aired on *The Wonderful World of Disney* in May 1964) with a film of the animatronic Lincoln's performance that did not appear in the televised segment. Judging by the audience's clothing, they are attending either a 1964 or 1965 performance at the World's Fair, or the Lincoln show at Disneyland soon after it opened there in 1965.

35. Robert Alden, "Lincoln at Fair Gains in Viewers," *NY Times*, May 24, 1965.

36. "Lincoln Voice Heard in Debut at Disneyland," *LA Times*, Jul. 19, 1965.

Chapter Thirteen: Reviving the Emancipator

1. Garry Wills, *Lincoln at Gettysburg: The Words That Remade America* (New York: Simon & Schuster, 1992), 38.

2. John Saar, "Rites at Lincoln Memorial Attract 200 on Birthday," *WA Post*, Feb. 13, 1973.

3. John F. Burns, "Very Little of Lincoln in Lincoln's Birthday," *NY Times*, Feb. 13, 1976.

4. Sherwood, *Abe Lincoln in Illinois*, 138 (see chap. 11, n. 17).

5. Arthur Unger, "Holbrook Wants to 'Humanize' Lincoln," *Christian Science Monitor*, Sept. 5, 1974, 11; Jerry Buck, "Now Holbrook Is Abe Lincoln," *Hartford Courant*, Sept. 8, 1974.

6. Unger, "Holbrook Wants."

7. Sandburg, *Lincoln: The War Years*, 4:176–77 (see chap. 5, n. 4).

8. Gore Vidal, "Lincoln," in *Screening History* (Cambridge, MA: Harvard University Press, 1992), 67.

9. Vidal, "Lincoln," 70 ("six-volume scrapbook"), 86 ("national god"); Vidal, "Lincoln: 'His Ambition Was a Little Engine That Knew No Rest,'" *LA Times*, Feb. 8, 1981. Vidal reprinted this *Times* attack on Sandburg, and on the saintly Lincoln, in two later essay collections: "A Note on Lincoln," in Vidal, *The Second American Revolution* (New York: Random House, 1982), 273–78, and "First Note on Abraham Lincoln," in Vidal, *United States* (New York: Random House, 1993), 664–68.

10. Wilson, *Patriotic Gore*, 120, 123, 130 (see chap. 12, n. 21).

11. Vidal, "Lincoln: 'His Ambition Was a Little Engine.'" ("American nation-state"); Vidal, "Lincoln," in *Screening History*, 90.

12. Vidal, "Lincoln: 'His Ambition Was a Little Engine.'" Vidal was quoting from Herndon's letter to Jesse W. Weik, Jan. 1891 (no day given), in *The Hidden Lincoln*, ed. Emanuel Hertz (New York: Viking, 1938), 259. Fehrenbacher and Fehrenbacher, *Recollected Words*, xlvi, xlviii, 237–38 (see chap. 2, n. 2), casts general doubt on Herndon's reliability, while David Donald sums up the case against his syphilis account in *"We Are Lincoln Men": Abraham Lincoln and His Friends* (New York: Simon & Schuster, 2003), 98–99. Douglas L. Wilson mounts a partial defense of Herndon's account in *Honor's Voice: The Transformation of Abraham Lincoln* (1998; New York: Vintage, 1999), 127–29. I treat Herndon's claim in "Mr. Lincoln Went Down to Beardstown, But Did He Pick Up Syphilis While He Was There?" at http://richardwfox.com.

13. Edwin McDowell, "Publishing: Top Sellers among Books of 1984," *NY Times*, Jan. 18, 1985 (fourth-biggest-selling work); Walter Clemons, "Gore Vidal's Chronicles of America," *Newsweek*, Jun. 11, 1984, 74 (a first printing of two hundred thousand copies); Harold Holzer, "A Filtered Portrait of Lincoln Comes to the Small Screen," *NY Times*, Mar. 20, 1988 (over a million copies sold).

14. Vidal, *Lincoln: A Novel* (New York: Random House, 1984), 288–90.

15. Clemons, "Gore Vidal's Chronicles," 74–77. Clemons didn't mention that Oates knew about Herndon's syphilis claim and simply denied its credibility. Stephen B. Oates, *Abraham Lincoln, the Man behind the Myths* (New York: Harper & Row, 1984), 21.

16. Vidal, *Lincoln: A Novel*, 659. In the 1996 interview, David Donald repeated his glowing endorsement of the book: "one of the great portraits of the President" as "a heroic figure who moves to change the very nature of American government and American society." PBS "Online Forum," Feb. 12, 1996, http://pbs.org. In *"We Are Lincoln Men"* (2003), with no reference to Vidal, Donald dissociated himself from the syphilis story.

17. Vidal, "The Agreed-Upon Facts," in William Zinsser, ed., *Paths of Resistance: The Art and Craft of the Political Novel* (Boston: Houghton Mifflin, 1989), 149, 151. Vidal also told the audience (in the winter of 1988) that he "pretty much" accepted the view that "Lincoln really wanted the Civil War, with its 600,000 casualties, in order to eclipse the Founding Fathers and ensure his own place in the pantheon of great presidents."

18. Vidal, *Lincoln: A Novel*, 656.

19. Ibid., 490 (Gettysburg Address), 356 (freedom and colonization). For a decade after 1981, Vidal tangled publicly with such leading Lincoln scholars as Don E. Fehrenbacher, Richard Current, and Harold Holzer.

20. Michael E. Hill, "'Lincoln': A Fast-Forward through Vidal's Historical Saga," *WA Post*, Mar. 27, 1988. This three-page cover story gave special weight to Vidal's list of Lincoln's nonheroic physical features: "Lincoln was chronically constipated, and was the First Anorexic—he ate little and lost more than 30 pounds in his last year. He had had a nervous breakdown and suffered from poor circulation and had perpetually cold hands and feet. He also, Vidal added, had had syphilis, and Lincoln's law partner thought that it may have contributed to the difficulties with the boys [*sic*—Herndon thought it might have killed some of them] and that Mary Todd Lincoln may have had paresis, a brain disease cause by syphilis."

21. John J. O'Connor, "'Lincoln'—A Giant Seen as a Man," *NY Times*, Mar. 27, 1988.

22. Vidal, *Lincoln: A Novel*, 657. Schuyler Colfax did report in late April 1865 that one morning at breakfast in 1863, dejected by the calamitous war casualties, Lincoln had wished he could change places with one of the sleeping soldiers. Maybe this implied a momentary desire to die in battle, but it was not an inclination to be murdered.

23. Vidal, *Screening History*, 87.

24. William H. Honan, "The Lessons of War Sell in Peacetime," *NY Times*, Dec. 19, 1988 (revived popularity of military history books).

25. James M. McPherson, *The Battle Cry of Freedom: The Civil War Era*, Oxford History of the United States 6 (1988; Oxford: Oxford University Press, 2003), 508–9.

26. McPherson, "Who Freed the Slaves?" *Proceedings of the American Philosophical Society* 139 (Mar. 1995): 1–10.

27. Eric Foner, *Reconstruction: America's Unfinished Revolution, 1863–1877* (1988; New York: Perennial Classics, 2002), 6–7.

28. Vidal, *Screening History*, 87; Jeremy Gerard, "'Civil War' Seems to Have Set a Record," *NY Times*, Sept. 29, 1990.

29. Ken Burns, "Four O'Clock in the Morning Courage," in Robert Brent Toplin, ed., *Ken Burns's The Civil War: Historians Respond* (New York: Oxford University Press, 1996), 164.

30. In discussing his film, Burns explained that his emphasis on personal courage and loss stemmed from his own experience: "My own mother died when I was eleven, changing me and permanently influencing all that I would become. The Civil War defines us in just that way, at both an intensely intimate level and in a broad national sense." His great-great-grandfather, he added, was a Confederate blacksmith, captured in West Virginia and imprisoned in Ohio. Burns, "Four O'Clock," 183.

31. If no photograph of a black soldier sitting with his wife was available in the 1980s, the script for *Civil War* narrator David McCullough might well have stated that fact and noted the regrettable historical distortion imposed on the program by racially selective patterns of photographic preservation.

32. John Boston to his wife Elizabeth, in Ken Burns, *The Civil War*, episode 3, at 1:33 min.—also reprinted in Geoffrey C. Ward, *The Civil War: An Illustrated History* (New York: Knopf, 1990), 150. In episode 5 of *The Civil War*, at 2:04 min., Burns quotes a similar letter from Sgt. Lewis Douglass (Frederick Douglass's son) to "My Dear Emilia."

33. Eric Foner, "Ken Burns and the Romance of Reunion," in Toplin, *Ken Burns's The Civil War*, 114–15.

34. Shelby Foote, in Ken Burns, *The Civil War*, episode 9, at 1:08 min. ("superior people"; reprinted in Ward, *Civil War*, 264); episode 1, at 0:18 min. ("compromise"; also in Ward, *Civil War*, 264).

35. Foote was featured in all nine episodes (broadcast over five consecutive evenings). He appeared in sixty-seven separate screen segments over ten hours—not including his promo spots before and after some telecasts. Barbara Fields appeared in five episodes, for a total of eleven screen segments. Harshly critical of Lincoln's go-slow approach to abolishing slavery and of his persistent interest in colonization, she shared much of Gore Vidal's perspective. Yet unlike him (and unlike Burns's script), Fields did her best to put the self-emancipation struggles of African Americans at the heart of the war experience. In her eyes, it was this emancipation on the ground—not Lincoln's legal, politically motivated version, and certainly not his overriding concern for reunion—that gave the war a "higher" purpose, justifying its incalculable human cost.

36. Glenna R. Schroeder-Lein, *Lincoln and Medicine* (Carbondale: Southern Illinois University Press, 2012), 37. Speculation about Lincoln's possible homosexuality reached a peak in the early twenty-first century. See C. A. Tripp, *The Intimate World of Abraham Lincoln* (New York: Free Press, 2005); the book includes Michael Burlingame's "A Respectful Dissent," pp. 225–38, which argues that available evidence does not support the idea that Lincoln was gay.

37. Wills, *Lincoln at Gettysburg*, 130 ("founding document"), 132. Wills's book was followed by many others over the next two decades heralding Lincoln's eloquence. Among the best is Ronald C. White's *Lincoln's Greatest Speech: The Second Inaugural* (New York: Simon & Schuster, 2006).

38. On the post–Civil War reception of the Gettysburg Address, see Gabor Boritt, *The Gettysburg Gospel: The Lincoln Speech That Nobody Knows* (New York: Simon & Schuster, 2006), 163–203, and Jared Peatman, *The Long Shadow of Lincoln's Gettysburg Address* (Carbondale: Southern Illinois University Press, 2013), which examines its reception around the world.

39. *Chicago Tribune* blurb on the paperback edition ("intoxicating originality"). In a second blurb, Studs Terkel noted how *Lincoln at Gettysburg* restored the vitality "of what we rote-memorized as school children" in the era of the Lincoln cult. The single most perceptive review is Paul A. Raje's in *Reviews in American History* 21 (Jun. 1993): 218–24.

Chapter Fourteen: Lincoln Sightings at the Bicentenary: Obama, Disney, Spielberg

1. "President-Elect Obama Speech at Lincoln Memorial," Jan. 18, 2009, C-SPAN, http://c-spanvideo.org/program/283443-1, at 3:30 min.

2. Ray Suarez, "The New Presidential Library Showcases Legacy of Abraham Lincoln," Apr. 15, 2005, PBS NewsHour, http://pbs.org/newshour/bb/media/jan-june05/lincoln_4-15.html.

3. Obama speech, ALPLM dedication, Apr. 19, 2005, http://www.c-span.org/video/?186315-1/abraham-lincoln-presidential-museum-dedication.

4. Obama, "What I See in Lincoln's Eyes," *Time*, Jun. 26, 2005, http://www.cnn.com/2005/POLITICS/06/28/obama.lincoln.tm.

5. "Speech of Hon. Abraham Lincoln" [June 16], *CH Trib*, Jun. 19, 1858.

6. Peggy Noonan, "Conceit of Government," *Wall Street Journal*, Jun. 29, 2005.

7. Obama, *The Audacity of Hope: Thoughts on Reclaiming the American Dream* (New York: Three Rivers Press, 2006), 361–62. The Lincoln Memorial figures as an image of civil-rights idealism in Obama's *Dreams from My Father: A Story of Race and Inheritance* (1995; New York: Three Rivers Press, 2004), most compellingly when, reflecting on the dismal prospects for reform in 1980s Chicago, he imagines himself "standing at the edge" of it "looking out over an empty pavilion, debris scattering in the wind" (140).

8. Lerone Bennett Jr., speaking on Obama at the Covenant with Black America forum, 2007, Jamestown, VA, http://youtube.com/watch?v=QgrGwQo7MaU; Bennett, *Forced into Glory: Abraham Lincoln's White Dream* (Chicago: Johnson, 2000), 215, 230. Bennett's book received spirited rebuttals from Lincoln scholars—for example, James M. McPherson, "Lincoln the Devil," *New York Times Book Review*, Aug. 27, 2000, 12–13.

9. Henry Louis Gates Jr., "Abraham Lincoln on Race and Slavery," in *Lincoln on Race and Slavery* (Princeton, NJ: Princeton University Press, 2009), xvii–lxviii.

10. Don E. Fehrenbacher surveys the history of dissent from the cult of Lincoln in "The Anti-Lincoln Tradition," *Papers of the Abraham Lincoln Association* 4

(1982): 6–28; and Daniel Feller analyzes Adams and DiLorenzo in "Libertarians in the Attic, or a Tale of Two Narratives," *Reviews in American History* 32 (Jun. 2004): 184–95.

11. Charles Adams, *When in the Course of Human Events: Arguing the Case for Southern Secession* (Lanham, MD: Rowman & Littlefield, 2000), 2–3, 35–36.

12. Thomas J. DiLorenzo, *Lincoln Unmasked* (New York: Crown Forum, 2006), 8, 28, 186. *Lincoln Unmasked* is DiLorenzo's follow-up to his still big-selling *The Real Lincoln* (2002; New York: Three Rivers Press, 2003). An illuminating 2002 debate between DiLorenzo and Lincoln scholar Harry Jaffa is available on the Independent Institute's website: http://independent.org/events/transcript.asp?id=9.

13. DiLorenzo, *Real Lincoln*, 52–53.

14. "Abraham Lincoln," in *Official Program, 43rd Inauguration, 1957* (Washington DC: [Republican] Inaugural Committee, 1957), 15.

15. Bob Staake, *New Yorker* cover, Nov. 17, 2008; Arthur Hochstein, "Top Ten Magazine Covers, 2008," *Time*, Nov. 3, 2008, http://content.time.com/time/specials/packages/article/0,28804,1855948_1863163,00.html.

16. Eric Foner to Rick Rothschild [of Disney Imagineering], May 25, 1994; letter in the possession of Eric Foner. I am grateful to Foner for allowing me to see, and quote from, his file of Disneyland correspondence. He mentioned the Rodney King riots in a phone interview on January 6, 2013.

17. Disneyland president Paul Pressler, quoted in Mary Susan Herczog and Steve Hochman, "What Would Walt Say?," *LA Times*, Dec. 24, 1995. Sandy Spurgeon recalls that in August 1990, she and other *Great Moments* hosts informed visitors that within days the show was scheduled to be shut down for good, and to be replaced with a stage performance by the Muppets. (No public announcement had been made.) Those visitors told their friends, and a groundswell of opposition quickly developed. Phone interview with Spurgeon, May 22, 2013. See also Bob Pool, "Lincoln Liberated: Tourist Revolt Keeps 'Great Emancipator' on Display at Disneyland," *LA Times*, Aug. 24, 1990, which quotes Spurgeon: "The Muppets should go somewhere else."

18. "More Great Moments with Mr. Lincoln," unpaginated typescript (2001) in Eric Foner's possession; Foner e-mail to Steven F. Spiegel, Jan. 31, 2001, responding to Spiegel e-mail of the same date.

19. "More Great Moments with Mr. Lincoln"; Foner dialogue suggestions on emancipation in e-mails to Steven Spiegel, Nov. 18, 2000, and Jan. 28, 2001.

20. Dawn C. Chmielewski, "Lincoln Voice Is Talking Point," *LA Times*, Dec. 18, 2009.

21. Tony Kushner related the story of his 2010 telephone appeal to Daniel Day-Lewis on several occasions at the end of 2012, including his interviews with Janet Maslin at the Jacob Burns Film Center in Pleasantville, New York, on December 20, 2012, http://youtube.com/watch?v=qeY9Kg91xNA, at 2:22 min.,

and in "Angel in America," *Entertainment Weekly*, Nov. 9, 2012, 52. He added the Greenwich Village detail in his appearance at the University of Southern California: "An Afternoon with Tony Kushner," Oct. 6, 2013.

22. On her friendly "badgering" of Kushner to foreground the storytelling Lincoln, Doris Kearns Goodwin's remarks at the Richmond Forum, Richmond, VA, Jan. 5, 2013, http://youtube.com/watch?v=Ag9PGQez_Pg.

23. Chad Jones, "Spielberg, Day-Lewis Speak of 'Lincoln,'" *SFGate*, Nov. 12, 2012, http://www.sfgate.com/movies/article/Spielberg-Day-Lewis-speak-of-Lincoln-4001464.php; "Lincoln Q & A—Full Interview (2012)—Steven Spielberg, Daniel Day-Lewis," Oct. 11, 2012, quote at 3:20 min., http://youtube.com/watch?v=BERKF9rnBcQ.

24. "Lincoln Q & A," at 8:45 min. ("preposterous" and "outlandish") and 26:25 min. ("voice" reflections).

25. "The Woman Who Transformed Daniel-Day Lewis into Abraham Lincoln," KPCC Take Two (radio) interview, Nov. 19, 2012, http://scpr.org/programs/take-two. Lois Burwell, interviewed in *Lincoln*'s official "20 Minute Featurette" (2013), at 13:49 min. www.youtube.com/watch?v=z-w4A43wkGU.

26. Tony Kushner, *Lincoln: The Screenplay* (New York: Theatre Communications Group, 2012), 6–7.

27. Ibid., 16.

28. Tony Kushner, speaking at the Union League Club of Chicago, Feb. 22, 2013, http://youtube.com/watch?v=bfz8GteWD44 ("full, open-hearted affection" at 1:14:25 min.); Jones, "Spielberg, Day-Lewis Speak of 'Lincoln'"; official "20 Minute Featurette" (at 6:49 min.).

29. Louis C. K.'s *Saturday Night Live* Lincoln skit demonstrates its global grass-roots popularity by its continuous availability on Internet sites, often in more than one language.

30. *BioShock Infinite*'s 2011 gameplay demo is available at http://youtube.com/watch?v=kEBwKO4RFOU (three million views followed by sixteen thousand comments, as of April 2014). Photos of the George Washington and Abraham Lincoln "Heavy Hitters"—"motorized patriots" who qualify as "clockwork terminators" (relentless combatants)—are at http://bioshock.wikia.com/wiki/Motorized_Patriot. Thanks to Rubidium Wu for alerting me to BioShock.

31. Joshua Speed to William Herndon, Feb. 7, 1866, in *Herndon's Informants*, 197 (see chap. 6, n. 27).

Illustration Credits

Page ii: Courtesy Library of Congress Prints and Photographs Division
Page iv: Lincoln Financial Foundation Collection, courtesy of the Allen County Public Library and Indiana State Museum and Historic Sites
Page xiii: Photo by author; printed with permission of DreamWorks Studios
Page 1:   Lincoln Financial Foundation Collection, courtesy of the Allen County Public Library and Indiana State Museum and Historic Sites
Page 6:   Courtesy Library of Congress Prints and Photographs Division
Page 7:   Courtesy Library of Congress Prints and Photographs Division
Page 7:   Courtesy Library of Congress Prints and Photographs Division
Page 13:   Courtesy Library of Congress Prints and Photographs Division; photo by Christopher German
Page 33:   Currier and Ives lithograph, 1865; courtesy American Antiquarian Society
Page 41:   Courtesy Library of Congress Prints and Photographs Division
Page 41:   Courtesy Library of Congress Prints and Photographs Division
Page 48:   Lincoln Financial Foundation Collection, courtesy of the Allen County Public Library and Indiana State Museum and Historic Sites
Page 51:   Courtesy Library of Congress Prints and Photographs Division
Page 76:   Courtesy Library of Congress Prints and Photographs Division
Page 84:   Lincoln Financial Foundation Collection, courtesy of the Allen County Public Library and Indiana State Museum and Historic Sites
Page 100: Courtesy Library of Congress Prints and Photographs Division
Page 100: Courtesy Library of Congress Prints and Photographs Division
Page 120: Lincoln Financial Foundation Collection, courtesy of the Allen County Public Library and Indiana State Museum and Historic Sites

Page 122: Lincoln Financial Foundation Collection, courtesy of the Allen County Public Library and Indiana State Museum and Historic Sites

Page 125: The George F. Landegger Collection of District of Columbia Photographs in Carol M. Highsmith's America, Library of Congress, Prints and Photographs Division.

Page 162: Courtesy Library of Congress Prints and Photographs Division

Page 165: The George F. Landegger Collection of District of Columbia Photographs in Carol M. Highsmith's America, Library of Congress, Prints and Photographs Division

Page 170: Courtesy Cook Collection, Valentine Richmond History Center

Page 171: Courtesy Valentine Richmond History Center

Page 196: Courtesy Library of Congress Prints and Photographs Division

Page 198: Courtesy Abraham Lincoln Presidential Library and Museum

Page 211: Courtesy Library of Congress Prints and Photographs Division; photo by Carol M. Highsmith

Page 216: Courtesy Library of Congress Prints and Photographs Division; photo by Carol M. Highsmith

Page 220: Courtesy Library of Congress Prints and Photographs Division; photo by Carol M. Highsmith

Page 242: Courtesy Library of Congress Prints and Photographs Division

Page 265: Lincoln Financial Foundation Collection, courtesy of the Allen County Public Library and Indiana State Museum and Historic Sites

Page 294: Courtesy Liljenquist Family Collection of Civil War Photographs, donated to the Library of Congress in 2010. Courtesy Library of Congress Prints and Photographs Division

Page 320: Courtesy Library of Congress Prints and Photographs Division

Page 322: Courtesy Library of Congress Prints and Photographs Division

Page 323: Courtesy American Academy of Motion Pictures (Margaret Herrick Library) and DreamWorks Studios

Index

About the Author

An alumnus of Stanford University, where he received his BA and PhD degrees in history, Richard Wightman Fox has taught since 1975 at Yale University, Reed College, Boston University, the Ecole des Hautes Etudes en Sciences Sociales in Paris (where he held a one-year visiting professorship in American Civilization), and, since 2000, at the University of Southern California, where he offers an undergraduate research seminar titled "The World of Abraham Lincoln," among other courses on American cultural and intellectual history.

A recipient of fellowships from the Guggenheim Foundation, the American Council of Learned Societies, and the National Endowment for the Humanities, Fox is the author of four previous books: *So Far Disordered in Mind: Insanity in California, 1870–1930* (University of California Press, 1979, a revision of his PhD thesis); *Reinhold Niebuhr: A Biography* (Pantheon, 1985); *Trials of Intimacy: Love and Loss in the Beecher-Tilton Scandal* (University of Chicago Press, 1999); and *Jesus in America: Personal Savior, Cultural Hero, National Obsession* (Harper-SanFrancisco, 2004).

He has also coedited four volumes: *The Culture of Consumption in America: Critical Essays in American History, 1880–1980* (with Jackson Lears; Pantheon, 1983); *The Power of Culture: Critical Essays in American History* (with Jackson Lears; Pantheon, 1993); *A Companion to American Thought* (with James Kloppenberg; Blackwell, 1995); and *In Face of the Facts: Moral Inquiry in American Scholarship* (with Robert Westbrook; Cambridge University Press, 1998).

His website for this book (richardwfox.com) includes some of his short pieces on Lincoln that expand on issues broached in these pages.